DUMBARTON OAKS STUDIES

XXXVII

The Church of the Panaghia tou Arakos
at Lagoudhera, Cyprus:
The Paintings and Their Painterly Significance

The Church
of the
Panaghia tou Arakos
at
Lagoudhera, Cyprus:

The Paintings and

Their Painterly Significance

David and June Winfield

DUMBARTON OAKS RESEARCH LIBRARY AND COLLECTION
WASHINGTON, D.C.

For our children,
Nancy, Diana, and Edward

Frontispiece: Head of the apostle with closed eyes behind St. Andrew (Figure 221)

COPYRIGHT © 2003 BY DUMBARTON OAKS
TRUSTEES FOR HARVARD UNIVERSITY
WASHINGTON, D.C.
PRINTED IN THE UNITED STATES OF AMERICA

LIBRARY OF CONGRESS CATALOGING-IN-PUBLICATION DATA

Winfield, David.
    The Church of the Panaghia tou Arakos at Lagoudhera, Cyprus: The Paintings and Their Painterly Significance / David and June Winfield
        p. cm.— (Dumbarton Oaks studies; 37)
    Includes bibliographical references.
    ISBN 0-88402-257-9
    1. Mural painting and decoration, Byzantine—Cyprus—Lagoudhera. 2. Mural painting and decoration, Byzantine—Conservation and restoration—Cyprus—Lagoudhera. 3. Mural painting and decoration—Cyprus—Lagoudhera. 4. Mural painting and decoration—Conservation and restoration—Cyprus—Lagoudhera. 5. Panaghia tou Arakos (Church: Lagoudhera, Cyprus) I. Winfield, June. II. Title. III. Series.

ND2819.C93 L348 2000
751.7'3'095693—dc21
                                                            99-057805

CONTENTS

Contents

FOREWORD

From the early 1960s to the mid-1970s Dumbarton Oaks was actively involved in fieldwork on the island of Cyprus, conducting or sponsoring projects for cleaning, conserving, and studying medieval Byzantine frescoes in the churches of Asinou, Lagoudhera, Monagri, and Perachorio and at the monasteries of St. Chrysostomos and St. Neophytos. In addition, Dumbarton Oaks supported work on the early Byzantine wall and vault mosaics at Lythrankomi and Kiti and sponsored excavations at the Episcopal Basilica at Curium and at the castle of Saranda Kolonnes at Kato Paphos. The necessary publication of this ambitious program of fieldwork has followed as circumstances have allowed, either in the *Dumbarton Oaks Papers* or, when the importance of the monument so warrants, in a separate monograph.

With this book, one of the most important of the fieldwork projects undertaken by Dumbarton Oaks is fully published. The wall paintings in the church of the Panaghia tou Arakos at Lagoudhera can lay claim to being among the finest examples of middle Byzantine monumental art. Not only is their overall quality very high, but the paintings at Lagoudhera are in an excellent state of preservation, thanks, largely, to the protection provided by the secondary roof with which the structure has long been covered. The paintings were cleaned, conserved, and recorded by David and June Winfield between 1968 and 1973. At the same time the church was comprehensively documented through photographs and architectural drawings by Richard Anderson with the addition of detail photographs by D. Winfield. The resulting book provides details of the techniques and procedures employed by the Byzantine painters, and thus complements the recent iconographic study by Andréas Nicolaïdès, "L'église de la Panagia Arakiotissa à Lagoudéra, Chypre: Etude iconographique des fresques de 1192," published in *Dumbarton Oaks Papers* 50 (1996).

David and June Winfield present to us the paintings of Lagoudhera from the viewpoint of the artists who created them, rather than from the perspective of the patron, clergy, or congregation. Their richly illustrated book focuses on the Byzantine painter's practice of his craft—the limits and the potential of the training and techniques that he deployed to give physical form to the mysteries of his religion. The Winfields describe in detail the Byzantine painters' methods of plastering, and how they rapidly laid out their compositions with compasses, incisions, impressions, and preliminary drawings. We are told of the addition of secondary underdrawings, of the systems of modular proportions used to construct the figures, and of the techniques and the

sequence of color applications employed for the final layers of painting. The authors discuss the composition of pigments, the methods of gilding and silvering, and the frequent adjustments and corrections that were made as the work progressed. In addition, the Winfields detail the conservation methods that they themselves used to preserve the paintings. Their detailed descriptions of the paintings at Lagoudhera provide an excellent demonstration of the Byzantine artists' ability to vary the basic canons of their craft. We are shown how the technical procedures of Byzantine wall painters contributed to the characteristic aesthetic of medieval Byzantine painting and how these same procedures distinguished Byzantine murals from the art of medieval painters in the West.

The church of Lagoudhera is remote and still relatively difficult to access. Through this book its treasures are made more widely available. More importantly, David and June Winfield allow the viewer to approach Byzantine art through the hands of Byzantine painters as they worked. Byzantine church art was a supremely intellectual construct, but its all-encompassing ideology had to be translated into the individual strokes of the artists' brush; it is this process of transformation that is here described.

Henry Maguire
Urbana, Illinois

PREFACE

The purpose of this account of the Panaghia tou Arakos is to give a full description of the church and its paintings and to set down how Byzantine painters created this harmonious and collective work of art. We hope to make it apparent that, just as there was method and theme ruling the choice of subject matter, so also was there systematic method and technique in the execution of the decoration.

The book is divided into five parts. The first part contains a general description of the church and its history. The account of the iconography is no more than summary, since a detailed study of this aspect of the church by Andréas Nicolaïdès appears in *Dumbarton Oaks Papers* 50 (1996). The second part describes the paintings in the apse, which are undated but are earlier than 1192. The third part is the core of the book. It contains a detailed description of the paintings by the 1192 master and an analysis of their importance. His work is a fine example of the Byzantine language of church decoration.

The fourth part discusses the techniques involved in creating the decoration. Aspects of the methods of plastering and painting at Lagoudhera are of general importance in the development of medieval and Renaissance wall painting in Europe. With the limitation that no laboratory help has been available, we have endeavored to be precise in the descriptions of practices at Lagoudhera and the light that they shed on the general development of wall painting. The fifth part of the book gives an account of the later paintings.

Each painting is individually described. I had once thought that the craft of Byzantine wall painting was so highly systematized that descriptions could be reduced to a shorthand catalogue.[1] Many more years of careful observation have proved that the work of any painter of individual interest cannot be so arbitrarily listed. The general system of Byzantine painting remains valid for Lagoudhera, but each painting presents distinctive additions and variations to the rules, and each painting is an individual work of art.

It may be argued that any systematized craft such as is described in this book must inevitably inhibit the production of a work of art. A moment's reflection will show that this is certainly not

---

[1] D. C. Winfield, "Middle and Later Byzantine Wall Painting Methods: A Comparative Study," *DOP* 22 (1968), 136–38.

so. Plato's Athenian applauded the Egyptian approach, which restricted painters by law to reproducing only a limited number of gestures and movements that had been passed by the legislators as good. The result (he claimed) was that over a period of ten thousand years, paintings and reliefs were produced to a high standard, looking exactly the same at the end of the period as they did at the beginning. Byzantine painting was not quite so long-lived or rigid as that, but it is the last of the hieratic arts of the antique world, imbued with the power of Christian spirituality, and it is possible to look at a mosaic, such as the Sinai Transfiguration of about A.D. 550 and see that the master painters of Lagoudhera, six hundred years later, were following a similar set of conventions. So also was the journeyman painter who was responsible for the Transfiguration on the exterior of the north wall of the same church more than a thousand years later.

Despite its affinities with the art of the antique world, the decoration at Lagoudhera cannot be fully enjoyed if the beholder approaches it from the point of view of the humanist looking for the Hellenistic illusion of reality. It is fine painting that conveys its spiritual message through harmony of proportion, beauty of color, and linear form and movement. People and objects are deliberately separated from our idea of the illusion of reality by the linear forms. The conventions of Byzantine church painting made it essential that figures should be clearly recognizable, but for an image to become an icon it must not be given the destructive illusion of reality.

It is one of the happier quirks of history that the benefaction of Lord Leon and the work of his master painter of 1192 should have survived for more than eight hundred years in its quiet Cypriot mountain valley. It was a privilege and a pleasure to have worked on such fine paintings, and we hope that the reader may find in the beauty of the painting the instruction and the pleasure that would have gratified both patron and painter. For the Lagoudhera painter was like the master described by Alexander Pope in his "Essay on Criticism," as one who sought "Those nameless Graces which no methods teach / And which a Master Hand alone can reach."

David Winfield
Isle of Mull

ACKNOWLEDGMENTS

T he church at Lagoudhera was officially taken into the Dumbarton Oaks program by Professor Cyril Mango, then director of field studies. The work of cleaning and preserving the paintings at Lagoudhera was done under the direction of D. C. Winfield, with the assistance of J. C. Winfield, between 1968 and 1973. They and Dumbarton Oaks are indebted to the Department of Antiquities of the Republic of Cyprus and to the late Kyprianos, bishop of Kyrenia, for permission to undertake the work. The late Polykarpos Joannides, diocesan secretary of Kyrenia, always gave us his friendly encouragement. We are particularly indebted to the two now retired directors of the Department of Antiquities, Vassos Karageorghis and A. Papageorghiou, who always gave freely of their time and advice and gave permission for the publication of Figures 3, 4, and 6. Mr. Orphanou, the former chief foreman of the Department of Antiquities, gave us much practical help.

The meticulous plans and elevations of the church are the work of Richard Anderson, and much of the high quality of the photographic record of the church is due to his care and skill as a photographer. For help with the inscriptions of the church, we are indebted to Cyril Mango, Ihor Ševčenko, John Wilkinson, and John Parker.

The foreman throughout the work at Lagoudhera was Kostas Zaferiades, who went into retirement after twenty years of service with Dumbarton Oaks. His patience and skill contributed much to the success of Dumbarton Oaks' field projects and in particular to the work at Asinou and at Lagoudhera. We also owe much to our chief assistant, Haralambos Haralambides. His position as café proprietor and assistant head man of the village contributed greatly to easing the practical difficulties of setting up an expedition in a remote village, and he worked on the paintings with patience and care. We have also to thank the villagers of Lagoudhera and Sarandi for welcoming us and our children into their communities, and for transforming what might have been five years of difficulties into an interesting period of our lives. The kindness and hospitality of many Cypriot friends contributed to our happy years in Cyprus and we would particularly mention our old friends Georgos and Joan Georghallides.

For financial assistance while preparing this report, D. C. Winfield is indebted to Dumbarton Oaks, to the warden and fellows of All Souls College, to the warden and fellows of Merton College, Oxford, to the Leverhulme Trust, and to the British Academy. His greater debts for encouragement and financial support are owed to an old friend, the late Lawrence Strangman,

Acknowledgments

who assumed the role of patron at a time when unemployment and all things else seemed to conspire against fruition.

Finally, we are grateful to Henry Maguire, former director of Byzantine Studies at Dumbarton Oaks, to Glenn Ruby, publishing manager, and his staff for the care with which they have seen this volume through to publication. The anonymous reader provided helpful advice in revising the form of the publication and a number of useful suggestions and criticisms.

LIST OF FIGURES

13

List of Figures

List of Figures

Naos, north bay under the dome

Soffit of the north arch under the dome, roundels

Naos, lunette of the north bay under the dome, the Presentation of the Virgin [70]

Naos, north wall under the dome, east side of the door

List of Figures

List of Figures

LIST OF PLATES

List of Text Figures

List of Text Figures

LIST OF ICONOGRAPHIC NUMBERS AND
KEY TO THE ICONOGRAPHIC PLANS*

Throughout the text iconographic numbers are contained within square brackets.

Dome

1   The Christ in the center of the dome

2   Chevron pattern around dome central medallion

3   Etoimasia, dome, eastern medallion

4   Archangel, angel frieze, southeast medallion

5   Archangel, angel frieze, south-southeast medallion

6   Angel, angel frieze, south medallion

7   Archangel, angel frieze, south-southwest medallion

8   Angel, angel frieze, southwest medallion

9   Angel, angel frieze, northwest medallion

10   Archangel, angel frieze, north-northwest medallion

11   Angel, angel frieze, north medallion

12   Archangel, angel frieze, north-northeast medallion

13   Archangel, angel frieze, northeast medallion

Cupola

14   Pattern: vermiculated rectangles, east window reveals

15   The prophet Jeremiah, southeast quarter, east end

16   Pattern: bud and leaf, southeast window reveals

17   The prophet Solomon, southeast quarter, center

18   Pattern: vermiculation, south-southeast window reveals

19   The prophet Elijah or Elias, southeast quarter, west end

20   Pattern: vermiculated triangles, south window reveals

21   The prophet Elisha or Elisias, southwest quarter, east end

22   Pattern: bud and leaf, south-southwest window reveals

23   The prophet Daniel, southwest quarter, center

24   Pattern: vermiculated squares, southwest window reveals

25   The prophet Gideon, southwest quarter, west end

* See Text Figures 1–6 for the iconographic plan, p. 36 onward.

List of Iconographic Numbers

26 Pattern: bud and leaf, west window reveals

27 The prophet Habakkuk, northwest quarter, west end

28 Pattern: bud and leaf, northwest window reveals

29 The prophet Ezechiel, northwest quarter, center

30 Pattern: vermiculation, north-northwest window reveals

31 The prophet Jonah, northwest quarter, east end

32 Pattern: bud and leaf, north window reveals

33 The prophet Moses, northeast quarter, west end

34 Pattern: vermiculated squares, north-northeast window reveals

35 The prophet David, northeast quarter, center

36 Pattern: bud and leaf, northeast window reveals

37 The prophet Isaiah, northeast quarter, east end

Pendentives

38 Archangel Gabriel of the Annunciation, northeast pendentive

39 Jesus Christ Emmanuel, center

40 The seated Mother of God, southeast pendentive

41 St. John the Evangelist, southwest pendentive, east side

42 St. Luke the Evangelist, southwest pendentive, west side

43 St. Matthew the Evangelist, northwest pendentive, west side

44 St. Mark the Evangelist, northwest pendentive, east side

West Vault

45 St. Tryphon, medallion at west end

46 St. Vikentios, medallion to west

47 St. Viktor, medallion to east

48 St. Menas, medallion at east end

49 Pattern around medallions

50 The Anastasis, north half of vault

North Wall of the West Bay

51 Vermiculated pattern, west spandrel

52 St. Paul, east side

53 Imitation marble dadoes of 1192 decoration

54 The Baptism, wall of blind arch

55 St. Andronikos, west reveal of blind arch

56 St. Kosmas, soffit of blind arch, west side

57 St. Damian, soffit of blind arch, east side

58 St. Kyriakos the Anchorite, east reveal of blind arch

North Bay under the Dome

59 St. Sabas, west reveal of the blind arch

60 St. Anempodistos, roundel west end of arch soffit

61 St. Elpidiphoros, roundel west side of arch soffit

62 St. Aphthonios, roundel west of center of arch soffit

63 St. Pigasios, roundel center west of arch soffit

64 St. Akindinos (?), roundel center east of arch soffit

65 St. Gourias, roundel east of center of arch soffit

66 St. Samonas, roundel east side of arch soffit

67 St. Abibos, roundel east end of arch soffit

68 Pattern around medallions in soffit of arch

69 The Mother of God Eleousa, east reveal of arch

70 The Presentation of the Mother of God, lunette north wall

71 St. Nicholas, west side of north door

72 The Holy Tile, panel above lintel of north door

73 The 1192 Inscription, on lintel of north door

74 Presentation of Christ, Symeon and Christ child, east of door

75 St. John the Baptist, or the Forerunner, east side of north door

76 Cross with Latin graffiti, west reveal of north door

77 Cross, east reveal of north door

Sanctuary Vault

78 The Ascension, the entire vault

North Wall of the Sanctuary

79 St. Symeon the Younger, the Wonderworker (Thaumaturgos), west side

80 St. Joseph the Poet or Hymnwriter, east spandrel

81 St. Onuphrios, west reveal of blind arch

82 Cross, medallion at center of soffit of blind arch

83 St. Stephen the Protomartyr, east reveal of blind arch

84 Pattern at south edge of east reveal of blind arch

85 Cross in prothesis niche of east reveal of blind arch

86 St. Hypatios, north wall of blind arch

87 Patterns around niche in north wall

88 Patterns on east and west reveals of niche in north wall

89 Cross in niche

West Reveal of Bema Arch

90 St. Stachios, deacon, lower roundel on north side

90a Decorative roundels at springing of arch

91 St. John of Damascus, upper roundel on north side

92 The Holy Towel or Mandylion, center of arch

93 St. Kosmas the Poet, upper roundel on south side

94 St. Nikanor, deacon, lower roundel on south side

List of Iconographic Numbers

Pre-1192 Paintings in the Apse

    95   The archangel Gabriel, north side of conch

    96   The Mother of God and Christ child enthroned, center conch

    97   The archangel Michael, south side of conch

    98   St. Zenon, medallion of middle register, north end

    99   St. Nikon(?), medallion of middle register, north side

  100   St. Philagrios, medallion of middle register, north of center

  101   St. Auxibios, medallion of middle register, center east

  102   St. Herakleidios, medallion of middle register, south of center

  103   St. Makedonios, medallion of middle register, south side

  104   St. Tryphillios, medallion of middle register, south end

  105   St. Tychon, ground register, north side, north end

  106   St. Nicholas, ground register, north side

  107   St. Meletios of Antioch, ground register, north side

  108   St. John Chrysostomos, ground register, north side, east end

  109   St. Epiphanios(?), north mullion of apse windows

  110   St. Barnabas, south mullion of apse windows

  111   St. Spyridon, north roundel below windows

  112   Unknown St., south roundel below windows

  113   St. Basil, ground register, south side, east end

  114   St. Gregory the Theologian, south side

  115   St. Athanasios, ground register, south side

  116   St. John the Almoner, south side, south end

South Wall of the Sanctuary

  117   St. Theophanes the Poet, medallion in eastern spandrel

  118   St. Symeon the Elder, the Archimandrite, west side

  119   Floral pattern at western edge (later than 1192, 14th century?)

  120   Pattern, east reveal of blind arch

  121   Cross in diakonikon, east reveal of blind arch

  122   St. Romanos the Melode, east reveal of blind arch

  123   Cross, medallion in the center of soffit of blind arch

  124   St. Lazaros, west reveal of blind arch

  125   St. Kyprianos, wall of blind arch

South Bay under the Dome

  126   Dado with earlier twelfth-century painting fragment

  127   Jesus Christ Antiphonetes, east reveal of arch

  128   St. Akepsimas, medallion at east end of arch soffit

  129   St. Mardarios, medallion at east side of arch soffit

  130   St. Eugenios(?), medallion east of center of arch soffit

  131   St. Eustratios, medallion center east of arch soffit

List of Iconographic Numbers

167   Unknown bishop, upper register, right of door

168   St. Herakleidios, upper register, right of door

169   Unknown bishop, upper register, right of door

170   Four standing figures, lower register, west of door

171   Other fragments of painted plaster, lower register, west of door

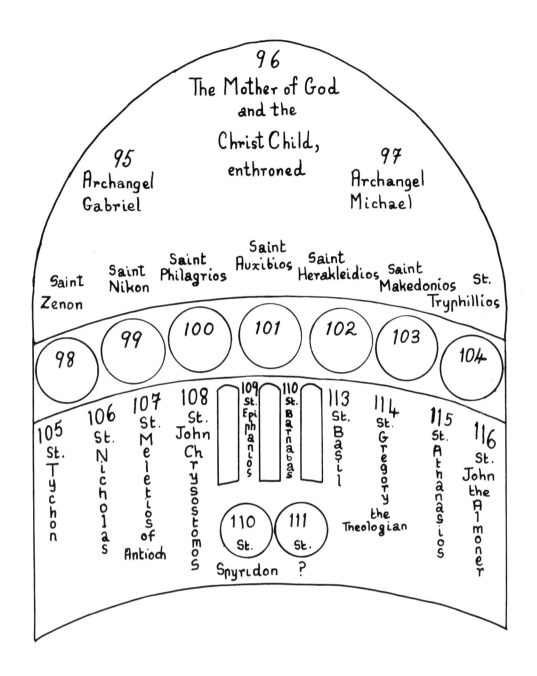

Text Fig. 1 Iconographic plan of the pre-1192 paintings in the apse

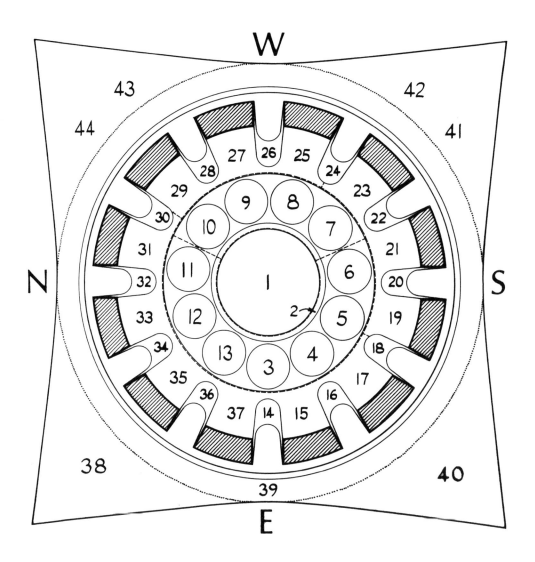

Text Fig. 2 Iconographic plan of the 1192 paintings in the dome, drum, and pendentives (R. Anderson). The dotted lines mark plaster joins.

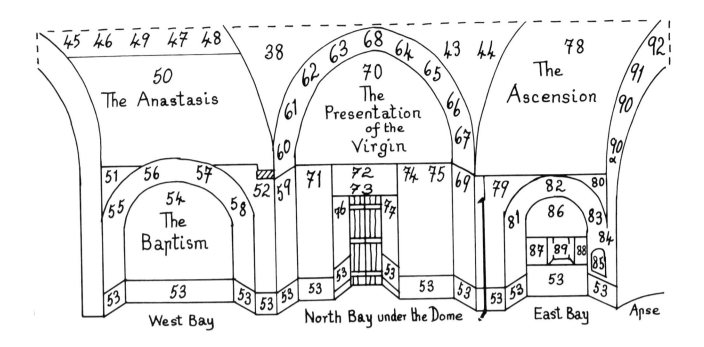

Text Fig. 3 Iconographic plan of the 1192 paintings on the north wall of the naos and the northern half of the bema

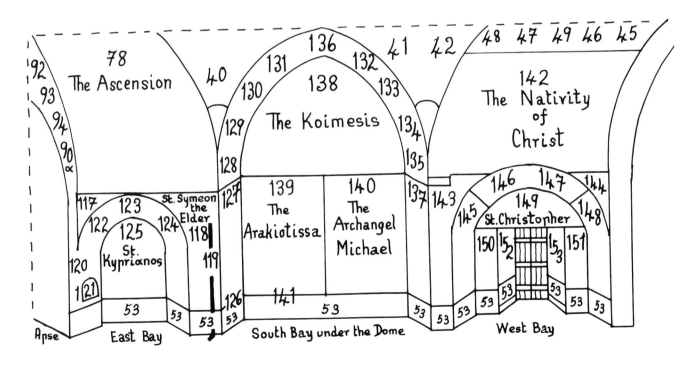

Text Fig. 4 Iconographic plan of the paintings on the south wall of the naos and the southern half of the bema

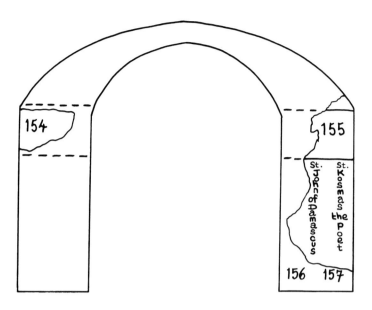

Text Fig. 5 Iconographic plan of the fourteenth-century painting on the east wall of the narthex

Mounted Saint	St. Theodore Stratilates	Saint Menas	Angel	Ancient of Days 163	Angel	Bishop	Prophet	The Transfiguration	St. Herakleidios	Bishop	Bishop
160	161	162		INSCRIPTION 159 Mother of God Achrantos 158		164	165	166		167 168	169

σ σ

North Door

170

4 Standing Figures

171

Fragments

Text Fig. 6 Iconographic plan of the late paintings on the exterior of the north wall

39

List of Abbreviations and Bibliography

AIPHOS	*Annuaire de l'Institut de philologie et d'histoire orientales et slaves*
Ἀρχ.Ἐφ.	Ἀρχαιολογικὴ Ἐφημερίς
BAR	British Archaeological Reports
BCH	*Bulletin de correspondance hellénique*
DOP	*Dumbarton Oaks Papers*
EtByz	*Byzantine Studies/Etudes byzantines*
HUkSt	*Harvard Ukrainian Studies*
JÖB	*Jahrbuch der Österreichischen Byzantinistik*
JÖBG	*Jahrbuch der Österreichischen Byzantinischen Gesellschaft*
Κυπρ.Σπ.	Κυπριακαὶ Σπουδαί
ODB	*The Oxford Dictionary of Byzantium,* ed. A. Kazhdan et al., 3 vols. (New York–Oxford,1991)
TAPS	*Transactions of the American Philosophical Society*

d' Arezzo, R. *La composizione del mondo di Ristoro d'Arezzo*, ed. E. Narducci. Rome, 1859.

Battisti, E. *Cimabue*. Milan, 1963.

Bear, L. M. *The Mineral Resources and Mining Industry of Cyprus*. Ministry of Commerce and Industry, Geological Survey Department, Bulletin no. 1. Nicosia, 1963.

Bomford, D., et al. *Italian Art before 1400*. National Gallery, exhibition catalogue. London, ca. 1989.

Buckler, W. H., and G. Buckler. "Dated Wall Paintings in Cyprus." *AIPHOS* 7, 1939–1944.

Du Cange, C. *Les Familles d'Outre Mer*. Edited by E. G. Rey. Paris, 1869.

Carr, J. M., and L. M. Bear. *The Geology and Mineral Resources of the Peristerona—Lagoudhera Area.* Memoir/Geological Survey of Cyprus, no. 2. Nicosia, 1960.

Cennino Cennini. *Il Libro del Arte*. Edited and translated by D. V. Thompson. New Haven, 1932–33.

Church, A. H. *The Chemistry of Paints and Painting*. London, 1901.

Cormack, R. *Writing in Gold*. London, 1985.

Demus, O. *Byzantine Art and the West*. London, 1970.

———. *Byzantine Mosaic Decoration*. London, [1948].

Doerner, M. *The Materials of the Artist*. London, 1935.

Bibliography

Gennadius, P. *Cyprus: Mineral Substances Utilized in the Arts.* Nicosia, 1905.

George, W. S. *The Church of St. Eirene, Constantinople.* Oxford, 1912.

Grigorovich-Barsky, V. G. "Странствованія Василия Григоровича-Барскаго по святымъ местамъ Востока, 1723–1747." In Православное палестинское общество. Vol. 2. St. Petersburg, 1886.

Gunnis, R. *Historic Cyprus.* London, 1936. Reprint, Nicosia, 1973.

Hackett, J. *A History of the Orthodox Church of Cyprus.* London, 1901.

Heaton, N. *Outlines of Paint Technology.* London, 1956.

Herringham, C. *Cennino Cennini.* London, 1899.

Hetherington, P. *The "Painter's Manual" of Dionysios of Fourna.* London, 1974. Revised edition, Torrance, California, 1996.

Hill, Sir George. *History of Cyprus.* Vol. 1. Cambridge, 1940.

James, L., *Light and Colour in Byzantine Art.* Oxford, 1996.

James, M. R., trans. *The Apocryphal New Testament.* Oxford, 1924, reprint 1966.

Karageorghis, V. "Chronique des fouilles à Chypre en 1966." *BCH* 91 (1967).

Kartsonis, A. *Anastasis: The Making of an Image.* Princeton, 1986.

Kazhdan, A. P. and A. W. Epstein. *Change in Byzantine Culture in the Eleventh and Twelfth Centuries.* Berkeley, 1990.

Kitzinger, E. "The Byzantine Contribution to Western Art in the Twelfth and Thirteenth Centuries." *DOP* 20 (1966).

———. "The Descent of the Dove." In *Byzanz und der Westen: Studien zur Kunst des europäischen Mittelalters*, Österreichische Akademie der Wissenschaften 432 (Vienna, 1984): 99–115.

Klerides, N. *25 Μοναστήρια στήν Κύπρο.* Vol. 2. N.p., n.d.

———. Χωριὰ καὶ πολιτεῖες τῆς Κύπρου. Nicosia, 1961.

Kyriazes, N. Τὰ μοναστήρια ἐν Κύπρῳ. Larnaca, 1950.

Laurie, A. P. *The Painters' Methods and Materials.* New York, 1967.

Maguire, H. *Art and Eloquence in Byzantium.* Princeton, 1981.

———. "The Iconography of Simeon with the Christ Child in Byzantine Art." *DOP* 34–35 (1980–81): 261–69.

———. "The Self-Conscious Angel." In *Okeanos: Essays Presented to Ihor Ševčenko, HUkSt* 7 (Cambridge, 1983): 377–92.

———. *The Icons of Their Bodies: Saints and Their Images in Byzantium.* Princeton, 1996.

Mako, V. *Lik i broj* (Figure and Number), Belgrade, 1998

———. "The Proportional Distribution and Age of the Frescoes in the Church of St. Basil in the Sea at Hilandar." In *Hilandarski Zbornik* (Belgrade, 1997): pp. 75–97

———. "Principles of Composition and Proportion in the 13th-century Wall Painting of Mileševo," in *Mileševo Notes* 3 (Prijepolje, 1998). Mako's book and articles are in Serbian.

Mango, C. *The Art of the Byzantine Empire.* Sources and Documents in the History of Art Series. Edited by H. W. Janson. Englewood Cliffs, N.J., 1972.

Bibliography

————. Appendix to D. C. Winfield, "The Church of the Panagia tou Arakos, Lagoudera: First Preliminary Report, 1968." *DOP* 23–24 (1969–70), 379–80.

Mango, C., and E. J. W. Hawkins. "The Hermitage of St. Neophytos and Its Wall Paintings." *DOP* 20 (1966), 119–206.

Mango, C., E. J. W. Hawkins, and S. Boyd. "The Monastery of St. Chrysostomos at Koutsovendis (Cyprus) and Its Wall Paintings." *DOP* 44 (1990), 63–94.

de Mas Latrie, L. *Nouvelles preuves de l'histoire de Chypre*. Paris, 1873. Reprint, Famagusta, 1970.

Megaw, A. H. S. "Background Architecture in the Lagoudera Frescoes." *JÖB* 21 (Vienna, 1972), 195–201.

Megaw, A. H. S., and E. J. W. Hawkins. "The Church of the Holy Apostles at Perachorio, Cyprus, and Its Frescoes." *DOP* 16 (1962), 277–348.

Megaw, A. H. S., and A. Stylianou. *Cyprus Mosaics and Frescoes*. UNESCO World Art Series. New York, 1963.

Meiss, M. *The Great Age of Fresco*. London, 1970.

Merrifield, Mrs. *The Art of Fresco Painting*. London, 1952.

Mesarites, Nikolaos. *Description of the Church of the Holy Apostles at Constantinople*. Edited and translated by G. Downey. TAPS 47, pt. 6 (1957).

Neale, J. M., ed. *The Primitive Liturgies*. London, 1875.

Neale, J. M., and R. F. Littledale, *Translations of the Primitive Liturgies*. London, 1869.

Nicolaïdes, A., "L'église de la Panagia Arakiotissa à Lagoudéra et la peinture byzantine du XIIe à l'aube du XIIIe à Chypre." Thèse de doctorat (Université de France, Aix en Provence, 1993), 3 vols.

————. "The Church of the Panagia Arakiotissa in Lagoudera, Cyprus, Chronological Survey." In *The Sweet-Land of Cyprus*, Birmingham Symposium 1991, ed. A. A. M. Bryer and G. S. Georghallides (Nicosia, 1993): 424.

————. "L'église de la Panagia Arakiotissa à Lagoudera, Chypre. Etude iconographique des fresques de 1192," *DOP* 50 (1996), 1–137.

Oddy, A., ed. *The Art of the Conservator*. London, 1992.

Oertel, R. *Early Italian Painting to Fourteen Hundred*. London, 1968.

Oxford Dictionary of Byzantium. New York and London, 1991.

Panofsky, E. "Die Entwicklung der Proportionslehre als Abbild der Stilentwicklung." *Monatshefte für Kunstwissenschaft* 14 (1921). Translated as "The History of the Theory of Human Proportions as a Reflection of the History of Styles," in *Meaning in the Visual Arts*. London, 1970.

Papadopoulos Kerameus, A. Ἑρμηνεία τῆς ζωγραφικῆς τέχνης. St. Petersburg, 1909.

Radojčić, S. *Masters of Old Serbian Painting*. Belgrade, 1955.

Papageorghiou, A. *Masterpieces of the Byzantine Art of Cyprus*. Nicosia, 1965.

————. "Εἰκὼν τοῦ Χριστοῦ ἐν τῷ ναῷ τῆς Παναγίας τοῦ Ἄρακος." In Κυπρ.Σπ. 32 (1968), 45–55.

————. *Icons of Cyprus*. Nicosia, 1992.

Bibliography

————. "Δύο βυζαντινὲς εἰκόνες τοῦ 12ου αἰώνα." *RDAC* (1976).

————. Ἱερὰ Μητροπόλις Πάφου. Ἱστορία καὶ Τέχνη. Nicosia, 1996.

Papageorghiou, A., and D. Mouriki. *Byzantine Icons from Cyprus*. Benaki Museum, exhibition catalogue. Athens, 1976.

Pelikanides, S. M., et al. *The Treasures of Mount Athos*. Vol. 2. Athens, 1975.

Report of the Department of Antiquities, Cyprus (*RDAC*). Nicosia, annuals.

Richard, J. *Documents Chypriotes des Archives du Vatican*. Paris, 1962.

Segers-Glocke, C. *Forschungsprojekt Wandmalereischaden: Arbeitshefte zur Denkmalpflege in Niedersachsen*. Vol. 2. Hannover, 1994.

Sophocleous, S. *Icons of Cyprus, 7th–20th Century*. Nicosia, 1994

————. *Panagia Arakiotissa in Lagoudera*, Cyprus. Nicosia, 1996.

Sotiriou, G. A. "Θεοτόκος ἡ Ἀρακιώτισσα τῆς Κύπρου." Ἀρχ.Ἐφ., 1953–54.

Steel, A. *Illustrated London News*. 6 February 1937.

Stylianou, A. "The Wall Paintings of the Church of the Panaghia tou Arakou, Lagoudhera." *Acts of the IX International Byzantine Congress, Salonika*. Athens, 1955.

————. Αἱ περιηγήσεις τοῦ Βασιλείου Γρηγορόβιτς Βάρσκυ εἰς τοὺς Ἁγίους Τόπους τῆς Ἀνατολῆς. Nicosia, n.d. [1957].

Stylianou, A. and J. "Donor and Dedicatory Inscriptions, Supplicant and Supplications in the Painted Churches of Cyprus." *JÖB* 9 (1960): 101.

————. *The Painted Churches of Cyprus*. Nicosia, 1964. Rev. ed., London, 1985.

Talbot Rice, D., ed., *The Church of Haghia Sophia at Trebizond*. Edinburgh, 1968.

Thompson, D. V. *The Materials of Medieval Painting*. London, 1956.

Torp, H. *The Integrating System of Proportion in Byzantine Art*. Institutum Romanum Norvegiae, Acta ad Archaeologiam et Artium Historiam Pertinentia, Series altera in 8°. IV, Bretschneider. Rome, 1984.

Vasari, G. *Vasari on Technique*. Translated by L. S. Maclehose and edited by G. Baldwin Brown. New York, 1907.

————. *Lives of the Painters, Sculptors and Architects*. Edited by W. Gaunt. London, 1963.

Vitruvius. *De Architectura*. Cambridge, 1962.

Walter, C. *Art and Ritual of the Byzantine Church*. Birmingham Byzantine Series 1. London, 1982.

Weyl Carr, A. *A Byzantine Masterpiece Recovered: The Thirteenth-Century Murals of Lysi, Cyprus*. Austin, Tex., 1991.

Wharton, A. J. *Art of Empire: Painting and Architecture of the Byzantine Periphery: A Comparative Study of Four Provinces* (University Park, Pa.–London, 1988).

Wharton Epstein, A. "Phases of Construction and Decoration in the Enkleistra of St. Neophytos near Paphos on Cyprus," *Byzantine Studies/Etudes Byzantines* 10 (1983).

Winfield, D. C. "Middle and Later Byzantine Wall Painting Methods: A Comparative Study." *DOP* 22 (1968), 61–139.

————. "Dumbarton Oaks' (Harvard University) Work at Haghios Neophytos, Monagri, Perachorio and Lagoudera, 1971, 1972 and 1973: A Final Report." *RDAC* (1978), 279–87.

Bibliography

Winfield, D. C. *Panagia tou Arakos, Lagoudhera: A Guide*. Department of Antiquities. Nicosia, n.d.

Winfield, J., and D. C. Winfield. *Proportion and Structure of the Human Figure in Byzantine Wall Painting and Mosaic*. BAR International Series 154. Oxford, 1982.

Part One: General Introduction

I

SITUATION AND HISTORY

The church of the Panaghia Arakiotissa is situated in the district of the Pitsilia, which comprises the higher parts of the southern end of the Troodos mountain range. It is at a height of just under 1,000 m and lies on a spur under the northeastern face of Madhari, the second highest of the Troodos peaks.

Two valleys with brooks join to form the main stream flowing down from this side of Madhari (Text Fig. 7). The eastern one is the Lagoudhera valley, known as Βασιλιτζί, and the westerly one

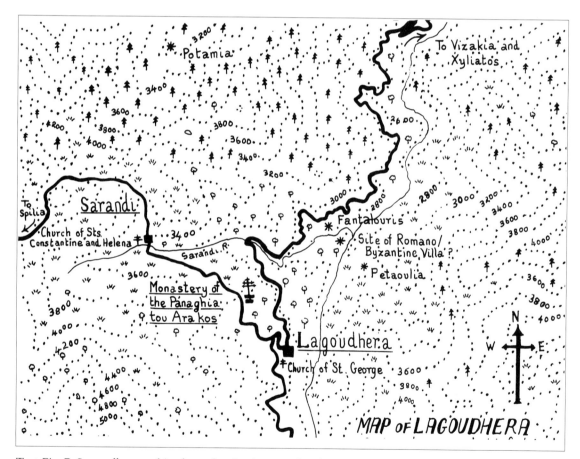

Text Fig. 7 Lagoudhera and its dependencies (contour heights in feet)

47

has the village of Sarandi at its head. Between the valleys is a spur of the mountain, at the end of which stand the monastery buildings and the church, about halfway between the two villages. Lagoudhera and Sarandi both have their own church, and as no village ruins are around the Panaghia Arakiotissa, it is unlikely that it was built as a parish church.

The mountain slopes are largely formed of gabbro, and they rise steeply so that they are only fit for terracing. The main crop is grapes, which are among the last to ripen on the island because of its elevation and northern exposure, and they are excellent in quality both for eating and for making wine. The olive and the almond both reach the upper limit of their habitat with the two villages, and the hazelnut and walnut flourish along the stream beds, or wherever there is a spring. Terraces grow vegetables enough for the families who till them. A certain amount of cereal was also grown on them by those villagers who, unlike the monastery, did not possess land farther down the valley. Villagers preserve the memory of a flour mill below the confluence of the two Lagoudhera streams. Nothing is now left of it, but when the waters ran high with the melting snow in spring it would have sufficed to grind the cereals grown by the villagers. The ruins of a similar mill still exist in the neighboring valley just below Platanistassa. The pollarded stump of a very ancient mulberry tree in the monastery's courtyard may indicate the production of silk at some period, since this was an important product of the island up to the eighteenth century.

The surrounding mountain ridges are now much denuded except for the forestry plantations of Pinus Nigrus and Pinus Brutus Rubea. When the church was built, the natural forest of cedars of Lebanon was probably still extensive. The undergrowth consists mostly of arbutus and scrub oak on the higher slopes, and sage and cystus lower down. The chief game are now partridge and hare, but in the medieval period there also must have been plenty of mouflon, the indigenous wild sheep of Cyprus. The hare, λαγός, probably gave its name to the village of Lagoudhera. Another derivation takes the origin of its name from the cyclamen that grow in abundance in these valleys. The petals of this flower look very like the ears of a hare and hence its name, λαγού τα φτιά, or "hare's ears," which the local dialect converted into λαουδχία, hence λαγουδερά.[1] Among the domestic animals, the chicken, the donkey, and the goat predominate, and every family kept its own pig, until it was recently forbidden to do so.

One of the major goat foods of the region is the wild vetch, whose beautiful purple blossoms cover the mountain terraces in the spring. In Greek it is called ἄραξ, and it gave its name as an epithet to the church of the Mother of God, Arakiotissa.[2] The use of a flower name as an epithet for Our Lady was not uncommon in Cyprus. The Panaghia Aphsinthiotissa, the Panaghia Mavriotissa, and the Panaghia Phorviotissa are among many other examples of like usage. However, the popular Cypriot explanation of the name and foundation of the church goes back at least to the first half

---

[1] N. Klerides, Χωριὰ καὶ πολιτεῖες τῆς Κύπρου, (Nicosia, 1961), 130–31.
[2] Ibid., 131–32.

of the eighteenth century when it was recorded by the Russian monk Barsky.[3] It relates that a princess was once attendant upon her husband on a hawking expedition. When the princess was resting, a hawk brought down a partridge not far from her, but when they sought to retrieve the bird, they found in its place an icon of the Mother of God. The princess enlisted the aid of her husband and built a church on the spot where the icon had been found, and she called it the Panaghia tou Ierakou, Our Lady of the Hawk. It is a pleasing legend, and current to this day among the villagers, but "Our Lady of the Vetches" must be preferred since it requires no change in the inscriptions (see below, p. 65).

The history of Cyprus in the Byzantine period is provided with scant documentation, and it is therefore not surprising that there should be nothing much to tell of an obscure valley such as Lagoudhera. Archaeological evidence has, however, provided some indication of the late Roman and Byzantine periods, and the picture could be considerably filled out by excavation.

The confluence of the Basilitsi and Sarandi brooks is about 200 m lower down than the present village of Lagoudhera. It is dominated by a low spur with rounded sides and on it are many fragments of ridged tile, potsherds, and broken-up masonry of mortared rubble. There are also the ruins of a small baths or cistern. The pottery is largely unglazed earthenware, but there are also fragments of sgraffito wares with green, brown, and cream glaze, and the site was certainly occupied from the Roman until well into the middle Byzantine period. On the northern slopes opposite to the confluence is another area of ground covered with plentiful potsherds and the fragments of a crude mosaic floor belonging to a small church. This area was partially investigated a few years ago.[4] The site is called Φανταλουρίς, and village tradition preserves the dedication of the church to St. Epiphanios. The nature of this early site could only be elucidated by excavation, but it must have been either a township or a great estate with a vicus around it. It seems unlikely that the valley could ever have provided support for a township, unless mines were in the area,[5] or that a village would have been wealthy enough to build baths. The most likely identification for the site, therefore, seems to be that of a fortified villa or castle on the spur, complete with its own baths or cistern, and a dependent village on the northern slopes with a small church.

The quality of the cistern suggests a date in the Roman period, but it could be as late as the seventh or eighth century. The carefully made tiled floor, the wall lined with a lime plaster with an

---

[3] V. Grigorovich-Barsky, "Странствования Василия Григоровича-Барскаго по святым местам Востока, 1723–1747," in Православное палестинское общество, vol. 2 (St. Petersburg, 1886), 302–3. For a Greek edition of the Cypriot sections, see A. Stylianou, Αἱ περιηγήσεις τοῦ Βασιλείου Γρηγορόβιτς Βάρσκυ εἰς τοὺς Ἁγίους Τόπους τῆς Ἀνατολῆς (Nicosia, [1957]), 94. For general reference, see Sir George Hill, *History of Cyprus*, vol. 1 (Cambridge, 1940); J. Hackett, *A History of the Orthodox Church of Cyprus* (London, 1901).

[4] Briefly reported in V. Karageorghis, "Chronique des fouilles à Chypre en 1966," *BCH* 91 (1967), 302.

[5] The detailed geological survey makes no mention of mineral workings in the upper parts of the valley, but there is an old slag heap that could indicate workings of a Byzantine date near the modern open-cast mines of Xyliatos, much lower down the valley (see below, p. 54). J. M. Carr and L. M. Bear, *The Geology and Mineral Resources of the Peristerona–Lagoudhera Area*, Memoir/Geological Survey of Cyprus, no. 2 (Nicosia, 1960).

aggregate of crushed earthenware fragments, and some fine water pipes are all indications of a period previous to the Arab invasion. The only other physical remains of note that may come from the site are a pair of very crudely carved leaf capitals, one of which is in the courtyard of a Lagoudhera village house, while the other is used as a base for a post supporting the eastern end of the secondary wooden roof over the monastery church. Higher up on the southern slopes near a spring and terraces called Πεταουλία is another reputed chapel site dedicated to St. John, and glazed potsherds confirm occupation of this site in the middle Byzantine period. The "Petaoulia" fields belonged to the monastery, as will be seen below.

The monastery church and the two present villages of Lagoudhera and Sarandi are at about the same height. If we assume that the valley became largely the property of the church, and that the church took over the functions of the lordship of the valley, then this may account for the desertion of the sites lower down the valley and the creation of the new villages. In support of this view, it may be noted that local tradition attributes the name of the village of Sarandi to the fact that the forty masons who built the church settled there and founded the village.

The church is older than the dated donor inscription (see below, p. 65), which gives the name of Leon Authentes and the date A.D. 1192 for the most important sequence of paintings. It is unlikely that the earlier sequence of paintings, which remain undated, could be ascribed to a

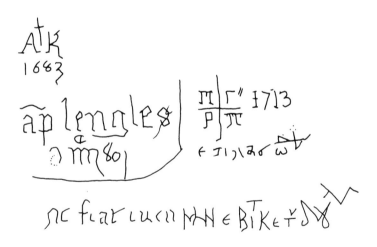

Text Fig. 8 Graffiti on the west jamb of the north door

period previous to the twelfth century,[6] and if so, the building of the church can only be ascribed to a date preceding its decoration in 1192 but still in the twelfth century. It has been plausibly

[6] These paintings had not been recognized as earlier than the 1192 A.D. paintings before Dumbarton Oaks' conservation work. Reasons for assigning them to a date previous to 1192 are given below as they are discussed. For a general account of the 12th and 13th centuries in Cyprus, see A. J. Wharton, *Art of Empire: Painting and Architecture of the Byzantine Periphery: A Comparative Study of Four Provinces* (University Park, Pa.–London, 1988), 68–90, and A. Weyl Carr, *A Byzantine Masterpiece Recovered: The Thirteenth-Century Murals of Lysi, Cyprus* (Austin, 1991), 63–110.

suggested that Lord Leon might have been a local governor of Cyprus,[7] but there is no evidence of this. All that can be said of this donor is that the word "αὐθέντης" attached to his name was an epithet given to upper-class Byzantine families; this sense of the word continued into Ottoman usage as *effendi*.

The date of the paintings is of interest since the 1192 series was painted after the conquest of the island by Richard I Lionheart. The disruption of trade and supplies caused by the Frankish invasion may well have been the reason the painters ran out of blue pigment for the upper backgrounds. This can be seen in the Ascension (see below, p. 197) and in some of the panels in the ground register (see below, p. 158).

The Byzantine aristocracy of an island like Cyprus would have been small in number. It must have been relatively easy for the Lord Leon, or his father, to institute enquiry as to where the best painters on the island were to be found. He chose the school or workshop associated with Bishop Cinnamos and the monastery of St. Neophytos at Paphos.

Until 1970 the church possessed two fine icons of the Mother of God and the Pantokrator made by the 1192 master. These were removed to the Department of Antiquities for safekeeping and for cleaning and restoration.[8] The evidence of the paintings suggests that restoration work in the church was carried out in the fourteenth century when the painter Leon or Leontios signed his name in an inscription around the exterior tympanum of the north door.[9] The restoration work was made necessary by water damage to the paintings, which almost certainly happened before the protective secondary roof was erected. If the church was not originally a monastic foundation, monastic life may have begun at the time of the restoration work. Other evidence of the Latin period is provided by a well-executed graffito on the west jamb of the north door with the name Ap Lengles in Gothic lettering (Fig. 143, Text Fig. 8). This name must belong to a member of the Lengles or Langlais family, and it is tempting to speculate that they might have taken over the lordship of the valley of Lagoudhera, but there is no evidence of this.[10] It seems possible that the name of the mountain, Madhari, and of this region in the Latin period was Presterone de la

[7] A. and J. Stylianou, *The Painted Churches of Cyprus* (Nicosia, 1964), 71; rev. ed. (London, 1985), 158. N. Klerides, *25 Μοναστήρια στήν Κύπρο*, vol. 2 (n.p., n.d.), 78, 79, less plausibly suggests that Lord Leon was governor of the whole island.

[8] These icons are discussed in A. Papageorghiou, "Εἰκὼν τοῦ Χριστοῦ ἐν τῷ ναῷ τῆς Παναγίας τοῦ Ἄρακος," Κυπρ.Σπ. 32 (1968), 45–55, pls. 1–4; and A. Papageorghiou, *Icons of Cyprus* (Nicosia, 1992), color dust jacket of the icon and p. 49. A. Papageorghiou and D. Mouriki, *Byzantine Icons from Cyprus,* Benaki Museum, exh. cat. (Athens, 1976), nos. 6, 7.

[9] See below, pp. 68–69, and C. Mango's appendix on this inscription in D. C. Winfield, "The Church of the Panagia tou Arakos, Lagoudera: First Preliminary Report, 1968," *DOP* 23–24 (1969–70), 379–80 and figs. 8, 9.

[10] C. Du Cange, *Les Familles d'outre Mer*, ed. E. G. Rey (Paris, 1869), 605. A member of the family is mentioned as an exile with Queen Charlotte at Rome in 1513. L. de Mas Latrie, *Nouvelles preuves de l'histoire de Chypre* (Paris, 1873; repr. Famagusta, 1970), 385, n. 1. Also see J. Richard, *Documents Chypriotes des Archives du Vatican* (Paris, 1962), 81, 93–94, 106, 126–27, 152–53, for a number of references to members of the family.

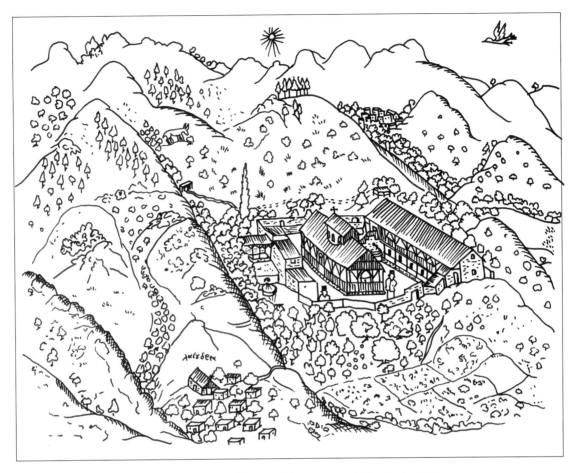

Text Fig. 9 Drawing of the monastery made by the Russian monk Barsky in 1735
(see bibliography Grigorovich-Barsky, redrawn to achieve greater clarity by J. C. Winfield)

Montaigne,[11] since the villages referred to under this name in Latin documents are in the Pitsillia. Richard suggests that the Logara de Condaran named in a land grant by King John II in 1440 may be Lagoudhera,[12] although earlier in the same book he identifies "Logara" as Louvaras.[13] The identification of Legora or Logara as Louvaras seems the most acceptable, since in the late fifteenth-century Venetian inventory of the island Legora appears as a *casal* of the Hospitallers, whereas Lagoudhera appears in its more or less correct form as "Lagodera," forming one of the *casals* of the royal demesne. It may be as a result of this royal overlordship that the Lagoudhera valley is known as Βασιλιτζί.[14]

The wall paintings of the little church of Sts. Constantine and Helena at Sarandi probably date from the sixteenth-century period of the Venetian occupation of the island, and an icon or

---

[11] I owe this suggestion to Peter Edbury of the University of Swansea.

[12] Richard, *Documents Chypriotes*, 143.

[13] Ibid., 68.

[14] Klerides, Χωριά, 131. De Mas Latrie, *Histoire*, 503–5.

two in the village church of St. George at Lagoudhera may also date from this period.[15]

The paintings along the exterior north wall of the Panaghia Arakiotissa are, unfortunately, undated. They are simple in execution and were made with a limited range of colors, and they tell us only that works of redecoration were carried out at some time between the fifteenth and seventeenth centuries. The paintings in the church of the Archangel at Vizakia, which was a dependency of the Lagoudhera monastery (see below, p. 54), are also undated, but they do not show any close relationship either to the work at Sarandi or to the monastery church. Gunnis gives a date for the church of the Archangel of around A.D. 1500,[16] but the paintings seem more likely to be of the late sixteenth or seventeenth century. Once again, all we can say is that painting was being carried out under the aegis of the monastery at this period.

The Turkish period in Cyprus seems to have brought back a prosperity to the Greek church, that had been lacking under the Latins. The rood cross in the Panaghia Arakiotissa has the date Α Χ Ο Γ, or 1673, inscribed upon it. The wooden iconostasis screen is certainly of the same date as the rood cross, and the elaborate carving and gilding are indicative of considerable prosperity (see Pl. 2). A carved wooden throne, an icon stand, and a carved wooden pulpit reached by a ladder that can be swung away from it probably also date from the seventeenth century. These furnishings are certainly not earlier than the building of the extension, since the pulpit depends partly upon its new walls. Wooden monastic pews of uncertain date were in the new extension, and this, together with the physical evidence that the pulpit belongs to the extension, may suggest that the west wall was knocked down in the seventeenth century to provide for a larger church, or even for the foundation of a new monastery. The north door of the new narthex has a sculpture of the Crucifixion inserted over it, with the date 1796.

Until recently, the church possessed an egg-shaped replica of a giant hailstone said to have been presented by the Turkish friend of a judge who was killed by it. The tradition runs that a Turkish judge, or *kadi*, who had heard of the fame and healing powers of the icon of the Mother of God at Lagoudhera, came with a party of men to deride the icon, and that he was miraculously killed by a hailstone as big as an ostrich egg. Villagers still point out the judge's burial site as the μνῆμα τοῦ καδή.[17]

In the early eighteenth century, the Russian monk Barsky visited Lagoudhera, and his account provides the first factual evidence that the church of the Panaghia Arakiotissa served as a monastery church. He recorded the legendary story behind the name of the church and drew a picture of the monastery complex (Text Fig. 9).[18] Barsky left his signature written carefully on the painting of St. Stephen the Protomartyr [83] in the apse: Βασίλειος μοναχός μοσχοβορῶσσος

[15] R. Gunnis, *Historic Cyprus* (London, 1936; repr. Nicosia, 1973), 311, 312, 424–25, for brief accounts.
[16] Ibid., 457.
[17] Ibid., 312. The story is told by Klerides, *25 Μοναστήρια*, 81, and it is still current in the village, but no one could say who had removed the miraculous stone from the church.
[18] Stylianou, Αἱ περιηγήσεις, 94, n. 3.

(Figs. 168, 176). It appears from his drawing of the monastery that the buildings stood then more or less as they do now. The building to the south of the church was an olive press knocked down in recent years.[19] According to Barsky, the church did have its secondary roof raised on a wooden framework. This framework depends upon stone buttresses that appear to be part of the masonry of the new extension. He states that the monastery was in the diocese of Kyrenia and that three monks were then living at the monastery, but he was saddened by their lack of observance of the rules of monastic life, particularly in allowing women into the monastery. His sketch shows an open water supply flowing from the spring in the corner of the valley; it flowed openly up to the time of the restoration of the monastery.[20] Earthenware pipes dug up along the course of the stream show that at one time there had been a piped water supply, perhaps at the time of the foundation. These pipes were of the same basic shape as those used for the cistern at lower Lagoudhera, but the crudity of the monastery pipes in comparison to those used for the cistern are witness to a sad decline in technology in the Byzantine period.

A manuscript account of the late eighteenth century, which was preserved until 1974 in the episcopal palace of Kyrenia, gives an inventory of the possessions of the monastery, and although it may be true, as N. Kyriazes states, that the monastery had a flourishing history,[21] the list of possessions suggests a house of moderate means at the date of the making of the list. It is a particularly valuable list since it gives the names of the lands that the monastery possessed. The terraces in the valleys to either side of it are still in its tenure and let out by the bishopric of Kyrenia, which has administered the property since it ceased to function as a monastery. The farms of Potamia were in a neighboring valley to the northeast of Lagoudhera. This area is now uninhabited and given over to forest land. The mention of two ruined hospices there suggests that the property was already in decay when the eighteenth-century inventory was carried out. All that can now be found there are fragments of ridged tiles, probably of Byzantine date, and sherds of unglazed earthenware. The farms of Vyzakia and gardens at Xyliatos are lower down in the foothills of the mountains, almost on a level with the plain. These were probably among the most valuable possessions of the monastery since the olives, cereal crops, and flax produced there would have provided a salable surplus over and above the needs of the monastic community. There is also an open-cast iron mine between Xyliatos and Vizakia, and near it are long-disused slag heaps. There are no records for the working of the mine, but if it had belonged to the church at the time of its foundation, this would have made it a considerably more prosperous place and would go far toward explaining the presence of high-quality wall paintings. These mines are also a source of high-quality red and yellow ochres and hematite, and a natural outcrop of pure umber is nearby, so that many of the basic pigments for the wall paintings could have been obtained locally.[22]

[19] It is now replaced by a press in the village, but the stone grinding wheel still lies in the monastery courtyard.

[20] Grigorovich-Barsky, "Странствованія," 302. The spring was originally tapped by cutting a small channel into the hillside and lining and roofing it with stones.

[21] The list is printed in N. Kyriazes, Τὰ μοναστήρια ἐν Κύπρῳ (Larnaca, 1950), 109–10, no. 95.

[22] Carr and Bear, *Geology and Mineral Resources*, also mention the occurrence of green earth and of gypsum in the

Situation and History

The date of the end of monastic life at Lagoudhera is unknown. No memory of monks at the monastery is preserved in either of the two villages, and it seems possible that the Turkish massacre in Cyprus in 1821 may have marked its end. At that time many of the clergy were executed, and the few monks of a small monastery like Lagoudhera may have been called away to repopulate the larger houses.

The history of the valley of Lagoudhera must rest for the moment as a matter of informed guesswork. In the late Roman and early Byzantine periods, the iron mine at the foot of the valley provided wealth for its owner, who may have built a villa nearby. In the period of the Arab invasions, from the seventh to the ninth centuries, life for a Christian subject was insecure, and the owner may have built himself a new fortified villa with baths or a cistern much higher up the valley on a naturally defensible site at the confluence of the Lagoudhera and Sarandi streams. The twelfth-century owner of the valley may have retired to a monastic life, building and decorating the church of the Mother of God that is the subject of this book. His son, Lord Leon, redecorated the church in 1192 in the best style of the period.

The repainting of the church in the fourteenth century, with additional work between the fifteenth and seventeenth centuries, may show that it served an active community with some money to spend. It may be that there was an extension of the monastic community in the seventeenth century and that the pulling down of the west wall, the building of a new iconostasis, and new monastic pews are evidence of this increase in prosperity for the church. The monastery seems to have flourished in a moderate way at least until the end of the eighteenth century. The community ceased to exist, perhaps in the early nineteenth century, leaving to posterity the remarkable beauty of its paintings.[23] By 1954 it had fallen into a ruinous condition, and in 1955 and 1956 a complete restoration of the structure was undertaken by the Department of Antiquities in cooperation with the bishopric of Kyrenia.[24] In the postwar period, some wall paintings in the ground register of the church, including the great panel of the Mother of God Arakiotissa, were cleaned by an itinerant schoolmaster who, unfortunately, removed several of the upper layers of paint. The monastic living quarters to the north of the church were in ruinous condition, and these were largely rebuilt in 1967 and 1968. Work on the cleaning and conservation of the paintings of the church was carried out by Dumbarton Oaks from 1968 to 1973.[25]

---

area. L. M. Bear, *The Mineral Resources and Mining Industry of Cyprus*, Ministry of Commerce and Industry, Geological Survey Department, Bulletin no. 1 (Nicosia, 1963), 162–68, has brief historical notes and a section on colors. See also P. Gennadius, *Cyprus: Mineral Substances Utilized in the Arts* (Nicosia, 1905).

[23] The first photographs of the paintings appeared in an article by A. Steel in the *Illustrated London News*, February 6, 1937. See also A. Stylianou, "The Wall Paintings of the Church of the Panaghia tou Arakou, Lagoudhera," *Acts of the IX International Byzantine Congress, Salonika* (Athens, 1955), 459–67; A. H. S. Megaw and A. Stylianou, *Cyprus Mosaics and Frescoes*, UNESCO World Art Series (New York, 1963); Stylianou, *Painted Churches*; A. Papageorghiou, *Masterpieces of the Byzantine Art of Cyprus* (Nicosia, 1965); D. C. Winfield, *Panagia tou Arakos, Lagoudera: A Guide* (Nicosia, n.d.).

[24] *RDAC* 1955, 10; 1956, 12.

[25] Ibid., 1971, 1972, 1973.

2

ARCHITECTURE

(Pls. 1–4; Figs. 1–6; Text Figs. 10–13)

The church in its present form consists of a rectangular naos with an extruded apse at the east. The naos is divided into three bays, of which the central one is the largest and is crowned by a dome set on a drum with twelve windows. A later extension is at the west end, and the whole of the church is covered by a secondary wooden roof that comes down on the north, south, and east sides to form an ambulatory around the church (Figs. 1–2).

The presence of a church that is earlier than the year A.D. 1192 is proved by the existence of a layer of wall paintings earlier than those executed in 1192 and by the fact that the floor level for this earlier painted decoration was some 10 cm lower than that for the second decoration of 1192. These earlier paintings survive in good order in the apse, and fragments of them are in the southeast corner of the naos under the dome. No clear structural divisions of an early nature exist, and it is difficult to say whether the 1192 decoration was accompanied by a substantial rebuilding program, or whether it was simply completed over the walls of an already existing building.[26] Perhaps there was a catastrophe such as an earthquake soon after the first church was built, and the structural repairs may well have consisted only in the filling of cracks and general repointing, but this would have necessitated pulling down all the paintings, if indeed they had not already been shaken down from the walls. The likelihood of an earthquake is further supported by the vertical structural crack down the center of the conch of the apse. The apse itself survived complete with semidome. It may be remarked that this has happened to many Byzantine churches; the apse remains standing because it is a strong, independent structure, while the rest of the church has disappeared or has been rebuilt. In the case of Lagoudhera, it is possible that the whole of the church was painted in the period before 1192, as shown by the surviving fragments in the southeast corner of the naos (see below, pp. 99–101, Fig. 41, Text Fig. 20). Or it may be that the earlier painter only completed the apse painting and a votive composition for the father of Lord Leon in the southeast corner of the naos.

[26] The repointing of the exterior in the course of repair work in the 1950s makes observation of the structure difficult, but there does appear to have been a large diagonal crack in the masonry of the south side, running roughly from the east side of the central bay at the top corner to its west side at the bottom corner.

Architecture

In the following description of the church it will be seen that much of the evidence for phases of building derives not from the structure but from the phases of painted decoration. This is inevitable because the comprehensive decoration conceals the structural evidence.

Phases One and Two: Twelfth Century

These two building phases are described together since there is no visible structural evidence for separating them. The structure consists of a rectangular, domed naos, with an apse to the east that is semicircular in shape both on the exterior and interior. The naos is divided into three bays, of which the central one is the largest and is crowned by a dome. The west and east bays are covered by barrel vaults, and the north and south walls of the bays between the piers are formed with blind arches (Pls. 1–4). A rectangular door is in the west bay of the south wall, and another is in the center bay of the north wall; both date back at least to 1192, since the painting covering the door jambs is of that date. The east bay is separated from the naos by the iconostasis, and it functions as a sanctuary space with niches in the eastern walls of the blind arches to serve as prothesis and diakonikon. The apse is lit by a group of three tall, narrow windows that have round arches and are separated by two mullions.

The west wall was demolished when the new extension was built, and the evidence for this demolition is clear. The painted plaster of the west vault of the naos ends with a broken-off section of red border all around the west end, and the plaster makes a steep right-angle bend along most of the length of the border, showing that there was at least a wall in the tympanum arch. The existence of the wall was further verified in 1970 by stripping off the covering plaster of the underside of the present arch. This revealed the rough face where masonry had been hacked away. It is reasonable to assume that an earlier narthex was destroyed when the present extension was built (see below, pp. 60, 62, 63; Figs. 4, 6), and there would also have been a west door to the church.[27]

The dome rests on a high drum with twelve windows, and this, in turn, is built over pendentives. The four piers divide the naos into three bays, and they also act as supports for the dome. Each has a plain, jutting cornice of wood to mark the level of the springing of the vaults and pendentives.

The walls are built of a core of mortared rubble with random-coursed facing stones. The majority of the stonework is of the local gabbro, which is extremely hard and difficult to cut. This accounts for the unevenness of the walls, which is evident in many places where the plasterer had to cover over stones that protruded considerably from the vertical faces. The second stone is a yellow limestone cut into small, rectangular blocks that are fairly neatly finished. Relatively few of these seem to have been employed, and they may perhaps have been taken from the site of the earlier Lagoudhera settlement mentioned above. They are apparent in the walls of the apse and in

---

[27] A. H. S. Megaw recalls that he saw evidence for an earlier narthex with north and south apses at the time of the 1955 to 1956 restoration, but we were unable to verify this.

the lower parts of the drum of the dome.[28] The internal surface of the apse walls appears to be more regular than the surfaces elsewhere in the church. It is impossible to give a definitive report on the masonry of the church, since the internal masonry surfaces are almost completely covered by plaster and paintings.

The third ingredient in the masonry is brick, and this was sparingly used.[29] The arches of the apse windows, the dome windows, and the tympanum over the south door all have brick voussoirs, and the dome itself may well be constructed of brick, but the covering plaster prevents observation. The only evidence was of one brick visible in a small hole in the horizontal, painted red border above the prophets in the drum. This may represent a brick course at the springing of the dome from the drum, or there may be more. The east side of the northeast pier under the dome has at least one brick in it, the existence of which could only be verified because there was a hole in paintings at about a meter above the ground level, but the hole was not large enough to allow measurements to be taken.

The vaults of the church were constructed of lime concrete and covered with ridge tiles of the normal Byzantine pattern, with imbrex tiles over the joints. The tiles were bedded in mortar to hold them in position, and a few still remain in situ, but the majority have gone since the addition of the secondary roof rendered it unnecessary to maintain the original tiling system (Figs. 3, 4, 5).

A marked change in the curvature of the dome occurs roughly at the level of the shoulders of the angels, painted in roundels beneath the central medallion of Christ. This change may represent the point up to which the dome was constructed without centering. Thereafter a wooden frame would have made building much easier.

It is not clear to what extent timber beams may have been used within the walls as a reinforcing element since they are not visible, but four massive beams were used to hold in position the central piers of the naos, which carry the dome. These were set in just above cornice level, but they were cut away during the restoration work of the 1950s in order to give a more open view of the paintings. The cornices of the piers are also made of wooden blocks; this is not a common feature in Byzantine church building, although it is found in other Cypriot churches. The windows of the drum each have a horizontal wooden support at the level of the springing of the window arch. These were presumably to hold the masonry in position at this level, but most of them are now loose in their sockets, and the window arches are noticeable more for their irregularity than for their uniformity. The lintels of the north and south doors are formed of beams that penetrate for a considerable distance into the wall on either side of the door. The beams are small and laid in series to extend across the thickness of the wall.[30]

---

[28] The exterior masonry of the drum is largely random-coursed gabbro, but it seems likely that it was squared up on the interior with a facing of ashlar sandstone.

[29] Brick does not seem to have been as commonly used in Cyprus as it was elsewhere in the Byzantine period. The surviving examples suggest a greater use of it in the 11th and 12th centuries A.D., e.g., the castle churches of St. Hilarion and Kyrenia, and the monastery churches of Apsinthiotissa and Koutsovendis.

[30] The movement of the lintel beams with changes in humidity and temperature has caused considerable damage

Architecture

A small, brick fireplace was built up against the western dado of the prothesis niche at some uncertain but early date, since the paintings behind it were quite free of dirt, in marked contrast to the grimy surrounding areas. The removal of this fireplace enabled us to see that the floor level of the church in 1192 was much the same as it is now, since one flat brick of the original floor remained in position. The brick measured 29 cm by 42 cm and was 3 cm thick. Two water-worn stones in the apse floor also appeared to be original, and thus the floor of the 1192 church may have consisted of a mixture of stones and flat earthenware bricks. The wall plaster of the 1192 paintings comes down more or less flush with the present floor level, although the painted red border of the painting is some 10 cm above the floor level. The wall plaster of the pre-1192 apse painting runs down to about 10 cm below the floor level of 1192, while the red border is a centimeter or two above it.

The floor foundations were made up as follows. The foundations of the church walls were 15 cm to 20 cm below the present floor level. Near the wall were uneven quantities of lime mortar, which had probably leaked away when the foundations were laid. Over this was about 10 cm of hard, tamped earth, probably laid down with water to ensure a firm base. It may be that the pre-1192 flooring was laid directly onto the tamped earth, but we were unable to carry out excavations to verify this. Over the packed earth was a setting bed, about 6 cm deep, of lime mortar with some charcoal fragments in it. This lime and ash mixture is the impure residue from lime burning, and it was economical to use it for such purposes as flooring. On this setting bed were laid the original tiles. The present tiled floor dates from 1956.

An original feature of the floor of the prothesis is a small dyke some 6 cm high in the northeast corner. It cuts off a corner of the floor space and seems to have been intended as a form of drain, although there is no pipe, and it could only have functioned as a soakaway. This was perhaps used for the disposal of the water used to rinse the chalice after Communion, since this water could not be thrown out in the normal way.

In the diakonikon floor, in front of the niche in the east wall, a small pythos is sunk into the ground with its lip below floor level. The "sunken" lip allowed a covering for the pot as well as a floor slab, and this was probably used for storing the Communion wine, unless it served the more romantic purpose of concealing a hoard of gold.

The altar is constructed of stones set in lime mortar with a lime plaster facing to it. A baldachino of wood was later built over it, but the roof of this was sawn off by order of the Department of Antiquities in the 1960s in order that the apse paintings might be open to view.

The original window frames have all disappeared, and those that replace them are in the style of Cypriot Byzantine windows, but date from the restoration of the 1950s.

---

to the paintings on either side of the doors at this level. At some period the north and south doors were partially blocked and formed into windows. Their appearance as windows can be seen in Mr. Wright's plans of the church, illustrated in Stylianou, *Painted Churches*, figs. 100, 102.

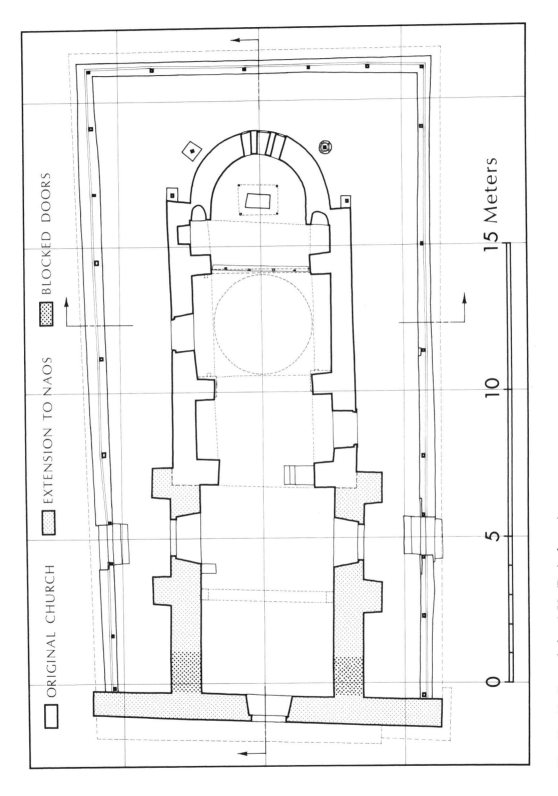

Text Fig. 10 Ground plan, 1:50 (R. Anderson)

ORIGINAL CHURCH

EXTENSION TO NAOS

BLOCKED DOORS

15 Meters

15

10

5

0

Phase Three: The Fourteenth Century

The surviving paintings of the old narthex are similar to the exterior paintings in the tympanum of the north door, which are attributed to the fourteenth century (see below, Chapter Twenty). In order to expose the figures on the east wall of the narthex, a part of the later extension wall that covered them was cut away. The cutting revealed that the fourteenth-century painting came to an end 20 cm within the thickness of the newer wall, at a right-angle turn marked by the vertical, red painted border. No further evidence was apparent as to the shape of this early narthex except for

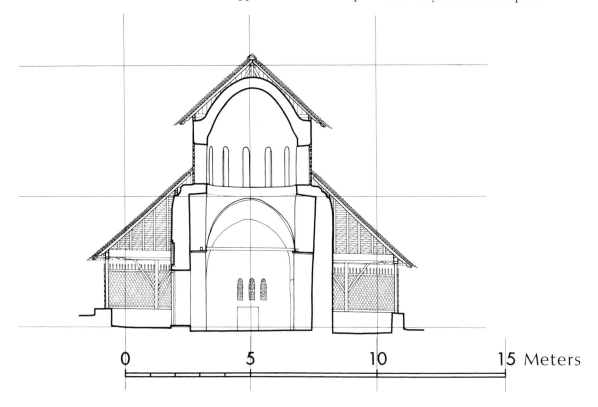

0   5   10   15 Meters

Text Fig. 11 North-south section through the church, facing east, 1:50 (R. Anderson)

the upper red border of the paintings on the south side. This runs diagonally at a lower level than the vaulting in the naos, and it indicates some lower form of roofing for the narthex. It is even possible that there was no proper narthex but only a porch with a gabled roof, the line of which is indicated by the painted red border.

In the naos, the paintings in the pendentives and elsewhere were also restored by this fourteenth-century painter, since the originals had been extensively damaged by water coming in through the windows of the drum. The restoration work is of poor quality, but it has not suffered much damage. This may indicate that a secondary roof was built over the church to protect it as early as the fourteenth century.

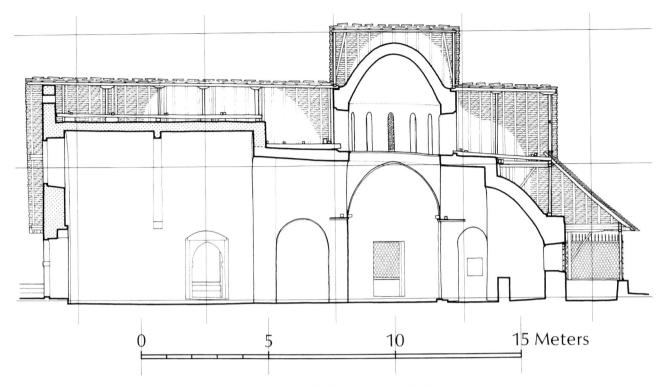

Text Fig. 12 East–west section through the church, facing north, 1:50 (R. Anderson)

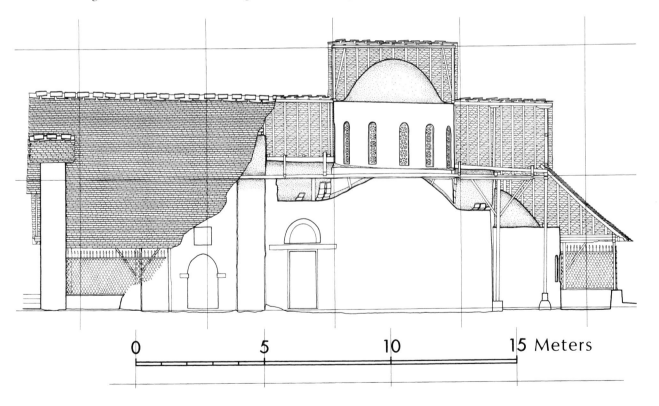

Text Fig. 13 South elevation of the church, with timber roof partially cut away, 1:50 (R. Anderson)

Phase Four: Fifteenth-Seventeenth Century

Between the fifteenth and early seventeenth centuries, a series of wall paintings was made along the exterior of the north wall at a height above the lintel of the door (Text Figs. 6, 10). There were probably more paintings in the lower register, but these have now fallen away. The gaps in the wall plaster for these paintings indicate that there were vertical supports on either side of the north door, probably made of timber. The plaster along the top of the paintings shelves outward a little, and it seems likely that a wooden beam lay horizontally along the wall here to act as a support to a sloping wooden roof. A timber-roofed structure was along the north side of the church at this period.

Phase Five: Perhaps 1673

If we assume that the present wooden furniture of the church is largely of one date, then the rood cross gives us the date 1673 for the making of a new iconostasis screen, a new throne, and a new pulpit. The pulpit, as we have noted above (p. 53), is supported upon beams built into the walls of the new extension, and it seems likely to be contemporary with it. If this is correct, then the demolition of the narthex and the building of the present extension may date to 1673. If the church did not serve a monastic community from the time of the foundation in the twelfth century, then the extension of 1673 marks another possible date for the foundation of the monastery (Text Figs. 11, 12, 13).

The new walls are of local stone built with lime mortar in much the same manner as the original church. The addition is in the form of a high, rectangular hall with a slightly pointed vault. Two doors to it were in the north wall and one door was in the south wall. The doors at the western end of the south and north walls were round arches with brick voussoirs. The door at the eastern end of the north wall has a pointed arch with some shallow moldings typical of the simple Cypriot Gothic style. Above the door is a naive relief of the Crucifixion with the date 1796. This was probably a late insertion, since the structural evidence indicates that the new western addition is of an earlier date. The west wall was originally a blank wall built straight up against the natural rock of the mountain. The roof was never covered with tiles, and it is clear from this, and from the form of the buttresses, that it was designed to be covered by a timber roof. This timber roof can be seen in Barsky's drawing of the monastery, and the present roof is a replica of it (Figs. 1–4, 6; Text Fig. 9). It is in itself an interesting structure of considerable complexity. The buttress on the north side to the east of the door of the extension covers up a part of the sixteenth- or seventeenth-century paintings. The buttress on the south side to the east of the extension door has a fragment of painted plaster with a grey background color and a red border. This is the only fragment of painting that appears to date from this phase.

Phase Six: 1955 and Afterward

The final period from 1955 onward saw the complete restoration of the structure by grout-

ing, repointing, and reroofing in lime concrete. The interior of the church was given a new floor, and earth was cleared away from the exterior walls where it had accumulated up to a meter or more in places. The rock face at the west was cut away to leave a free passage between it and the west wall of the extension, and a west door and a west window were added to it in order to give a better light for the paintings. At the same time, the western doors in the north and south walls of the extension were blocked up, and the two doors in the naos were opened up. The outlines of the blocked openings are clear in the exterior wall. The timber roof and the ambulatory around the church were rebuilt in the original pattern, and all the rotten timber was replaced.

The monastery buildings remained much as they appear in Barsky's sketch, but they became completely derelict. They were restored in 1967 and 1968, and electricity was brought to both the church and the monastery. In 1972 the western arch between the church and the extension was stripped of plaster in order to investigate the evidence for the destruction of the west wall of the church. The arch was then refaced with a honey-colored plaster in order to differentiate the earlier from the later periods of building.

The paintings were cleaned and conserved by a Dumbarton Oaks team from 1968 to 1973.

Undated Earlier Phases

At periods that are impossible to date but are certainly earlier than the exterior paintings of the north wall, the exterior of the apse was rendered with a lime plaster. On the south side, this has traces of crosses painted in red, and on the upper parts of the apse wall above window level the plaster has had pebbles stuck into it, resembling an early version of pebble dash. This technique for external surfacing appears in some other Cypriot churches. The north wall was rendered with a coarse plaster of mud and straw, which underlies the paintings.

3

HISTORICAL INSCRIPTIONS

The North Door in the Naos

The donor's inscription, giving the date of the decoration, is painted in white letters on the interior lintel of the north door below a representation of the Holy Tile [72] (Fig. 7). It is in three lines and measures about 1.12 m in length:

ἀνιστορήσθ[η] ὁ πάνσεπτος ναὸς τῆς ὑπ[ε]ρ[αγίας] θ[εοτό]κου τοῦ Ἄρακος // διὰ συνδρομ[ῆς] καὶ πολλ[οῦ] πόθ[ου] κυροῦ Λέωντ[ος] τοῦ Αὐθέ[ν]τ[ου] μηνὶ Δεκαιβρίο / / ἰνδ[ικτιῶνος] ια' τῷ ͵ςψα' ἔτους //

The most revered church of the All Holy God-Bearer of the Wild Vetch was repainted by the contribution and great desire of the Lord Leon (the son) of Authentes in the month of December (in the) indiction 11 (in) the year 6701.

This gives us the date of December 1192 for a redecoration of the church. The appearance of ἰστορῶ as a verb to describe the decorating of a church with painting is not uncommon in Byzantine usage. The inscription previously has been published four times; two of the readings are in agreement with ours as to date.[31] Only two variations are of note. The first is that W. H. and G. Buckler read Ἀράκου for the epithet of the Virgin. This is the form in common use in Cyprus, but the inscription reads quite clearly Ἄρακος, and it was correctly read by A. and J. Stylianou and Nicolaïdes. The second is that the Buckler, Stylianou, and Nicolaïdes translations have "was painted," whereas our reading takes into account the prefix ἀν and we have translated "was repainted." This accords better with the fact that the apse paintings were made by an earlier painter, and that there are traces of a similar, earlier layer of painting in the naos.

---

[31] A. Nicolaïdes, "L'église de la Panagia Arakiotissa à Lagoudéra, Chypre: Etude iconographique des fresques de 1192," *DOP* 50 (1996), 4–5. W. H. Buckler and G. Buckler, "Dated Wall Paintings in Cyprus," *AIPHOS* 7 (1944), 48–49. A. and J. Stylianou, "Donor and Dedicatory Inscriptions, Supplicant and Supplications in the Painted Churches of Cyprus," *JÖBG* 9 (1960), 101. G. A. Sotiriou, "Θεοτόκος ἡ Ἀρακιώτισσα τῆς Κύπρου," Ἀρχ. Ἐφ (1955), 87–91. The text of the final part of the inscription is difficult to construe as it stands. For a recent attempt at interpretation, see Nicolaïdes, "Panagia Arakiotissa," 4–5.

The inscription therefore tells us nothing about the building of the church but gives a firm date for the repainting of it. The use of the word "ναός" only indicates church and does not tell us whether Leon's redecoration was for a funerary chapel, a monastery church, or simply a parish church. There are no signs of foundations of any buildings around the church other than those of the present monastery buildings. It might be expected that if the village had originally clustered around the church, or if there had been castle walls enclosing it, some physical traces of these might remain in the form of masonry foundations or potsherds. The lack of such remains suggests that the church was designed as a funerary chapel, and perhaps Lord Leon was following the Byzantine practice of giving over his own land to form a monastery.

The name of the donor, Leon Authentes, is not known from any other source, and we can only assume that he was lord of the valleys of Lagoudhera and Sarandi. His name is repeated in dedicatory verses around the votive image of the Mother of God Arakiotissa (see below). These verses tell us that he had a family and suggest that he was still alive, since he prays for redemption.

Two facts suggest that the redecoration of the church was finished in December 1192. The first is that the frosty winter weather at Lagoudhera makes plastering work impossible, and therefore December is the latest possible end for a season of painting, rather than a time for the beginning. The second is that the inscription is on the register of paintings at ground level, and these were the last paintings to be executed, since Byzantine painters began in the dome and vaults of a church and worked downward to ground level.

The letter forms of the inscriptions are the same as those throughout the paintings, with the exception of the apse and of smaller areas of repainting. Therefore we know that the redecoration covered the whole of the church except for the apse. The inscription does not indicate how long the work may have taken, but perhaps it could have been completed in one season of painting, with the work beginning in the early spring of 1192 (see below, p. 318).

The Arakiotissa [139]

(Pls. 4, 32; Figs. 9, 224)

The image of the Mother of God Arakiotissa, to whom the church is dedicated, is painted on the south wall of the naos in the ground register. In this large panel, the tall and slender figure of the Mother of God stands upright in front of an ornate, backless throne; she enfolds in her arms the Christ child, while two angels hover around her head holding instruments of the Passion in their hands. Below them on the blue and green background, a long votive inscription is written in spindly, white letters. The script is aligned horizontally in two columns to either side of the figure and throne. Five broad lines of writing on either side give way to eleven shorter lines that become increasingly constricted as the background space narrows between the throne and the red border.

The first line reads horizontally and greets the Virgin with two of her titles, then follows the

invocation, which is written in dodecasyllabic verses running down each vertical column starting to the left of the figure. The inscription has been previously published, and cleaning and conservation have added little to previous interpretations.[32]

The first line on the left gives the Virgin her local title as Our Lady of the Wild Vetch, then the prayer of intercession proceeds as follows:

+Μήτηρ Θεοῦ ἡ Ἀρακιότησσα /// κὲ καιχαριτομένη

To the left of the figure is written the following:

Ἄχραντον ὁ σὴν ἐκμορφώσας // εἰκόνα χρώμασι φθαρτοῖς Πάναγνε // Θεομ[ή]τω[ρ] πόθω σὺν [πο]λλῷ καὶ θερ // μω[τάτη] πίστει Λέων [πε]νιχρὸς εὐ // τελὴς σὸς οἰκέτης // ὁ τοῦ Αὐθέντος //πατρώθεν // κεκλημέ // νος σὺν ὁ // μοζύγω καὶ // συνδούλη // . . . . // αἰτοῦσι // πιστῶς // δάκρυσιν // ἀμέτροις ///

To the right of the figure is written the following:

εὔθυμον εὑρεῖν βίου λοιποῦ // τὸ πέρας σὺν ὁμοδούλοις // κὲ παισὶ σοῖς [οἰ]κέταις // καὶ λήξεως τύχουσι τῶν // σε[σω]σμέν[ων] // [μό]νη γὰρ ἔχεις // τὸ δοξάσθαι // Παρθένε // εἰκαι τῶν // θέλειν δυ // σωπηθεῖσα // πάντως // τούτοις // παρασχεῖν . . . . . . ///[τ] . . . . . .

Arranged in verses and with normalized spelling, the inscription would read as follows:
Μήτηρ θεοῦ ἡ Ἀρακιώτισσα καὶ κεχαριτωμένη

Ἄχραντον ὁ σὴν ἐκμορφώσας εἰκόνα
χρώμασι φθαρτοῖς, πάναγνε θεομήτωρ,
πόθω σὺν πολλῷ καὶ θερμοτάτη πίστει
Λέων πενιχρὸς εὐτελὴς σὸς οἰκέτης
ὁ τοῦ Αὐθέντος πατρόθεν κεκλημένος
σὺν ὁμοζύγω καὶ συνδούλη . . . . .
αἰτοῦσι πιστῶς δάκρυσιν ἀμέτροις
εὔθυμον εὑρεῖν βίου λοιποῦ τὸ πέρας
σὺν ὁμοδούλοις καὶ παισὶ σοῖς οἰκέταις
καὶ λήξεως τύχουσι τῶν σεσωσμένων.
μόνη γὰρ ἔχεις τὸ δόξασθαι, παρθένε,
ἱκετῶν (οἰκετῶν?) θέλειν δυσωπηθεῖσα πάντως
τούτοις παρασχεῖν . . . . . τ . . . . . .

All-pure Mother of God, he who has portrayed
your immaculate image in perishable colors

32 See above, note 31.

67

with great yearning and most ardent faith,
Leon, your poor and worthless servant,
called after his father Authentes,
together with his consort and fellow servant [name of wife]
request faithfully with countless tears
to find a happy conclusion to the rest of their life
together with their fellow slaves and children, your servants,
and receive the death of the saved.
For you alone, Virgin, are able to be glorified
When entreated to provide these people with.....t....

The text of the final part of the inscription is difficult to construe as it stands; for a recent attempt at interpretation, see Nicolaïdes, "Panagia Arakiotissa," DOP 50, 1996, pp. 4–5.

This inscription brings to life the piety of the Byzantine donor of the paintings, speaking to us across a gap of eight hundred years. It indicates that Lord Leon, the donor mentioned in the above inscription, was still alive at the time that he had the church redecorated, since he prays for the salvation of himself, his wife, his children, and his household at the Day of Judgment. It mentions Lord Leon's father, who may have been the builder of the church.

The Exterior Tympanum of the North Door [159]

(Figs. 8, 303)
This inscription was first published by C. Mango,[33] and his rendering in conventional orthography, together with modified comments upon it, is given below:

+ Ἤχῳ εὐλάλῳ προδιαγνοὺς Ἀμβακοὺμ ἀραρότως ἐκ σοῦ, Παρθένε, Λόγου τὴν σάρκωσιν καὶ κόσμος λελύτρωται τῆς ἀρχεγόνου ἀρᾶς. Εὔχεσαι τῷ γράψαντι τὴν δέλτον ταύτην Λεοντ[ίου δια]κόνου. | Ἀμήν.

With a clear sound Habakkuk firmly foretold the Incarnation of the Word through thee, O Virgin, and [so] the world has been delivered of its original curse. Pray for him who has written this tablet, Leontios the Deacon. Amen.

With regard to the missing part, there can be little doubt that the penultimate word should be completed διακόνου, even if this is the wrong case. We are thus left to choose between Λέοντος and Λεοντίου. The second alternative appears the more likely because above the missing letter following the tau is a sign that looks like a rough breathing, but may have been meant as an accent.

33 Mango, appendix to Winfield, "Church of the Panagia tou Arakos," 379–80, figs. 8, 9. A correct manuscript copy of it taken in the 1930s was found in the papers of the late Father Gervase Matthew, O.P.

The spelling and accentuation of the inscription are, however, so erratic that no certain conclusion can be drawn. A parallel may be drawn with the accentuation of the same name accompanying a donor portrait in the narthex of the church at Asinou, which might be by the same hand:

Δέ[ησις] του δούλου του θ[εο]υ Λαιῶντιόυ

The final formula, which Mango suggests was copied from the colophon of a manuscript, is unsuitable for a wall painting. The first part of the inscription was identified by Mango. It is from a heirmos by George Sikeliotes (seventh or eighth century),[34] of which the published version runs as follows:

Ἤχῳ εὐλάλῳ προδιαγνοὺς Ἀββακοὺμ
ἀραρότου [sic] Λόγου τὴν σάρκωσιν
κέκραγεν ἀναφανδόν. ἀκοὴν ἀκήκοα
θείας βουλήσεως. Θεὸς γὰρ ἀτρέπτως
τοῖς βροτοῖς ὁμιλήσει ἐξ ὅρους
ἐρχόμενος παρθενικῆς ἐκ γαστρὸς
καὶ κόσμον λυτρούμενος
ἀρχεγόνου ἀρᾶς.

Mango points out that in line two, ἀραρότως, as in the Lagoudhera inscription, would make better sense.

Paleographically, this Lagoudhera inscription is extremely close to the one dated 1333 in the narthex at Asinou as well as to other inscriptions of the same period in the latter church. At Lagoudhera the inscription is associated with the tympanum painting of the Mother of God Achrantos ([158] pp. 334–35, Fig. 8), and stylistically it can be linked with the narthex paintings and with repair work on the paintings in the naos. The work in the two churches of Asinou and Lagoudhera is so similar as to suggest paintings by the same school, and if this assumption is correct, then the Lagoudhera inscription gives the name of one of these painters, Leontios the Deacon. The Asinou inscription of 1333 repeats the name Leontios and gives a date when this school was at work.

---

[34] Εἰρμολόγιον, ed. Sophronios Eustratiades, vol. 3 (Chennevières-sur-Marne, 1932), no. 154.

4

ICONOGRAPHY

The Church in December 1192

(Text Figs. 1–6)

Lagoudhera is a centrally planned church with a dome over a rectangular naos and an apse and bema to the east. It is small in size, measuring some 10 m in length by 5 m in width, and the dome is about 10 m high.[35]

This architectural setting for the painted decoration has two focal points. The major one is the dome, to which the eye constantly returns, and is occupied by the waist-length figure of Christ [1], painted to a larger scale than any other figure in the church. The secondary focal point is the semidome of the apse, which is occupied by the Mother of God with the Christ child [96], flanked by her two guardian archangels Michael [97] and Gabriel [95].

These two images of Christ and the Mother of God proclaim the church of the New Dispensation. The program of paintings illustrates a few of the main events of their lives, which were the subject of the major feast days of the church, and it illustrates the celebration of the redemption of the world through Christ in the form of the Liturgy, eternally celebrated by the church fathers and the company of saints and martyrs.

The church is dedicated to the Mother of God, and two dedicatory images are appropriately placed for the worshipper who enters the church from the door on the north side. The importance given to the north door suggests this was designed for a monastery church, since the living quarters for the monastery are on the north side of the church and the monks would have entered by this door for the celebration of their offices. The first image to be encountered is the half-length orans figure of the Immaculate Mother of God, the Panaghia Achrantos [158], painted in the tympanum over the exterior of the north door. The present painting dates from the fourteenth century, but the

---

[35] A comprehensive iconography of Lagoudhera has been published in A. Nicolaïdes, "L'église de la Panagia Arakiotissa à Lagoudéra, Chypre: Etude iconographique des fresques de 1192," *DOP* 50 (1996), 1–137. The present account is only a summary attempt to view the decoration from the point of view of patron and painter.

colors of an earlier painting can be seen where the fourteenth-century paint has eroded, and it is reasonable to assume that such an image formed part of the 1192 decoration.

On entering through the north door, the worshipper is faced with the full-length figure of the Mother of God Arakiotissa [139], painted life size on the ground register of the south wall, with her attendant guardian, the archangel Michael [140] (Pl. 4).

Below the Christ in the dome, the Second Coming is symbolized by a roundel of the Etoimasia [3] and the attendant angelic host of six archangels and four angels [4–13]. The two standard conventions for depicting the angelic host were either in the form of full-length figures moving forward to the east and bending in adoration, or as waist-length figures in roundels. Both conventions seem to have been current over a number of centuries, and it is typical of the precise style of the 1192 master that he should have chosen roundels for his angelic host, with the eastward movement achieved in a controlled manner by the series of circles that appear to roll forward, aided by the powerful sweep of the wings of the angels (Pl. 1) .

Below the angels and between the windows of the drum are twelve figures that are the only ones from the Old Testament represented in the church. These Old Testament figures were retained because they foretell the coming of Christ on earth, depicted below in the naos and bema, and the Second Coming in the form of the Etoimasia and the angelic host above their heads.

Christ's ministry on earth is foreshadowed by the Annunciation [38, 40] in the eastern pendentives and by the roundel of Christ Emmanuel [39] in the arch between the archangel Gabriel and the Mother of God. In the western pendentives are the four Gospel writers who told the story of the Word Incarnate.

The four surviving scenes of the life of Christ are the Nativity [142] in the south half of the west vault; the Baptism [54] in the western blind arch of the north wall; the Anastasis [50] or Descent into Hell, in the north half of the west vault; and the Ascension [78], covering the whole vault of the bema. The essential scene of the Crucifixion is missing, and it was probably painted on the west wall, now demolished. The iconography of the four scenes is unremarkable except for the precision and economy with which the painter treated these essentially narrative scenes. One further event in Christ's life on earth is the Presentation in the Temple, which was often painted as a narrative scene, but the Lagoudhera master used the symbolic image of Symeon holding the Christ child in his arms [74] on the ground register of the north wall to the east of the door.[36]

The life of the Mother of God is represented by the two narrative scenes of her Presentation in the Temple [70] in the lunette of the north wall under the dome and of her death and Assumption, the Koimesis [138], in the lunette of the south wall under the dome. The presence of both these scenes is warranted by the dedication of the church to Mary, but they have additional warrant in the fact that the Presentation foreshadows the Nativity, and the Koimesis is one of the twelve Great Feasts of the church (Pls. 3, 4, 22–24).

---

[36] H. Maguire, "The Iconography of Symeon with the Christ Child in Byzantine Art," *DOP* 34–35 (1980–81), 261–69.

General Introduction

The Second Coming, which is symbolized by the Etoimasia, halfway up to Heaven in the dome, has its accompanying earthly symbol of the Last Judgment, painted in the ground register on either side of the arch into the sanctuary. It takes the simplified symbolic form of St. John the Baptist and the Mother of God Eleousa [75, 69] on the north side and Christ Antiphonetes [127] on the south side. St. John and the Mother of God pray for the redemption of mankind in words that are written in black on the scroll held by her, and Christ gives his cautionary answer in red letters, on the same scroll (Figs. 136, 137, 283). The Deesis as a symbol of the Last Judgment, with its theme of salvation through prayer and the intervention of the redeemer, forms a natural link with the celebration of the Liturgy. This is symbolized in the apse by a number of figures of the church fathers and deacons. The eight principal celebrants in the ground register of the apse hold texts from the Liturgy of St. John Chrysostomos.[37]

The register above the church fathers is often given to the prefiguration of the Liturgy in the form of the Communion of the Apostles, but at Lagoudhera the universal theme is pleasingly modified by local patriotism, and seven Cypriot bishops are depicted in roundels. They are, from north to south, St. Zenon [98], St. Nikon (?) [99], St. Philagrios [100], St. Auxibios [101], St. Herakleidios [102], St. Makedonios [103], and St. Tryphillios [104]. To these were added the most important of Cypriot saints, the apostle Barnabas [110] and the archbishop Epiphanios (?) [109] on the mullions of the west window. There are two further bishops in roundels below the apse windows; one of them is the Cypriot Bishop Spyridon [111]; the inscription for his companion is destroyed, but he was almost certainly another Cypriot bishop [112]. The local Cypriot emphasis is continued with three more saints who were added by the 1192 master: St. Lazaros [124], St. Hilarion [148], and St. Kyprianos [125].

The saints celebrating the Liturgy in the apse all belong to the earlier period of painting at Lagoudhera, but the theme of the Liturgy is continued in the paintings of 1192 in the bema. To either side of the apse arch are the deacon saints, Stephen [83] and Romanos the Melode [122], swinging their censers in toward the altar, and two further deacons, St. Stachios [90] and St. Nikanor [94], are in attendance in roundels. St. Romanos the Melode officiates not only as a deacon but also as a hymn writer, and his Akathistos hymn appropriately celebrates the Mother of God. The three other important hymn writers, St. John of Damascus [91], St. Joseph the Poet [80], and St. Theophanes the Poet [117], are also represented in roundels in the bema. St. John of Damascus can also claim a double role similar to that of St. Romanos, in that his second homily on the Koimesis is a source for the iconography of this scene. Bishop Hypatios of Gangra [86] seems to have no special connection with Cyprus. His image appears in the face of the blind arch in the north side of the bema. St. Nicholas [106] appears in the earlier apse painting, among the church fathers celebrating the Liturgy. His image is the only one to appear twice, for he was painted for a second time by the master of the 1192 paintings on the north wall of the central bay to the west of

---

[37] C. Walter, *Art and Ritual of the Byzantine Church*, Birmingham Byzantine Series 1 (London, 1982), for the development of liturgical programs in apse decorations.

the door [71]. Perhaps the popularity of St. Nicholas may account for this second image since the laity, who looked to the saint for all manner of help in their difficulties, would not have been able to find and venerate him in the apse.

Another allusion to the Liturgy is at the west end of the naos on either side of the south door. Here St. Zosimos [151], on the west side of the door, administers the final Communion to St. Mary of Egypt [150], to the east of the door.

The remaining spaces in the church are filled by a selection of the company of saints who bear witness to the theme of salvation through Christ. In the place of first importance come the "pillars of the church," the apostles Peter [143] and Paul [52], placed symbolically on the two western pilasters under the dome. There was no need of further images of the apostles since they all appear in apostolic groups in the scenes of the Ascension [78] and the Koimesis [138], and the evangelist apostles appear in the pendentives.

A pair of images that were necessary to the general scheme of Christ's church were Constantine and Helena. St. Constantine was necessary as the first Christian emperor and convoker of the First Ecumenical Council at Nicaea. St. Helena, his mother, was celebrated as the discoverer of the true cross and as the founder of the Cypriot monastery of Stavrovouni. For this reason, she was a saint particularly venerated in Cyprus, and it is highly probable that the traditional images of Constantine and Helena holding the true cross between them were painted on the ground register of the now-destroyed west wall.

The hermits and the monks play their part in the imagery, together with the church fathers and the bishops. There are eight monk saints [55, 58, 59, 79, 118, 137, 145, 148], and most of these were anchorites, though they wear the regular habit of monks. There are two specifically anchorite extremists denoted by their near nakedness. St. Onuphrios [81] is on the western reveal of the blind arch of the bema. He was a monk of Hermopolis who lived for sixty years in the desert, and he is depicted naked, with a long beard, and a shrub to cover his private parts. Only one dedication of a church to St. Onuphrios is recorded in Cyprus, in the hills below the monastery of Makhairas. The other anchorite has already been listed in connection with the Liturgy, St. Mary of Egypt [150], who paid for her harlotry by an ascetic life in the desert, and she is depicted as a half-naked skeletal figure. She has the distinction of being the only woman among the company of saints at Lagoudhera. The remaining twenty-five images are mainly of the glorious company of martyrs, and of those classified as Anargyroi, the holy moneyless ones, who healed the sick without taking a fee.

St. Christopher [149] is in a roundel in the lunette over the south door. This was an appropriate place for him, since he was the patron of travelers and anyone who looked at him would come to no harm that day. Since the north door was probably for the monks, any visitor to the church would normally leave by the south door, with St. Christopher watching over him.

Iconographic numbers are not given for the destroyed west wall, but the likely subject matter would have been a large painting of the Crucifixion in the lunette, Constantine and Helena to one side of the west door, and possibly St. Mamas, the most popular of all Cypriot saints, and St.

George, another very popular saint in Cyprus, on the other side of the door.

Thus, by December 1192, the church decoration was finished to represent the City of God of the New Dispensation. Lagoudhera is a good example of the hieratic scheme of imagery that apparently evolved out of the iconoclast controversy for application to the centrally planned church with a dome. Narrative schemes of decoration that seem to have evolved from the fourth to the sixth centuries continued in use side by side with hieratic schemes, since narrative was a more apt method for decorating the long walls of a basilican church. The hieratic scheme applied to the centrally planned church represents the most complete and systematic decorative exposition of the Christian faith that has ever been evolved. Otto Demus traced the evolution of it in mosaic at Hosios Loukas, Chios, and Daphni, and although the parts of the scheme may never have been as rigidly ordered as he suggests, this does not invalidate the existence of a system.[38] Lagoudhera provides firm evidence for the system, and it is the latest example that we have of it before Byzantine church walls become increasingly cluttered with inessential, if picturesque, narrative.

At Lagoudhera, the narrative element is strictly confined within the red borders of each scene. Some events have totally abolished narrative in favor of symbolic representations. These are the Etoimasia, the Deesis, and the self-contained figure of St. Symeon holding the Christ child. The dedication of the church to the Mother of God warrants the two narrative scenes of the Presentation and the Koimesis. But the once-sumptuous image of her in the ground register of the south wall, although embellished with gold and silver leaf, reverts from narrative to the severe symbolism of the Mater Dolorosa.

Maguire has shown the relevance of religious writing as a source for the evolution of the iconography of many religious paintings, and for the particular placing of scenes and single images on church walls. At Lagoudhera, the dedicatory image of the Mother of God of Sorrows refers directly to the scene of the Koimesis above it. On the north wall opposite to these paintings, Symeon holding the Christ child is a reference to the Presentation of the Virgin above him.[39]

The treatment of the real and pictorial space in the church is in keeping with the hieratic system of decoration. The broad, empty background spaces of vermilion or blue abolish any illusion of real space in favor of a mystical vision that thrusts both the individual figures and the narrative scenes out of our time and space and into a magical presence in the church. This paranormal reality is fostered by a baroque handling of composition that incorporates the sacred figures

[38] O. Demus, *Byzantine Mosaic Decoration* (London, 1948). I lost my copy of this seminal work in a fire. When the text of the present book was almost completed, I found that my notes of forty years ago on Demus's book had survived the fire and I reread them. Although this was not our intention, it will become apparent to the reader that our text is in part a technical and factual analysis of the evidence that Demus had intuitively observed. Lagoudhera may change some of the reasoning and deductions that he made. In particular, it shows that the system of mosaic decoration was just as well suited to wall painting in the hands of a painter who understood it, whereas Demus (pp. 61–62) thought that the spread of wall painting helped in the dissolution of the system. His explanation of the asymmetrical frontal portrait and the three-quarter-profile head may need modification, but his observations of these phenomena, and the spatial arrangements of Byzantine church decoration, were astonishingly accurate.

[39] H. Maguire, *Art and Eloquence in Byzantium* (Princeton, 1981), 64–65, for specific mention of Lagoudhera.

into the real architectural space of the church.[40] None of this spatial treatment and probably none of the iconography represents original creation by the 1192 painter, but what is original is the masterly skill with which he melded all the elements of the system into a coherent whole.

The internal evidence for those seminal meetings that must have taken place in the winter of 1191 between Lord Leon and his master painter to decide upon the program of paintings is slight but of interest. If the church contained only the apse paintings and the votive image or images commissioned by Lord Leon's father, patron and painter would have discussed the preliminary planning of the repainting of an otherwise bare-walled church. We may imagine Lord Leon suggesting a list of saints. The experienced master painter would size up the ground register in his mind's eye and explain to Lord Leon that if he wanted life-sized figures he could have about a dozen saints on each of the north and south walls and four more on the west wall. He could also have twenty or thirty waist-length figures in the soffits and other odd spaces. When they discussed scenes, the really important decisions would have had to be made. They were in agreement that they would have large scenes filling vaults and lunettes, and settle for only seven of them. The church was to have an austere iconography, but it was to be painted on a large scale to give the maximum effect of majesty in the small spaces available.

We can conjecture that the Authentes family was from a locally based, land-owning aristocracy of perhaps many generations' standing in Cyprus, since Lord Leon's father had insisted upon so great a concentration of Cypriot saints in the apse. We can also conjecture that they were a modestly conservative family since Lord Leon apparently did not ask for a picture of himself in supplication at the feet of the Mother of God. This latter point is not entirely certain since there could have been a portrait of him and his family on the lost west wall or in the narthex, if there was one.

The fact that the apse paintings were left as a decoration and not overpainted, as was common practice, may bear witness to the filial piety of Lord Leon. It also shows a remarkable tolerance on the part of the master of the 1192 paintings. Or perhaps he even appreciated the totally different bold style and coloring of his predecessor. Certainly he seems to have agreed and accepted the Cypriot emphasis of the scheme since he strengthened it by adding St. Lazaros, St. Kyprianos, and St. Hilarion.

Lord Leon probably provided as much gold and silver leaf as he could afford or obtain for the embellishment of the dedicatory image of the Mother of God Arakiotissa. It is clear that he wanted his little church to be as fine as possible, but he was unable to afford, or more likely, unable to obtain the variously colored marble pieces necessary for real opus sectile revetments. And so he asked for the painted marble dadoes [53] and opus sectile [90a] and the imitation glazed tile revetment [87–89] to be simulated as carefully as possible. The painter carried them out with the same care and precision that he devoted to his figural work. The 1192 dado is in strong contrast to the often perfunctory dado work that was carried out in quite grand churches elsewhere.

---

[40] See below, pp. 311–16, for further comment on the means by which images and scenes became a real presence for the Byzantine viewer.

The most striking fact to be gained about the painter is his mastery of the internal layout of the paintings. He must have been an experienced master with many church decorations to his credit since the whole Lagoudhera ensemble gives an impression of unity of purpose, with no hesitancy as to the harmonious division of walls and vaults, and none in the relative size and proportion of his ninety or more figures.[41]

The Fourteenth-Century Paintings [154–159]

(Figs. 300–303; Text Figs. 12, 13, 50)

A few fragments of painting remain from a now-destroyed narthex. These are similar in style to the image of the Mother of God Achrantos [158] in the tympanum over the north door and to the paintings dated 1333 at Asinou (see below, pp. 334–35). The iconographic program of the naos and apse were not altered, and the painter of this period contented himself with repairing the damaged earlier paintings.

Later Paintings on the Exterior of the North Wall

(Figs. 304–308)

The Panaghia Achrantos [158] and the inscription [159] have been mentioned above, (see p. 69). The upper register of paintings, reading from east to west, consist of an unidentified mounted warrior saint [160]; St. Theodore Stratilates, mounted and killing a dragon [161]; and St. Menas as a mounted warrior [162]. The Ancient of Days with archangels censing him is over the tympanum of the north door [163] along with a bishop [164] and a prophet [165]; the scene of the Transfiguration [166]; a bishop [167]; St. Herakleidios [168]; and another bishop [167].

In the lower register are fragments of painted plaster [170, 171], but no subject matter is distinguishable. Not enough of these paintings remains to form any impression of an organized program. They are described below (see pp. 329–44).

---

[41] See below, pp. 275–79, for a more detailed discussion of planning and layout.

5

Conservation and Restoration

The major physical damage to the paintings is the result of the destruction of the west wall in order to enlarge the church with the consequent loss of all the paintings on it, and those of the narthex beyond it. A structural crack running more or less vertically down the semidome of the apse may indicate earthquake damage before 1192.

With the exception of the ground register, the paintings were neither very dirty nor very badly damaged. The dirt above the ground register was made up of soot from candles and oil lamps, mingled with the dust of eight centuries. The lack of a heavy coating of soot may suggest that the church began life as a funerary monument rather than as an active monastery.

In the ground register, paintings suffered damage probably from the casual movement of church furnishings and from the construction of new furnishings, such as the large iconostasis screen of 1673. Paintings that extended over the wooden lintels of doors or wooden cornices suffered from the movement of the wood, since in some cases the plaster ground was not flexible enough to move with the wood, and it fell off the wall.

It was reported that earlier in the twentieth century an itinerant schoolteacher had tried to clean the Mother of God Arakiotissa and the archangel in the ground register of the south wall. This may account for the loss of paint layers, particularly in the face and hands. It is possible that this cleaning also destroyed most of what was left of the gold and silver leaf in the Arakiotissa, although centuries of kissing and devotional attentions had probably removed most of it by 1960. We made no great attempt to clean these areas since it was felt that future methods might achieve a better result with less risk of removing the remaining fragments of gold and silver leaf. The same cleaner may have coated the Koimesis in the lunette above them with some form of preservative. This would account for the slightly blurred and hazy effect of the colors, in contrast to the rest of the work of the 1192 master, which is characterized by crisp, clear colors.

Other casual damage was caused by the crush of congregations on feast days, and by the churchgoers' ritual of lighting a candle to their patron saint and sticking it onto the paint surface of his image, where it burned until gutted. The result is either darkened patches of color, or, in the case of yellow ochre, the heat was usually intense enough to transform it into red ochre. Considerable portions of the imitation marble dado pattern in the naos were missing or damaged by contact with the boots of the congregation.

General Introduction

The paintings of 1192 suffered from water seepage in some areas of the drum of the dome, the pendentives, the west vault of the naos, and the semidome of the apse. With the exception of the apse and the drum of the dome, these are all areas that were repainted to some extent, probably in the fourteenth century. This repainting shows little sign of water damage, which suggests that the secondary wooden roof over the whole church may have been added at an early date or soon after the repainting was carried out. The fine condition of most of the twelfth-century painting is certainly due to the secondary roof. This not only shelters the masonry structure from the severe winter gales bringing rain and snow, but it also protects the structure from too much temperature change by avoiding direct sunlight on roofs and walls. It has also made the church darker so that light damage was reduced.

The painting in the semidome of the apse suffered from patchiness due to water-soluble salts. We found, by experience, that the easterly winter gales were driving rain and snow through a vertical, rectangular space in the secondary structure so that they fell on the external roof of the semidome. This no longer had any tiles to protect it. They had been allowed to fall off, since the secondary roof was thought to be sufficient protection. We covered the open rectangular space with glass to prevent further damage. This has been improved upon by the Cyprus Department of Antiquities and no further damage should occur. The heavy saturation of water in the apse is evidenced by the fact that we colored in the white salt efflorescence, but further efflorescence of salts has in turn destroyed our toning down of damage. Efflorescence may well continue for a further fifty years or so until the plaster has completely dried out.

In the drum of the dome, it is evident that some of the windows must have remained without glass for quite a long period. This caused water damage to the prophets on the northwest side, and to the western pendentives, with some lesser damage to the Virgin of the Annunciation in the southeast pendentive.

In the west vault of the naos there was damage from water seepage that must have occurred before the construction of the secondary roof. More severe damage in the upper eastern section of the Nativity was caused by rain coming in through the broken windows of the drum.

The paint surfaces of the apse paintings and of the 1192 paintings suffered general flaking in the background areas and wherever the paint layers were thinly applied. The painters mixed into their plaster considerable quantities of chopped straw and chaff. The plaster ground only thinly covered this addition of organic binders. Also, the plaster was frequently reworked to bring up moisture to the surface before painting, and this may have helped bring the binding materials up toward the surface before painting began. The chaff and straw would dry out more quickly than the plaster around them. As the fragments of binder contracted, perhaps over a period of a hundred years or more, the plaster surface above them flaked off, together with the pigment, exposing the particles beneath. This reaction would be very slow, as the interior body of lime plaster will hold moisture for long periods. It is only the thin upper surface layer of lime with pigment in it that quickly converts from calcium hydroxide to calcium carbonate to form an impervious surface layer.

Conservation and Restoration

Aside from this damage, which would not have occurred in the lifetime of the painters, the paint surfaces are in remarkably fine condition. The only pigment to suffer notable damage is vermilion. This was applied with a glue medium, and where it was laid over a yellow ground, as in the background to the Christ in the dome, it has powdered away in some areas. Vermilion also undergoes a chemical change toward black as a result of exposure to light or contact with lime. Most of the vermilions of the dome and pendentive areas have darkened considerably. This contrasts with the brighter appearance of the same pigment in the bema, where no sunlight and little daylight penetrate.

The colors of the areas repainted in the fourteenth century are in good condition. They are readily distinguishable from the colors used by the 1192 master because they are thinner in texture and have different tonal values. The workmanship of the repainting in the higher areas is slipshod in comparison with the original work by this painter on the east wall of the narthex. The explanation may be that he was using an insecure ladder rather than scaffolding, and he frequently covered perfectly good original work that was not in need of repair. Where this occurred, we have removed the overpaint.

Our first task was to carry out a preliminary survey of the surface condition of the colors and the security of the plaster ground. We then experimented with a general purpose cleaning fluid (see below) and with dry cleaning by soft rubbers. Work began in the dome and continued downward through the vaults and semidome of the apse to finish in the ground register.

The Christ in the dome, the chevron pattern, and the angels were initially cleaned by gently dusting over the surfaces with soft brushes followed by working over the surfaces with india rubber. We then found that most areas responded further to the use of harder rubbers pared down with a knife so that individual pigments could be cleaned following the brushstrokes of the painter. Finally, pencil-type erasers were used to follow the complicated layering pattern of pigments that build up the detail for faces, hair, and jeweled garments. Throughout the church as far down as the ground register, we proceeded with the same cautious treatment of preliminary cleaning followed by experimental further cleaning until we were satisfied that we had removed all dirt that could be safely removed.

The ingrained mixture of soot, sweat, and drops of oil from lamps in the ground register was more difficult to handle. We used a solution of Lissapol N with water, and small amounts of white spirit and ammonia. It was found that a warm water solution greatly helped in dissolving the dirt. Candle wax was first pared down as far as was safe with medical scalpels or dental tools. Where patches of dirt proved very resistant we used the above solution combined with fine dental-grade pumice powder and soft brushes.

In general, the plaster and paint surfaces were firm, and there was no need to apply surface fixatives. In the areas damaged by water seepage there was some detachment of plaster from the wall. As a fixative, we injected a lime slurry with a small admixture of polyvinyl emulsion. The loose area was held under gentle pressure, using a sponge rubber pad backed by a wooden press, until the fixative had dried.

General Introduction

For plastering, we brought in rock lime and slaked it in our own pit in the churchyard. Slaked lime improves over the years, and areas like the dado, which were the last to be replastered, should benefit from the increased slaking time for the plaster used. In a few areas where the pigments tended to be powdery, they were repeatedly sprayed with a saturated solution of lime water.

The methods of restoration used at Lagoudhera were the decisions of the authors. Our views are pragmatic and apply only to wall paintings where the layers of color are quite distinct and separate, and there is no problem with the blending of colors, as in oil painting.

In a church that had large areas of plaster and paint missing, the remaining original work can be made more readable by toning down the whiteness of new plaster with a neutral color. Where the paintings have only small holes, no neutral color can be found for the repair, and it is better to supply a weak imitation of the original.

At Lagoudhera we followed compromise measures that allow the eye to concentrate on the original painting rather than the damaged areas. In background areas we restored a blue grey to the missing areas of blue background, and we put in the missing red in the damaged background of the Christ in the dome. Where areas of repetitive pattern were missing, most noticeably in figures with imperial robes, we restored the patterns.

The missing areas of plaster were replaced with a lime plaster of a different texture from the original. The only major areas of loss were in the lower part of the prophets along the rim of the drum, the fractured areas over lintels of doors and the wooden cornices of the piers, and the dado areas. In the case of the prophets and the missing figural areas, such as the head and halo of St. Mary of Egypt, we painted in the missing forms in sympathetic tones of color. No attempt was made to repaint detail or to simulate the buildup of colors characterizing the technique of the original paintings. The myriad, small white flecks where straw or chaff had flaked off the surface of the painted plaster were colored with a tone close to the original.

The one major area of repainting was the 1192 dado pattern, where the severe and irregular damage upset the balance and harmony of the painted registers above. We therefore replastered the lost areas, giving to the surface of the plaster a rough texture quite different from that of the smooth, original surface. We then repainted the opus sectile patterns but left out the imitation veining of the marble as simulated by the original painter. These two measures make the restoration easily recognizable.

The restorations were carried out mainly with earth colors, some of which we found locally and ground for ourselves. The media used were lime water and/or a casein or glue. All painted repairs are water-soluble, and the paint is thin without the thick opacity of the original, so it can be readily distinguished by the inquiring eye.

Part Two: The Apse Paintings

6

DESCRIPTIONS

The earliest painted decoration in the church is found in the apse (Text Fig. 1). There are three registers of painting. The upper register in the conch contains the enthroned figure of the Mother of God and child accompanied by archangels. The middle register consists of a continuous narrow band running around the apse, with red borders above and below it. It contains seven roundels, each with the waist-length figure of a Cypriot church father. The lower or ground register extends down to just above the present floor level, and it is interrupted at its center by a window formed of three narrow lights. Eight more church fathers are assembled here. The two window mullions each contain a small figure, and beneath the window, in a rectangle outlined in red, are two further roundels with waist-length figures.

The apse paintings are undated, but it is quite clear that they were made before the adjacent 1192 paintings, since the plaster of the bema arch overlaps the plaster of the panels in the apse.

Two additional fragments of painting that belong to this earlier period of decoration were found at dado level in the naos. The first was in the damaged dado beneath the 1192 painting of the Arakiotissa [139] on the south wall at the east end of the naos. This fragment was removed from the wall, remounted, and now hangs in the west end of the church. A smaller fragment was seen through a hole in the damaged dado under Christ Antiphonetes [127]. No other traces of a previous decoration were found under the 1192 sequence of paintings. The technical evidence (see above, pp. 56–59 and below, p. 276) suggests that these two fragments belong to the period of the apse decoration, and it can be assumed that the earlier decoration was not confined to the apse but that it was meant to extend through the sanctuary and into the naos.

The Mother of God and Child with Archangels [95–97]

The Enthroned Mother of God and Child, flanked by the Archangels Michael and Gabriel (Pls. 5, 6; Figs. 10–13; Text Figs. 15–17)

Along the base line the conch measures 6.12 m, and its height at the center, measured along the surface, is 2.65 m. These measurements include the red borders defining the perimeter of the

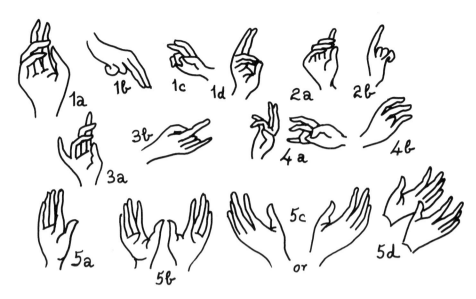

Text Fig. 14 The articulations of the hand in gestures of blessing and exortation throughout the twelfth-
century decorations

conch. The figures appear against a plain backdrop of an upper ground of blue and a lower foreground of green; the ratio of green to blue is approximately 1:6 (Plate 5; Fig. 10).

The conch is dominated by the central figure of the Mother of God seated upon a throne
with her slippers resting on a broad footstool edged with jewels. With her hands Mary steadies the
figure of the Christ child against her breast. The child's legs are bent as if he were seated, and he
clutches a rolled scroll in his left hand while extending his right hand in blessing (Text Fig. 14.1c).[42]

The throne has a tall back that extends as high as Mary's shoulders, and it is magnificently
patterned and decorated with jewels. The fat, tasseled bolster that rests on the patterned seat is
partly covered by a broad, white cloth. The bolster is sunk convincingly at the center to suggest
Mary's weight, and the fringed ends of the white cloth reappear to either side of the seat to give
some suggestion of depth. In contradiction of this illusion of depth, the white cloth falls vertically
from the bolster without contouring its bulk. The whole upper surface of the footstool is revealed,
as well as the front and the two lateral edges.

The archangel Gabriel advances from the left, and his right hand gestures across his body
toward Mary, while in his left hand he holds a stave. The archangel Michael stands to the right
with his left hand clasping a stave, while with his right hand he gestures toward Mary. The heads
of both the archangels are turned toward Mary and their faces are in three-quarter profile. Their
gazes, however, are turned away from her in the most unnatural manner as they look toward the
naos. In nature, this would involve a painful contortion of the eyeballs, but in the painting it serves

[42] The various positions of the fingers of a hand held up in blessing, or allocution, throughout the whole 12th-
century decoration are illustrated and listed in Text Fig. 14.

Descriptions

as a very useful device to link the congregation in the naos to the central figures. Both archangels are dressed in the traditional himation and chiton with clavus. Their feet are clad in boots richly decorated with pearls, and the tips of their staves of office are also bedecked with pearls.

The four figures in the conch all have haloes with vermilion inner and white outer outlines, whereas the other figures in the apse all have black inner and white outer outlines to their haloes.

The Mother of God and Child [96] (Fig. 13, Text Figs. 15, 16)

The inscription "The Mother of God" is placed to either side of Mary's halo in the normal abbreviated form. The large, vermilion letters and accents are outlined in fine white line and would have shone out grandly with the original brilliance of the vermilion. The letters for this inscription are twice the size of the white lettering used for naming the archangels.

Mary sits very stiffly upright, but her bent legs drift sideways to the right. She wears a close-fitting wimple of bright blue under the maphorion, which contours and flows over her head, shoulders, and upper arms before falling into narrow, vertical folds to the right of each leg. The maphorion is somber; it has a dark red ground, with black lines and fold lines, and washes of thin sky blue that produce the effect of shot silk of a dark purple color.[43] Her tunic has a dark grey ground, black lines and outlines, and solid areas of cool blue highlights. Touches of bright color are provided by the double bands of yellow on her cuffs and at the edges of her maphorion where it outlines her face. There are also traces of decorative vermilion lines on the inner side to the hem folds of her maphorion. The segmenta on her forehead, shoulders, and cuff are small, yellow rings, each picked out with five pearls. The narrow white sash, whose ends tumble through her fingers, has decorative red lines on it, and her slippers are colored bright vermilion with four white pearls decorating the toes. The upper part of Mary's figure, as far down as the bolster, is contoured with a thick, white line

At the center of the somber and cool figure of the Mother of God, the Christ child appears luminous with bright color. His chiton has a bright blue ground with thick white highlights, and a single vermilion line marks his clavus. His himation has a yellow-brown ground, vermilion lines, umber fold lines and outlines, and the whole is threaded with linear, creamy yellow highlights to imitate chrysographia. The scroll in his left hand is white with narrow, red tie ribbons. The cross bars of his halo are white, and each has a central vermilion jewel.

The figure of the child is placed directly under his mother's head so that the same notional vertical axis would bisect both figures. The top of the child's halo is tangent to the notional base of Mary's halo at a point one nose length from Mary's chin.[44] Both figures have faces shown in the

---

[43] Cennino Cennini, *Il Libro del arte*, ed. and trans. by D. V. Thompson, New Haven, 1932–33, chap. LXXVI, p. 53. Pliny, *Natural History*, Ch. 35, para. 26, section 45, mentions a similar compromise for the simulation of purple.

[44] The nose length is that of Mary above, measured from the nasal incision to the base of the nose. The top of the Child's halo lies three of these nose lengths from the notional eye line in Mary's face. Proportion and construction

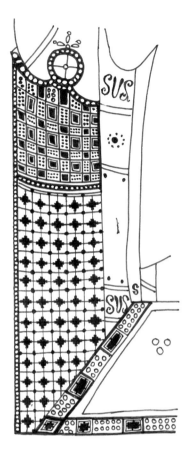

Text Fig. 15 Decoration on the upper part of the throne of the Mother of God [96]

Text Fig. 16 Decoration of the lower part of the throne of the Mother of God [96]

frontal asymmetrical aspect; Mary's gaze is directed sideways across the wider plane of her face toward the archangel Gabriel on the left, and the child's gaze is directed toward the archangel

are covered more fully in J. Winfield and D. C. Winfield, *Proportion and Structure of the Human Figure in Byzantine Wall Painting and Mosaic*, BAR International Series 154 (Oxford, 1982). See also H. Torp, *The Integrating System of Proportion in Byzantine Art*, Institutum Romanum Norvegiae, Acta ad Archaeologiam et Artium Historiam Pertinentia, Series altera in 8°, vol. 4, Bretschneider (Rome, 1984). Torp writes from a point of view different from ours and some of our respective conclusions differ, but we are in agreement about the broad outlines of the system. D. C. Winfield, "Middle and Later Byzantine Wall Painting Methods: A Comparative Study," *DOP* 22 (1968), 63–140. See also V. Mako, *Lik i broj* (Belgrade, 1998); V. Mako "The Proportional Distribution and Age of Frescoes in the Church of St. Basil in the Sea, at Hilandar," in *Hilandarski Zbornik* (Belgrade, 1997), pp. 75–97; V. Mako, "Principles of Composition and Proportion in the 13th-century Wall Paintings of Mileševo," in *Mileševo Notes* 3 (Prijepolje, 1998), pp. 21–36. Mako's work (all in Serbian) is based on a slightly different interpretation of the proportional system used by 13th-century Byzantine painters.

Text Fig. 17 An archangel's [95, 97] boot and stave

Michael on the right. The child's head measures less than half that of his mother, and he has the figure of a small adult.[45]

The child is given the appearance of an infant with his chubby cheeks and wide, high forehead. However, the ratios of the vertical measures for his head are those of a miniature adult, except that the forehead area is increased at the expense of the hair.

The frame of the back of Mary's throne is yellow, and it is filled with alternating rectangles and squares containing pearls or single jewels (Text Fig. 15). The whole frame is outlined with a continuous, narrow black band dotted with single pearls. The knobs and upper rail are trimmed with an edging of pearls. The black panel within the frame has a design of semicircles, with outlines that have a single row of round jewels with white outlines. These outlines encircle a corridor filled with a delicate vine meander with bunches of grapes outlined in fine vermilion, blue, or white lines. The central circles and the interstices of the design are filled with leaf pattern outlined in white. The front of the throne is visible to either side of the figure, and each side is topped by a round, jeweled knob on top of two panels containing diaper patterns (Text Fig. 16). The lower pattern is made up of interlinked, stepped crosses and the upper pattern of intersecting jeweled bands; both are built up on a yellow ground.[46]

The bolster on the seat has a dark red ground, black lines and outlines, and vermilion highlights, and each end is gathered by a white loop. A blue band with white outlines contours the bolster on either side, and this is studded with a single jewel picked out with pearls. The footstool is yellow, and its upper surface is decorated with groups of three large pearls in horizontal rows along the center. The three jeweled edges have a dark red ground that is decorated with single jewels of red, blue, or green. These alternate with double rows of pearls. This footstool is identical

[45] Winfield and Winfield, *Proportion*, 91–95, fig. 17.

[46] Both these interlacing diaper patterns appear in the work of the 1192 Lagoudhera master, who used them to decorate the loroi of his archangels.

with the one portrayed on the fragment of painting that was removed from beneath the dado of the 1192 paintings [141] (Fig. 41, Text Fig. 20.2c).

The Archangels Gabriel [95] and Michael [97] (Pls. 5, 6; Figs. 10–12; Text Fig. 17)

 The titular inscriptions are white. The letters are similar to those elsewhere in the apse, but flaking at the edges has deprived them of their serifs, and they have lost much of their original elegance.

The archangels each carry a tall, vermilion staff of office with elongated knobs decorated with drop pearls. Their wings are each built up in similar colors, and one of them is furled up behind the halo while the other is unfurled down the back in each figure. The body of the wing has a dark red ground with vermilion striations, and the long feathers are built up in black and white. Both angels wear a wispy, white hairband with a blue jewel at the center. Their chitons have a light grey ground, dark grey shadows, black lines and outlines, white washes, and highlights in thick paint applied in both blocks and lines. The clavus of both archangels is made with two bands of vermilion.

Their himations are different in color, but they both have the same striking characteristic of being painted on two different ground colors within the same garment, so that some groups of folds are built up with a darker range of tones than other groups. Thus Gabriel has dark folds around his waist and along the hem; these are made on a dark red ground with black lines and fold lincs, and red highlight lines. The lighter sections of his himation have a light umber ground, red lines and fold lines, and highlights made in blocks and lines of thick white, as well as with fine line and wash. On his upper right thigh, the area of white highlight is further emphasized by a curving row of white dots.

Michael's himation has dark folds at his waist and down his right side, which are built over a dark red base with black lines and fold lines and vermilion highlight lines. The lighter sections of his himation have a light red ground, red lines and fold lines, white washes, and thick white highlights in blocks and lines.

Both archangels are shod in red boots decorated with rings of pearls. The boots have double black bands dotted with single pearls across the toes and ankles (Text Fig. 17).

The Roundels of Church Fathers [98–104]

(Pl. 7; Figs. 14–22; Text Fig. 18)
Seven roundels float within a narrow band that runs around the apse at the base of the conch. The central roundel lies due east over the center light of the window. Each roundel contains the waist-length figure of an elderly Cypriot church father, each with a closed book against his left side and with his right hand held in front of him. From north to south the figures are as follows: St. Zenon [98]; St. Nikon [99]; St. Philagrios [100]; St. Auxibios [101]; St. Herakleidios [102]; St. Makedonios [103]; and St. Tryphillios [104].

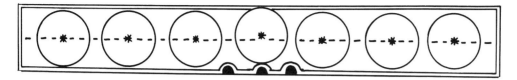

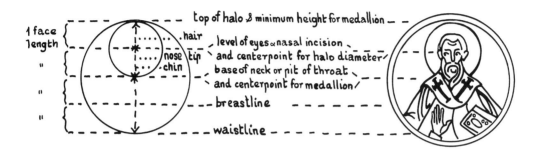

Text Fig. 18 Diagram showing the method of alignment and construction of the roundels in the middle
register [98–104] in a horizontal panel

The width of the roundel band from north to south is 6.12 m at the top and 6.28 m at the
base. The height of the band is irregular and averages about 80 cm. The roundels stand free of the
red borders outlining the panel, but the central roundel is perched over the east window and
overlaps both red borders.

The internal diameter of the roundels is 66 cm and that of the haloes is 33 cm. The southern
end of the panel is narrower by a few centimeters than the central and northern areas so the painter
reduced the size of the diameter of the roundel, but not the measures of the figure and its halo,
which remain the same in each roundel.[47]

The medallions were constructed around a notional median line, roughly bisecting the height
of the band. All the medallion centerpoints can be aligned along this line, and the bases of the
haloes are all tangent to it. The evidence for the constructional system is present in the compass
marks for the centers of circles and in the preliminary drawing lines, and it is further supported by
the regularity of the measures both in the geometry of the circles and in the figure (Text Fig. 18).

The background to the roundels is blue and green. The green foreground extends to approximately a quarter of the height of the band. In the upper ground of blue, the brushwork is very

[47] The diameter of all the haloes is standard. The haloes are not tangent to the roundel borders with the
exception of that of St. Tryphillios. The top of his halo overlaps the border of his roundel, which is smaller than that of
the others. The nose measure (nasal incision to base of nose) and the chin measure (base of nose to chin) are equal to
each other and from one head to another. The vertical head measure (vertex of head to base of chin) is equal to four
nose measures. The height of the forehead varies in measure due to the variety of hair styles.

clear in the form of broad, horizontal brushmarks, except for a single broad brushstroke that contours each roundel as far as the green. The inscriptions are painted high up on the blue background to either side of each roundel, and all are written in spindly white letters.

The roundel frames are yellow with black outlines and white outer outlines, with the exception of the roundel of St. Herakleidios [102], which has a single outer outline in white. The backgrounds to the figures within the roundels alternate in color. Roundels 98, 100, 102, 104 have a red ground over which a broad band of vermilion was painted toward the outer edge. The vermilion is now badly discolored to a greyish black. The other three roundels [99, 101, 103] have a plain, dark red background. The haloes of the figures are yellow with a black inner and a white outer outline. The books held by the church fathers each have a vermilion spine and a cover with a yellow ground decorated with a varied pattern of gems and pearls.

All the church fathers are seen in the frontal aspect. Their faces are asymmetrical in relation to the median of the nose, and the gaze of their eyes is directed to one side.[48] Their white hair and beards vary in style, but their faces differ little from one to the other, except for a variation in the highlight patterns within the forehead. Each church father wears a phelonion, which falls in voluminous folds. Each has an omophorion decorated with a long, black cross on each shoulder.

St. Zenon [98] (Pl. 7; Fig. 22)

The saint's inscription is unabbreviated. He has smooth hair parted at the center and a long beard that falls to a point under the neatly rounded chin. His right hand holds the top of his slanting book. His omophorion has a thick white ground, blue wash shadow lines at the edges, and opaque black crosses. His phelonion has a light green ground, green shadow lines, and thick white highlights.

St. Nikon (?) [99] (Fig. 18)

The inscription is damaged and incomplete. The upper layers of paint in the halo and at the top of this saint's head have flaked away, exposing preliminary drawing and the washes that form the base colors.

The damage to the halo reveals that its circumference follows a preliminary outline in grey on the white plaster. Damage within the head shows preliminary drawing outlines in grey marking the central curve of the hair over the forehead, and a horizontal brush line marking the nose bridge and upper lid line. There are two layers of yellow within the halo: the base yellow overlaps the base layer of green laid in for the head; both base colors were applied over the white plaster. The second and final layer of yellow for the halo underlaps the second green of the ground laid in for the head.[49]

[48] For a discussion of the asymmetrical face, see Winfield and Winfield, *Proportion*, 83–87, 136–44, and below, pp. 287–90, and Text Fig. 45.

[49] For a comparison with the 1192 painter's method of laying in color, see below, pp. 307–11.

Descriptions

The saint's book is upright and his right palm is turned inward. His beard and his omophorion are similar to those of St. Zenon. His phelonion has a yellow-green ground, umber fold lines, and thick white highlights over which was applied a rather slapdash wash of light blue.

St. Philagrios [100] (Figs. 15, 20)

His inscription is complete, save for some missing accents and the missing tail of the final ς. The upper head, halo, and roundel borders have suffered much from the flaking away of the upper layers of pigment.

Two preliminary drawings for the head are revealed by the damage. One in pale red defines the contours of the hair and marks a horizontal eye line. A second definitive and enlarged drawing in grey defines the outline to the skull, the shape of the hair over the forehead, and the placing of the right ear. A horizontal eye line was also drawn, and it forms a T-junction with a descending vertical to the right side of the nose.[50] Further grey lines define the outlines to the roundel borders and the circumference of the halo. Both drawings were executed on the white plaster in broad brush lines. It is evident that the painter blocked in the whole of the head with his base wash of green, and the yellow base of the halo did not extend under it.[51]

The beard of this saint divides beneath the chin into two square-ended locks. His omophorion is similar to that of Zenon, and his phelonion has a light green ground, green fold lines, and thick white highlights, over which a blue wash was applied so hastily that it intrudes into the green ground. The saint's right hand extends palm downward across the central panel of his omophorion, and his book is upright.

St. Auxibios [101] (Fig. 17)

The second and third letters of his name are damaged. His hair is smooth, with a tuft at the center of his forehead, and his long beard divides beneath the chin, one side swirling gracefully to a point over the other. His omophorion is similar to that of St. Zenon. His phelonion has a yellow ground, red and dark red fold lines, and thick white highlights. His damaged right hand is raised with the palm outward, and his book lies aslant his left arm (Text Fig. 14.5b).

St. Herakleidios [102] (Figs. 14, 21)

The inscription is complete. The saint's head is damaged, revealing further evidence as to the initial preliminary drawing in light red brush line, followed by the corrective drawing in grey

---

[50] Winfield and Winfield, *Proportion*, 160–62. The T-junction formed by the horizontal eye line and the vertical nose line were the formative framework around which Byzantine painters constructed the face. It can often be seen in damaged manuscript illuminations, icons, and wall paintings.

[51] He did not cover the whole of the halo with a preliminary base wash of yellow. In this the apse painter differs from the 1192 master, who washed in a base yellow for the whole halo area. See below, p. 305. The second green or ground color upon which the apse painter built up the definition colors for the head has a vivid emerald tone rather in contrast to the yellow-green of the ground used by his successor.

brush lines that formed the basis of the final painting. This roundel is distinct from the others in that the painter omitted the outer black outline to the roundel, which has only a single contour outline in white.

The saint's beard comes to an undivided point below his chin. His book is upright, and his right hand is raised in blessing, with the two forefingers upright (Text Fig. 14.1a). The tips of the two other fingers touch the top of his thumb. His omophorion has a ground of thick white, but unlike those of the other church fathers, the edges are picked out with vermilion lines. His phelonion has a light green ground, green fold lines, and thick white highlights.

St. Makedonios [103] (Fig. 19)

The inscription is uncertain because of the absence of some of the letters, but since these are all Cypriot church fathers, Makedonios seems likely. He has a neatly rounded, short beard that reveals his neck and the yellow bordered neckline of a blue undertunic. His omophorion is similar to that of St. Zenon, and his phelonion has a light brown ground, light and dark umber fold lines, and thick white highlights. His book is upright and his hand lies palm down across his omophorion.

St. Tryphillios [104] (Fig. 16)

His inscription is complete. His hair is styled into a cluster of tight curls that gather horizontally across his forehead. His long beard divides into wispy tresses below the chin. His right hand is palm downward, and the fingers rest on his book, which is placed in a diagonal position. His omophorion is like that of Zenon but the pale blue wash at the edges is reinforced with dark blue. His phelonion is light green with green fold lines, white wash highlights, and thick white highlights, of which some are applied very broadly.

The Standing Bishops [105–108, 113–116]

(Pl. 8; Figs. 23–38; Text Fig. 19)

The ground register has two panels on either side of the central window lights, each containing the standing figures of four bishops. The panels each measure an average 1.68 m in height and 1.65 m in width. In the north panel, running north to east, stand St. Tychon [105], St. Nicholas [106], St. Meletios of Antioch [107], and St. John Chrysostomos [108]. In the south panel, from east to south, stand St. Basil [113], St. Gregory the Theologian [114], St. Athanasios [115], and St. John the Almoner [116]. The inscriptions for the figures are written in spindly white letters to either side of their haloes.

All eight bishops turn toward the center of the apse, and their figures are in the three-quarter-profile aspect, with the head and shoulders inclined forward. Their stances are more or less identical. With their inner hand they hold up to shoulder level the top of an unfurling scroll. The outer

Descriptions

arm is bent across the body so that the hand can support the base of the scroll.

The white scrolls each bear an inscription from the liturgy of St. John Chrysostomos. These are written in watery black letters, line below line, with no horizontal dividing lines. The outlines of the scrolls are drawn in umber.

The bishops wear the traditional episcopal garments.[52] A white omophorion fits around the neck, and is marked by a black cross on each shoulder; the long center panel falls vertically and then loops up over the outer arm of the figure. Exceptionally, the omophorion of St. Gregory has an unhindered vertical fall. Under their omophorions, the bishops all wear a phelonion, which falls loosely from the shoulders and is caught up in rippling folds over their inner arms, revealing a triangle of the epigonation. The phelonions worn by St. Meletios and St. John Chrysostomos are covered with a design of bold, black crosses and should more properly be called polystavrions. All the bishops have an undergarment or sticharion that falls in a stiff vertical before heaping into horizontal folds over their black slippers. At the wrist, each forward arm reveals a heavily ornate cuff, or epimanikion, and some figures have a thick black clavus. Each bishop wears an epitrachelion, but only part of the vertical front panel is visible where it falls from beneath the phelonion. The patterns on each epimanikion, epigonation, and epitrachelion are executed in fine, dark umber lines upon a yellow ground. The pattern panels on each epigonation are separated by an intervening wide bar in dark umber. Each epimanikion has a pattern at the wrist formed of yellow circles outlined in a black band. Otherwise, the patterns are as follows (Text Fig. 19):

a single, large asterisk with dots at the end of each arm;
a square net pattern with alternating yellow and umber squares;
a diamond net pattern with alternating yellow and umber diamond shapes;
a diamond net pattern with a single bar bisecting the base angle;
a diamond net pattern with a single bar bisecting all the angles;
a vermiculated pattern with scroll and palmette;
a repetition of concentric circles with the outer circles tangent to each other, the inner circle containing a single cross; the corridor between circles filled with dots; and the interstices filled with vermiculation.

Each omophorion has white tassels hanging from its hem, and the edge of each epigonation is fringed. These garments are much damaged, and some of the decorative detail has gone.

The bishops are tall and slender, but the width of the phelonion gives to each figure a central mass and an appearance of authority. Each of the saints has the face of an old man with little variation, even in the patterned highlighting of the forehead. The eyes are very striking, with thick, arched black eyebrows, thick black rims to the eyes, and large, solid black pupils. The main distinction between the heads lies in the variation of hair and beard styles.

[52] For the significance of episcopal vestments, see Walter, *Art and Ritual*, 7–26.

93

Text Fig. 19 Ornamentation of the bishops' [105–108, 113–115] episcopal robes

St. Tychon [105] (Figs. 23, 27)

The titular inscription is complete and unabbreviated. The scroll carries a quotation from the Prayer of the Third Antiphon.[53] St. Tychon has the receding hair and the long, pointed beard of an old man, but the coloring for the hair is that of middle age, with the addition of white highlights. His omophorion has a thick white ground, umber edges, and black crosses. His phelonion has a

dark red ground, black lines and fold lines, and red highlights. His sticharion has a light grey ground, black lines, and white highlights.

St. Nicholas [106] (Figs. 23, 28)

His inscription is widely spaced on two lines on either side of his halo. The inscription on his scroll is taken from the prayer of the Second Antiphon.[54] The saint has the receding white hair of an old man, and his beard is short, smooth, and neatly rounded, exposing his neck and the collar of his sticharion, which is light blue with umber outlines. His omophorion is similar to that of St. Tychon, and his phelonion has a light red ground, dark red fold lines, and broad, thick white highlights. His sticharion is grey, with dark grey and black lines, and thick white highlights. St. Nicholas's light-colored phelonion contrasts well with the dark phelonion of St. Tichon and the bold polystavrion of St. Meletios.

St. Meletios of Antioch [107] (Pl. 8; Figs. 24, 29, 37)

His inscription is complete and is to either side of the halo. The text on his scroll is taken from the First Antiphon.[55] The saint has receding hair and a long, pointed beard with the coloring of a middle-aged man, but with the addition of thick white highlights. His omophorion is similar to that of St. Tichon. His polystavrion has a thick white ground with umber fold lines, and it is overlaid with a pattern of black crosses that has no regard to the garment folds. His sticharion is light grey, with dark grey and black fold lines, and thick white highlights.

St. John Chrysostomos [108] (Pl. 8; Figs. 24, 30, 35)

The first two letters of his inscription are abbreviated and lie to the left side of his halo, and the epithet "the golden tongued" is written on two lines to the right of the halo. The text on his scroll is taken from the Prayer of Prothesis.[56]

The saint has receding hair and a beard that is short and trim. Both hair and beard are colored like those of a young man. His omophorion is similar to that of St. Tichon. His polystavrion has a thick white ground and blue fold lines, and it is overlaid with a complex pattern of equal-armed black crosses set between bracketing crosses. His sticharion has a thick white ground with two black clavus lines on either side.

St. Basil [113] (Figs. 25, 31, 36)

The first words of his inscription are damaged, but his name is complete. The inscription on

---

[53] J. M. Neale, ed., *The Primitive Liturgies* (London, 1875), 116; J. Neale and R. F. Littledale, eds., *Translations of the Primitive Liturgies* (London, 1869), 95–96.

[54] Neale, ed., *Liturgies*, 116; Neale and Littledale, eds., *Translations*, 95.

[55] Neale, ed., *Liturgies*, 115; Neale and Littledale, eds., *Translations*, 94.

[56] Neale, ed., *Liturgies*, 113.

his scroll is taken from the prayer said by the priest during the singing of the Cherubic Hymn.[57] The saint has receding hair and a long beard with a wavy outline; the coloring of the hair is that of a middle-aged man. His omophorion has a thick white ground, grey wash outlines, and thick black crosses. His phelonion has a dark red ground, black lines and fold lines, and light red highlights. His sticharion has a yellow ground, thin red shadows, dark red fold lines, and yellow-tinted white highlights.

In a contemporary alteration to St. Basil's phelonion, the painter extended the area of the folds falling down from behind his left hand. This was a happy change, as it widened the upper part of the figure, giving it more substance and balance.

St. Gregory the Theologian [114] (Figs. 25, 32, 38)

His long inscription is divided into three lines to either side of his halo. The text on his scroll is taken from the prayer of oblation.[58] The saint has receding hair, and his abundant beard divides neatly under his chin into two generously rounded masses. His omophorion is like that of St. Basil, but it is not caught up over his arm, and so it covers most of his epitrachelion. His phelonion has a light red ground, red and dark red fold lines, and thick white highlights. His sticharion has a light grey ground, dark grey fold lines, some black lines, and thick white highlights.

St. Athanasios [115] (Figs. 26, 33)

His inscription is unabbreviated, and it is written on three lines to either side of his halo. The text on his scroll is taken from the priest's prayer after the creed.[59] The saint has receding hair and a long white beard divided under the chin. His omophorion has a thick white ground, blue shadow lines at the edges, and black crosses. His phelonion has a yellow ground, light red lines and fold lines, and thick white highlights. His sticharion has a light grey ground, dark grey shadows, black lines and fold lines, and thick white highlights.

St. John the Almoner [116] (Figs. 26, 34)

The first two words of his inscription are abbreviated, but the epithet is complete. The text on St. John's scroll is taken from the prayer before the consecration.[60] The saint's figure is much damaged and particularly badly scorched. The head is well preserved and portrays an old man with receding hair and a long, pointed beard divided into tresses below the chin. His phelonion has a dark red ground, black lines and fold lines, and wash highlights in light red. His sticharion has a yellow ground and black lines and fold lines, but it is much discolored by burning.

---

[57] Neale, ed., *Liturgies*, 125; Neale and Littledale, eds., *Translations*, 106.
[58] Neale, ed., *Liturgies*, 129; Neale and Littledale, eds., *Translations*, 110.
[59] Neale, ed., *Liturgies*, 132; Neale and Littledale, eds., *Translations*, 112.
[60] Neale, ed., *Liturgies*, 133; Neale and Littledale, eds., *Translations*, 113.

St. Epiphanios (?) [109], St. Barnabas [110], St. Spyridon [111], and an unknown saint [112]

(Figs. 39, 40)

The panels on the north and south mullions of the apse window each contain the standing figure of a bishop. The identification of St. Barnabas seems fairly certain, and Archbishop Epiphanios is often linked with him, since it was to him that the location of the apostle Barnabas's tomb was revealed. These are the two most important Cypriot saints, and although the images are small, they hold pride of place in the center of the apse.

Each figure holds his right hand up in blessing while the left hand, enveloped in clothing, seems to steady the jewel-covered closed book in the crook of his left arm.

The height of the panels within the borders is 74 cm and their width averages 24 cm. The northern figure measures 68 cm and the southern figure only 66 cm. The ratio between the height and the head length in these figures is rather short, but this may be due to the limited height of the panel itself, so that the painter shortened the bodies to emphasize the heads. Damage within the heads of both figures reveals that the painter enlarged the heads in his final painting, for they are larger than those in the preliminary drawing beneath. The background of each figure is made up of a blue upper and a green lower ground. The green occupies approximately a quarter of the panel height.

The plaster joins for these panels can be found in the red borders contouring the windows, but not in the border separating them from the panel beneath. It is, therefore, clear that these panels were plastered at the same time as the ground register. The surface and edges of the panels are much damaged. This was probably caused by weathering through the window openings at a time when the church was not cloaked with its secondary roof.

St. Epiphanios (?) [109] (Fig. 39)

The inscription has fallen away, save for an encircled alpha to the left of the saint's halo. The head is that of an old man with receding hair and a long, pointed beard. He wears a white omophorion with black crosses over a polystavrion with a pattern of bracketed crosses like that worn by St. John Chrysostomos [108]. His sticharion is light blue with dark grey fold lines and white highlights. His epimanikion, epigonation, and epitrachelion all have a yellow ground upon which are black linear patterns similar to those on the costumes of the adjoining bishops. His book has a red spine with umber definition lines and a yellow cover with pearls scattered about a central oval jewel.

St. Barnabas [110] (Fig. 39)

All that remains of the inscription are the letters B and A at the beginning of the saint's name to the right of the halo. The saint wears a chiton and himation over which is draped an omophorion

with a vertical panel, the end of which is caught up over his left arm. The omophorion has a white ground, blue outlines, and black crosses, one on each shoulder and another at the bottom of the panel beneath the book. His himation has a ground of indeterminate color and red fold lines; his chiton has a light blue ground with grey fold lines and white highlights.

St. Spyridon and an unidentified saint [111, 112] (Fig. 40)

Beneath the windows and on the same plaster section as the rest of the ground register is a rectangular panel containing two roundels, each with a waist-length figure of an elderly bishop. Exclusive of the red borders, the panel measures 120 cm in width and 102 cm in height. The roundels are level and separated by 1 cm. They are tangent to the red borders on either side and their diameter is 59 cm. The haloes of the figures have a diameter of 29 cm and are tangent at the base to the center point of the roundel. In the case of the unidentified saint, the halo is also tangent to the base of the neck.

The upper background to the roundels is blue, and the base of their circumference lies some 4 cm above a lower foreground of green. The green foreground occupies approximately one-third of the panel height. Both the roundels and the haloes have black and white outlines.

Both saints are represented as old men and are dressed in a phelonion over which falls an omophorion. Each figure gestures with his right hand and carries a closed book with a jeweled cover propped against his upper left arm. The books have red spines with umber lines to mark the ties and clasps. The covers have a yellow ground and are decorated with pearls and bright vermilion and green jewels.

The panel is much damaged, with extensive losses under the window openings, at the edges, and in the green foreground. There is considerable scoring, flaking, and burning in the surface layers of the painting. This damage interrupts and weakens the original linear strength of the painting and the intensity of the colors.

Most of the letters for St. Spyridon's name are still visible above the roundel. The background to the figure has a red ground with traces of vermilion on it. The saint wears his traditional conical, basket-weave hat. He has white hair that falls low over his forehead, and his long white beard divides to a point beneath the chin. His hat has a yellow ground with umber lines. His omophorion has a white ground with grey shadow lines and black crosses, and his phelonion has a white ground with blue fold lines.

The figure of the unidentified saint is set against a dark red background. His hair is clustered into tight, white curls that come low down over his forehead, and his beard is short and rounded, revealing at the neck the border of the phelonion beneath it. His omophorion has a white ground with umber shadow lines and black crosses, and his phelonion has a white ground with blue fold lines.

Descriptions

Fragments of pre-1192 painting [126, 141] found in the Naos

(Fig. 41; Text Fig. 20)

In the course of preservation work in the naos, two fragments belonging to an earlier decoration were found under the dadoes of the 1192 paintings of Christ Antiphonetes [127] and the Mother of God Arakiotissa [139]. Both fragments have shaved edges and were scored with holes to allow the 1192 plaster to adhere over them. Examination of other areas of deep damage in the upper registers of the 1192 sequence of painting failed to reveal any further trace of an earlier plaster layer. It must be assumed that the earlier decoration to which these fragments belonged either fell from the walls or was scraped from them.

Fragment [126] under Christ Antiphonetes [127] (Text Fig. 20.1)

This section was painted with the fore part of a sandaled foot resting on the remains of a vermilion footstool with a jeweled border. The buildup of the flesh colors is very similar to that used for the flesh of the apse figures. The quality of the vermilion is similar to that used in the apse and differs from the carmine value of the vermilion used in the 1192 paintings. The edge of the footstool was much damaged, but it was made up with a dark red ground and decorated with large white pearls (Text Fig. 20.1).

Fragment [141] beneath the Arakiotissa (Fig. 41, Text Fig. 20.2a–d)

The larger fragment was removed from the wall and remounted on an independent foundation and hung in the west end of the church. At its widest, it measures 108 cm, and its maximum height is 31 cm. The painting shows parts of two panels (Fig. 41; Text Fig. 20.2). The base of an upper panel depicts the boots of an archangel alongside a footstool bordered with jewels. To the right of the footstool is a piece of blue robe and a triangular fragment with part of a throne with decorations on it.

The boots in the upper panel are similar in color and design to those worn by the archangels in the conch [95, 97] (Pl. 5; Figs. 10–12; Text Fig. 17). The footstool fragment is similar in color and decoration to that of the Mother of God in the conch (Pl. 5; Fig. 13; see also above, pp. 84–85). The only difference between the footstools lies in the angle of vision. The footstool in the conch exposes the jeweled border on the left side, whereas the one in the naos fragment reveals no border at all on that side. On the far right of the fragment is a small patch of blue with black fold lines that must represent the hem of a garment. Rising to the left side of the footstool is a decorated triangular shape that would appear to be part of a seat front. The decoration is in the form of a stepped, cross-diaper pattern similar to that found on the seat front of the throne of the Mother of God in the apse [96] (Pl. 5; Fig. 13; Text Fig. 16). The close similarity between this naos fragment and similar elements in the conch suggests that the naos painting belonged to a decoration that must have formed part of the apse master's sequence of painting. The subject of the panel remains

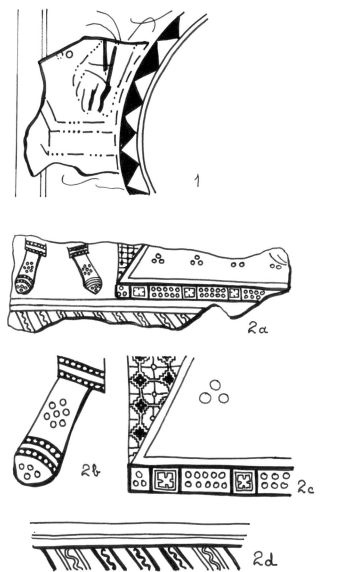

Text Fig. 20
Remains of pre-1192 decoration in the naos
1. Fragment [126] visible through a hole in the dado beneath Christ Antiphonetes [127];
2 a–d. Details from fragment [141] removed from under the dado below the Arakiotissa [139].
See Fig. 41

uncertain, but the pieces indicate that it is likely to have been an enthroned figure, possibly an enthroned Mother of God. It lay under the 1192 dedicatory icon of the Mother of God Arakiotissa [139] who stands on a footstool and in front of a very ornate seat.

The dado is separated from the panel above by a red horizontal line that runs below the boots and the footstool; here, a pattern was painted directly onto the plain white plaster. A horizontal yellow line runs parallel to the red border line and beneath it is a linear pattern contained by an upper line of black. The linear pattern follows a repetitive sequence consisting of two black diago-

nal lines with a wavy line between them on a green ground; two black diagonal lines containing between them a wavy black line on a white ground; and two red diagonal lines with a wavy red line between them on a yellow ground. These are repeated and the intervals are white. There is no dado pattern in the apse, and nothing else in the church can be compared with this diagonal pattern. It is not uncommon in other Byzantine churches and represents marble revetments.

The whole of the naos fragment was removed from the wall, consolidated and cleaned, then mounted on a metal grid and hung in the west end of the church. It was badly damaged, since holes had been made in it in order to key on the 1192 plaster.

7

METHOD, STYLE, AND DATE

The plastering for the apse follows conventional post-Iconoclast Byzantine practice, and the paintings were executed on a foundation of two layers of plaster.[61] A roughcast of lime plaster with an aggregate of sand and small stones, the arricio, was applied directly over the masonry. The second rendering of plaster forms the direct foundation for the paintings, the intonaco. It averages 1 cm in thickness, and has an aggregate of black sand with finely chopped straw and chaff as a binding material. The straw and chaff are particularly apparent at the center of the conch where the thin layer of lime that covered them has flaked off. This has caused fragments of the paint layers to flake away.

The apse was plastered in three sections. The first section extends over the whole area of the conch. The second served for the seven roundels of the bishops, and the last section covered the area for the lower register of paintings and the window jambs, extending downward below the present floor level (see pp. 59, 83). The plaster joins can be observed in the red border lines that define the three registers. There is no evidence of the insertion of plaster patches, nor did the apse painter impress or incise the surface plaster in an attempt to retain permanent guidelines for his composition. However, the plaster sections are relatively large by Byzantine standards, and a considerable amount of ridging in the plaster probably indicates that the painter gave his surfaces a general reworking in the course of painting, in order to bring up the moisture to the surface. There are small, shallow depressions within the roundels that mark the centerpoint for the circumferences of the halo and roundel borders. The halo and roundel outlines are defined with geometrical precision both in the preliminary drawings and in the final painting, and they were executed with a compass.

Clear evidence as to the presence of two preliminary drawings was apparent in damaged roundels of the middle register (see above, pp. 88–97) (Figs. 20, 21). The painter first made a drawing in a thin, red color.[62] If major alterations were required, he resorted to a grey color to

[61] For a discussion of Byzantine plastering methods see Winfield, "Methods," 64–78.

[62] It is likely that the painter habitually used a wash of light red, rather than grey, for his preliminary drawings. The only evidence as to the use of grey was found in the roundels, where an original drawing in "pink" was replaced and redrawn in grey. Thin, light red or sinoper is a particularly suitable color for preliminary drawing, since it is not used as a base wash under any ground color and provides a useful contrast to those that are.

distinguish them from the initial red drawing. The drawings were cursory and executed with broad brushstrokes. Indents in the plaster at the center of roundels and haloes confirm the use of a compass. This would also have been used to relay measure modules.

The layout of the apse panels is largely dictated by the architecture and the windows (Text Figs. 1, 10, 11). The height of the roundel panel is approximately one-third of the panel in the conch above it. The height of the bishop panel in the ground register is approximately twice the height of the roundel panel, and the figures within it are life-sized.

The panel in the conch is aligned around a central median running through the center of the figures of the Mother of God and Child. The pattern of construction for the roundels is quite clear (see above, p. 89, Text Fig. 18).

The figures in the apse differ slightly in size in the three areas of painting, but all the figures relate to each other in mathematical harmony.[63] This suggests the use of a modular canon similar to the modular canon used in the 1192 sequence of paintings.[64]

In the conch the figure of the Mother of God is constructed to a larger scale than those of the archangels. These angels are carefully placed at the further edges of the conch so that they do not appear foreshortened to the viewer in the naos. From thence the four heads appear powerfully grouped, like a constellation at the top of the conch.

The upper outlines of the throne appear to converge sharply inward toward the seated figure because no account was taken of the distortion that would be caused to the viewer by the curvature of the conch.

The proportions of the figure of the Christ child relate more readily to those of an adult in miniature than to those of an infant.[65] His head can be bisected horizontally along the eyeline, whereas in nature, the upper head of the infant (vertex to eyeline), is larger than the lower head (eye line to chin). Some of the characteristic appearance of childhood is suggested in the head of this Christ child; the painter has plumped out the cheeks and enlarged the forehead area at the expense of the hair. The child is seated in direct vertical alignment with his mother's head, and the top of his halo is tangent to the notional base of hers.

The hands of the Mother of God are large, and her fingers long and spatulate; their size is in

[63] In most Byzantine figural panels, the leading characters in the drama are constructed to a larger scale than the lesser participants. While the figures may differ in size according to hierarchical precedence, their proportional relationships remain the same.

[64] For a discussion of the canon of proportion used by the 1192 master, see below, Part Four, Ch. 16, pp. 283–97. For a wider discussion see Winfield and Winfield, *Proportion*, 133–65. There is enough material in the 1192 paintings to establish the use of a modular proportional system. In the apse there is only enough painting to confirm parts of that system. Canons of modular proportion were also used by good quality painters in Romanesque churches, and in due course it will be interesting to learn what connection exists between the Western and Byzantine systems.

[65] For a discussion of the measures and proportions of the Christ child, see Winfield and Winfield, *Proportion*, 91–94, 154–60.

keeping with her figure, and the hand measures at least as long as her face (three nose lengths), which conforms with natural proportion.[66]

The heads of the figures in the apse are presented in the two characteristic Byzantine stances.[67] The painter used the three-quarter profile aspect for the archangels and the standing church fathers; and the asymmetrical, frontal aspect for the Mother of God and child, the heads of the church fathers in roundels and those of the two little figures in the window jambs. In the three-quarter profile faces, the gaze is usually directed across the narrow side of the face, and only one nostril is shown, and the narrow side of the face reveals no temple. An exception occurs in the case of the archangels, whose gaze is directed back into the church.

In the asymmetrical frontal faces, both nostrils are illustrated, although one nostril is usually more pronounced than the other, and it alone has a "contour" white highlight. Both temples are visible as well as both of the ears, although one ear may be larger than the other. The gaze is indirect, and the glance is focused across the wider plane of the face. This is achieved by placing the pupil of the larger eye slightly off-center towards the outer corner of the eye.[68]

With the exception of the Christ child, the proportional relationships of the measures in the heads of the apse figures and their relationships between head and halo are very similar to those of the 1192 paintings (see below, p. 287).

The technique of the apse painting follows standard Byzantine procedure.[69] The painter first completed the background, together with any inanimate elements within it, such as the throne of the Mother of God. He then proceded to complete the garments of the figures before painting the hands, feet, and heads. He painted the heads of the figures with more precision than the garments. At the final stage, he completed the inscriptions and other white details requiring thick, white paint, such as pearls and perhaps some additional touches of highlight.

[66] See Winfield and Winfield, *Proportion*, 59, 64–65, 83–100, 106. Vitruvius, Dionysios of Fourna, Panselinos, and Cennini all agree that the length of the hand (wrist to tip of finger) equals three nose lengths or one face length. None of them makes any exception for the female hand. The 1192 painter shortens all the hands of his female personages (see below, p. 293).

[67] For a discussion of characteristic aspects used by Byzantine painters for representing the human head, see Winfield and Winfield, *Proportion*, 64, 65, 83–100.

[68] The master of the apse paintings at Lagoudhera, together with other post-Iconoclast Byzantine painters, followed the general principles for the construction of an asymmetrical frontal face that were to be formulated in the text describing the technique of the painter Panselinos. Panselinos's instructions for the asymmetrical frontal head emphasize the difference in size between the eyes. The eye in the wider side of the face is longer and narrower than the smaller and rounder eye in the narrow plane of the face. The smaller eye is at a lower level than the larger eye. With regard to the frontal heads in the Lagoudhera apse painting, the faces are clearly asymmetrical in relation to the median of the nose; the larger eye is in the wider side of the face and is longer than the smaller eye, which is not necessarily very rounded; and both eyes are level. For the measures of Panselinos, see A. Papadopoulos-Kerameus, Ἑρμηνεία τῆς ζωγραφικῆς τέχνης (St. Petersburg, 1909), appendix A, 237–39. For a particular discussion of these measures, see Winfield and Winfield, *Proportion*, 68–71, 82–87.

[69] Winfield, "Methods." 99–129.

Method, Style, and Date

The technique employed is straightforward and lends itself to rapid execution. It is briefly summarized here since it makes an interesting comparison with the methods used by the master of the 1192 paintings (see below, pp. 305–11).

A preliminary drawing in light red wash outlined the contour of the halo and head, and it also gave rough outlines for the hair and beard, if any, and the shape of the chin, neck, and ears. A vertical line was drawn to mark the side of the nose, and this ran perpendicular to a horizontal line marking the eyeline. These formed a T-shape around which the face could easily be built. There was probably also a mouth line and a line to mark the cleft of the chin, if this were beardless. If an error was made at any stage, then corrections were carried out in a contrasting line wash, such as grey, as in the case of the roundels in the middle register.

For the base colors, a wash of thin green was applied over the head, the neck or beard areas, and the ears; then a wash of thin yellow was painted over the remaining white plaster within the halo. There is no trace of yellow under the ground colors for the face and hair. The ground colors for the hair and the beard, if any, were blocked in with an opaque light umber while the face, neck, and ears were blocked in with an opaque green; a second coat of opaque yellow was applied within the remaining areas of the halo. The halo was probably completed at this stage, since the double outlines to it are clearly compass-drawn and the centerpoint of the halo lies within the face. The compass point made a mark which would have to be painted out.

The lines and outlines characterizing the contours and shapes of the features were drawn in umber over the green ground of the flesh areas. The buildup of colors for the hair and beards was carried out at the same time that the colors for the face were laid in, but the color procedures for both are distinct and varied, and they will be described separately. The first flesh color in light yellow was applied in mask fashion, mapping out all the prominent areas and leaving green the eye cavities and other hollows of the face, as well as the shadowed areas and the edges of the face. The second flesh color, in creamy white often tinged with pink, was applied in blobs and broad lines within the areas already mapped out by the first flesh color.

Dark red lines were then used to reinforce the feature lines and outlines, and as a further shadow. Vermilion was used to reinforce certain areas; it was added to the highlighted areas of the forehead, the cheeks, and cheek hollows, and it was used for the lips. Black lines were then used to emphasize and outline the face and its features, the ears, and the hair. The final application, of thick white highlights, was applied in fine line or broad brush or blobs to all the salient points of the face, neck, and ears, to a corner of each eye, and to define the prominences in the broad foreheads of the elderly church fathers. These highlights do not overlap onto the green ground of the shadow areas.

This is a very simple and speedy method of building up a face. There are two flesh colors, one shadow color not counting the green ground, and vermilion and white are used as highlights. The eyebrows are sweeping black lines and there is no inner lid line. The pupil and iris form one solid, dark circle. There is no careful buildup of color layers within the eye socket, although in some heads the eyelids are emphasized with pink flesh color. The face colors are built up in stencil fashion on the green ground, and there is no delicate attenuation of the colors at the edges, such as

can be achieved by lifting the brush. The method of painting is thus startlingly linear and severe. The painter built up the face like a relief map with dark valleys and prominent light areas defined by contour lines to mark the features of the face.

The other flesh areas, such as the hands, were built up in a similar manner to the face. Where the flesh paint overlaps onto garments, as in the hands of the church fathers in the roundels and the feet of the Christ child, the flesh colors were built up over the ground color of the garment beneath.

Three types of color buildup occur for the hair: one for young men, one for middle-aged men, and one for old men. All three were built up on an umber ground color. The coloring for beard and mustache follows that for the type of hair. For the white hair of old men, a coat of opaque, light green was applied over the light umber ground, leaving the umber exposed at the edges. Upon the light green, lines in red and black were drawn, defining the hair style and shape. Finally, the hair was articulated with fine striations in white. The hair of men of middle age was painted on a layer of red, which was applied over the umber ground. The red was outlined and shaped with black and striated with fine lines in white with an occasional grouping of blue lines. The hair of young men was painted directly onto the umber ground, and it was then shaped and outlined in black and articulated with fine, yellow lines. The hair was mostly completed before the painting of the face, but the final white highlights and the black lines that tidied up and finished off a head were added afterwards.

The painter was clearly aware of the technique of using a wash of one color over another color of a darker tone to give the effect of a further color, as in a shot silk garment. Thus, Mary's maphorion has a dark red ground over which washes of light blue were laid in broad patches to give the suggestion of a purple hue.

A technique peculiar to the apse master is that of building up different areas of the same garment with different colors or tones of colors. The standard Byzantine technique for building up garments is to lay in an overall ground color of an intermediate tone and to build upon it grades of dark and light tones of the same color. In general, the apse master follows this method, but in the case of the himations of the archangels, the garment is divided into light and dark sections, each with different grounds and with different hues and tones laid upon them. For example, Michael's himation has dark folds at the waist and down one side that are built up of black definition lines and vermilion highlights upon a dark red ground. The rest of his himation is built up with red fold lines, white wash, and thick, white highlights upon a light red ground. The contrast is startling, since the division of the garment into light and dark areas is arbitrary and made with little regard to the natural body forms beneath, or to a particular source of lighting.

The use of a combination of vermilion and dark red is echoed in the background of three of the medallions, where the overall vermilion ground of the roundel is overlaid toward the center by a coat of crimson vermilion between halo and shoulder. The apse master shows other idiosyncrasies in color technique. The four figures in the conch each have a halo with an inner outline in vermilion and the usual white outer outline, whereas all the other apse figures have the standard

black and white outlines to their haloes. The Mother of God has a continuous white contour line around her figure from waist level upwards. Such white outlines in Byzantine painting seem to appear more frequently from the thirteenth century onwards. The other figures in the apse are conspicuously lacking in any continuous dark or light outlines to the body, although the heads are outlined in black.

Blue is often used over the final layers of white wash and thick, white highlights on the phelonions of some church fathers in the roundels. Blue is also used over white garments as an intermediate highlight. If this blue wash had been applied according to the standard method, directly on to the green ground of a garment, the blue would not have retained its color value.

The speed at which he painted is confirmed by minor imprecisions in applying colors to garments. However, the faces are carefully painted. All the lines and outlines that give finish and form to the figures are rapidly brushed in. This is particularly clear with black, since the painter used smooth paint, and the widths of his line work vary according to the pressure on the brush. Apart from the thin blue of the background, the colors are strong and opaque, and there are few, if any, black reinforcing lines in the robes. The lack of black lines and outlines in the clothing has the effect of adding greater substance to the garments, as if they had the weight of heavy woolen cloth.

In contrast to his method for the garments, the painter made a free use of bold, black lines for the heads of the figures in the roundels, and he gave them stark, black pupils for their eyes. There is little character differentiation between the heads, other than the style of hair and beard, but the strong, black lines impose a rigid authority on their blank gaze.

The apse paintings were the work of a confident master who followed conventional Byzantine rules. The masklike buildup of the faces of the church fathers in the ground register will instantly be recognized by anyone accustomed to looking at Byzantine painting. The figures are simple and were painted at speed, but they are, nevertheless, impressive and powerful in fulfilling their role of attending at the Liturgy.

The painter worked to a harmonious constructional system, and perhaps the best proof of this is that the more fastidious and careful master of the 1192 painting was content to let the apse paintings stand in unity with his own work, rather than resort to the common practice of repainting. The coloring technique is sophisticated, with a preference for strong contrasts between light and dark areas, both within the figures and in their backgrounds. The apse painter was a master of broad sweeping brush-work, and it is this quality, together with the bold choice of color, that gives the paintings their powerful effect. It projects the Mother of God, Christ child, and the archangels forward into the naos, looming as almost tangible figures against the de-materialized background. The present seventeenth-century iconostasis unfortunately vitiates much of this effect, since it is larger and more solid than the original screen, which would have been lower and more open. This color technique is particularly effective in the roundels, where the light colored phelonion of each church father contrasts with the dark red and vermilion backgrounds. The use of light hues for

figures against dark grounds has the effect of thrusting the figures forward, and it also adds to the notion of depth. This is very successful in the case of the Mother of God and Christ child. The child is luminous with the creamy chrysographia of his garments, and he stands out vividly in contrast to the somber figure of the Mother. The black panel back to her throne, with its fine but colorfully intricate filigree of linear patterns provides an excellent foil to the solid figure of the Virgin.

No inscriptions within the apse offer firm evidence as to a date for the paintings. Stylistically, they do not relate very closely to the early twelfth-century paintings in other Cypriot churches. A date in the second half of the twelfth century is supported by the detail of the swirling folds of the archangels' garments. These are convoluted patterns that herald the style of late twelfth-century painting. In both of the dedicatory inscriptions of 1192, Lord Leon mentions his father, and this is powerful circumstantial evidence that the original church was built by the father.[70]

---

[70] For the suggestion of a more precise date, see Nicolaïdes, "Panagia Arakiotissa," pp. 6, 7, 134.

Part Three: The 1192 Decoration

8

THE DOME

The Christ [1]

(Pls. 1, 9; Figs. 42–45; Text Figs. 21, 22)

A large, waist-length figure of Christ is painted in the center of the dome. Although Christ has the characteristics and position traditionally assigned to the Pantokrator, the only inscription is the sigla $\overline{\text{IC}}$ $\overline{\text{XC}}$ placed within two small roundels on either side of his head. The figure is contained within a circle that has a swing radius of 1.45 m.

In a concave dome, a swing radius centered on the dome center is the only way to create a perfect circumference. The area within such a saucer dome will be larger than implied by the swing radius, and when a dome has as many irregularities as at Lagoudhera, the surface area will be even more asymmetrical. Measured along the flat, the north-south diameter is 3.36 m and the east-west diameter 3.26 m; the difference between them being 10 cm.

The great circle was plastered in a single section with the plaster join running in the white outline of the chevron pattern that outlines the circumference. The lime contains a larger proportion of straw and chaff than is common elsewhere in the church. It also contains particles of crushed brick or earthenware. A dome is the most difficult area to plaster and an increased quantity of binding material gave a better chance of adherence. The success of the mix is proven by the fact that, after eight hundred years, the plaster is still sticking firmly to the dome. However, pigments will not adhere firmly to the shiny surface of straw or chaff, and when the painting dried out, the thin layer of lime and pigments flaked off those particles too close to the surface.

The thickness of the plaster could only be observed where there was damage. It appears to be in a single layer, and at the top center it was 10 cm thick, whereas lower down it was as thin as half a centimeter. The regular outline of the plaster patch suggests a circle may have been marked out on the masonry with a compass, or possibly that the perimeter follows a circular course of brickwork in the masonry of the dome.

The surface shows extensive irregularities where areas of plaster have been reworked to bring moisture to the surface, and quite a lot of the design was scored into the plaster with a spatula. The

base of the south side of the neck of Christ has very clear undulations caused by the reworking.[71] Around the edges of Christ's hair, the polish of the color surface shows that the plaster was reworked after the second yellow of the halo was painted in. The area of his hand held up in blessing also shows such careful reworking as to suggest a separate patch of plaster, but no evidence of a join could be found (Fig. 45, Text Fig. 22).

The upper western half of the great circle contains the two small inscribed roundels and the powerful dominating head of Christ within its halo. In keeping with Byzantine convention, he is portrayed as a young man with the flowing hair of the Nazarene gathered to one side in a loose tress. He wears a thin mustache and his short beard divides into twin curls below the chin. The eastern half of the circle contains the upper body of Christ enveloped in the voluminous folds of his himation. His right hand emerges out of these folds and is raised in blessing. His left hand lies palm downward across the cover of the closed book that he steadies against his chest. Under the himation, he wears a chiton with clavus.

The head of Christ is shown in the frontal aspect and his face has the asymmetry characteristic of post-Iconoclast Byzantine painting, with the wider plane of the face to the right of the nose.[72] The hair is also wider and more voluminous on this side of the head. The two nostrils are shown, and the shadow of the nose falls to the right side. The left eye is narrower and longer than the right eye, which is more rounded. The pupil of the right eye is slightly off-center, whereas the pupil of the left eye is placed toward the nose. The gaze is directed sideways to the right, across the wider side of the face. This indirect gaze becomes more pronounced when seen from ground level. It is this slight squint position of the eyes that causes the often-remarked effect that Christ's eyes seem to look directly at the onlooker wherever he stands, whereas the actual gaze is directed over the shoulder and beyond the onlooker.

The head is not placed symmetrically within the halo; the left and upper cross bars are tangent to the halo, but the bar to the right of the head is not. The methods used by the 1192 painter to resolve the problems inherent in constructing a waist-length figure in a dome are discussed below (pp. 114–20), and the actual measurements are listed below (pp. 119–20).

Within the great circle, the background of the figure and of the inscribed circles is a bright, shiny vermilion; the circumference of the great circle is defined by a line in thick white. The circles with sigla are blue, and both the outline of the circles and the letters within them are in thick white. The head of Christ has the young features and light brown hair that characterize the heads of other young men in the 1192 decoration, and the colors are built up in a similar manner.[73]

---

[71] A similar corrugation of the reworked plaster can be observed in the lower body mass of the Mother of God Arakiotissa [139], which can be found in the center bay of the south wall.

[72] See Winfield and Winfield, *Proportion*, for a wider discussion of Byzantine proportion. For a discussion of the asymmetrical frontal face in post-Iconoclast painting, see ibid., 82–87; and for particular reference to the asymmetrical heads in the 1192 sequence of painting at Lagoudhera, see ibid., 136–39. See also below, pp. 287–90.

[73] For a detailed analysis of the 1192 master's methods of building up colors for the hair and flesh, see below, pp. 307–11.

However, in the case of this great icon, much care and attention were given to the brushwork, particularly to the painting of the beard, and to emphasizing the effect of the finely striated eyebrows and the rims of the eyes.[74]

Christ's halo is yellow with black inner and white outer outlines. The black and white outlines were drawn with a pair of compasses, though only the white shows any sign of brushmarks, and the paint is uniformly even and thick. It would have been impossible to paint such regular outlines without some mechanical device attached to the compass or dividers. The cross bars of the halo are light blue, but an impression of pictorial space is given by the addition of a white highlight and a blue shadow underlined in black line; the jewels within the bars are vermilion with black outlines.

Christ's chiton has a red ground, umber shadows, black fold lines and outlines, and blue linear highlights. His clavus has a yellow ground, red shadows, and umber lines. His himation has a grey ground, and black fold lines and outlines with broad washes of thick blue between them. The Gospel book has a yellow cover with bright red jewels outlined in black, and white pearls; the page ends are vermilion and the ties and clasps are black (Text Fig. 36.1a).[75]

Christ's young face gives an impression of linear severity that is relieved by the soft curve of the hair. His expression might be described as intense, but it depicts no particular human emotion since the eyebrows and mouth are not articulated but remain in repose. The deliberate, if standard, asymmetry of the face, with its unequal face planes and differentiated eyes, contributes interest and character to an otherwise bland physiognomy. This leaves the beholder free to read into it the imprint of his own personal feelings about the Almighty. The careful buildup of the shadow tones gives some volume to the face, but the final dominating effect is linear and incorporeal, stressed by the strong definition of the sweeping black curves of the eyebrows and rims of the eyes.

The painter has ensured that the head is not dwarfed by the mass of the shoulders and the torso beneath it by enlarging the neck. This adjustment was made to counteract the foreshortening effect of the concave dome surface. Christ's body is in the frontal aspect, but the fact that his right hand is slightly foreshortened and that the left or north side of his head is narrower than the right gives the figure a recessive effect to the left side. The right half of his body contains the gathered himation folds, the bejeweled book, and his left hand. All of these elements help to break up this large area. The lesser mass of the left half of his body is given extra stress, and a sense of balance in the whole figure is achieved by the voluminous folds of the himation that sweep around and up to envelop his right hand.

[74] The type of finely striated eyebrow also appears in the face of the Christ in the Holy Tile [72] (Fig. 188) and that of the Christ Antiphonetes [127] (Fig. 140). In the 1192 decoration, the other faces of Christ have similarly curved eyebrows, but each is formed of a single, smooth, solid black line in the manner used by this painter for the eyebrows of the faces of young men.
[75] The pattern on the book is very similar to that on the book held by St. Nicholas [71] in the lower register of the naos (Fig. 113, Text Fig. 36.1a).

It seems to have been the custom for Byzantine wall painters to use the best colors for the most important paintings in a church, but while gold and silver are used for small details in the figure of the Mother of God Arakiotissa [139], and in the figures of Symeon and the Christ child [74], none appears on the Christ in the dome. Next to gold and silver in value come bright blue and vermilion, both in the aesthetic and in the monetary sense. The background of the figure of Christ and the inscribed circles show a lavish use of vermilion, while his himation was built up with a generous use of blue. There is a definite impression of polish to the vermilion background, but it was impossible to discover how this was done. For the chiton, the painter would have needed imperial purple, but this was made from the exclusive murex dye, which would not have been suitable for wall paintings. He therefore contrived to suggest it by using blue highlights over a red ground.

The meticulous and almost over-solicitous care given to the painting of the head of Christ stands out in marked contrast to the bold treatment of his clothing and Gospels. His garments were painted with broad brushstrokes that show no trace of hesitation. This was rapid painting by a master who knew precisely what he wanted and cared little about details like the precise placing of colors for the jewels of the book cover, where he knew that the imprecision would not detract from the general effect of majesty.

The credit for this great masterpiece can be attributed to the Lagoudhera painter's knowledge of the standard Byzantine system for painting, informed and brought to life by his own artistic sense. He was a consummate craftsman who put his best skills into the delineation of this, the most important image in the church.

Construction (Text Figs. 21, 22)

Before proceeding to plaster within the dome and drum, the painter would have worked out on the masonry a rough layout of the panel sizes.[76] The projected circle for the Christ had to allow for the angels and the standing figures of prophets beneath him.

Once the basic layout had been established, the painter was faced with the problem of constructing a waist-length figure of Christ in a wide, shallow saucer. The size and curvature of the dome made it impossible for him to survey his whole composition while he was at work, and it is unlikely that he ever had a satisfactory overall view of it until the last of his scaffolds were down, after completing all the painting in the main body of the church. Moreover, in order to reach and paint the dome, the floor of the scaffolding where the painter worked would have been above the level of the windows in the drum. He would have worked in comparative darkness, relieved only by the light of candles or oil lamps. Some drips of wax were found on the surface of the paintings in the drum. These were at first thought to be the remains of an encaustic medium, but it is more

---

[76] A description of the construction of the Christ in the dome at Lagoudhera was first published in Winfield and Winfield, *Proportion*, 163–65.

Text Fig. 21 Diagram of the Christ in the dome [1] showing construction of the figure
★···★··· indicate the notional perpendicular diameters that guided the basic construction; ▬ indicates impressed guide lines in the plaster; ┼┼┼ indicate incised guide lines in the plaster; - - - - indicate a preliminary outline to Christ's halo. ★···★ = 1 nose length; 3 nose lengths = 1 face length from the top of the forehead to the chin.

likely that they were, in fact, spatterings from candles, probably held close to the wall by a pupil while the painter worked at some particularly delicate area.

When the painter was working on the lower part of the figure of Christ at the east side, the head would be behind his back on the west side. In order to relate the different parts of his design to each other and to maintain each part in correct proportion to the whole, the painter followed a set of rules and established points of reference and guidelines. To build up his composition, he relied on a modular system of proportion based on the nose measure.[77]

The evidence for the method of construction used by the 1192 painter to design and control his composition is to be found in the painting itself. The presence of incised and impressed lines

[77] The measurements used for the construction of the Christ in the dome are based on the same modular proportional system that the 1192 master used for the drawing of his figures. The method of construction for the head and its proportional canon are described below in the section on proportion (pp. 287–90). The method used in the construction of a Christ in the dome is not dissimilar to the method used in constructing any other waist-length figure in a roundel. (See below, pp. 284–86, Text Figs. 23, 25, 45.)

and of a distinct pattern of measure relationships between the parts and the whole form a framework, or armature, upon which the painting was constructed. The actual measurements and distances are listed below (see pp. 119–20). Text Fig. 21 illustrates the pattern of these measure relationships and the position of the impressed and incised lines that are visible in the surface plaster and paint. The text figure is necessarily schematic, since the actual painting is on a concave surface and distances cannot be accurately drawn on flat paper.

The painter first had to locate the centerpoint of his circle. It is impossible to determine how the centerpoint of the Lagoudhera dome was originally plotted, but it is possible to run intersecting strings from the top of the north, south, east, and west windows, and, with the use of a plumb line, arrive at the point which the painter used for the centerpoint of the dome circle. However, it could be that, as in the dome of the church of St. John Chrysostomos at Koutsovendis in Cyprus, a suitable concentric course of brick or stone in the dome masonry was used as a guideline for the circumference.[78] The centerpoint used by the 1192 painter does not correspond to the point of insertion of the iron hook and ring, from which hung the central corona until the ring and hook were removed in 1969.

After establishing a limit for the circle that left adequate room for the angels and the prophets, the painter used the centerpoint to draw a circumference with a swinging radius to form the central circle. He was then able to draw a flat radius along the surface of the dome to establish the basic module (the face length), which controls the structure of the figure. For the construction of the heads and other smaller measures, a subdivision of the face measure was used—the nose length. This is equal to one-third of a face length. Starting from the centerpoint, he needed six equal lengths, and a further length that was flexible in size. The six equal parts, each a nose length in measure, comprise the neck, the chin, the nose, the forehead, the hair, and the distance between the top of the head and the halo outline. The adjustable seventh part was the area between the upper edge of the halo and the roundel border.

When he had established the perimeters and the size of his basic module, the painter then plastered the central area of the dome. He would have plastered a larger area than the circumference marked on the masonry because he knew that the chevron design would eventually conceal the irregularities of the plaster join with the angel panel beneath. He then proceeded to map out his design rapidly, in order to lay in his base colors before the plaster surface became impervious.

To establish his drawing, he used the east-west and the north-south diameters as his main nominal guidelines. He first redrew the roundel circumference upon the fresh plaster. Then, proceeding from the centerpoint along the west radius and measuring out a distance of three nose-length modules along the surface, he came to the point that marks the centerpoint of the halo circle. This point also determines the perpendicular junction of the horizontal eyeline with the vertical of the radius of the dome circle. It is this axis that controls the measurements within the

[78] C. Mango, E. J. W. Hawkins, and S. Boyd, "The Monastery of St. Chrysostomos at Koutsovendis (Cyprus) and Its Wall Paintings," *DOP* 44 (1990), 73, 93.

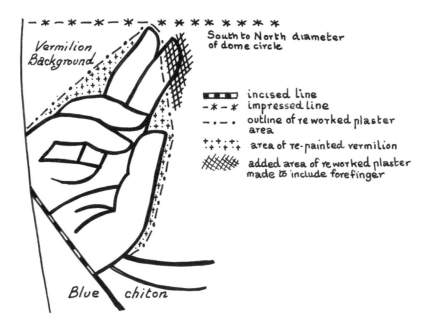

Text Fig. 22 Schema of the right hand of the Christ in the dome [1] (see also Fig. 45)

head.[79] The horizontal eyeline/halo diameter was extended to either side to help locate the centerpoints of the circles with the sigla. The diameter of these circles is equal to one nose-length module. To delimit the shoulders, the painter measured three nose lengths along the north-south diameter to either side of the centerpoint to the dome, thus allowing six nose lengths for the width of the shoulders. This width is equal to the diameter of the halo.

In the lower eastern semicircle, the painter placed Christ's right hand with its fingertips tangent to the north-south diameter. It is likely that the placing of the book, Christ's left hand, and the himation folds were also controlled by regulated measurements. Some evidence of this lies in the presence of incised and impressed lines in the plaster. These lines delimit particular elements in the composition so that the main points of the preliminary drawing can be retained as guidelines throughout the procedure of laying in the colors.

There is an incised line marking the left outline of Christ's neck, and the cover of the book has incised lines along its upper edge and down the left side separating it from the pages. A further short, diagonal, incised line cuts through the top of the pages. This line presumably marks the top of the pages as in the preliminary drawing, but at a final stage of painting the painter altered it and extended the vermilion pages higher up. A short, vertical, incised line on the east-west diameter

[79] In the asymmetrical frontal faces the centerpoint of the halo rests on the eye line of the face, so it was simple to mark out measure reference points for the top of the forehead, the top of the head, the base of the nose, and the base of the chin, since all these lengths equaled one nose length or one-third of the radius of the halo. See below, pp. 287–90.

marks the junction of the vertical and horizontal himation folds. This incised line is continued by lines impressed in the plaster which delineate the curving folds of the himation. Where the himation folds overlap Christ's left shoulder, their inner edge is outlined with an impress line. Three more lines delineate between them the area where Christ's chiton is revealed. A short, impressed line marks the wrist of Christ's left hand at a point higher than the present himation edge. A further impress line along the southern end of the north-south diameter extends as far as the top of the fingers of Christ's right hand. The impressed lines serve a similar purpose to the incised ones, but a blunt tool was more successful than a sharp one for making curved lines in a still-moist plaster, and probably the painter used a spatula.

Having marked out his composition in the manner described above, the painter proceeded to lay in his colors, or perhaps the coloring would have already begun, with pupils working alongside the master in the comparatively easy task of laying in the base colors.

While the construction of the Lagoudhera Christ followed the sequence outlined above, there is also evidence of two adjustments to the original design. Both these adjustments were made at an intermediate stage in the painting. The original design was painted out when the modifications were made. First, on the south side of the halo rim there are disturbances that indicate that the original halo rim ran some centimeters further to the south. This rectification was carried out before the completion of the face and neck areas. The reason for the adjustment appears to have been an attempt to balance the head more symmetrically within the halo. Both halo outlines were compass-drawn with a swing radius. A second alteration shows where the cross bar to the left of his head was adjusted so as to extend further over to the south, and the northern side of the bar was correspondingly cut back by an overpaint in yellow to conceal the white paint beneath it.

Perhaps the greatest problem in painting any figure upon the curved surface of a dome was the optical distortion of certain areas in the composition. The Lagoudhera painter seems to have resorted to a number of expedients to cope with this problem. The central neck area of the figure was made much larger than usual. The height of the neck for a figure painted on a flat wall surface is one nose measure, and the notional base of the halo is tangent to the base of the neck. For the Christ in the dome, the height of the neck is two nose lengths and the notional base of his halo runs through the green shadow in his neck. His neck is also very wide. These enlargements were made to counteract the foreshortening effect of the center of the dome where it reaches maximum concavity. The cross bars within Christ's halo, which appear from below to be in neat perpendicular alignment with his head, were, in fact, painted in a diagonal relationship to it.[80] Similarly, the neat alignment of the sigla when seen from below is achieved by placing the letters diagonally within their circles.

[80] An understanding of the optical illusion caused by curved spaces goes back at least as far as the Iconoclast period. The distortion caused by the semidome of the apse was allowed for in the making of the great cross of St. Eirene. See W. S. George, *The Church of St. Eirene, Constantinople* (Oxford, 1912), 47.

The Dome

Surface Measurements

The east-west diameter measures 3.26 m and is 10 cm shorter than the north-south diameter. The centerpoint of the dome circle lies at a point below the right curls of Christ's beard and the green line marking the curve of his Adam's apple. The diameter of the circles for the sigla measures 24 cm, and these circles lie 48 cm above the notional north-south diameter. Christ's halo has a diameter of 144 cm and its centerpoint lies to the right of the nose and above the inner corner of the right eye on a notional eyeline. This line runs tangent to the nasal incision and the upper rim of both eyes, and it marks one of the standard divisions of the Byzantine face.

The halo centerpoint is also located on the notional east-west diameter. The base of the halo is tangent to the north-south diameter at the centerpoint of the circle.

The measures for the head are taken down a notional vertical to the right side of the nose using the following reference points: the apex of the head; the top of the forehead, which lies at the end of the parting of the hair; the top of the nose or the nasal incision, which corresponds with the eyeline; the base of the nose; and the base of the chin, which lies at the top of the divide between the two beard curls.

The vertical measurements are as follows: the hair, forehead, nose length, and chin length are each 24 cm. The total head length is 96 cm and the face length is 72 cm. The length from the base of the chin to the centerpoint of the dome circle is 24 cm, and from the base of the chin to the neckline is 36 cm.

The horizontal measurements for the head are taken along the eyeline; this is a notional line that can be drawn tangent to the upper rim of each of his eyes and that runs through the nasal incision. The width of the head is 85 cm; the width of the face is 48.5 cm.

From left to right along the eyeline the measurements read as follows: the hair (left side to edge of face) is 16.5 cm; the temple (edge of face to closed corner left eye) is 5 cm; the left eye (corner to corner) is 12 cm; the distance between the inner eye corners is 8 cm; the width of the right eye (corner to corner) is 13 cm; the right temple (outer corner right eye to edge of face) is 10.5 cm; the edge of face to outer edge of hair is 20 cm.

The width between the pupils, centerpoint to centerpoint, is 24 cm. The height of the left eye (between the rims at the center) is 7.5 cm; the height of the right eye is 7 cm. The irises of the eyes are oval; their height is 4.5 cm and their width is 5 cm.

The north-south notional diameter is tangent to the top of the fingers of the left hand and to the highpoints of the shoulders. The distance between the highpoints of the shoulders is 144 cm, which is equivalent to 6 nose lengths, and this measurement is the same as the diameter of the halo. The length of the left hand from below the thumb to the top of the fingers is 2.5 nose lengths, but the heel of the hand is concealed. The length of the right hand, across the book from the wrist to the fingertips, is 72 cm or three nose lengths. The cover of the book is 34 cm wide by 57 cm in height and the side (page ends) is 12 cm wide.

The Chevron Pattern [2]

(Pl. 1, Fig. 42)

The circumference of the great circle in the dome [1] and the upper border of the band of roundels [3–13] are separated by a chevron pattern averaging about 11 cm in width, excluding the white outlines. The pattern band is executed for the most part on the plaster rendering for the figure of Christ, and it is contained between the white outlines that delimit the compositions above and below it.

The chevrons are well balanced as to size but are not executed with geometric accuracy. The painter commenced his design with double upward parallelograms at a point above the angel [9] on the northwest side of the dome, but he also completed it with a double upward parallelogram, and some confusion in the color adjustments ensued. The irregularities suggest that the pattern was set out freehand and not with a stencil.

The inner part of the chevron has downward-slanted parallelograms in vermilion and upward-slanted parallelograms in light red with a white highlight line. The lower part of the chevron has downward-slanting blue parallelograms and upward-slanting light blue parallelograms which have a dark blue shadow line and white highlight lines. A thin black line separates the shapes and marks the vertical divisions. The triangular interstices above and below the chevron are filled in with black.

The distribution of dark and light tones of color within the chevron gives to this pattern an illusionist three-dimensional quality that enhances the importance of the figure above. It has the effect of both physically separating Christ from the other images in the church, and of elevating him into an ethereal sphere. The deacon, Nikolaos Mesarites, writing in the twelfth century, described the Pantokrator in the dome of the church of the Holy Apostles in Constantinople. He described Christ as "looking forth through the window, leaning out down to his navel through the lattice, which is near the summit of the dome."[81] The chevron border at Lagoudhera serves very well as the frame of the lattice in Mesarites's simile.

[81] Nikolaos Mesarites, "Description of the Church of the Holy Apostles at Constantinople," ed. and trans. G. Downey, *TAPS* 47, pt. 6 (1957), 869–70; C. Mango, *The Art of the Byzantine Empire*, Sources and Documents in the History of Art Series, ed. H. W. Janson (Englewood Cliffs, N.J., 1972), 232. Mesarites's reference to lattices, as he himself states, is inspired by Song of Songs 2:9: "Behold, he standeth behind our wall, He looketh in at the windows, He showeth himself through the lattice." Mesarites' description is of further interest in that he suggests that the worshipper reads into Christ's expression the emotions that are the reflections of his own state of mind. See above, p. 113.

The Band of Roundels [3–13]

(Pls. 1, 10–12; Figs. 46–59; Text Figs. 23, 46b)

Between the chevron pattern and the springing of the dome from the drum, there is a continuous band containing a series of eleven roundels. The eastern roundel contains the Etoimasia [3], and the ten roundels to either side of it each contain the half-length figure of an angel or archangel. There are six archangels [4, 5, 7, 10, 12, 13] and four angels [6, 8, 9, 11]. The Etoimasia [3], the symbolic image for the Second Coming of Christ, is the focus of the whole roundel band, and the ten angels incline their heads eastwards toward it, as if in an act of homage.

The centerpoints of all the medallions are set along a median line that roughly bisects the panel. A similar constructional layout occurs in the medallion band in the apse (see above, p. 89; Text Fig. 18) and for medallions in arch soffits (see below, pp. 149, 223; Text Fig. 25). The diameters and the centerpoints of the medallions form the framework upon which figures are constructed, and the module controlling their measures could not be determined until these were established. The height of the panel varies as much as 10 cm in the northwest section. The diameter of the medallions [7–10] in that section is larger than the others, but the figures within all the medallions are similar in size. The difference of 10 cm in height between the two sections may be accounted for by the need to adjust the painting scheme to some constructional peculiarities of the dome in this area. Just above the level of the springing of the dome there is a break in the otherwise even curvature, perhaps marking the point where the builders ceased to build brick upon brick and resorted to timber centering to support the final inward curve of the dome. On a level with the

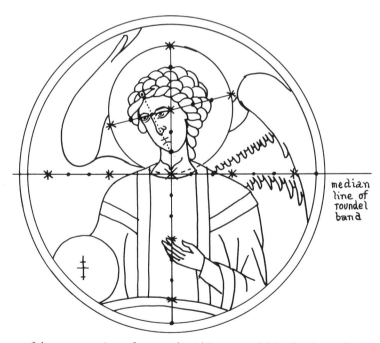

Text Fig. 23 Diagram of the construction of an angel within a roundel in the dome [4–13]

breasts of the angels, the curving profile changes in angle to a sharper, upward curve.

The plaster for the roundel band was rendered in two sections. The eastern section was plastered first, and this contains roundels [3 to 6] and [11 to 13]. The height of this section averages 108 cm. The shorter, western section was plastered second, and this contains roundels [7 to 10], and has an average height of 117 cm. The eastern medallions have an average diameter of 75 cm and those of the western section are 79 cm. There is evidence to suggest that the borders of the western roundels were enlarged at an intermediate stage of painting.

The ten angels were all constructed to similar measurements. Their halo diameter is standard, and its notional base is tangent to the notional median construction line that forms the horizontal diameters of the roundels. The heads are all inclined in the oblique aspect, their bodies are frontal, and their arms follow the sideways direction of the heads. The flat, modular, geometric construction underlying the design is responsible for the peculiar stiffness of the inclined stance of the head (Text Fig. 23). Its arbitrary angularity makes no concession to the plastic nature of movement in the human figure.

Each of the outlines for the roundels is marked out in the plaster by a trowel or spatula, and there is a contrast between the number of spatula marks within the roundels and the smooth surface of the plaster of the backgrounds. Impressed marks occur quite frequently within the roundels, marking out the contour of a shoulder, a wing, or a hand. There is also evidence of retroweling in order to bring moisture to the surface of the plaster.

There is a contrast between the smooth plaster surface for the heads and the roughness of the remaining area for the roundels. This may be because the detailed brushwork would have been difficult to execute on a rough plaster surface. There is also a contrast between the smoother plaster surfaces of angel [6] and archangel [7] at one end of each plaster section, and the altogether rougher plaster surfaces of archangel [10] and angel [11] at the further end of those sections. This could indicate that the painter began the sections with roundels [6] and [7] when the plaster was fresh and moist, but that he had to rework the plaster more on roundels [10] and [11], which were the last to be painted.

The roundel band has an upper ground of blue and a foreground of green, and both grounds were painted over a grey base. The green occupies approximately a quarter of the height of the band. In the eastern section, about one third of the green was given a wash of thin white with a wavy upper edge; this was painted out with the standard background green, and it illustrates an interesting change of thought on the part of the painter. There is no trace of a similar wash in the foreground of the western section. The roundels appear to float in a narrow sea of green against a plain blue background, where the only interruption is the inscription on either side of the roundel of the Etoimasia [3]. The roundel borders are yellow with black outlines and they average 3.5 to 4.5 cm in thickness. Five roundels have a background color of vermilion, three have blue backgrounds, and three have green backgrounds.

The Etoimasia [3]

(Pls. 10a, 11a, b; Figs. 46, 47)

The inscription is written in white letters with delicate serifs, placed on either side of the roundel and a little above it on the blue background of the roundel band.

The central feature of the Etoimasia is a seat inset with pearls and surmounted by a plump, much decorated bolster. The bolster is covered by a broad cloth whose flat folds do not contour to the rounded form beneath it. Upon the cloth stands a closed book with a decorated cover. The upper half of the roundel is dominated by a two-armed cross of rounded poles that looms up from behind the seat. To the left of the cross stands a thin spear and to the right another spear with a sponge upon it. At the center of the composition, perched in front of the cross, is a dove in profile with its narrow wings outstretched and its head turned back over its shoulder.

The Etoimasia shows considerably more evidence of plaster working than do the roundels of angels, and it is reasonable to assume that this is the roundel where the painter started work. It also seems likely that the painter took greater care with it since it was the focal point of the roundels. The small area covering the shape of the dove has been marked in with a spatula, and the primary feathers of its wings have been marked by sketchy, incised lines (Fig. 47). The lance and the sponge are each marked out by a vertical incised line in the plaster. The shapes of the cross and parts of the outlines of the cloth over the bolster are impressed into the plaster.

The background within the medallion is a bright, shiny vermilion applied over a yellow base. The shine of the background is so marked as to make it certain that it was polished after the colors had been laid on.

The throne has a yellow ground with umber pattern lines, vermilion and green jewels, and white pearls; the decoration on the seat is similar to pattern I on Pl. 11a, but the corridor pattern on the legs has only single rows of pearls. A vermiculated pattern runs between the legs of the throne. The gathered ends of the bolster have a yellow ground, patterns in umber lines, and a single pearl at either end; the central area has a black ground with a pattern of concentric circles painted in vermilion and green line and picked out with white pearls (Pl. 10a). The cloth has a red ground, umber shadows, black lines and outlines, and blue highlights. The page ends of the book are vermilion with black ties and clasp, and the cover is decorated with pattern II (Pl. 11b, Text Fig. 36.1b). The cross has a yellow ground with umber and then black shadows, and black outlines. The spears, sponge, and bird are all painted in thick lime white.

The incision lines of the preliminary drawing for the composition and the evidence of the paint overlaps make it clear that the painter originally envisaged a smaller-scale composition. The present upper outline to the top of the book and the cloth is 4 cm higher than the incised line demarcating the top of these features, which lies along the horizontal diameter of the medallion circle. In the earlier version the horizontal seat did not project at the sides. At a final stage, important alterations were made to the dove. The wings were fined down by scraping away the paint,

and the bird's head was changed around from facing south to facing north (Fig. 47). All of these changes much improved the balance and the abstract geometry of this composition.

The flat folds of the cloth are, in reality, incompatible with the rounded volume of the bolster beneath it, but they perform a painterly role by giving a recessed effect to the lower half of the composition. This would otherwise have dominated the more important semicircle containing the heavily shadowed cross and the luminous white bird to the front of it.

The Angel Roundels [4–13]

(Pls. 1, 11a–c, 12; Figs. 48–59)

The half-length figures of the ten angels are all slightly turned, and they incline their heads sideways to the east. Their forward wings furl backward and upward behind their haloes, and their rear wings fold downward behind the shoulders, revealing the inner feathers. All the angels have the faces of young men, and the only difference between them lies in the degree of damage they have sustained over the years. They all have their rounded, wig-like hair styles arranged into tight, clustered curls with a single tress down the back of the neck; a delicate ribbon band threads the hair with a jewel at its center and a single end floating loose behind the head. The four angels [6, 8, 9, 11] wear the chiton with clavus under a voluminous himation that enfolds the forward-bending arms and hands. The archangels [4, 5, 7, 10, 12, 13], each hold an opaque white globe that conceals their forward hands. Each globe is decorated with a small, two-armed black cross. The archangels' other hands lie diagonally, palms downward, across their chests. They all wear the imperial loros over their chitons, from under which only the decorated cuff of the undertunic is visible.

The wooden stance of the figures is counterbalanced by the whirling effect of their wings, which appear to bowl the roundels forward towards the central eastern medallion of the Etoimasia. When seen from the naos, the figure of Christ in the dome looms above the Etoimasia, and the angels appear to converge eastwards and upwards toward him.

The color buildup for the angels' hair is standard, both for the figures in the dome and for the other angels in this 1192 decoration. It has a light umber ground, shadow delineations in umber, highlight lines in yellow, and final lines and outlines in black. The hair ribbon is white with blue shadow lines, a black underline, and a central, round, blue jewel picked out with four white pearls.

The loroi worn by all the archangels and kings in this decoration have a basic design of jeweled, black borders and a central panel with a choice of three different jeweled patterns built up on a yellow ground. (Patterns I–III, Pl. 11a-c). The broad, black borders have a yellow, linear corridor filled with double (sometimes triple) rows of pearls that alternate with square red, blue, or green jewels within yellow setting lines.

The central areas of these loros panels are yellow and are overlaid with one of two patterns in the case of the archangels in the dome. A third pattern appears in the loros of figures lower down in the decoration.

The Dome

Pattern I (Pl. 11a) can be seen within the loros of archangels [4, 7, and 12] and consists of a linear diamond net pattern of intersecting corridors lined with a double row of pearls. A blue, red, or green jewel is set within the square formed where the corridors intersect. The diamond-shaped interstices to these corridors are bisected by linear diagonals, and the ensuing triangles are filled with palmettes and vermiculation in red line.

Pattern II (Pl. 11b) can be seen within the loros of archangels [5, 10, and 13]. It consists of a square net pattern in umber line with single pearls at the intersections. The square "lattices" contain at their center a solid, stepped square with a fine, white outline. Each stepped square is linked to the other by a fine, white line imposing a white net pattern over the umber one.

The loroi worn by the archangels in the dome consist of three sections or panels; the two upper panels are either crossed diagonally over the chest or one panel enfolds the shoulders and is overlapped by a central vertical panel that falls from a rounded neckline; in every case a third section is partially visible as it enfolds the body horizontally at the base of the roundel. The cuffs to their undertunics are decorated with pattern Ia (Text Fig. 24).

The globes carried by the archangels have a white ground painted over a yellow base, and each has a circular block of blue shadow at the center upon which a thin two-armed black cross is painted.

The color buildup for the wings of the angels, both in this roundel series and elsewhere in the 1192 paintings, is carried out in a consistent and similar manner, though some variation can be found in the colors used for the inner feathers. The painter began with a yellow base that was laid in at a preliminary stage to map out the form of the scapula or body of the wing, and this was overlaid with an opaque ground of light umber. Over the light umber he then made very broad outlines in umber to shape the scapula, and then the whole wing was defined by a final, broad outline in black. The inner area of the scapula was striated with fine, light green lines, and the tops or inner edges of the wings were given shorter, yellow feather lines. The feathers of the wings were built up in a diminishing sequence of length and in colors of a diminishing darkness of tone proceeding inward from the long, black, primary feathers through the rows of covert feathers ending in short thick, white feathers below the scapula. The meeting of the covert feathers with the scapula was tidied up by the final addition of a row of stubby black feathers.

Angels [4, 6, 7, 9, 11, 13] have covert feathers whose colors are graded from vermilion to pink; angels [5, 12] have covert feathers graded from dark green to pale green; and angels [8, 10] have feathers graded from dark yellow to pale yellow.

Archangel [4], the southeast roundel (Figs. 49, 293, 296, 299)

The background is green. His chiton has a light red ground, and black lines and outlines. Some discolored lines, now of a greyish tone, suggest that it may have had vermilion highlights. His loros is decorated with a variation of pattern I (Pl. 11a). Above the globe is a crack in the plaster, and impress marks with thumb prints show how the painter pressed the edges together

with his fingers and thumbs before he overpainted the damaged area in green (Fig. 293). The green of the overpaint is darker in tone than the background green. Perhaps the darker tone may have been caused by greasy fingers. There are clear impress marks in the plaster of the hands and the face and in the borders of the black loros (Fig. 299). The hand was retooled (Fig. 296).

Archangel [5], the south-southeast roundel (Fig. 53, 58)

The background is vermilion, and there is evidence of reworking in the plaster. The angel's chiton has a red ground, umber shadows, black lines and fold lines, and blue linear highlights. His loros is decorated with pattern II (Pl. 11b). The painter retroweled the area of the archangel's hand after the painting of the patterned loros had already been completed. This caused a disturbance in the pattern, which was repainted after the hand was completed (Fig. 58). The impressing of the black decorative border of the loros is very clear, as in roundel [4] (Fig. 296).

Angel [6], the southern roundel (Fig. 51)

The background is green. The angel's chiton has a red ground, black lines and fold lines, blue wash highlights and broad, thick, white highlights. His himation has a green ground, black lines and fold lines, white wash, and thick white highlights. To the right of this angel runs the plaster join separating the east and west section of the band on this southern side. This plaster join is vertical, except where it meets and follows up the curve of the roundel.

Archangel [7], the south-southwest roundel (Fig. 57)

The angel is seen against a blue background and his chiton has a light red ground, red shadows, black lines and outlines, and vermilion highlights that have now become discolored. His loros is decorated with pattern I (Pl. 11a). Traces of a light red preliminary drawing for the face were observed in the much damaged head. Where the paint layers had fallen away, chaff can be seen on the surface of the plaster, showing that in the case of this archangel there is no fresh plaster patch for the face.

Angel [8], the southwest roundel (Figs. 55, 59)

The background is vermilion. His chiton and himation have a ground color that can only be described as bright apricot, a color not noted elsewhere in this decoration, and that probably came either from the successful mixing of red and yellow pigments or from a particularly orange ochre. The ground for the chiton was then overpainted with an opaque ground of light umber upon which were built up umber shadows and black lines and outlines, followed by white wash and thick, white highlights. The himation also received a further ground of opaque, light grey, grey shadows, black lines and outlines, and thick, white linear highlights. The original "apricot" ground is visible where the later paint layers have fallen away.

The Dome

Angel [9] , the northwest roundel (Fig. 56)

The background is green and he wears a chiton with a light red ground, over which broad, thin washes of white were painted. The shadows and fold lines were made in red, with black lines and outlines, and the whole garment was finished off with light blue wash highlights and thick, white linear highlights. His himation has a light umber ground, umber shadows, black lines and fold lines, blue wash highlights, and thick, white, linear highlights. The painter retroweled the plaster for the face so vigorously that he built up a ridge of plaster at the base of the neck.

Archangel [10], the north-northwest roundel (Fig. 52)

The background is vermilion. His chiton has a red ground, umber shadow lines, black lines and fold lines, and linear blue highlights. His loros panels are decorated with pattern II (Pl. 11b). At a final stage in the painting, the shoulders of this figure were enlarged and heightened. This alteration was made so late in the procedure of painting that much of the plaster and paint was already dry. The areas of the loros that were extended over onto the background around the shoulders have now flaked away because of the lack of bonding between the paint layers of the alteration and that of the dry vermilion background. A plaster join runs in an irregular vertical line through the side of this roundel. Most of the roundel is on the new section of plaster and it is marked by the same retroweling of the surface as in the other roundels. The outline of the roundel is marked in the plaster except for the portion that runs over the adjacent plaster section. The plaster of this older, eastern section must have set too hard to take the impress marks. This roundel, like that for the Etoimasia, exhibits an untidy plaster surface at the level where the curvature of the dome changes. It was difficult both to plaster and to paint over this changing curvature without creating a distortion.

Angel [11], the north roundel (Fig. 54)

The background is blue. His chiton has a light red ground, red shadow lines, black lines and fold lines, and broad patches of thick, white highlight. His himation has a green ground, yellow-green shadow areas, black lines and fold lines, blue wash highlights, and thick, white linear highlights. An impressed line marks the original outline for the figure's right shoulder. At a final stage of painting this shoulder and arm were narrowed 2 to 3 cm. The marks of scraping where this rectification was made can be seen to the left side of the figure. A blue wash was used to conceal the alteration and the vertical brushmarks of the blue paint can be seen running over the scraped area. Most of the plaster join marking the end of the west section runs through the north side of this roundel. There is a very marked impress line for the shape of the west side of the body.

Archangel[12], the north-northeast roundel (Fig. 50)

The background is vermilion. His chiton has a red ground, black lines and fold lines, and linear blue highlights. His loros panels are decorated with pattern I (Pl. 11a). At the western edge of the face of this figure, at eyebrow level, there is an uneven length of plaster that seems to

represent the edge of a fresh plaster patch for the face. But, just possibly, it could have resulted from some careless retroweling of the plaster. The retroweling of the plaster area for the hand, as in other archangels, caused a disturbance of the already completed pattern of the loros. When he had finished the hand, the painter repainted the pattern over the disturbed plaster, but the repainted design is not in accord with the original pattern alongside it.

Archangel [13], the northeast roundel (Fig. 48)

The background is blue. The ground color of his chiton is now a grey brown, but originally, this was probably vermilion; this was overlaid with red shadows, and black lines and fold lines. His loros panels are decorated with pattern II (Pl. 11b). The shape of the body was clearly impressed into the plaster before painting. In the head, the spatula impress marks for the curls of the hair on the eastern side can be both felt and seen in the plaster, showing that not only broad outlines, but also, sometimes, small details were "drawn" into the plaster. On the west side, the impressed shape and the final painted shape of the body correspond fairly clearly. On the eastern side, at some intermediate stage of painting, the upper left arm and the globe were reduced in size. The original paint was scraped away and the alteration was concealed under a fresh coat of blue paint.

The painter's adjustments in this otherwise repetitive band of angels and in the Etoimasia call for some comment. It is quite possible that work on such an area would be shared between the master painter and an experienced pupil. In no other place did we find the rather clumsy expedient of adjusting the texture of the plaster by pressing the thumb into it. The fastidious attention to detail of the Lagoudhera master suggests a temperament that would have shied away from such a crude solution to a problem. The various other adjustments detailed above may all represent a quick tidying up of a pupil's work by the master. The major changes in the Etoimasia that give so much better a balance to this composition could also have been the result of allowing a pupil to draw it out, followed by the master's decision to improve the balance of the painting.

A contrast can be made between the broad and speedy brushwork of the wings of the angels and the thin and precise linear quality of the painting of other areas. And finally, it is possible to detect a change of shaping in the eyes of some of the angels that gives them a slightly different character, perhaps the work of another hand.

9

The Drum of the Dome and the Pendentives

Drum

[4–37] (Pls. 11, 14–18; Figs. 60–75, 264–275, Text Figs. 2, 24)

The drum of the cupola has a circumference of approximately 11 m and a vertical height of an average 1.73 m. The upper edge is marked by the red border at the base of the band of angel roundels and the lower edge is marked by a red-painted cornice or sill, 7 cm wide and 5 to 7 cm thick. The wall of the drum is broken by twelve windows, three in each quadrant. The windows are tall, narrow, and round-arched, and all their measurements are irregular. Each window has one or two wooden tie beams about 15 cm below the soffit, and these are part of the original structure. There is no longer any trace of medieval glass or of the fittings for it, and with the exception of the eastern window, each light is fitted with modern, rounded glass panes set in cement frames that date from the restoration of 1955.

The windows have an average height of 144 cm. The width of the sills at the interior edge of the reveals varies from 26 cm to 30 cm, but this width often narrows to half its size at the springing of the arched soffits. The reveals are splayed so that the exterior width of the sill is greater than the interior, but this is partly because the plastering of the reveals did not extend to the exterior edges. The length of the sill could only be measured at the east window, where the frame had been removed for access purposes in the course of work, and this measured 61 cm from the interior to the exterior edges. The plastering of each reveal was carried out in a single, continuous rendering, and the width of the plaster band is approximately half the width of the reveals. The sills were unplastered. A plaster join runs round the red border that outlines each window where it meets with the plaster rendering for the flat surfaces of the wall of the drum.

The twelve mullions have an average height of 1.73 m and their width at the base varies from 65 to 81 cm. The windows do not occupy the full vertical space of the drum and the area between their soffits and the springing of the dome varies from 25 to 37 cm in height. On the face of each mullion stands the gesturing figure of a prophet.

The surfaces containing the prophets were plastered in three sections, and plaster joins appear above the south-southeast window [18], the north-northwest window [30], and the south-south-

west window [22]. The eastern section contains six figures [15, 17, 31, 33, 35, 37], the northwest section three figures [25, 27, 29], and the southwest section also contains three figures [19, 21, 23]. The plaster joins were well worked over and it is unclear which section was plastered first. It seems likely that the western sections with three prophets in each patch of plaster were plastered first. The painter could have planned originally to have four plaster sections, with three prophets in each section. But he gained confidence in painting the western sections, and, as with the angel roundels, he could have decided to speed up the work and paint the remaining six prophets on a single patch. Or these plaster joins may represent evidence of different painters (Text Fig. 2).

The Patterns in the Window Reveals [Even Nos. 14–36] (Pl. 11d, e, f)

All the window reveal patterns (Pl. 11) have a wide, red border at their interior edge that is flush with the red border to the mullions, but at their exterior edge there is no containing red border. The patterns correspond to three different designs: Design 1, in windows [14, 20, 24, 34], has its yellow base color over-painted with three broad stripes of green, white, and yellow, which form the ground for a design in umber line. The design consists of repeated squares, each bisected by diagonals that form triangles filled with vermiculation (Pl. 11, reveal pattern d). Design 2, in windows [18 and 30], has a ground similar to Design 1, but the stripes are overlaid with a continuous scroll pattern filled with vermiculation in umber line (Pl. 11, reveal pattern f). Design 3, in windows [16, 22, 26, 28, 32, 36], has elements of the design painted over a yellow base and consists of a continuous yellow chevron outlined in black and enclosing a wavy black line within it. Each triangle of the chevron is filled with a leaf-and-bud design formed by two yellow leaves on either side of a central green one, with a rounded red bud set between them. The whole pattern was embellished with curlicues in umber line. There are some variations: window [28] has a green chevron with a leaf-and-bud design in yellow only, and windows [22 and 26] have an extra black outline within the triangles formed by the chevron (Pl. 11e).

The Twelve Prophets on the Mullions [Uneven Nos. 15–37]

(Pls. 13–18; Figs. 60–75, 264–275; Text Figs. 2, 24)

The twelve Old Testament figures are all given the title of prophet, though only seven of them are included in the list of prophets: Jeremiah [15], Solomon [17], Elijah [19], Elisha [21], Daniel [23], Gideon [25], Habakkuk [27], Ezechiel [29], Jonah [31], Moses [33], David [35], and Isaiah [37]. All are painted life-size, one to each mullion of the cupola. The height of the drum between the sill and the upper red border is approximately 1.73 m. The spandrels between the window arches are used to accommodate the titular inscriptions and the gesturing hands of the prophets.

The parading figures are set against an upper background of blue and a lower ground of

green; the green ground occupies about two-fifths of the panel. The titular inscriptions are painted in fine, white letters on the blue ground. Each prophet clasps an unfurling scroll, the colors for which are built up in a similar manner. They have a light green ground, with some umber shadow lines in the folded ends, while broad horizontal bands of white delimit the areas of green upon which the black lettering is inscribed. In the lettering of the scrolls, there is frequent confusion between the use of epsilon, alpha, eta, and iota. In some cases the master painter made corrections and modifications, and perhaps the inscriptions were the work of a pupil. For the most part, the confusion may be attributed to the lack of a standard orthography in Byzantine Greek. There is also a constant and arbitrary use of shortenings in order to ensure that the whole of the desired text for each prophet could be indicated (Figs. 264–275).

The courtly figures of Daniel and the kings Solomon and David are seen in the frontal aspect, but David's head is in three-quarter profile. The other figures stand in a more lively variety of stances and their heads are all in three-quarter profile. Solomon, Daniel, and Habakkuk are portrayed with the unlined faces of young men; the other prophets have the furrowed faces of old men, but their heads are differentiated by a variety of hair styles. Daniel, Solomon, and David wear courtly and royal robes; the other figures wear the chiton with a black clavus under a swirling himation, and their bare feet are shod in sandals with fine, black straps. Daniel alone wears a single, pearly earring. Traditionally in Cyprus, the single earring worn by a man is regarded as the sign of a great destiny, and in the 1192 decoration, the heads of the Christ child all feature this singular earring. In the earlier decoration, however, the Christ child held by the Virgin in the apse does not wear one.

Jeremiah [15], southeast quadrant (Pls. 15, 18; Figs. 60, 264)

His titular inscription is aligned on either side of his halo. The inscription on his scroll is taken from Baruch 3:36, in the Septuagint. The prophet is represented as an old man with his face in three-quarter profile turning back to look to the left over his shoulder. The whole head is a fine example of the masterly fluency and precision in brushwork at which the 1192 painter excelled. His white hair falls in flowing tresses, with a long lock straying over his shoulder, while his beard and mustache ripple to a point beneath his neatly shaped chin. His upper body is in the frontal aspect, but his right leg swings forward to the right, while his left leg extends behind it, so that his body spirals stiffly from left to right. With his left hand he holds up the top of his scroll, while with his right hand he steadies the lower end against his waist. His heavy, upper body and the long, slender legs advancing on tiptoe are counterbalanced by the belling folds of his chiton, and the narrow, free-hanging folds of his himation.

His chiton has a light green ground, green shadow, black lines and outlines, white wash, and thick, white highlights. His himation has a light red ground, red shadow, umber fold lines, black lines and outlines, white wash, and thick, white highlights. Some alterations were made at a final stage of painting to improve the balance of the figure. The left arm was narrowed and the free-hanging himation folds were widened to balance the heavy left shoulder. The right shoulder was

heightened by the addition of an arbitrary, thick, black outline.

Solomon [17], southeast quadrant (Pls. 10c–e, 11c; Figs. 61, 265)

The titular inscription is placed on either side of the halo and is unabbreviated. The inscription on the scroll is badly damaged and only part of it is legible. The text is a quotation from the Book of Proverbs 31:29, in the Authorized Version, and 29:29 in the Septuagint (Fig. 265). There is a corrected error in the scroll at the end of the top line where a patch of grey was painted on to cover up an epsilon. A linked alpha iota was then painted over the grey.

Solomon is portrayed as a beardless young man with brown hair falling in loose curls to chin level. He is shown in the frontal aspect; his left arm lies alongside his body and his forearm is foreshortened as he grips the top of his unfurling scroll. His right arm sweeps across the top of his chest, and the hand extends upward as if to indicate his name. He is clad in formal, imperial regalia. Upon his head is a mitered crown with pendilia, and he wears a dalmatic with a jeweled hem and white sash under a heavy bejeweled loros. A rich, soft cloak is thrown back over his shoulders and his feet are shod with boots studded with pearls. Under the dalmatic, he wears a narrow-sleeved tunic with a yellow cuff.

The sleeve of his tunic and the body of his dalmatic both have a red ground, umber shadows, black fold lines and outlines, and vermilion highlights that have now faded to grey. The rich hem panel to the dalmatic, with its jewel-studded circles, is similar to that of the prophet David [35] (Pl. 10e). The collar has a yellow ground overlaid with a pattern of circles and vermiculation in umber line. The cuff was probably similar to the collar but only the damaged, yellow ground color remains. The dalmatic was tied at the waist with a white sash and the whole was overlapped by the stiff vertical and horizontal panels of the jeweled loros.

King Solomon's loros is decorated with pattern III (Pl. 11c). Within its jeweled, black borders, the central yellow panel is overlaid with a net pattern in umber line forming intersecting corridors lined with double rows of pearls. The quadrilaterals of the lattice pattern and the squares formed by the intersections of the corridors are each filled with a single jewel. The jewels are red or green and are set within white lines that imitate claw settings of gold. Each jewel is divided diagonally into triangles of dark and light tones that well simulate jewels cut into facets. This pattern also decorates the loros of the prophet David [35] and that of the archangel Michael [140].

His cloak has a vermilion ground, shadow lines in red, and black folds and outlines. A narrow, yellow band lined with single pearls borders the hem. His miter crown has a yellow ground and is outlined in dark red line. It is decorated with red, green, and blue jewels. The narrow pendilakia are black and dotted with white pearls, and each terminates in a square jewel outlined with seed pearls from which hangs a large singular pearl (Pl. 10d).

The figure was considerably damaged as it was exposed to the worst of the local weather. The central areas of the body and the lower scroll are much flaked and eroded, as is the area around his feet.

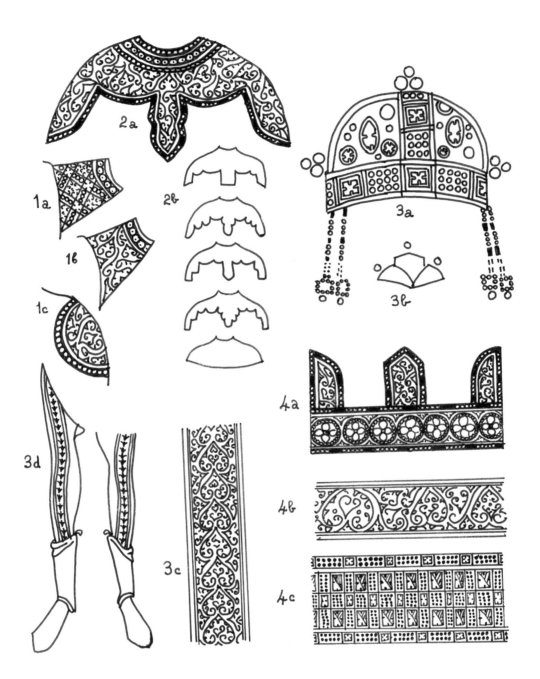

Text Fig. 24 Decorative garment details

This figure of Solomon is static under the heavy richness of his formal costume, which restricts his movement. The sumptuous stiff garments do, however, enrobe his figure with an air of authority that is lacking in the youthfulness of his face.

Elijah or Elias [19], southeast quadrant (Figs. 62, 266)

The unabbreviated titular inscription is placed on either side of the halo. Originally the iota in the name was written as an eta, but the right vertical and the horizontal bars were scraped off and two dots added above the left vertical bar to make an iota, with the accent left far over to the right. Elijah's scroll is much weathered and the lower part of the text has become indecipherable. The text seems to have been taken both from the story of Elijah at the brook Cherith (3 Kings 17:1, according to the Septuagint, and, in the Authorized Version, 1 Kings 17:1) and from the story of his translation up to Heaven (2 Kings 2:2.4.6, and in the Greek Bible, 4 Kings 2:2–4) (Fig. 266).

The prophet is portrayed as an old man with long, white hair that falls in flowing tresses, with one long lock trailing across his left shoulder. His beard and mustache ripple to a point beneath the neatly outlined chin. His face is in three-quarter profile, and it is turned to the left. His figure is seen in the frontal aspect, and his right arm is folded upwards so that the hand lies palm downward across his chest. His foreshortened left arm thrusts forward while the hand grips the top of the unfurling scroll. He wears a chiton with clavus under a fur-lined cloak that is thrown back over his shoulders.

His chiton has a light yellow ground, yellow shadows followed by red shadows, umber fold lines and black outlines, and thick, white linear highlights. His cloak has a dark yellow ground, grey-green shadow lincs, and black lines and fold lines. The fur collar has a yellow-green ground. A thin, white wash is used to outline the tufts, and there are thick, white linear highlights.

At a late stage in painting, some adjustments were made to the left side of the figure to counterbalance the mass of the foreshortened right arm and scroll. The left shoulder was heightened, and the sleeve falling from the left arm was enlarged outward and downward. He now appears as a solid and relatively static figure, but greater impetus of movement was probably provided by the articulation of his chiton. A large area of this is now lost where plaster has fallen away, leaving no evidence as to the shape of it. In the course of restoration, a general shape was given to the chiton in order to make the figure visually acceptable, but no attempt has been made to restore any articulation within the garment.

Elisha [21], southwest quadrant (Figs. 63, 267)

The titular inscription is unabbreviated and lies to either side of the halo. The text on the scroll refers to the Translation of Elijah (Elias) as witnessed by Elisha, but the Lagoudhera text misses the phrase referring to the horsemen. The words are taken from 2 Kings 2:12 (Fig. 267).

The prophet is portrayed as an old man with brown hair that has receded to the back of his head; two long tresses trail over his right shoulder, while his rippling beard comes to an irregular point beneath the outline of the chin. His head is seen in three-quarter profile as it turns to the right. His shoulders are in the frontal aspect, while the rest of his body twists sideways as his left leg steps out to the right. His right leg remains strictly frontal with the foot extending vertically downward, as if on tiptoe. The prophet's right arm is bent at the elbow as he clutches the top

of his scroll against his chest. He steadies the lower end of his unfurled scroll in the fingers of his left hand.

His chiton has a light red ground, red shadows, dark red fold lines, and further black fold lines and outlines. The highlights are formed of thin, white washes and both linear and block highlights in thick, white paint. His himation has a light umber ground, umber shadows, dark umber fold lines, and further black fold lines and outlines, and the white highlights are painted in thick blocks of white, as well as in fine white lines. There is no intermediate highlight for the himation, as the ground color is already extremely pale.

The rather solid figure of this prophet was relieved by the rippling folds of his himation, but the flaking of the paint layers has much weakened the effect of linear movement.

Daniel [23], southwest quadrant (Pl. 13; Figs. 70, 74, 268; Text Fig. 24.3b, c, d)

The titular inscription is unabbreviated and lies to either side of the halo. The epithet "Prophet" now lacks the final sigma. The text of the scroll is taken from the Book of Daniel 2:44 (Fig. 268). The prophet is represented as a beardless young courtier with a calotte on his head and smooth brown hair falling to chin level. A single, large, pearl earring hangs from his left ear. His figure is shown in the frontal aspect and his right arm is extended upward and outward in exhortation. His left arm is foreshortened as he holds the top of an unfurled scroll in his hand.

Only the cuff and sleeve of his undergarment are visible under his richly decorated short tunic. This garment has short, wide sleeves and the broad decorated hem reaches only to mid-thigh level. It is further decorated by a vertical panel descending from the round neckline to the base of the belly, and it is tied loosely at the waist by a white sash knotted into a bow at the center. A long cloak fastened below the neck with a single pearl is thrown back over his shoulders. His legs are clad in close-fitting, decorated hose and plain, soft boots.

His calotte is vermilion with black outlines, and three, large, single pearls pick out the corners. His cloak has a vermilion ground, umber shadows, black fold lines and outlines, and some white highlights upon the interior; the hemline is decorated with a thin, yellow band lined with pearls. Both the sleeve of his undergarment and the body of his tunic have a green ground, dark green shadows, black fold lines and outlines, white wash, and thick, white linear highlights. The cuff of his undertunic, the rounded shoulder decoration on his cloak, the central panel, and the hem border of his tunic all have a yellow ground with broad white highlighting down the center to simulate the luster of silver and gold thread. Upon this ground is overlaid a vermiculated decoration in umber line (Text Fig. 24.3b–c.). All these decorated panels are outlined with narrow black bands picked out with single pearls. The stockings have a red ground, black lines and outlines, and broad areas of blue wash highlighting. The blue wash over red gives a striking impression of shot silk, just as in the chiton worn by Christ [1].[82] Running down the front of each stocking is a design in light yellow consisting of two vertical parallel lines outlining a narrow vertical corridor

---

[82] See Cennini, *Il Libro del Arte*, 50–53.

filled with single trefoils (Text Fig. 24.3d). Daniel's boots have a yellow ground, light yellow highlights, and black lines and outlines. A narrow, white loop projects at the back of the boot. A similar loop extrudes from the cuff of Daniel's undergarment. At a late stage of painting, the left forearm was narrowed, and the loose, short sleeve of the tunic above it was widened downward.

The decorative figure of the prophet Daniel well illustrates the slim and elegant proportions favored by the 1192 painter. The length of the legs is further emphasized by the continuation of the inner thigh line up to the groin and the base of the belly, and by the unforeshortened length of the dorsum of the frontal foot. The figure has a high waist because the 1192 master gave a rather short proportional allowance to the area between the chin and the breast line.[83] Two small examples of the particular affectations of this painter can be observed in this figure. One is the extrusion of white loops from the cuff and boots. Such narrow, white loops are frequent in the garments of the 1192 figures, particularly where clothes are tight-fitting, as in the case of narrow sleeves. The other is the placing of two large, thick, white dots on the black outlines at the exterior edge of some garments. The white dots can be seen at the lower edge of the sleeve of Daniel's tunic.

Gideon [25], southwest quadrant (Figs. 64, 269)

The titular inscription is placed on the left side of the halo and the final sigma to the title is missing. The text on the scroll is taken from the Book of Judges 6:36 (Fig. 269).

The prophet is portrayed with the lined face of an old man, with white hair that ends in a long tress over his back. His white beard and mustache are in fine tresses that are squared off just below the neatly rounded chin. The three-quarter profile head and neck are set on shoulders that are shown in the three-quarter posterior aspect. The result of this unnatural stance is that the meeting of the head and shoulders is clumsy and disconcerting to the viewer. The abdomen is in three-quarter profile, and while the left leg advances forwards to the right, the right leg steadies the figure to the rear. Only the thumb and forefinger of his left hand can be seen where they hold the top of his uplifted scroll. His right arm extends downward to the right, and his right hand firmly grips the bottom of the scroll.

The prophet's chiton has a light yellow ground, yellow and light red shadows, black fold lines and outlines, and thick, white linear highlights. His himation has a light yellow ground, yellow shadows, black fold lines, and thick, white, linear highlights.

The free-hanging folds of the himation at the back of the figure were lengthened and widened at a final stage of painting, and a further, pointed fold to the hem of the chiton was also added at the back. The back of Gideon's left hand, at the top of the scroll, was painted green, but the flesh

---

[83] For a discussion of the proportional system followed by the 1192 master, see below, Proportion, pp. 283–98. Byzantine perspective allows for full-length "flipper" feet, as if they were seen from above. Seen from the naos below, such a frontal overview of the dorsum of the foot gives figures a better balance than the stumpy foreshortening of the frontal view in correct optical perspective.

colors were never added, though the fingers were properly built up with flesh colors. This is a rare example of an oversight in the otherwise meticulous finish that is characteristic of the Lagoudhera master.

The figure of Gideon well illustrates the dilemma of a painter who had the choice of only two settings for the face: the frontal and the three-quarter profile. Gideon's stance, with shoulders in the semiposterior aspect, would fit more fluently with a profile head, rather than the three-quarter version painted here. It is to the painter's credit that the eye is so beguiled by the streaming folds of the garments and the fine painting within the head that the distortions pass almost unnoticed (see below, pp. 284–85, 298).

The lower part of the figure is much damaged and the loss of the surface layers of paint reveals the original dark grey brush drawing for the himation folds. It was the frequent practice of the Lagoudhera painter to make the opaque grounds for his robes in very light tones of color so that the grey preliminary drawing of the garment folds might remain visible enough to act as guidelines for the placing of the shadows that articulate the garment.

Habakkuk [27], northwest quadrant (Pl. 17, Figs. 65, 270, 291, 298)

The titular inscription is placed on the left side of the halo. The final sigma of his title is indicated by a dot, and the final mu of the Greek spelling for Habakkuk is omitted. The text on his scroll is Habakkuk 3:3.

The prophet is portrayed as a beardless young man with long, brown hair that falls into loose tresses over his left shoulder. His face is in three-quarter profile and turned to look over his right shoulder. The upper part of his body is turned to the right, and his extended right arm reaches upward and forward across his body. His left arm descends alongside his body, and the forearm is foreshortened as his hand grips the top of his unfurled scroll. His right leg is turned to the front with the foot extending vertically downward, whereas his left leg, seen in profile, steps forward to the right.

His chiton has a light green ground, green shadows, black fold lines and outlines, white wash, and thick, white, linear highlights. His himation has a light red ground, red shadows, black fold lines and outlines, white wash, and thick, white highlights.

At an early stage of painting, there was an alteration to the placing of the arms. Originally, the right arm of the figure was destined to hold the scroll and his left arm to extend upward. The alterations are clearly marked in the plaster (Fig. 298). Originally, there was also a gap between his left thigh and the scroll, but, at a final stage, this was painted out and made into a solid area of garment.

There is some contortion in the figure, particularly where the left leg is put into the anterior aspect, but this disposition gives a better balance to the figure.

Ezechiel [29], northwest quadrant (Pl. 16, Figs. 66, 271, 292)

The titular inscription is written on either side of the halo. The text of his scroll is taken from the Book of Ezechiel 1:19 (Fig. 271).

Ezechiel is portrayed as an old man with long, flowing, white tresses, one strand of which falls over his shoulder. His beard flows in loose strands over his chin before gathering to a blunted point above his larynx (Fig. 292). His face is in three-quarter profile and turns to the right over shoulders that are shown in the posterior aspect; his abdomen is shown in three-quarter profile and his legs are seen in profile, walking away toward the left. His left arm, seen in the posterior aspect, extends outward and downward to the left as the hand holds the bottom of an unfurled scroll. The thumb and forefinger of his right hand grip the top of the scroll. The different sections of the body do not relate to each other in a natural manner, and indeed, the figure is contorted beyond the wildest possibilities of nature. The painter retrieved this potentially disastrous figure once again by the skill of his compositional rhythms (see below, p. 144 n. 86, pp. 284–85).

The prophet's chiton has a light yellow ground; yellow shadows; further shadows in red; black and dark umber fold lines and outlines; and thick, white linear highlights. His himation is a very light yellow, with yellow shadows, black fold lines and outlines, some white wash, and thick, white linear highlights.

The convoluted folds at the end of the himation, to the right of the figure, were originally designed to reach higher into the blue area of the background. This is clear from the impress lines in that area and an overpaint of blue. The lowering of the massed folds gives a much better balance to the figure, which would otherwise be heavily weighted toward the top left side by the mass of the shoulder and scroll.

The 1192 master was clearly so aware of the visual effects of a correct balance and symmetry within his figures that he was prepared to make considerable adjustments to them at a late stage in painting. It is an apparent paradox that so able a painter could allow such a major contortion as occurs in Ezechiel and in Gideon. The distortions result from the compartmentalized system of proportion that Byzantine painters used in place of observation from nature.

Jonah [31], northwest quadrant (Figs. 67, 73, 272)

The titular inscription is aligned on either side of the prophet's halo. The text on his scroll is taken from the Book of Jonah 1:1–2 (Fig. 272). In the last line of the scroll the last letter should be an iota, not an eta.

Jonah is portrayed as an old man with a high, domed, bald head. A thin strip of hair lies above his left ear, and his beard and mustache are neatly rounded beneath his chin. His head is in three-quarter profile and turned to the right, while his body twists away to the left. His right leg advances forward to the left, while his left leg extends backward in the frontal aspect. His left arm curves outward and downward behind him, and the hand grips the top of his unfurling scroll. His right arm is raised outward and upward with the hand held up in exhortation. The end of his himation

sweeps forward over his left shoulder and under his raised right arm to fall over the elbow in a triangular ripple of folds.

A segment of his chiton is visible at his neck, and it reappears from beneath his himation to fall into a mass of bell folds over his ankles. The two sections of the chiton are colored differently. The upper section at the neck has a yellow-green ground, green shadow, white wash and thick, white, linear highlights. The lower section has a light yellow ground, yellow shadows, then thin umber shadows, black and umber fold lines, black outlines, and finally, green wash highlights and thick, white, linear highlights. His himation has a light yellow ground, yellow shadow blocks, thin umber darker shadows, black and dark umber fold lines and outlines, and thick, white, linear highlights.

Some alterations were made to the figure at a late stage in painting, when the pendant folds of his himation were carefully separated from his body by the insertion of a narrow corridor between them, painted in the blue of the background; a similar corridor in the blue and green of the background colors was inserted between the inner edge of the scroll and upper thigh of the figure.

This dynamic figure of Jonah is made up of echoing curves that unite within the body to form a powerful rhythmic tension. The most striking rhythms are formed by the horizontal S-curves made by the arms and shoulders, the forward-thrusting arch of the body, the line of the hollow back, and the looping curves of the himation folds. These are answered and balanced by the articulation of the folds in the garments, whose curving patterns encircle the belly, ripple across the thighs, and mass into bell folds along the hem of the chiton.

Moses [33], the northeast quadrant (Figs. 68, 75, 273)

The titular inscription is placed on either side of the halo. The text on the scroll is taken from the Book of Genesis 1:1 (Fig. 273).

Moses is portrayed as an old man, without a beard, but his hair has the characteristic coloring of a middle-aged man, and falls in smooth, pointed locks that reach to the shoulder. His face is particularly interesting, as it shows the buildup of linear patterns that are characteristic of old age, but Moses's face is clean-shaven (Fig. 75). The head is in three-quarter profile as the prophet turns to the right, while the rest of his body moves toward the left. His chest is in the frontal aspect, his abdomen in the three-quarter profile aspect, and his legs are in profile with his left leg moving as if to the left. He raises his right arm upward and outward in exhortation, while his left arm hangs downward with the forearm foreshortened as the hand grips the top of the unfurling scroll.

The prophet's chiton has a light red ground, red shadows, black fold lines and outlines, white wash, and thick, white, linear highlights. His himation has a light yellow ground, yellow shadows, black fold lines and outlines, white wash, and thick, white linear highlights.

The prophet's garments were adjusted at an early stage of painting. The yellow ground of the himation was extended outward over the blue and green of the background in order to enlarge the

figure. When at a final stage the enlargement proved to be an exaggeration, a corridor area of background was painted in blue and green over the clothing to separate the body from the figure's left arm, and from the scroll and the pendant himation folds. A further attempt to reduce the width of the body was made by placing the black outlines of the torso and thigh within the yellow ground and not at its edge. The shoulders were also heightened at the final stage. There is a lack of attention to the finish where the corridor area between the right side of the scroll and the red border of the window aperture was only partially painted in. The upper area should have been painted in blue to match the level of the background, but this was omitted, and most of the corridor remains as uncolored plaster.

The prophet Moses provides a lively companion figure to Jonah [31] as he strides forward with one arm high and the other thrusting forward with his scroll. The contouring belly folds and the agitated bell folds on the hems of both his garments break up the voluminous robes and form an emotive pattern of movement. This pair of prophets unites in a great surge of upward, rhythmic emphasis toward the Christ above them in the dome.

David [35], northeast quadrant (Pls. 10d, e, 11c; Figs. 69, 71, 72, 274, 290, 297)

The titular inscription is placed on either side of the halo, but in this case the last five letters of the word "prophet" are written out in full and aligned to the right above the abbreviated form of David. The text on his scroll is taken from Psalms 45:10, in the Authorized Version of the Bible, and from Psalms 44:11, in the Septuagint (Fig. 274).[84]

King David is portrayed as an old man with white hair reaching to the level of his chin and a neatly rounded beard. His head is in three-quarter profile and turned to the right, but his body stands in the frontal aspect. His right arm is extended outward and upward, the hand gesturing in exhortation, and his left arm curves outward and downward, while the hand grips the top of the unfurling scroll. His feet are both in the frontal, unforeshortened aspect. He is clad in the imperial dalmatic and loros, and wears a miter crown with pendilia. His feet are shod in boots ornamented with bands of single pearls. His costume resembles in every respect that worn by his son, Solomon [17] (Fig. 61). The buildup of colors within this costume is similar for both figures, except that David's dalmatic has a bright pink ground, vermilion shadows, red fold lines, and black outlines.

At a final stage of painting, the folds of David's cloak to the left of his body were narrowed and his right hand was adjusted. His right boot was enlarged and moved further inward to fit under the narrow hem of his dalmatic (Fig. 297). The decoration of single pearls and black bands with pearls was also enlarged. This could be seen where flaking paint revealed the original decoration under the overpaint. The enlarged foot bears a more correct proportional relation to the rest of the figure.

[84] The figure of David is directly above the Annunciation, and the text that he holds was traditionally regarded as a prefiguration of the Annunciation. See E. Kitzinger, "The Descent of the Dove," in *Byzanz und der Westen: Studien zur Kunst des europäischen Mittelalters*, Österreichische Akademie der Wissenschaften 432 (Vienna, 1984), 99–115. For other examples of the placing of interrelated images, see Maguire, *Art and Eloquence*.

Isaiah [37], the northeast quadrant (Pl. 14, Fig. 275)

The titular inscription is distributed on either side of the prophet's halo. A contemporary alteration was made to the iota of the name; this was originally formed as the letter eta, and when it was changed to an iota the accent was left in its original position. The text for the scroll is taken from the Book of Isaiah 7:14 (Fig. 275). A contemporary alteration occurs in line five of the scroll, where the αι of τέξεται was originally τέξετε.

The prophet Isaiah is portrayed as an old man with long, white hair falling into two long tresses over his shoulder, while his beard and mustache ripple into a point beneath his neatly rounded chin. His head is in three-quarter profile and turns toward the right while his body turns as if to move to the left. The frontal shoulders give way to a three-quarter profile abdomen and a profile right leg. His left leg stretches backward in the frontal aspect. His right arm curves upward with his hand raised in exhortation, and his left arm curves downward to a foreshortened forearm with the hand gripping the top of the unfurling scroll.

His chiton has a light red ground, red shadows, black fold lines and outlines, white wash, and thick, white, linear highlights. The himation has a light yellow ground, yellow shadows followed by dark yellow and red shadows, black fold lines and outlines, and the finishing touches of white wash and thick, white highlights.

At a final stage in the painting, the prophet's right shoulder was heightened and a corridor of green and blue background was introduced between the scroll and his body to the right of the figure.

This dynamic figure of Isaiah is articulated in a similar manner to that of the prophet Jonah [31], except that Isaiah's loose himation folds fall behind the figure. The oval folds over the abdomen, rippling diagonal folds over the thigh, and the bell folds of the hem of the chiton are very similar in both figures.

The lively figures of the prophets provide an exciting contrast to the formal angels in their roundels, the static and stately Etoimasia, and the all-imposing figure of Christ himself.

Within the technical limitations of his art, the painter sought to give a wide variety of stances to the twelve prophets. Eight of his figures are shown as if in arrested movement, and the varied articulations of their bodies draw the eye in a circular and upward pattern of movement around the dome. Only four figures are in a static frontal stance, and in the case of three of these, that stiffness is due to the heavy and ornate nature of their costumes. This is particularly true for the regal figures of David and Solomon, whose heads are weighed down by their miter crowns and whose bodies are enveloped in the heavy, jewel-encrusted panels of the imperial loros. But even the ponderous authority of these figures is relieved by the alternating curves of the arms. Most of the gestures of the prophets distantly descend from antique gestures of greeting. The Lagoudhera master was clearly attracted by echoing curves. He has a predilection for placing one arm of his figures curving upward in exhortation and the other curving downward to clutch the scroll, thus forming a horizontal

S-curve that is repeated several times. The master's repertoire of fluent rippling folds is illustrated by the massing of bell folds along hemlines, rippling diagonal folds across the upper thigh, the circling folds around the belly, and the skillful use of flying himation ends to balance the stance and mass of the figure.

The series of prophets forever gesturing their prophecies in a stately, circular movement around the drum may be compared to dancing variations upon a musical theme. The theme of the prophets is the mainstream of Byzantine iconography, and the variations are the interpretations of the Lagoudhera master. We already see him in the dome paintings as an outstanding master of linear pattern, which he weaves at will into evocations of volume and of movement, of tension and of peace, culminating and unifying in the majesty of Christ.

The Pendentives [38–44]

(Pls. 1–4, 19, 20; Figs. 76–87)

The four pendentives under the dome were plastered in two sections. The first section comprises the two eastern pendentives, with a composition of the Annunciation, and the second section comprises the two western pendentives, which contain the four evangelists seated at their task. The plaster joins dividing the two sections lie at the center of the north and south arches. The lower plaster joins run along the red borders outlining the arches and the upper perimeter join runs around under the ledge at the base of the cupola. Four horizontal incision lines were made for guidance in the painting of the building behind St. Luke, but no other such guidelines were found. A fresh plaster patch was inserted for the head and neck of the archangel Gabriel, and the plaster for his hands was heavily reworked.[85]

The average height of each pendentive, measured flat up the center, is 2 m, and the average width, measured across the center of this height, is 1.2 m.

The two southern pendentives and the northwestern pendentive have suffered considerable damage from water leaking down from the windows above. This damage was repaired, probably in the fourteenth century, with crude colors carelessly daubed over the flaking areas.

The complex architectural backgrounds are a striking element in the painting of the pendentives (Pl. 1; Figs. 76–83). They form a closure screen, or backdrop, to the actions taking place. The need for real perspective, implying angles of vision and horizon points, does not enter into the design, since this would lead the gaze beyond the figures that are the visual and spiritual focus of the compositions. However, from a narrative viewpoint, the actions took place inside buildings. Buildings are therefore provided, and the drapery over them is a Byzantine convention for representing an interior. If the figures had been correctly contained within architecture, this would have dwarfed

---

[85] The use of plaster patches for heads in the 1192 decoration is discussed in Part Four, Technique. See below, pp. 279–82.

them and upset the whole spiritual and hierarchical emphasis.

Although the buildings sometimes appear flat and lacking in three-dimensional substance, they were given some depth partly by varying the color of the wall surfaces, and partly by the plethora of architectural features ornamenting the facades. These are built up in light and dark colors, which give them strong relief. They include windows; doors, which are sometimes open and sometimes closed, and which are equipped with ring handles and bolts; arched colonnades, which have capitals and columns; cornices and pediments; and flights of steps. There are also ornamental plaster reliefs, merlons, and ornamental ironwork.

The tiled roofs are festooned with voluminous draperies, except for the building behind St. Luke, where the drapery is entwined in swags around the colonnade of the facade. Where visible, the roofs have a yellow ground, within which are tiles overlapping each other in the manner of fish scales. They are defined in umber line and highlighted in thick white. The draperies are either vermilion or they have a dark red ground, black lines, and blue, linear highlights. The walls are built up with two different sets of colors. They are either painted with a ground in a variety of tones of light yellow with yellow or light umber shadows, washes of white, and thick, white highlights, or they have a light red ground with red shadow and white wash, and thick, white highlights. The shadows tend to be placed to the side of the building that is away from the figures. The embrasures of the windows are yellow, with a dark yellow inner band and black denoting the interior. Some have their receding sills marked with diagonal lines in umber. Columns, capitals, and ornamental details are painted blue, with black defining lines and thick, white highlights. The merlons and ironwork are white. The flights of steps are ambiguous in perspective and could be interpreted as being seen either in profile or from the front. They have a light yellow ground, yellow shadow, and white wash highlights, and are strewn with squiggles in umber line to simulate marble. The ambiguity in perspective is similar to that of the asymmetrical frontal faces in the heads of figures.

There are four cornice patterns repeated throughout the façades, and all of them are built up on a light yellow ground: a continuous, single chevron in the alternating colors of blue and white or red and light red, with umber vermiculation filling the interstices of the chevron; a succession of dentils with white upper surfaces and yellow lower surfaces that have a black band down one side; a continuous band of leaf pattern in yellow, with the scalloped edges picked out in umber, and heavily highlighted in white; and a series of stepped, vermilion blocks outlined in white line, with a single red dot also outlined in white in each upper interstice.

The fourteenth-century repairs to the yellow roofs were carried out in a muddy yellow that is quite distinct from the color of the original painting. The tiles of the repair period are square in shape and contain two or three diagonal lines in thin black. The drapes over the buildings were repaired in a purplish red ochre that is distinct from the 1192 red. A number of messy fourteenth-century alterations were made to the fall of the draperies. In the course of conservation the overpaint was removed where it was found to overlap the original design below.

The Annunciation [38, 39, 40]

(Pls. 1, 2, 4, 19, 20; Figs. 76, 77, 81a, b)

The Annunciation is painted across the eastern pendentives. In the northeastern pendentive, the elegant figure of the archangel Gabriel springs eastwards with wings streaming behind him; one foot is painted across the red border of the scene in baroque fashion, so that he appears to be advancing across the actual space of the arch. In the southeastern pendentive sits the figure of the Mother of God, stiffly upright between two tall blocks of architecture. The Spirit of the Lord streams down upon her from a small semicircular segment of heaven above. At the center of the eastern arch is a roundel with the waist-length figure of the Christ child, Emmanuel. This provides the theme linking the two figures. The narrowing base to each pendentive contained floral patterns that are now almost completely lost under a repaint in yellow and black.

The inscriptions are from St. Luke 1:28 and 38. The painter frequently used κέ for καί and substituted omicron for omega, as he has done in this inscription.

The archangel Gabriel [38] (Pl. 19; Fig. 81a)

The titular inscription lies to the right of the figure and the letters gamma and alpha are reduced to a smudgy outline. The head of the archangel is in three-quarter profile, but his shoulders are twisted into a semi-back view that is totally at odds with the stance of the head above.[86] He has the face of a young man, and his hair style and fillet are similar to those of the angels in the roundels of the dome. The buildup of colors within his wings is also similar, and the covert feathers are graded from pale vermilion through vermilion to dark red.[87] Part of his stave and his left arm are concealed by the forward movement of his body. He wears a chiton with a black clavus and a himation, and sandals on his feet.

[86] For a discussion of the posture, see H. Maguire, "The Self-Conscious Angel," in *Okeanos: Essays Presented to Ihor Ševčenko*, HUkSt 7 (Cambridge, Mass., 1983). He suggests that it illustrates Gabriel's hesitation as to how to address the Virgin without alarming her. Our own explanation of the posture, which does not necessarily exclude Maguire's, is that the figure is a sum of correctly proportioned parts, although their integration is arbitrary.

Observation of the human figure in nature was not a part of the training of a Byzantine painter, but painting according to structural proportional rules was fundamental to his work. Those flat, sectional rules do not take into account the plastic, three-dimensional changes within the figure in movement, such as in this figure of Gabriel, whose forward-lifting shoulder is at odds with his three-quarter-profile head. This distortion of the upper body is duplicated in the figures of Ezechiel [29] and Gideon [25] in the drum above, and in the Announcing Angel of the Nativity [142]. Similar disjoinings in the figure appear in mosaics in Venice and Sicily and in metalwork in the altarpiece of Nicholas of Verdun at Klosterneuberg. None of these examples is in the Annunciation scenes, but that does not mean that the posture does not mean hesitation.

More research is needed into the grammar of Byzantine gesture and stance. It seems unlikely that the posture would have a classical prototype, as suggested by Weitzman, since the classical artist did work from observing nature, and so would avoid impossible distortions.

[87] The buildup of colors for the wings of angels and archangels is standard (see above, p. 125). Only the covert feathers vary as to their colors and the graded tones with which they are built up.

His chiton has a green ground, with grey and then dark green shadows, and black fold lines and outlines. The highlights are made with a white wash and then thick, white, linear highlights. Both the white wash and the thick white are painted over with a blue wash. His himation has a light red ground with red shadows and dark red and black fold lines and outlines. It is highlighted with washes of white and thick, white, linear highlights, and the flying folds of it are picked out with a white dot at their point. His stave is vermilion with black outlines and a white top.

The Christ child, the Emmanuel [39] (Pl. 20)

On the blue background on either side of the roundel are placed the sigla $\overline{IC}$ $\overline{XC}$, and within the roundel on either side of the figure is written the title "The Emmanuel." The white outline of the roundel overlaps the upper red border of the eastern arch and intrudes into the recessing under the cupola ledge. This overlapping of the roundel borders can be seen elsewhere in the church, and it was designed to have the effect of thrusting the roundels forward into the real space of the church. This roundel has a horizontal diameter of 45.5 cm and a vertical diameter of only 40.5 cm, due to the flattened upper edge.

The waist-length figure of the Christ child is seen in the frontal aspect. His right hand is raised in blessing but seen in profile, and the other hand clasps a furled scroll. His head is characterized by well-rounded, ruddy cheeks and a very high forehead below a narrow band of hair that gathers into a tight cluster of curls just beneath the prominent ears. He wears a chiton with clavi under a himation.

Within the roundel, the background of the figure is a shiny vermilion that gives the impression of having been specially polished. The halo is yellow with red and white outer outlines, and it has three cross bars that are light blue with black shadows and white highlights. His chiton has a dark yellow ground, umber fold lines and outlines, a bright blue neckline, and vermilion clavus. His himation is blue with black fold lines and outlines.

The painter's awareness that proportions within the head of an infant are different from those within the head of the adult are clearly illustrated within this painting. The lower face (the distance between the nasal incision and base of chin) is shorter than the upper head (the distance between the nasal incision and the apex of the head). The difference in the ratio between them is 2:3 nose lengths instead of 2:2, which the painter used when depicting adults. The effect is to enlarge the skull and to puff out the cheeks, thus emphasizing the characteristics of the young child. The child's ears measure well over a nose length.[88]

The Mother of God [40], (Pls. 1, 2, 4; Fig. 81b)

The sigla are aligned on either side of her halo. To the top left of the figure, Heaven is represented by a double scalloped semicircle, painted white on the blue background. From it three

---

[88] The proportions governing the Christ child are discussed in the section on Proportion (see below, pp. 293–98). For a discussion in a more general context see, Winfield and Winfield, *Proportion*, pp. 154–60

linear white shafts of light slope toward the Mother of God as she sits on her backless stool. Her figure is shown in the frontal aspect, but her head turns to the left, toward the advancing Gabriel. Her right hand is laid across her breast in a gesture of submission, and her left hand grips a now-faded spindle, which rests on her knee. The top of her stool is tilted forward to reveal the bolster, which is overlaid with a white cloth. The front of the seat is decorated with a jeweled net pattern. Her slippered feet repose on a footstool with a jeweled border.

She wears a close-fitting, light blue wimple covered by an ample maphorion of dark red, with umber and black fold lines and linear blue highlights. The hem of her maphorion is decorated with double yellow bands picked out with light yellow highlights. There are traces of light yellow tassels on the lower hem, and the segmenta on her shoulders and forehead are also yellow. Her tunic is blue, with black lines and fold lines and double yellow bands at the cuffs. Her slippers are now obscured by the late overpaint of red that covers both them and the cushion of the footstool. Originally the footstool had an elaborate, jeweled border, but it was crudely overpainted in black with a few grey-white pearls. The bolster is red with yellow ends, each with a white loop tassel. The white cloth on the bolster has horizontal bands of vermilion that have now discolored to grey. The top of her throne has a greyish yellow overpaint, but it was probably yellow like the sides, which are decorated with a diaper pattern similar to the design within the borders of loros pattern I (Pl. 11a).

This figure of the Mother of God is much weakened by damage and by the overpaint in dull and rather dirty colors. The effect of the overpaint is to fudge the linear clarity of the original painting and to obscure the clean character of the high-quality colors used by the 1192 master. Some of the original paint layers were revealed during cleaning and conservation work, but in many areas they had totally disappeared.[89] Nevertheless, Mary's figure still retains a dignified serenity that reflects the pride of the Hebrew maiden chosen to bear the Messiah, and she provides a placid and somber foil to the luminous leaping archangel with his streaming wings and agitated garments. The architectures surrounding Mary seem to hold her earthbound, and their pastel hues contrast with her dark garments. The Christ Emmanuel, in the shiny bright vermilion roundel, forms a warm focus at the center of the cool, blue arch. The scene of the Annunciation links the heavenly occupants of the dome and drum with the congregation beneath, since it is a veiled representation of the Incarnation of Christ, and it prefigures the Holy Eucharist. It provides a suitable subject for transferring the attention of the worshipper from the arch into the sanctuary. There is no iconographic innovation, but the painter excelled in the aptness with which he married his linear composition with the actual architectural surfaces and the real space of the church.

---

[89] The damage caused by dampness is pronounced on the south side. The face and hands of the Mother of God were particularly badly flaked. Probably in the 14th century, the repair painter lowered the maphorion over her forehead and daubed the face with an orange-yellow. Brick-red paint was daubed over the damaged bolster and can still be seen on Mary's knees and the robe folds between them. The sides of the throne were smeared with yellow overpaint regardless of the original decorative patterns below. In the course of work in 1970, these overpaints were removed to expose the original painting where it still survives.

This skillful use of space, of color contrast, of decorative elements, and of contrasting movement has created a successful and inspiring interpretation of a familiar subject.

The Evangelists

St. John the Theologian and St. Luke [41, 42], (Pls. 1, 4; Figs. 78, 79, 83, 86, 87)

The two evangelists in the southwest pendentive are seated opposite each other and are separated by a table upon which lies an unfurled scroll, while sand trays and ink flasks lie on the floor between them. Both figures are seen in the three-quarter-profile stance as their heads and shoulders bow forward over their work. Behind each figure rises tall architecture draped with rich cloths (Figs. 78, 79).

The titular inscriptions to the two evangelists were overpainted, but this overpaint was removed to reveal the original lettering. The scroll on the table is inscribed with a cursive script that is not Greek (Fig. 83). Both of the figures and the central table were much damaged by water leaking from the western windows of the drum. They were repaired with an overpaint that was smeared extensively over the original paintwork. Where the original work survived, the overpaint was removed. Both of the heads are repaints, as are St. John's hand and Gospel, together with the garments, the feet, and the footstools. The colors of the repaint are dull, thin in quality, and greyish in tone. The haloes of both saints were repainted in yellow with a greyish tinge, and this halo color served as the ground upon which the feature lines and hair styles were drawn with a brush in thick, black line with no further addition of color. Both of the evangelists were originally depicted as writing on tablets, with a pen in one hand and with the tablet held by the other. In the repaint, St. John clutches a closed book within the curving fingers of his left hand and a pen in his right hand. A fragment of the original tablet survives at the upper edge of the book. St. Luke's tablet has been reduced in size and painted to look like a book by the repainter, and none of the original lettering survives.

St. John wears a chiton of blue, with black fold lines and outlines and thick, white linear highlights; the repaint of it was made in a powdery "copper" blue with thin, grey-white highlights. His himation was originally a light yellow, but the repaint is in a grey-yellow, with black lines and fold lines. St. Luke's chiton is yellow with red shadows and black lines and fold lines, but it is much overpainted with a greyish yellow. His himation has a light red ground, darker pink shadows, umber fold lines and black outlines, and thick, white, linear highlights. The feet of both saints were repainted in brick red. St. Luke's footstool shows traces of a yellow border with jewels. The bolsters are vermilion with yellow gather lines, and the points are decorated with a linear pattern in umber line, and with a pearl at their tip. Their seats are yellow and are decorated with a vermiculated and jeweled diaper pattern similar to that of loros pattern I (Pl. 11a).

The writing desk has a yellow surface with a curved edge at the top that is fitted with round knobs; the yellow pedestal leg has central cross ties and a stepped base. Behind the table lies a yellow tray with two round and two rectangular, black sand containers. Two white flasks half-

filled with black ink stand in front of the table.

St. Matthew and St. Mark [43, 44], northwest pendentive (Pls. 1, 3; Figs. 80–82, 84, 85)

The two evangelists in the northwest pendentive are seated on either side of a central writing table, and they are flanked by draped architecture. The titular inscriptions for both saints are aligned horizontally above their haloes.

St. Matthew sits on a stool with a bolster, and his right foot rests on a plump footstool. His head and shoulders are bowed forward as he writes on a tablet that rests upon his left forearm, and he holds a pen in his right hand. His figure is shown in the three-quarter-profile stance. He is portrayed as an old man, with receding white hair and a pointed beard. He wears a light red chiton with red shadows, black lines and fold lines, white wash, and thick, white, linear highlights; at the shoulder and on the leg the chiton has been repainted in brick red. His himation has a yellow ground, light umber and dark umber shadows, black lines and fold lines, white wash, and thick, white, linear highlights. The cushion of his footstool has a light blue ground, blue shadow, and black lines; the border is yellow with double bands of pearls alternating with single jewels.

St. Mark turns his head toward St. Matthew, but his seated figure is in the frontal aspect. He holds his right arm across his chest with pen in hand, and with his left hand he steadies the top of the tablet that rests upon his knee. His head is in three-quarter profile and he is portrayed as a middle-aged man with receding hair falling loosely to below his ear. He has a neatly rounded beard. St. Mark's himation is built up in similar colors to those of St. Matthew's chiton but it was repainted with brick red over the area of the abdomen. His himation has a light blue ground, blue shadows, black fold lines and outlines, white wash, and thick, white, linear highlights. His footstool has a red ground, black lines and outlines, and blue highlights; the border is yellow with alternating pearls and jewels. The bolsters and seats are similar to those depicted in the southwest pendentive, as are the table and writing accessories, except that the scroll lying on the table has lost all its "writing." In their present form, the tablets held by the saints are mostly repaints in grey-white. St. Matthew's left foot was also overpainted, and it now has seven toes. Originally, it appears to have been painted in a foreshortened frontal view from slightly below, with the balls of the toes showing. But it is impossible to be certain about this ambitious piece of foreshortening because of the damage. The triangle at the base of the pendentive contains a scroll design that is a later repaint executed in black on a yellow ground.

The compositions in the western pendentives each form an introverted vignette wherein the curving surfaces of the pendentive are used effectively to emphasize the studious self-absorption of the evangelists at their task. The architecture and the figures are all designed to attract the eye of the viewer toward the central features of the pedestal desk and writing materials. The reduced proportions of the ornamental background architecture serve to emphasize the importance of the figures in a similar manner to the architectural backgrounds in the Annunciation. Unfortunately, these pendentive compositions lack some of their original crispness because of the damaged surfaces and the later repairs in poor colors.

10

The Center and North Side of the West Vault, and the Northwest Bay of the Naos

The Roundels in the West Vault [45–49]

(Figs. 88–91; Text Figs. 25, 26)

Along the center of the west vault, from west to east, runs a narrow band containing four roundels set within a background of faded floral pattern (Text Fig. 26). Each roundel contains the waist-length figure of a martyr. These roundels are constructed in a similar manner to the angel roundels and to those in the apse by placing their centerpoints along a notional median that bisects the panel. The difference in this vault is that the median bisects the figures vertically because they are placed one above the other along the crown of the vault. In both the horizontal and the vertical bands of roundels the diameter lines perform a similar constructional framework for the figures (Text Fig. 25).

The band measures an average 84 cm in width and 2.85 m in length, exclusive of its red borders. The roundels have an interior diameter of 63.5 cm, and their border averages 3.5 cm in width. The haloes to the figures have a diameter of 27.5 cm, and the nose length used in the construction of the figures is standard at 4.5 cm.

The rectangular band was plastered in one section, and the plaster joins run along the red borders at the edge of the east and west arches and at the upper edges of the Anastasis [50] and the Nativity [142].

The roundels each have broad, yellow borders outlined in strong, black lines. The borders of the two central medallions are tangent, but the borders of the two terminal medallions each overlaps that of its neighbor. The interior background of the figures in the roundels alternates from red to green from west to east. The titular inscriptions in white are aligned vertically within the roundels on either side of the figures.

The heads of the figures are aligned, with the top of their heads to the east, and both the head and the figure of each martyr are seen in the frontal aspect. Each figure holds a two-barred white

149

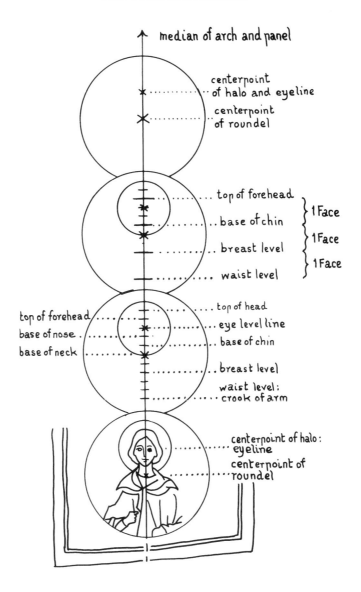

Text Fig. 25 Diagram of the construction of figures within the roundels in the west vault [45–48] in vertical alignment

cross in his right hand, and each conceals his bent left arm within the folds of his cloak. The figures are similarly dressed in undergarments of which only the decorated cuffs are visible. Over the undergarment, they wear tunics with elaborate "gold" collars. The collars have a yellow ground with white highlighting over the yellow to simulate sheen, and the whole is overlaid with a fine, vermiculated, scroll-and-palmette pattern drawn in umber (Text Fig. 24.1a–c, 2a, b). Both the necklines and the collar hems are decorated with black bands filled with single pearls. Over his shoulders, each saint wears a cloak, but the hanging folds of it are different for each figure.

Center and North Side of the West Vault and Northwest Bay

St. Tryphon [45], the westernmost roundel (Fig. 88)

His inscription survives complete on the vermilion ground of the roundel. He has the beardless face of a young man. His hair falls smoothly in loose curls to below his ears, of which only the lobes are visible. His tunic has a light green ground, grey shadows, black lines and outlines, white wash, and thick, white, linear highlights. His cloak has a green ground, grey shadows, and black lines and outlines with no highlights. The clasp for the cloak is made up of a "star" of five pearls.

St. Vikentios (?) [46], second roundel from the west (Fig. 89)

Dampness at some period caused the flaking of the green background within the roundel. The name of the saint is mostly lost, except for the OC at the end and the trace of an iota above the C, and higher still parts of a K and an E. The spacing is suitable for the letters of ΒΙΚΕΝΤΙΟΣ, who is normally listed with Sts. Viktor and Menas.

St. Vikentios is portrayed as a clean-shaven young man, and he could easily pass as the twin brother of St. Tryphon, who is next to him. His tunic has a light red ground, red shadow, black fold lines, white wash, and thick, white, linear highlights. His cloak, which is thrown back over one shoulder, has a dark red ground, dark grey shadows that are possibly discolored vermilion, and black lines and outlines. Unlike those of the other martyrs in this band, his cloak is edged with a yellow band lined with pearls.

St. Viktor [47], the second roundel from the east (Fig. 90)

His inscription is on the vermilion background of the figure. St. Viktor has long, smooth hair falling to loose curls below his ears, but he has the face of a middle-aged man, with tilted eyebrows, a short mustache, and a neat, rounded, short beard. His tunic has a light green ground, grey shadow, black lines and outlines, white wash, and thick, white, linear highlights. His cloak is swept up over both shoulders, with one end coming forward under his right arm to enfold his waist and left arm. The cloak has a green ground, black fold lines and outlines, and no highlights; the clasp is formed by a single large pearl.

St. Menas [48], the eastern medallion (Fig. 91)

His inscription is on the green background within his roundel. The martyr is portrayed as an old man with a lined face and white hair in the style most frequently associated with that given to the hair of St. Peter. The hair is clustered in tight curls around his head, concealing all but the lobes of his ears, and his beard is short and rounded. His tunic has a light red ground, red shadows, black fold lines and outlines, and white highlights. His cloak has a vermilion ground, dark red shadows, and black lines and fold lines.

Text Fig. 26 Patterns surrounding the roundels in the west vault [49] and the roundels in the soffit of the south arch under the dome [136]

The Pattern around the Roundels [49] (Figs. 88–91; Text Fig. 26a)

The rectangular band in which the roundels are set has a yellow ground decorated with a foliated meander design that fills the spaces between the roundels. The upper layers of paint have now all gone, and only the template of the design is left in a pale yellow tracery. Beneath this tracery lies the preliminary drawing in broad red lines. This appears to have been deliberately left visible in some places so as to form a shadow guide to the final painting. There is a similar pattern to this one in the background to the roundels in the soffits of the north and south arches under the dome [68 and 136], but there the pattern includes a decorative use of blue, of which there is now no trace in the west vault pattern.

The broad band of roundels along the crown of the vault serves a useful visual purpose. It separates the two large scenes of the Anastasis and the Nativity, which occupy the north and south sides of the vault, and it reduces the amount of distortion that would have been inevitable if the painter had extended these scenes to the crown of the vault.

The North Side of the West Vault

The whole side is devoted to the representation of the Anastasis [50] which complements the other major scenes of Christ's life, the Nativity [142] in the south half of the vault and the Baptism [54] in the bay below. It is very likely that the scene of the Crucifixion would have been placed on the now destroyed west wall.

Text Fig. 27 The scroll of St. John the
Forerunner in the Anastasis [50]

The Anastasis, or the Harrowing of Hell [50]

(Pl. 21; Figs. 92–99; Text Fig. 27)

The Anastasis at Lagoudhera is a very large painting, and allowing for the irregularity of the vault, the average width from west to east is 2.88 m, inclusive of the red borders which average 4 5 cm in width. The height of the painting is 2.59 m, inclusive of the borders. The shape of the panel is, thus, not far short of a square.

The inscription to the scene runs just below the upper border and is written in letters 4 to 4.5 cm high. The original letters were overpainted at a later period, and their present appearance lacks the crispness and angularity of the original. Each figure has its individual titular inscription and St. John holds an unfurling scroll with a damaged inscription (Text Fig. 27).

The composition follows a standard iconography. The scene combines elements of three separate events: the Descent into Hell, the breaking open of the Gates of Hell, and the Ascent with the freed souls of the precursors of Christ.[90] The whole scene is set against a background of mountains, and it is dominated by the central figure of Christ, as he straddles the sundered doors of the Gates of Hell. With his left hand, he grasps a great cross. With his right hand, he takes a firm grip of Adam's forearm, as if hauling him out of the depths of his gaping "marble" sarcophagus. Adam appears to levitate above his tomb in a half-kneeling position. Behind him stands the praying figure

---

[90] For a discussion of the iconography of the Anastasis, see A. Kartsonis, *Anastasis: The Making of an Image* (Princeton, 1986); Nicolaïdes, *DOP* 50, 1996, pp. 87–92.

of Eve. To the right of Christ, the two impassive figures of Solomon and David stand upright within their marble sarcophagi. Above them, the half-length figure of St. John the Baptist, scroll in hand, appears from behind a fold in the mountains. The undamaged mountains on the right are formed into highlighted gargoyle shapes appropriate to this Stygian realm. The black river in the abyss of Hell is strewn with locks, keys, and bolts. The composition is reduced to the essentials, and it does not include the chained figure of the Devil.

The scene is painted on a single patch of plaster with the joins running along the red borders that outline it. This was a large patch of plaster, and it is clear from the disturbances in the surface that the painter made considerable efforts to keep it fresh by reworking it. There are relatively few incised and impressed guide lines; two horizontal incised lines outline Adam's arm, and impressed lines mark the contour of St. John's shoulder.

The painter inserted fresh plaster patches for the heads of Adam and Eve, and these are the best-preserved heads in the painting. The patch for Adam's head is skillfully attenuated at the hair edge, but to the right side of his neck there is a high ridge of rucked plaster. Minor damage in the face revealed that it was built up over a base or proplasmos of green rather than yellow.[91] The painter also reworked some of the flesh areas of the figures, such as the hands of Christ, St. John, Eve, and Solomon, and Adam's left forearm. The plaster area for both of Christ's feet was also reworked. At a later stage, Christ's right foot was enlarged and extended to improve the balance of his figure. The paint layers of this adjustment have now flaked away.

The panel is much spoiled by discoloration and by the flaking away of the upper layers of pigment. Some of this damage is due to the seepage of water through the vault at a time when the church had no secondary roof. At some period the upper background was overpainted with copper blue, and the twelfth-century inscriptions were repainted upon it, roughly following the lettering beneath, but their present appearance lacks the crispness and angularity of the original. The damaged areas were also overpainted in the fourteenth century, and in the course of conservation, the blotchy colors of this overpaint were removed where they overlapped surviving original work.

The Background

The upper background or sky has a blue ground that was overpainted. The mountains have a light umber ground, thin, dark umber shadows, dark umber and black shaping lines, and thick, white highlights on the summits. There was probably some variation in the coloring of the mountains, but damage and repaints in grey and umber have obscured the delicate buildup of the original colors.

In the foreground, the pit of Hell is black, and its jagged border is outlined in white. The coffered gates have a yellow ground, black and umber construction lines, and a light yellow high-

---

[91] The heads of figures were usually built up with layers of colors upon the initial yellow base or proplasmos that covered the whole halo (see below, p. 305). But when the painter put in a fresh plaster patch for the head, he used a green proplasmos on the new white plaster, and upon this he built up the colors for the head. He reinforced the damaged halo with a further coat of yellow.

light line. The coffering has red rims and dark red at the center. The door fittings are painted in white, and in a meticulous detail that shows them to be types still to be found at Lagoudhera and elsewhere in Cyprus, where machine-made fastenings have not replaced handmade fittings.

The sarcophagi have black interiors, yellow rims with black definition lines, and white highlights that have umber wash over them. The front panels are painted in imitation of marble, and they have a yellow ground over which are broadly brushed swirls of light umber, light grey, and white; the whole surface is overlaid with linear squiggles in umber. The panels are inset with roundels in imitation of verd antique and porphyry. The verd antique roundels have a black ground and are flecked with light green and white; the red porphyry roundels have a dark red ground and are flecked with light red and white; the rims of the roundels have a white corridor outlined in black and filled with black triangles, in imitation of marble inlay. These panels are very similar to the dado below the 1192 decoration [53] (Pls. 3, 4).

Christ (Pl. 21; Fig. 92, 93)

Christ dominates the scene, and he is drawn to a larger scale, in a ratio of 5:4 to the other figures. The sigla of his inscription are placed to either side of and above his halo. The letters are a repaint, but part of the original XC is visible beneath the "copper" blue of the repainted upper background. Christ's figure is in three-quarter profile as he springs up and marches off eastwards with his cross in one hand, but his head is turned back, as if to urge Adam upwards. The cross with its three bars is made up of a long, narrow pole to which each of the three bars is attached by a single cross tie. Though nearly as tall as Christ, the cross is narrow enough to be clasped in his hand.

The ground for his halo is yellow and the cross bars within it were painted with grey and blue shadows. Each bar was decorated with a cluster of five vermilion circles with black outlines, from which the vermilion paint has now flaked away. Christ's hands and feet are each marked with a small, light brown circle to indicate the stigmata. He wears a tunic of which only the sleeves are visible, under a chiton with a black clavus, and a himation whose flying tail billows up high behind him in a conical mass of folds.

The cuffs of his tunic are decorated with a diaper design (Pattern 1a, Text Fig. 24), and each has a little free-hanging white loop at the lower corner. His tunic and chiton both have a similar light red ground, red shadows, and black defining lines, but the highlights on the sleeves are plain white, whereas his chiton has thick, white highlights washed over with blue. His himation has lost most of the surface layers of paint, but enough fragments remain to indicate that it had a light yellow ground, yellow shadows, black lines, white wash, and thick, white, linear highlights. The great cross has a light umber ground, dark umber shadow, black outlines, and a linear white highlight on top of the bars and to the left side toward Christ.

Eve (Pl. 21; Figs. 92, 95, 99)

Eve's titular inscription, which is simply her name with the definite article, is placed behind her head. The first two letters are thicker and were probably painted over by the fourteenth-century painter in order to emphasize them. She is shown in three-quarter profile as she leans forward with her arms bent, the hands extended in prayer, reaching out to Christ. She is portrayed as an old woman, but since no separate convention existed for the face of an old woman in Byzantine painting, she has the furrowed face of a beardless old man. The lines searing the cheeks of Eve are similar to the lines in the aged, unbearded faces of St. Lazaros [124] and the prophet Moses [33] (Figs. 183, 75, respectively). However, Eve's face is narrower, and it lacks the curling line that contours the cheekbone. This is a particular linear characteristic in the faces of old men as portrayed by the 1192 painter, and it is very pronounced in the beardless heads of Lazaros and Moses. This portrayal of the lined face of an old woman, with contorted age lines giving the impression of intense and pent-up emotion, is probably unique for this period in Byzantine portrayals of women. The Nerezi master used similar contorted eyelines for the face of the Virgin in his Pieta, but at Nerezi the face is more plastic, and it lacks the linear emphasis of age.

Under a voluminous maphorion, Eve wears a close-fitting wimple of light blue. The maphorion has a light umber ground, grey shadows, black fold lines and outlines, and no highlights. The upper edges of the maphorion were outlined with a white hem line. The circle of small pearls in greyish white that decorates the folds over her forehead belong to the fourteenth-century repaint. Eve's tunic has a light red ground, red shadows, and thick white highlights washed over with light red.

Adam (Pl. 21; Figs. 92, 97–99)

The titular inscription is placed above his halo and consists simply of his name, Adam, in original lettering. He is represented as an old man, with long white hair and a long white beard flowing over his chin. This type of head is used at Lagoudhera to represent St. Andrew, and several prophets in the dome have a similar head and hairstyle, but only Ezechiel [29] has the same type of free-flowing beard over his chin. Adam's figure is shown in a half-kneeling stance, with his head and torso in three-quarter profile. His right arm is bent forwards at the elbow, while the other arm is fully extended with his wrist in the firm grip of Christ's right hand. He wears a chiton with black clavus and a himation, and both garments are generously articulated into rippling folds and bell folds.

Adam's himation has a light yellow ground, shadows in yellow and then light umber, black lines and fold lines, white wash, and thick, white highlights. His chiton has a light green ground, black lines and fold lines, and white highlights. The thick, white highlights at the edges of his sleeves bear traces of a blue wash, but these were overpainted with pure white. This alteration was clearly a contemporary change of mind, perhaps where the master was guiding a pupil. The plaster for Adam's hands was not reworked and the surface paint layers have flaked off to reveal the preliminary drawing.

David (Pl. 21; Fig. 92)

The titular inscription includes no epithet, and his name takes the usual abbreviated form ΔΑΔ. The letters are original. They were partially washed over with a careless repaint in light umber. His head is much damaged, but he was clearly portrayed with the facial type of an old man, similar to his portrait in the dome [35] (Fig. 72); also similar is the imperial miter with pendilia crowning his head (Pl. 10d). His face is in three-quarter profile as he turns toward Solomon on his left, but his body is in the frontal aspect. He stands upright within his tomb, with his right hand palm-down across his chest and the other hand concealed within his cloak. His garments are rich, but no imperial loros entwines his figure. His cloak is pinned at the front but drawn back to fall from his left shoulder in vertical folds that mold, yet conceal, his right arm. His chiton has a decorated semicircular collar, and the decorated cuff of an undertunic is visible on his right arm.

His chiton has a light red ground, red and grey (possibly discolored vermilion) shadows, black lines and outlines, and thick, white highlights. His cloak has a light red ground, red shadows, black lines and fold lines, and no highlights. The hem of the cloak and the lower edge of the collar have a black border filled with a continuous line of single pearls. The cuff of his tunic is yellow, and it bears traces of a decorative pattern.

Solomon (Pl. 21; Figs. 92, 94)

The titular inscription lies to the right of his halo and, like that of David, his name carries no epithet. The lettering is original, and the last three letters are abbreviated. He is portrayed as a young man, and his head and his crown and pendants are similar to those in his portrait in the dome [17] (Pl. 10d; Fig. 61). His head is in three-quarter profile as he turns toward his father on his right. His right hand is raised in blessing in front of his chest, and his left hand is concealed beneath the folds of his cloak. His clothes are similar to those of David. The cuff of his undertunic is decorated with Pattern 1a (Text Fig. 24), and his collar has a yellow ground and is decorated with a vermiculated scroll design in umber. His chiton has a light green ground, green shadows, black lines, white wash, and thick, white, linear highlights. His cloak is vermilion with dark red shadows, black lines, and outlines.

St. John the Forerunner (Pl. 21; Figs. 92, 96; Text Fig. 27)

His titular inscription is original and it is given in an abbreviated form, to the right of his halo. He holds a scroll with a damaged inscription, the text of which remains obscure, but which could refer to Luke 24:7, or possibly John 18:8, both of which contain references to the Resurrection of Christ (Text Fig. 27).

St. John's half-length figure looms out of a cleft in the mountains behind the two kings. His head is seen in three-quarter profile as he turns toward Christ. He has the face of an old man with tousled brown hair and beard. His torso is seen in the frontal aspect. His right arm is bent upright at the waist as his hand gestures in exhortation. His other hand lies at waist level and grips the top

of his unfurling scroll. He wears a chiton and a himation, and both of these have been crudely overpainted. The chiton has an orange-yellow ground with sketchy shadow lines in thin umber and a few white, striated highlights. His himation is completely overpainted, and it is made with a thin, umber ground, and a more intense umber is used to mark the fold lines. Another full-length figure of St. John [75] appears in the ground register as part of a Deesis (Figs. 133, 135), but in this case, his head is in the frontal aspect, and he is clothed in an animal skin.

This traditional interpretation of the Anastasis is dominated by the large, galvanic figure of Christ, whose twisting body with its windswept flying himation folds links the static groups of figures to either side of him. The buildup of lights and darks is much confused by washes of overpaint. Nevertheless, it remains clear that the background hills are highlighted on the side nearer the central figure of Christ, and he himself is painted in luminous colors that contrast with the somber tones of the rest of the painting. The other figures and elements of the composition are built up in lights and darks that show no relationship to a particular source of illumination. The suggestion of depth within the painting is achieved by overlapping figures and elements and by revealing the upper surfaces of features like the sarcophagi.

The static stance of the figures around Christ is reinforced by the quiet diagonals and verticals that characterize the fold lines of their garments. However, the garments of the stolid figure of Adam appear to derive animation from his contact with Christ, and his himation falls into rippling, repetitive folds that impart to the figure the energy of a spring uncoiling. Despite the surface damage, Christ remains a wondrously powerful and triumphant figure with the great wooden cross seemingly as light as a feather in his hand, and the heavy wooden Gates of Hell lie puny beneath his feet.

The Northwest Bay [51–58]

The north wall has a patterned spandrel [51] to the west and St. Paul [52] stands on the pier to the east. The arch reveals are occupied by St. Andronikos [55], to the west and St. Kyriakos the Anchorite [58], to the east. The single panel in the soffit of the arch contains the half-length figures of the Anargyroi, St. Kosmas [56] to the west, and St. Damian [57], to the east. The Baptism of Christ [54] fills the lunette of the center bay. The dadoes [53] contain "marble" roundels. Each panel was plastered separately and the plaster joins run within red borders.

With the exception of the panel at the center of the arch soffit, all the panels in this ground register were given an upper background in green and a lower background in a darker green, perhaps because the painter was running short of his imported blue pigment.

At some period before the fourteenth-century repaint, the upper green backgrounds were overpainted with a copper blue. In the course of this overpaint, the inscriptions were either obliterated and repainted in letters not dissimilar from the original, or the forms of the original letters, which stood out in relief under the overpaint of blue, were gone over once again in white by the

repainter. In the fourteenth century, damaged areas were crudely overpainted. The overpaint was removed where it overlapped original painting.

The Pattern in the West Spandrels of the North and South Walls [51] [144] (Pls. 3, 4; Text Fig. 28)

These patterns are so similar that they are best described together. Each is enclosed by a black perimeter line with the standard red border and white inner line. The panels measure 57 cm in height at the west side; their length at the top is 73 cm, and their height at the center is 47 cm. The pattern consists of a linear scroll and palmette design picked out with vermiculations and executed in black line on a ground that is half yellow and half green.

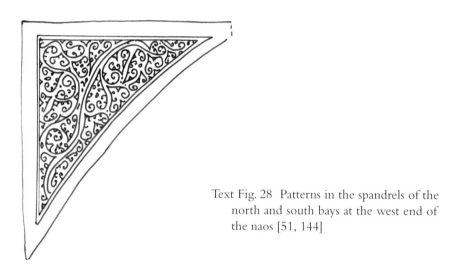

Text Fig. 28 Patterns in the spandrels of the north and south bays at the west end of the naos [51, 144]

St. Paul [52], *east side*

(Figs. 100, 285; Text Fig. 30a)

This panel has an irregular upper outline, but it measures 1.48 m in height at the center, and below the springing of the arch it has an average width of 66 cm. It was plastered in a single section, and the plaster joins correspond to the red borders defining the panel. The plaster areas for his hands and one foot were reworked.

There is major damage at the bottom of the panel where the borders and the left foot of the saint were lost. During conservation, a foot was sketched in on new plaster work, in order to restore balance to the figure. No attempt was made to build up the flesh colors within this sketch. The saint's himation is much discolored by candle burns from the small offertory candles that were lit by pious supplicants.

The titular inscription is placed above and to either side of the halo and consists of an

overpainting of the original inscription, except for the I and the C of the epithet. The I is an independent letter painted to the right of the original, which is still faintly discernible beneath the blue overpaint of the background. The C is a completely new letter (Text Fig. 30a).

The saint carries a scroll bearing a text from St. Paul's Epistle to the Galatians, 5:22, 23. The word Ἀδελφοί with which the Lagoudhera scroll begins, is an interpolation from Galatians 5:13. The effect of repainting has been to thicken the original letter forms so that they have lost their original, crisp quality.

The life-size figure of St. Paul stands upright with his head in three-quarter profile as he turns toward the east. His head is slightly tilted backward so that it is not quite centered within the halo. The backward inclination of the head was emphasized by the heightening of the left shoulder so that it stands level with his mouth (rather than the base of his neck). The measure relationships between head and body follow the 1192 canon (see below, p. 285), with the exception of the halo diameter that extended one nose length further to accommodate the tilting head. Its centerpoint lies above the eyeline, in the lower forehead.

The saint is represented as an old man, and his brown hair and beard are styled in a manner traditionally associated with St. Paul. On the top of his bald pate are two minuscule, linear curls and a further trace of hair appears behind his ear. His brown beard is of medium length and shapely, as it comes to a point beneath the neatly outlined chin. The saint gestures across his body with his right hand, while in his left hand he holds up the roll of his unfurling scroll. His chest is in the frontal stance, but his lower body twists sideways to the east. He wears a chiton with black clavus under a himation with loose folds.

His chiton has a light red ground, vermilion shadows and fold lines, black lines and outlines, and thick, white, linear highlights. His himation has a ground of thick white with light red wash over it, light red, then light umber shadows; black lines and outlines; and thick, white highlight lines.

This slender figure is given greater substance and authority by the amplitude of the himation folds and the widening of the chiton beneath the scroll. However, the widened chiton does not relate naturally to the width of the torso above. The articulated hands are not made according to the correct proportional measures and, as a result, they appear insubstantial and slender. His right forefoot has a realistic solidity. His left foot, as mentioned above, is a reconstruction. The figure of St. Paul is complementary to that of St. Peter on the south pier opposite, so that these two major saints conform to their traditional images as "pillars of the church."

The Painted Dadoes [53]

(Pls. 3, 4)

The walls of the naos and the sanctuary all have a base register of rectangular painted dadoes. All were plastered on patches separate from those of the paintings above them, and the plaster joins

can be observed in the red borders separating them. The bases of the plaster patches are all attenuated flush to floor level, below the present red borders that define the painted panel.

The dado patterns are contained between red borders, outlined in white. The vertical side borders run flush with the architectural corners. The base border lies an average 10 cm above floor level. The red borders average 5 to 6 cm, and the height of the panel contained within averages 42 cm. The width of the panels is dictated by the architectural features.

The pattern consists of one or more roundels of simulated dark marble, each with a patterned border set against a background of simulated light marble. When the space is narrow, as beneath St. Paul, the dado panel contains only one roundel. The continuous long dado which runs under the panels of the Arakiotissa and the archangel Michael in the south bay under the dome contains ten roundels side by side; that of the dado under the Baptism in the northwest blind arch has six roundels; and the dado under the panel with the figures of St. Symeon and St. John, to the east of the north door, has three and one-half roundels with their border patterns intertwined.

The backgrounds to the roundels have a yellow or pale umber ground, over which are painted swirling lines in browns, greys, and white. The roundels themselves are painted to imitate verd antique or dark red porphyry. Both have a somber ground of dark red, but the latter is speckled with flecks of lighter red, black, and grey white, while the former is speckled with green and pale grey. Each dark marble circle is outlined by a white border with a dark red outline. The white border is decorated either with a band of saw-edged pattern triangles, a variation on the Greek meander pattern, or a line of circles joined low to one side.

The base of the walls was much damaged, but the plaster was repaired in 1972 with a different surface texture so that it is readily distinguishable from the original. The pattern was restored in the fashion of the 1192 painter, but the restored areas do not have a marbled background.

The patterned dadoes provide a solid footing for the paintings above them, while at the same time they serve to separate the sacred images from the spectator. They also provide a decorative and unifying feature running along the north and south walls of the naos and sanctuary. For this reason, it was thought desirable to restore them, so that the harmony of the wall decoration above was not disturbed by jagged edges at floor level.

The Epiphany, or the Baptism of Christ in the River Jordan [54]

(Figs. 101–103; Text Fig. 29)

The arched panel in the bay measures 2.28 m in height at its center, exclusive of the red borders which average a width of between 4 and 7 cm. The width of the panel at the base is 1.9 m. The painting was plastered in a single section, and the plaster joins correspond with the red borders around it. There are no plaster patches for the heads, but some reworking of the plaster was carried out for the head of Christ. The surface damage to the panel is extensive, particularly in the upper central area and in the lower parts. The fourteenth-century overpainting of the damaged areas was

carried out in muddy colors with little regard for the original work.

The titular inscription to the scene lies above the head of Christ, and to either side of his halo are placed the sigla $\overline{\text{IC}}$ $\overline{\text{XC}}$. All the visible inscriptions are crude overpaints of the 1192 lettering that lies below them. The inscription for St. John the Baptist, or Forerunner, which is placed above his halo, was also repainted, but the final OC is visible in its original form at the end of the line, while the repainted OC was added beneath it, so that the letters appear twice.

In the river to the left of Christ are the partial remains of a tall, pedestal cross. Above his knee level, near the river's edge, is the cross, with two short, horizontal bars. Below, separated by a large area of damage, and at the level of his feet, is the pedestal, together with a short length of the turned vertical shaft. To the left side of the cross are the letters Φ repeated twice, one above the other. These are perhaps part of the sigla φχφπ : φῶς Χριστοῦ φῶς παντοκράτορος. To the left of the pedestal below, there is a damaged fragment of a contemporary votive inscription located to the left of Christ's feet.[92] (Text Fig. 29.1b) Only traces of the lettering now survive. It was in three lines, and the lettering that remains suggests the traditional formula, "Remember Thy servant," followed by the name of a person, which is now lost, but who was a monk. This may have been an inscription by the painter of the church. The lettering would appear to be of similar form and quality to that of the 1192 paintings. To the right of Christ's feet are the traces of a single-armed cross and part of a psi shape, which could be lettering or the base of a three-branched candlestick (Text Fig. 29.1a).

The iconography of this painting of the Baptism is very simple. The springing of the actual blind arch was used by the painter to mark the meeting of the foreground and background, which lies 1.15 m from the base line. At the center of the composition, the nude figure of Christ stands in a rippling River Jordan, which springs out of a conical mountain behind him. High above him, two shallow linear arcs indicate the arch of Heaven, whence three broad rays descend to a dove hovering above his head. A third undulated semicircle now outlines the arch of Heaven, but this is a late overpaint. The combination of damage and overpaint obscures the dove, whose form is no longer very clear. To the left of Christ, bowing forward with the curve of the arch, stands the figure of St. John the Forerunner, with his right hand extended to touch the head of Christ beneath him. There is no indication of any woodman's axe in the cleft of the tree behind St. John. To the right of Christ, a group of three angels bows forward in unison, their curving figures echoing the arching soffit behind them; the foremost angel extends his arms forward toward Christ, and his hands are concealed in the enveloping bell folds of his himation, which he tenders like a towel before him.

Apart from the various inscriptions described above, the river appears to contain no further elements. There is no trace of a personified Jordan, or of fish and other swimmers, dragons, etc., within the waters of the river.

---

[92] For a hypothetical reconstruction of this inscription, see Winfield, *Panagia tou Arakos*, 12, 13.

Text Fig. 29 Elements from the Baptism [54]

The Background

The conical mountain was originally painted with a light red ground and umber shadows, and trees or bushes were painted upon it, in the manner of the bushes painted on the mountains in the scene of the Nativity of Christ [142] (see below pp. 254–56; Pl. 22). Later, in the fourteenth century, the mountain was overpainted with a dirty brown ground that obscured the bushes, and it was given red rocks with grey highlights. This crude overpaint formerly extended into the river, but the overlap was removed in the course of cleaning, revealing the original thick, white, jagged outlines to the stream. The river had a glossy, light grey ground with thin, horizontal, wavy lines in paler grey; it was later crudely overpainted with a dark grey with black horizontal lines.

Christ

Christ is seen in three-quarter profile turned toward St. John. He stands in a dignified, yet submissive, pose, with his head bowed. His arms are slightly bent at the elbow as they hang loosely to either side of his body, and the fingers of his right hand are articulated in the gesture of blessing. His legs appear unnaturally long because the painter has omitted his genitals, and the inner thigh line continues without interruption up the groin. The long legs are steeply crossed at the knee, and both feet point diagonally downwards. Christ's head inclines toward John, whose hand intrudes within his halo. Much of the original painting of the head and halo survives. The body of Christ retains its original outlines, but it has lost most of the original 1192 buildup of flesh colors; traces of the original work can be seen at the edges where there are remains of the yellow of the base color and the pink of the preliminary drawing. The original buildup of flesh colors can be seen in his face and in his right hand. In the fourteenth century, the figure was totally overpainted with a ground of dull ochre upon which red lines mark the forms of the thorax and abdomen.

The 1192 Decoration

St. John

The Forerunner is shown in three-quarter profile as he bends over toward Christ. The upper part of his body remains a confusion of damage and fourteenth-century overpaint, but the head retains his characteristic tousled hair style. His halo is overpainted with an orange-yellow, and the features of his face were badly redrawn with umber lines. His himation has a yellow ground, grey shadow, black lines and no highlights; the overpaint in the belly area is a reddish yellow. His chiton has a yellow ground, light red shadows, and dark red fold lines reinforced with black. There are no highlights. The hem of his chiton is an overpaint in orange-yellow, and the shadows are thin lines in red outlining folds, in a sad attempt to imitate the 1192 bell folds. Some trace of the original folds can still be in seen in black line beneath the orange-yellow.

Angels

Three angels appear high up to the right of Christ. Only the angel in the forefront is shown in full length. He bends stiffly forward; his head and torso are in three-quarter profile, while his legs and feet are in profile. His left wing curves round and down behind him, while the other wing descends behind his halo and extended arms. He wears a chiton with clavus under a himation, and both garments partly conceal his jeweled boots. Apart from a few traces of original pigments, the whole of the head of this angel and the lower edge of his halo were repainted in the fourteenth century. The painting is soft and blurred, giving a false three-dimensionality that is in strong contrast to the precise linear work of the 1192 painter. His wings are damaged, but it is clear that they were built up in the standard manner of the 1192 painter, and the covert feathers are graded in shades of red.[93] His chiton has a yellow ground, red shadows, some thin umber shadows, red and black lines and outlines, white wash, and thick, white highlights. His himation has a light yellow ground, grey shadows, dark grey fold lines and black outlines, white wash, and thick, white highlights. Where these garments have been overpainted, the fourteenth-century painter attempted to imitate the original white highlights using his own grey-white color. His boots are similar to those of other booted angels and have a red ground, a black outline that is particularly thick under the foot, double black bands lined with pearls across the base of the toes and round the ankle, a ring of pearls on the dorsum, and a single pearl on the point of the boot.

The middle angel is mostly concealed by the overlapping angel in front of him, and only his head, some stubby wing feathers, and a portion of robe are to be seen. Much of the head retains its original paint, and he resembles the angels in the dome. His robes have a red ground and umber shadow lines, and his wing is similar in color to that of the leading angel. The rear angel is indicated by the presence of part of a halo, head, and wing tips behind them.

The Baptism is now much damaged, but it was originally an elegant composition. It was well designed to fit into its architectural setting, with complementary curves that echo the shapes of the

---

[93] With the exception of the archangel in the Ascension [78], all the wings of the angels in this decoration were built up in a similar manner (see above, p. 125). Only the covert feathers vary as to the tonal grading of colors.

arched recess. Despite the heavy overpainting, the figure of Christ retains its elegance of proportion and stance, thanks to the survival of the original outline. He takes hierarchical precedence at the center of the scene and he is drawn to a larger scale than the secondary figures of John and the angels. In its present damaged state, the lower part of the painting appears empty and out of balance with the well-occupied upper area. In the undamaged original version, the hillside supported bushes, and the long inscriptions, the candelabra, and the crosses would have furnished the river. The illusion of a three-dimensional relationship between the figures is established by the Byzantine conventions of overlap and the placing of figures one above the other. The figures of John and the angels are brought forward by the device of placing John's hand across Christ's halo and by placing the leading angel's foot across the river outline. While these baroque conventions are contrary to the accepted laws of modern ocular perspective, they do succeed in bringing the principal figure forward and out into the real space of the church itself.

St. Andronikos [55]

(Figs. 104, 106, 276)

The figure occupies a panel 198 cm high by 63 cm wide, exclusive of the red borders, which average between 5 and 7.5 cm in width. The panel was plastered in a single section, and the joins correspond with the outer edges of the red borders. There is some surface damage, and there are some losses in the lower area of the panel. The original green of the upper background was overpainted with blue at some later period, and the damaged areas were overpainted in the fourteenth century, in the manner of the other repaints in the lower register of the naos.

The lettering of the titular inscription is a repaint following the original forms beneath it. The inscription itself is aligned vertically on either side of the halo.

St. Andronikos, the monk and martyr, is tall and slender, and he stands upright in the frontal aspect as he faces eastwards. He is portrayed with the heavily lined face of an old man, but his receding hair and long rippling beard are brown, with a few white hairs, to suggest middle age. There is a particularly pronounced asymmetry in his frontal face, and his gaze is directed into the church. The head and the halo retain their standard measure relationships, but the centerpoint of the halo has been placed half a nose higher within the head. Presumably, this was done to accommodate the high shoulder line of the monastic garment, which comes up to the level of the mouth rather than to a level well below the chin.

The saint holds a white, double-barred cross in his right hand. In his left hand he holds an unfurling scroll (Fig. 276).[94] He is attired in somber monastic garb. Over a shirt, of which only the cuff is visible, he wears a long tunic whose hem spills over his black slippers. His habit is pinned at the neck and falls into short folds over his chest. His stole and his knotted black girdle hang down

---

[94] See Nicolaïdes, "Panagia Arakiotissa," pp. 121–22.

from beneath these folds. At the middle of the figure, the rope girdle divides into two diagonal arcs to either side of his tunic.

The cuff of his shirt and his tunic have an umber ground, light red and dark red shadows, and black lines and outlines; the cuff has a double black line at the wrist. His habit has a greyish yellow ground, grey shadows, and black fold lines and outlines. His stole has a red ground, grey shadows, black lines and outlines, and a decorative pattern in white lines. This has a single row of short crosses between double parallel lines, with a single cross marking the center of the area between the bands of pattern. The scroll has a green ground, and the rectangular spaces for the lettering are framed in thick white. The black lettering overrides both the green and the white.

The authoritative height of this figure is weakened by its slender width, but the weakness is partially corrected by the additional bulk provided by his scroll. The painter also strengthened the figure by adding extra folds to his tunic, on the right side beneath the scroll. Both the figure of St. Andronikos and that of St. Kyriakos opposite him, on the east side of the bay, were drawn with their heads and shoulders painted on the curve of the springing of the arches. This has the effect of tilting them slightly forward.

Sts. Kosmas and Damian [56, 57]

(Figs. 108, 109)

The half-length figures of the two Anargyroi are painted head to head on either side of the arch soffit, on a single panel. The panel measures 162 cm from east to west and averages 65 cm in width, exclusive of the red borders. It was plastered in one section, and the flesh areas of the faces and hands were all reworked before the painting was completed. The figures have suffered damage from surface flaking, and several candle burns are visible.

Because of the damage, the figures were touched up in the fourteenth-century repaint, and each was given the doctor's skull cap with a red bobble to it. The paint for the caps had largely flaked off, and what was left was removed in the course of conservation, since the crude blobs of paint detracted from the original clarity of line. The ghost shape of the skull cap can be seen in the different tone of yellow in the halo above the head of St. Kosmas.

The background was overpainted at a later period, but before the fourteenth century, with a dark "copper" blue, but this was removed in the course of conservation to reveal the original lettering and the original yellow background. This background was decorated with an overall, foliated, meander pattern of which only the traces in light yellow can now be seen. The pattern is very similar to the pattern surrounding the roundels at the center of the west vault [49] and to those in the soffits of the arches of the center bays of the naos [68] and [136] (Fig. 196, Text Figs. 26a–b). In the case of the pattern around the Anargyroi, it is uncertain that the blue flowers and green leaves were ever completed, since the titular inscriptions would have been obscured by the pattern. In the case of the other panels, the inscriptions are contained within the roundels so that

they were not concealed by the complex colors of the completed pattern. Here the titular inscriptions are painted over the yellow pattern and are placed on either side of each saint's halo. The overpaint was removed, and the present letters belong to the original 1192 decoration.

Both saints are portrayed as young men with mustaches and incipient beards. Their hair recedes to allow high foreheads, and it then falls smoothly to above their ears. Each face is in the frontal, asymmetrical aspect, and the gaze is directed toward the interior of the church. Each saint carries an instrument case in the crook of his left arm. St. Damian grasps the top of his case with the fingers of his right hand. St. Kosmas grips a fine scalpel-like instrument between the fingers of his right hand. Both figures wear an undergarment of which only a single decorated cuff is visible. Out of each cuff a single white loop protrudes at the lower edge. Over his undertunic, each saint wears an ample tunic, of which part of a broad collar is visible on one shoulder. Their loose overgarments have square, decorated necklines and broad, decorated bands running along the hem edge.

St. Kosmas wears a tunic with a green ground, dark green shadows, black lines and outlines, and fine, white, linear highlights. His overgarment has a red ground, umber shadows, black lines and outlines, and vermilion highlights that have now turned a greyish hue. His scalpel has a yellow shaft with a white blade. St. Damian has a tunic with a very light umber ground, umber shadows, black lines, and white, linear highlights. His overgarment has a green ground, grey shadows, and black lines. Their collars and cuffs have a yellow ground and are decorated with designs in umber and black lines. The cuff has the standard pattern (Text Fig. 24.1a). The collar and overgarment hem are decorated with a vermiculated scroll pattern, but the latter has an inner border of pearls. The instrument cases have a red ground with an umber shadow to one side and a vermilion highlight to the other; they have black outlines and are tied with black strings.

The two saints have youthful faces and their facial hair is painted with great delicacy over the completed flesh colors. The hair was made with a thin umber wash overlaid with fine lines in umber and black that delineate the drooping mustaches and the youthful beards. The cheeks are plump, and there are no lines to mar the smooth, glossy skin. Their short hairstyle reveals the 1192 master's characteristic method of painting ears with neat, shapely, highlighted contours and plain, shadowed interiors. Although both of these saints are portrayed as young men, their foreheads are very high, at the expense of the normal measure allowance for the hair. Since they were both doctors of medicine it is possible that Byzantine painters equated wisdom with a high forehead. These two saints are painted to look very alike, both in their faces and in their garments, and even to the instrument cases that they carry. This is in keeping with the tradition that they were twin brothers who both practiced medicine.

St. Kyriakos the Anchorite [58]

(Figs. 105, 107, 277; Text Fig. 30b)

His austere figure occupies a panel measuring 197 cm by 63 cm surrounded by red borders that average 5 cm in width. The panel was plastered in a single section. The plaster for the head

Text Fig. 30 Examples of overpainted inscriptions: the black letters belong to the 1192 inscriptions and
the dotted lines to the overpaints. a. St. Paul [52]; b. St Kyriakos the Anchorite [58]; c. St. Chariton
[145]; d. St. Maria of Egypt [150]; e. the lower inscriptions belong to St. Christopher [149].

168

and hands was reworked before these features were completed. In a later period, the upper background of the figure was overpainted with a "copper" blue. The painting has suffered some damage from flaking and considerable defacing has occurred beneath knee level.

The titular inscription is aligned vertically to either side of the head and shoulders, but the present lettering belongs to the period of overpaint. Some traces of the 1192 lettering of the word "anchorite" can still be observed beneath the blue background (Text Fig. 30b).

The saint stands upright in the frontal aspect, but his head is turned in three-quarter profile as he directs his gaze into the central space of the naos. He is portrayed as an old man, with a bald head that is relieved only by a single white curl on top and two white curls above his ear. His long, white beard is forked beneath the neatly outlined chin. In his left hand he grips the rolled part of an unfurling scroll, and in his right hand he holds the stem of a white two-armed cross (Fig. 277).[95] Both the forearms are foreshortened. He wears monastic clothes similar to those of St. Andronikos [55] on the reveal opposite him, and the colors of his garments are built up in a similar manner. Like that of the other monks in this register of painting, his halo diameter was increased one nose length to accommodate the high collar of his habit.

The severe monastic figure differs little from those of his companions in this register, and his only individual characteristics are the inscriptions and his particular hair and beard style. Monastic saints were usually given the faces of old men, but the great, bald pate and the long, elegant beard lend an air of wisdom and authority to St. Kyriakos.

[95] See Nicolaïdes, "Panagia Arakiotissa," p. 121.

II

The North Bay under the Dome

The Center Arch [59–69]

The reveals of the arch contain St. Sabas [59] to the west and the Mother of God Eleousa [69] to the east. The central panel in the soffit is occupied by eight roundels [60–67], each containing the waist-length figure of a martyr. The space around the roundels is filled with the remains of a delicate flower pattern [68].

St. Sabas [59] (Figs. 110, 112, 278)

The figure in the west reveal of the center arch occupies a panel measuring 225 cm by 64 cm contained between red borders that average 5 cm in width. The panel was plastered in a single rendering, exclusive of the dado beneath. The flesh areas of the head were not given a fresh plaster patch, but they were reworked prior to the buildup of the final layer of color. The plaster area for the hands was also reworked. Originally, the upper background was green, but this was overpainted with a coppery blue at a later date, and the inscription was rewritten. Some flaking of the surface pigment has occurred, and the lower part of the panel is severely damaged.

The titular inscription is placed on either side of the halo, and the lettering now visible belongs to the period of the overpaint. The saint is shown standing upright in the frontal aspect but his head and shoulders are slightly turned to the left. His head is in three-quarter profile as it turns toward the central space of the church. In his left hand he holds an unfurling scroll, while his right hand is held palm downwards across his chest; both forearms are foreshortened (Fig. 278).[96] The saint is portrayed as an old man with a single white curl on the top of his bald pate and a few curls above his ear. His broad, white beard is cut short and square under the hairless chin.

His garments are similar to those worn by St. Andronikos [55] (see above, pp. 165–66), but the colors vary. His habit has a yellow ground, light red shadow, some thin umber shadow, and black lines and outlines. His tunic has a red ground, umber shadows, black lines and outlines, and thick, white highlights. His stole has a red ground, black lines and outlines, and a design in thin, white line, similar to that of St. Andronikos [55].

[96] See Nicolaïdès, "Panagia Arakiotissa," pp. 118–19.

The head is a fine example of the Lagoudhera master's skill, and the quiet diagonals and strong verticals of his somber garments emphasize the calm authority of the figure.

Roundels in the Soffit of the Blind Arch [60–68]

(Pl. 24; Figs. 114–121, Text Figs. 25, 26b)

The eight roundels, each containing the half-length figure of a martyr, are contained within a single panel whose width is irregular and narrows sharply at the western end. The panel measures 602 cm from west to east, and its width reaches 62.5 cm at the western end, and 75 cm at the eastern end, inclusive of the red borders. The four roundels in the western half of the panel have a maximum diameter of 62 cm and those in the eastern half 63.5 cm. The width of the borders is 7 cm. The background is filled with a leaf-and-flower meander pattern [68], most of which is now lost. The meander pattern has faded and its basic outlines were much retouched. It is likely that the completed pattern resembled the design surrounding the roundels in the soffit of the center bay on the opposite or south wall [136], which is illustrated above (Fig. 196; Text Fig. 26b). The method of constructing this band of roundels is the same as that used for the other bands of roundels (Text Fig. 25).

The panel was plastered in two separate sections, and a plaster join between them runs across the center of the soffit of the arch between roundels [63] and [64]. The head of St. Abibos was painted on a fresh plaster patch, and the plaster for the flesh areas of some of the other heads and for the hands was reworked at an intermediate stage of painting. It is possible that the head of St. Gourias [65] was also painted on a plaster patch. Figure 119 illustrates the reworked plaster for this figure and shows that interpretation can sometimes be difficult, but the border of the new patch of plaster can be seen fairly clearly at the left side of the head, as can the spatula impress marks along the left shoulder. The figures in the roundels show no sign of repainting, but the much faded meander pattern was retouched, and in some places the underlying linear design was emphasized in black. The black retouching can be seen to the right of the roundel of St. Abibos [67], and it was done as part of the fourteenth-century repaint. The two central roundels of St. Pigasios [63] and St. Akindinos [64] have suffered from the seepage of moisture, causing the paint within both faces to flake badly and the loss of most of one inscription.

The titular name of each martyr is written within the roundel and aligned vertically on either side of the figure. The lettering is original. All the saints are shown in the frontal aspect, and the heads are asymmetrical. The wider side of the face is placed on that side of the soffit nearest to the interior of the church, and the gaze of all the figures is directed into the naos and not toward the wall.

The background of the figures alternates between green and vermilion from roundel to roundel. All the saints are martyrs, and each carries in his right hand a two-armed cross ornamented with splayed ends. All the crosses are plain white, with the exception of that of St. Abibos, the

Text Fig. 31 Examples of impedimenta: censers carried by deacons and bishops: 1a. bishop in the
Koimesis [138]; 1b. St. Stephen [83]; St. Romanos [122]; Incense boxes carried by deacons: 2a. St.
Abibos [67]; St. Stephen [83]; St. Romanos [122]; St. Joseph [135]; 2b. St. Stachios [90]; St. Nikanor
[94]. 3a. Chalice carried by St. Zosimos [15]; 3b. Medicine box carried by St. Panteleimon [147]

deacon, whose cross is painted yellow to contrast with his white surplice or sticharion. Each figure
conceals his left hand beneath the folds of his garments, and St. Abibos supports an incense box on
his forearm (Text Fig. 31.2a).

Apart from St. Abibos, the martyrs all wear similar garments that differ only in the articulation of the robe folds. Each saint wears an undertunic of which only the embroidered, yellow cuff
is visible, and three of these cuffs have a small, white loop protruding from the bottom corner.
Each saint wears a tunic with a broad collar that has an indented and scalloped lower edge. These
collars have a yellow ground with a wash of white highlight to imitate the sheen of gold. They are
patterned with a vermiculated design in umber line (Text Fig. 24.1–2b). The lower edge of the
collar is outlined with a narrow black band beaded with single pearls. Each of the saints wears a
cloak fastened at his breast with a clasp in the form of a single pearl.

Each roundel is painted with individual care, particularly as to the face and hair, and the colors are clean and bright in pleasing contrasts. The overall effect is decorative, despite the bland yellow of the bleached pattern between the roundels.

St. Anempodistos [60] (Fig. 114)

The background is green. The saint is portrayed as a beardless young man with smooth, brown hair which falls to a scalloped edge at chin level. His tunic has a green ground, grey shadows, black lines and fine, white highlights. His cloak has a vermilion ground, umber shadows and fold lines, black delineating lines, and a narrow, yellow band along the hem that is lined with single pearls.

St. Elpidiphoros [61] (Fig. 115)

The background is vermilion. The saint is characterized as a young man with an incipient mustache and beard. Apart from his facial hair, he could pass as an identical twin to St. Anempodistos, but his clothes are differently colored and differently arranged. His tunic has a green ground, green shadows and fold lines, black shadow lines, white wash, and thick, white highlights. His cloak has a light red ground, with some umber and black lines, and blue wash highlights. His cloak is not edged with pearls like that of St. Anempodistos.

St. Aphthonios [62] (Fig. 116)

The background is green. The saint is portrayed as an old man with smooth, brown hair flowing to just beneath the ear. His short beard is neatly rounded beneath the outline of the chin. It is brown, striated with white. His tunic has a light grey ground, blue shadow lines, and black lines and outlines. His cloak has a vermilion ground with the deep hollows between the folds colored dark red, and black lines and outlines.

St. Pigasios [63] (Fig. 117)

The background is vermilion. The head of this saint is much damaged, but the coloring of the hair suggests that he was represented as an old man. His tunic has a light red ground, black lines and outlines, a white highlight wash with blue, and thick, white highlights. His cloak has a blue ground and black lines and outlines.

St. Akindinos (?) [64] (Fig. 118)

The background is green. The title ὁ ἅγιος is complete, but only the final ος remains to suggest his name. It is likely that he is St. Akindinos, who is regularly portrayed in the company of the other martyrs in this panel. The saint is portrayed as a middle-aged man with brown hair and a long, pointed beard. His tunic has a yellow-green ground, green shadows, black lines, white wash, and thick, white highlights. His cloak has a vermilion ground that is now discolored, dark red shadows, and black lines and outlines.

The 1192 Decoration

St. Gourias [65] (Fig. 119)

The background is vermilion. The saint is represented as an old man with smooth, white hair flowing to beneath the ear lobes, and he has a long beard flowing to a point at the neckline. His tunic has a yellow-green ground, green shadows, black lines and outlines, and thick, white, linear highlights. His cloak has a light red ground, dark red shadows, and black lines and outlines with no highlights. The hem has a narrow, yellow border beaded with single pearls.

St. Samonas [66] (Fig. 120)

The background is green. The figure of St. Samonas could be the identical twin of St. Aphthonios [62] above. Their garments are very similar, but St. Samonas has deeper folds to his cloak, and the indentation to his collar is slightly different in outline. His cloak is like that of St. Aphthonios. His tunic has a light red ground, umber shadows, black lines and outlines, white wash, and thick, white highlights.

St. Abibos, Deacon and Martyr [67] (Fig. 121; Text Fig. 31.2a)

The background is vermilion. The saint is portrayed as a young man with a slight mustache and incipient beard. His brown, layered hair frames his head as far as the ears and then reappears below them in a short cluster of tight curls. He wears a long-sleeved tunic of which one embroidered cuff is visible under his sticharion, and his narrow orarion is draped vertically over his left shoulder. In the crook of his left arm he carries a jeweled incense box.

His tunic has a red ground, umber shadows, black lines and outlines, and no highlights. His sticharion has a thick, white ground, light grey shadows, and light blue lines and outlines. His orarion has a yellow ground with red outlines, and a single motif in umber of a thick horizontal bar between two thin lines. His incense box has a yellow ground, which is decorated with a diamond net pattern in umber line; the corridors are filled with single pearls and the lattices with vermiculation in umber. The rim has a horizontal line of linear rings between two narrow black bands filled with groups of single pearls. The lid has a petal design and is topped with a single pearl (Text Fig. 31.2a).

The Mother of God Eleousa [69] (Figs. 137, 139, 283)

The slender figure of the Compassionate Mother of God standing at the entrance to the bema forms part of a Deesis or supplication composition that unites her to the figure of Christ Antiphonetes [127] on the east reveal of the south blind arch under the dome. St. John the Baptist [75] appears alongside the Eleousa, in the panel to her left on the north wall, and the three figures are so placed as to make use of the real architectural space of the church (see pp. 144–46 and 311–16).

The panel measures 2.35 m in height and 74 cm in width, inclusive of the red borders. It was plastered in a single section, and the head was not given a fresh plaster patch. Some flaking has occurred in the upper figure, but the major damage is confined to the area below the knees, where

there are losses and bad flaking. Repairs were carried out by the fourteenth-century repainter, but most of his retouching was removed in the course of conservation. Unlike most of the ground register in the naos, the upper background to the Eleousa was painted blue to give her due honor. At a later date, this original blue was overpainted with copper blue, even though this was unnecessary.

The abbreviated titular inscription is placed on either side of the halo, and the epithet is aligned vertically at the back of the halo. The lettering is a bad overpaint of most of the original inscription. The scroll held by the Mother of God contains the words of a dialogue between the mother and her son as she pleads successfully for him to grant redemption to the human race. Her words are written in black letters and his replies are written in red letters.[97] The lettering is all by the 1192 painter (Fig. 283). The dialogue runs as follows:

Christ: Mother, What dost thou request?

Mary: The salvation of mankind.

Christ: They have provoked me.

Mary: My commiserations, O my son.

Christ: But they do not revert.

Mary: Spare them.

Christ: They are redeemed.

Mary: Thanks are said.

The upright figure of the Mother of God fits tightly into the panel. She stands in three-quarter profile, her head inclined forward in the direction of the Christ Antiphonetes on the other side of the naos. Her left arm is folded across her breast with the hand palm downward, in a gesture of humility. Her right hand, which is enfolded within a loose fold of her maphorion, grips the unfurling scroll. Her feet are in slippers, and they rest upon a jeweled footstool. She wears a long tunic under a voluminous maphorion, and her face is closely encased in a wimple. The maphorion has segmenta on the forehead and shoulders. The hem is banded with yellow, and the upper folds are enriched with tassels.

Mary's wimple is blue with black outlines. Her maphorion has a red ground, grey shadows, black lines and outlines, and blue wash highlights. The hemline is decorated with single or double bands of yellow picked out with highlight dots of thick, light yellow. The segmenta and the long tassels are yellow. Below the halo, the black outline to Mary's maphorion is reinforced with a second outline in white, which contours her figure and possibly serves to indicate the heavenly light surrounding her. Her tunic has a yellow ground but is too damaged for the further buildup of colors to be ascertained accurately. Her slippers are vermilion. The footstool is slightly wider at the front than at the back and three sides of it are visible. The upper surface is decorated with a diamond net pattern in umber line on a yellow ground. The corridors of the "net" are lined with single pearls and the lattices filled with vermiculation in umber line. The three narrow sides of the

[97] For the history of the Deesis composition, see *ODB* 1: 599–600.

stool are decorated with a continuous black band upon which pearls and jewels alternate within a yellow, linear outline, similar to loros pattern I (Pl. 11a).

The poise of her bowed head is gracefully designed in counterpoint to the curve of her arms and halo. Beneath this wide circling movement, the massing of vertical folds and the long narrow scroll establish a sense of quietude. There is no concession to femininity in Mary's face, which is constructed in a similar manner to those of the angels and young men. However, her hands measure less than one face-length, which is the normal measurement for male hands in the 1192 proportional canon.

The North Wall [70–77]

The lunette is occupied by the Presentation of the Virgin [70]. The ground register is interrupted by the north doorway, whose reveals are decorated with inscribed crosses [76, 77]. A narrow, rectangular panel above the doorway contains the Holy Tile [72] with the 1192 inscription beneath it. St. Nicholas [71] stands to the west of the doorway, and to the east stands St. Symeon, holding the Christ child [74] and accompanied by St. John the Forerunner [75].

Working from the lunette downward, the wall was initially plastered panel by panel, including the dadoes; the plaster joins are contained within the red borders.

The Presentation of the Mother of God to the Temple [70]

(Pls. 24, 25; Figs. 122–132; Text Figs. 32–34)

The panel in the lunette measures 3.56 m at its base and has a height at the center of 2.18 m. The curve of the arch is irregular, but the painter seems to have used a notional, central vertical running through the center of the angel's halo and down through the center of Anna's halo and figure. A notional horizontal could also have been drawn to run through the shoulder line of the lower row of maidens through the breast line of Joachim and Anna, tangent to the base of Zacharias's halo and through the top of the capitals to the fenestration in the eastern architecture. To the viewer, the scene divides into three or four vertical sections: The maidens and their architecture; Joachim and Anna; Mary and Zacharias; and the eastern architecture. These can be divided along the central horizontal: 102 cm; 65 cm; 80 cm; 53 cm. A notional horizontal, running along the upper edge of the cornice to the altar ciborium, neatly serves to separate the lower tableau from that of the feeding of the Virgin above.

The red borders average 6 cm in width, and the plaster join runs along the red line at the base of the panel. Along the curve of the lunette, the plaster joins can be traced along the inner edge of the red border where the plastering of the soffit above was extended into the lunette beneath it.

Text Fig. 32 The Presentation of the Virgin [70], indicating work on the plaster surface. ·—·— indicate incised lines; — indicate impressed lines; ——— outline areas that were given fresh plaster patches before the painting was completed. Hatched lines mark areas where the plaster was reworked before the application of the final paint layers.

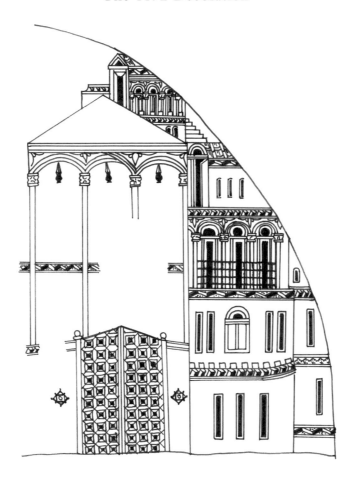

Text Fig. 33 The architecture to the right of the altar ciborium at the Presentation of the Virgin [70]

The panel was originally plastered in a single section. Text Fig. 32 illustrates the positions of impressed and incised lines, the insertion of plaster patches, and those areas where the plaster was reworked prior to painting. All of these show that in the course of painting, alterations and adjustments were carried out on some figures. In the fourteenth century, damaged areas were retouched with a yellowy orange color and with grey-white lines.

Five inscriptions are within the panel, and all the lettering is original. The titular inscription "The Holy of Holies" refers to the altar ciborium painted below and to the right of the inscription.[98] All the inscriptions appear to have been painted freehand, and there are no traces of painted or incised guidelines for them. The scene title is well spaced and almost geometrically horizontal, but the lettering for Joachim and Anna, and for Zacharias, drifts upward from left to right. All are painted on the blue upper background of the scene, except that the abbreviated title for the standing Virgin is painted on the architecture rising from behind her. All the lettering was painted in

---

[98] There is no sign that the scene was ever given its more usual title of Ἡ εἴσοδος τῆς Θεοτόκου.

thick white, but the letters of the scene title and the inscriptions for Joachim and Anna were overpainted with vermilion. The vermilion has now faded to a reddish brown. This additional adornment is an original addition by the 1192 painter that he did not repeat elsewhere in the church. All the letters are elegantly proportioned with fine serifs, and it needed great care and steadiness of hand to go over them again so neatly in vermilion. The iconography follows the account of this event in the apocryphal protoevangelium of St. James.[99]

The central upper background to the scene is blue. The only foreground is the green strip on the left, where the maidens stand. The three central figures tread no ground, as the wall behind them extends directly downward to the red border at the bottom of the scene. Joachim's feet overlap the red border, and the three figures appear to float out into the actual space of the church. The buildings of the inner temple complex also extend directly downward to the red border at the bottom of the scene, and the temple gates overlap Zacharias's legs so that he appears to stand beyond them. The painter skillfully manipulated the architectural backgrounds in a manner that places in recess the smaller and less important figures of the maidens, and thrusts forward the larger and most important figures of Joachim and Anna.

The placing of some of the architectural elements was reinforced by permanent guidelines put in at a preliminary stage of painting (Text Fig. 32). An impressed line marks the upper outline of the curving drapery of the building to the left. A vertical impressed line marks the side of the same building and continues down Joachim's back, separating him from the maidens. A further impress line marks the right side of the triangular canopy of the altar ciborium, and a horizontal incision marks the bottom line of it. A further horizontal incised line marks the top of the wall behind Zacharias. A long, vertical, incised line runs down the right side of the altar ciborium and continues down the side of the temple entrance wall. Another incised line marks the top of the temple door and of the wall to the right of it.

The altar ciborium is a large feature that has some plausibility in size in relation to the figure of Zacharias, which it seems to enfold. The architecture behind him is miniature in scale in relation to the figures in the scene. All the buildings have a compositional role, suggesting a pictorial space appropriate for the figures adjacent to them, but nevertheless, they remain a flat and unobtrusive backdrop. Like the architectural backgrounds to the figures in the pendentives, they are highly decorative and ornamented with a fine variety of architectural features.[100] These include tiled roofs; pointed and rounded gables; cornices in five different patterns; windows, short, tall, square, and round-arched; doors, open and shut; pilasters with "Corinthian" capitals and ornamented spandrels; arcades with rounded and horseshoe arches; crenellations; coffered gates with ball-topped gateposts; stairs; decorated "ironwork"; pendant lamps; furling drapery; and decorative insignia.

---

[99] The historical source for this scene is in the Protoevangelium of James and the Gospel of Pseudo Matthew, 4, in the *Apocryphal New Testament*, trans. M. R. James (Oxford, 1966), 41, 42, 7:2, 3.

[100] A. H. S. Megaw, "Background Architecture in the Lagoudera Frescoes," *JÖB* 21 (1972), 195–206.

The 1192 Decoration

The architectural features are each built up in light and dark colors to imply three-dimensional relief, but they do not impart a coherent suggestion of volume to the buildings that they decorate. There are three exceptional pieces of illusionism in the architecture. One is the crenellated cornice on the eastern building, which curves around and upward at the east side to create the impression of a rounded building (Text Fig. 33). A second example is the central arch to the ciborium, which is broken at its center where the right curve overlaps the left curve. This deliberate crossing within the arch suggests a convention to indicate the interior three-dimensional space within the canopy.

The third feature is that wall and roof surfaces are not made with flat and uniform colors. They are given differential coloring that indicates the play of light on a surface and a source of light. Thus, in the buildings at the east side, the ground color of an intermediate tone is shadowed toward the lateral border of the panel, and highlighted toward the edges nearest to the center. And in the ciborium, a rounded shape is suggested by darker coloring to the right and lighter coloring to the left. This disciplined orientation of lights and darks is not rigidly adhered to in architectural features such as columns, capitals, and cornices. And, in the block of architecture behind the seated Virgin, the shadows are in a reverse direction, with highlights toward the edge of the painting.

Joachim and Anna, Mary, and Zacharias (Pl. 25; Figs. 123, 126–132; Text Figs. 32, 34)

The four figures of Joachim, Anna, the child Mary, and Zacharias form a close-knit group in the center of the painting. Joachim is seen in three-quarter profile as he strides firmly forward. His left arm is bent and his hand articulated in admonition to the hesitant Anna. His right arm extends downward, as he ushers Mary forward. His feet overlap the red border so that he seems to float out in front of Anna. Anna stands still, her head turning back to Joachim. Her right arm is bent, with the hand palm downward across her breast, while her left arm extends downward, reaching for the head of the child below her. Mary's figure is half the size of that of her mother. She stands upright, her head slightly tilted back and her arms bent as she appears to reach up to Zacharias's welcoming hands. Zacharias bows deeply forward as he extends his arms, reaching for the child. The painter has skillfully linked these figures so that the eye focuses on the intimate drama taking place in the center of the painting. They are further distinguished from the other characters in the scene by their size, as they are constructed to a larger scale than the figures of the angel and the maidens. Also, the rims of the haloes of these four figures are made up of single black outlines filled with rows of four single pearls alternating with red or green jewels. The only other figures with similar outlines to their haloes are the Mother of God in the Nativity of Christ [142] and the Christ in the Mandylion [92]. All the other haloes in the paintings of 1192 have plain outlines drawn with a compass in black and white paint.

Joachim the Just stands off-center behind Anna. He is portrayed as a man in middle age with white striations in his loosely curled, receding, brown hair and short, tufted beard, but his face is lined like that of an old man. He wears a chiton with black clavus beneath a voluminous himation, and sandals. His himation has a light vermilion ground, red shadows, black lines and outlines,

broad, blue wash highlights, and fine, white, linear highlights. The light vermilion has become discolored and the translucent blue washes are now grey, with the exception of those areas where the white highlights have flaked off to reveal the bright blue beneath. His chiton was built up with similar colors, but without any blue wash highlights.

Joachim's head was painted on a fresh plaster patch, inserted at a late stage in painting. Flaking paint layers also reveal that originally the painter gave Joachim the usual black and white outlines to his halo, but the newer halo has but a single, black, jeweled outline. Both versions of the halo have roughly the same diameter, but the new head on its plaster patch was made smaller than the original head. In a further alteration, the head on the plaster patch was once again reduced in size. This can be seen where the final yellow of the halo has flaked to reveal the preliminary drawing on the plaster patch (Fig. 129).

Impressed lines in the plaster mark the outlines of Joachim's shoulders, and there is a vertical impress line to mark the separation between him and the maidens behind him (Text Fig. 32). The painter did not rework the plaster in the flesh area of the hands, and these are badly flaked, revealing the now powdery, yellow ground color. Joachim's raised left hand shows evidence of alteration, and the jutting index finger was repainted to place it closer to his chin, presumably to make a clearer separation between his hand and the enlarged shoulders of Anna. The plaster area for his feet was reworked, and these have the glossy finish of well-preserved, properly built-up flesh color. They also appear to be massive in proportion, especially in relation to the elegant feet of the standing maidens, who are constructed to a smaller scale than Joachim. His feet measure the canonical head length, from heel to toe, but that head length (apex to chin) was taken from the initial larger version of his head. The pendant folds of his himation were lengthened at a late stage in painting at the same time that alterations were carried out to Anna's maphorion.

The Holy Anna is portrayed with a young face, and her hair is concealed within a close-fitting wimple. Her head and shoulders are covered with a long maphorion that conceals all but the cuffs and skirt of her long-sleeved tunic. The golden hem of it overlaps her slippers. Her wimple is blue, and her maphorion has a vermilion ground, dark red fold lines, and black lines and outlines. In the fourteenth century, the repainter added grey-white highlights. Her tunic was overpainted at a late stage in the course of the original painting, when the 1192 master carried out a number of alterations to her figure. In his first version, he gave the tunic a light green ground, dark green shadows, black lines and outlines, and thick, white, linear highlights. In his final version he gave it a green ground, grey shadows, and thick, light blue, linear highlights. The hem of this version of the tunic was overpainted with yellow and articulated with blue fold lines and black lines. Her slippers are vermilion.

In further modification to the design, the painter made major changes to Anna's figure (Text Fig. 34). Her head was reoriented so that she now looks back toward Joachim, whereas in the original version, she looked toward Zacharias (Figs. 126, 127).[101] The change was achieved by

[101] The master painter frequently made very late adjustments to his paintings, for instance, by altering a shoulder

making a fresh plaster patch for the new version of the head, and by painting out the initial halo and making the new one with a jeweled black outline. The painter does not seem to have been thoroughly satisfied even with his second version of the head of Anna, since he enlarged it by extending the maphorion 1 cm outward into the halo all the way around the head. Most of this extension has now flaked away. In order to reconcile the enlarged and reoriented head in harmony with the figure beneath it, the painter had, of necessity, to enlarge and heighten the shoulders. This enlargement has mostly flaked away to reveal the outline of the original figure belonging to the initial version of the head. There is an incision line at the shaping of the left shoulder of the original figure.

The lower part of Anna's figure was also adjusted so that it should no longer crowd into Joachim (Figs. 126, 128, Text Fig. 34). The left sides of the maphorion and undertunic were narrowed by overpainting them with a color marking the continuation of the background wall; at the same time, the left foot was moved further over to the right and the right side of Anna's garments was extended outward a little way. However, in moving the left foot, it became necessary to adjust the lower folds of her tunic, as these were articulated to outline the full leg descending to the foot in the previous position. Hence the overpaint of the tunic hem.

The overpainted adjustment to the shoulders was particularly unsuccessful, and the overpaint layer has completely come away, leaving its imprint on the blue background but revealing the initial version of the shoulders. This first version of the shoulders was clearly narrower and lower than those of the repaint, and there are guidelines in the form of impressed lines in the plaster marking the curved outline to this initial version (Text Fig. 32). All of these alterations and adjustments outlined above were contemporary changes initiated by the 1192 master, who obviously became dissatisfied with the design of his composition. His final version of Anna was an improvement in terms of composition, but his carefully judged alterations proved unsatisfactory because of the dry ground upon which they were painted.

The little figure of Mary is half the size of her mother, Anna, and her proportions are in keeping with her age (Fig. 123). Despite her youth, her garments are those of the demure, married female, and unlike the bare-headed young maidens in her escort, Mary wears a close-fitting wimple

---

or an arm, enlarging a garment or reducing it, or enlarging a halo. It was by such changes that the painter improved the balance of his compositions and their final appearance. It is when he misjudged the moisture content of the plaster at the time of these adjustments that he reveals the whole process. The plaster for the Presentation had already dried out too much, and the incorporation of pigment and lime into the fresco process had already been completed, so that the late changes in the composition eventually fell away. The painter's confidence in carrying out these changes shows clearly that they were common practice, and in this case his misjudgment has revealed to us the extent to which he was prepared to go to achieve a satisfactory final composition. There is no trace of a 14th-century repair on the Presentation scene, so the paint layers must have survived to a much later period, and his misjudgment was more a piece of ill luck than a major error. Another example of the reorientation of a feature occurs in the Etoimasia [3], where he redesigned the bird representing the Holy Spirit so that it was better balanced against the mass of other features in the roundel.

Text Fig. 34 Contemporary changes and adjustments
made to the figure of Anna in the Presentation of
the Virgin [70]. The continuous black line indicates
the final version of the figure, the dotted line
indicates the preliminary version of the figure, and
the dashed line an intermediate version of the head.
All versions are 1192 in date.

that conceals her hair. An ample maphorion envelops her head and shoulders, and her long-sleeved
tunic is revealed at the cuffs and where the skirt of it overlaps her slippered feet. Her wimple is
blue, and her maphorion has a red ground, dark red fold lines, black lines and outlines, and broad
washes of blue. Her tunic has a blue ground and black lines and fold lines. Her slippers are vermilion, now faded, and they are underlined with black line. The segmenta on her maphorion and the
double borders on her cuffs are yellow.

Mary's figure was painted on a fresh plaster patch inserted at a final stage in the painting of the
scene. The plaster join for this patch runs from the red border, up across Anna's left foot, and up
the right side of the tall painted window behind Mary's legs; it then follows the outline of the edge
of the folds of Anna's maphorion, enters within Mary's halo rounding her head and descends along
the top of her hands to the newel post of the Temple gate, whence it descends vertically to the base
line (Figs. 130a–b, Text Fig. 32). The western or left edge of the plaster patch must not be confused

with the structural crack to the left of it. The reason for this late insertion of a fresh plaster patch must be that Mary was the last figure that the painter completed and that the plaster was too dry for alterations. It may be that the painter thought that the figure of Mary was initially too near to that of Anna. It is thanks to the fresh plaster patch that the figure of Mary remains totally undamaged, with its colors in fine condition. Exceptionally, the top left of her halo, together with the rim of the halo and Anna's intruding hand, have flaked badly because they were not painted on the new plaster. The painter inserted a narrow window behind Mary, painting it directly on to the vertical plaster join in an attempt to conceal the roughness in the surface. In an alteration with a similar purpose in the Ascension [78] (see below, p. 197), the painter endeavored to disguise the plaster joins in the vault by painting the inscriptions over them.

The Holy Zacharias is portrayed as an old man, with a short, white, pointed beard and long, softly waved hair. A small calotte is perched precariously on the top of his inclined head (Figs. 131, 132). Over a long-sleeved undertunic he wears a shorter wide-sleeved tunic with a richly embroidered hem and a collar with a long central panel. A loosely knotted sash enfolds his waist, and the broad cloak thrown back across his shoulders is hemmed with single pearls and gathered to his neck by a clasp marked by a single pearl.

His hat is vermilion with black outlines. It was overpainted in the fourteenth century with grey-white pearls and grey-white highlights. His undertunic has a light blue ground, blue shadows, black lines and outlines, and thick, white, linear highlights. The long sleeves are built up with the same colors as the wide sleeves of the short tunic overlapping them. This short tunic has a yellow-green ground, dark yellow-green shadows, black lines and outlines, blue wash highlights (now discolored), and thick, white, linear highlights. The cuffs, the hem of the tunic, the collar, and the center panel all have a yellow ground with a patch of white highlight to suggest the sheen of gold. On this ground various linear patterns were made in dark red and black lines. The cuff is decorated with a diamond net pattern; both the hem of the short tunic and the central panel are filled with a vermiculated palmette pattern; and the collar is decorated with a vermiculated scroll pattern (Text Fig. 24.1a, 3c). Each decoration is outlined with a narrow black band lined with groups of single pearls. The sash for his waist is blue with black outlines. His cloak has a vermilion ground, dark red fold lines, and a narrow, yellow border lined with single pearls.

The head of Zacharias was painted on a fresh plaster patch, and the original halo was altered (Fig. 131). The original yellow of the halo was painted out with blue paint where it extended beyond the final black outline of the new halo. This blue overpaint has now flaked away revealing the original yellow ground of the initial halo but no black and white outlines. This, in association with overlaps of color and adjustments at the neckline, suggests that the insertion of the plaster patch was made at the time that the painter returned to complete the head, when he had already completed the background details and the garments of the figures and, possibly, some of the other heads. The plaster for the priest's hands was not reworked before they were completed, and the pigment layers are badly flaked as a result. Both the damaged hands and the halo were poorly repainted with orangy yellow in the course of the fourteenth-century repairs.

The Seven Hebrew Maidens (Pl. 24, Figs. 122, 124, 125, Text Fig. 32)

These slender young girls with their flowing hair and diaphanous garments form a compact group behind Joachim as they advance toward the Temple. They saunter along with their dainty slippers treading upon a narrow strip of green ground in front of a tall building. A row of four full-length figures in front (maidens 4–7, left to right) conceals the lower body of three others behind them (maidens 1–3, left to right). The heads of the figures in the back row appear to be framed by arches decorating the upper story of the building behind them.

The figures are all in the three-quarter-profile aspect. Some of their heads are turned toward the center of the scene, but others turn away to the left, so that the girls appear to converse with each other. Each girl's face is framed by her long, smooth hair which streams back over her shoulder. Pearl earrings hang from their ear lobes. The heads are very similar, one to the other, and the young faces are built up like those of young men, although they lack the vermilion highlights given to most faces of young men in this decoration.[102] The right arm of each maiden is flexed forward, and their hands grasp tall thin tapers. The paint of the tapers has flaked badly and only traces can now be seen. The left arms are concealed by the garments of the figures in front of them. The figures in the front row step forward with their right feet, steadying themselves with the left legs to the rear. They are not quite level, and there is an upward tilt to the figures from the left toward the center.

Each of the four maidens in the front row has an undertunic of which only the skirt is visible as it swirls down into bell folds that overlap their slippers. All the maidens wear short, long-sleeved tunics with broad, decorated hems that reach to just above the knee. These tunics have embroidered collars and armbands. A loose stole is hitched over one shoulder, leaving a long, pendant fold to hang down their backs.

The maidens' earrings consist of a white ring with three pendant teardrop pearls, each topped with a round one. The decorative bands within the garments all have a yellow ground, sometimes with a white wash highlight to indicate the gleam of gold. Apart from the hem band to the undergarment, all these features are decorated with linear patterns in dark red lines, some picked out with pearls, and each is outlined with a narrow black band lined with groups of four single pearls with no intervening jewel. There are three basic patterns: a "washer" pattern that appears at the wrist-edge of cuffs; a vermiculated palmette decoration that appears on all the collars, cuffs, stole hems, and on the hems of the tunics of maidens 5 and 7; and a diamond net pattern, which can be found on all the arm bands and on the tunic hems of maidens 4 and 6 (Text Fig. 24.1a, 4b). The hem on the skirts of the front row of maidens consists of a yellow band painted over the green color of the garment. The upper edge of this band is an arbitrary horizontal that disregards the

---

[102] The lack of vermilion shows further recognition of the difference between the sexes. Tanned or rosy cheeks have never been much admired in the Middle East, where pale complexions are much sought after to this day.

articulation of the garment folds, but within the band these folds are indicated with red shadows, black lines, and light yellow highlights.

The heads of the maidens in the upper row were all painted on fresh plaster patches, and the yellow of the flesh color was extended over into the blind arches of the building behind them. The plaster in the area of the heads of maidens 4 and 7 in the front row was reworked, but this has not prevented flaking in the head of maiden 7. The heads of maidens 5 and 6, in the center of the front row, are in slight bas-relief, which could indicate that fresh plaster patches were also put in for these heads, but there is no trace of a plaster join for them. Perhaps they were reworked before the final painting. In the case of the four maidens in the front row, the plaster in the area of both the hands and the flesh area of the feet was reworked prior to the completion of the flesh colors. Deep impress marks outline the shoulders of all the maidens, but no other permanent reference marks were observed (Text Fig. 32).

The colors used for the robes of the maidens are standard and well preserved. The only exception is the light vermilion or "pink," which is frequently discolored to a grey-pinkish white. There is an extensive use of blue wash highlights over the light vermilion and the green grounds, and the transparency of these washes gives to the garments the appearance of gauzy, silken fabrics. Little other concession was made by the painter toward the femininity of these figures whose features and general proportions follow the standard formula for young men. However, he has made their hands and feet considerably smaller than the standard measures laid down for men. The hands of the maidens are very small, and even if their candle-grasping fingers were extended, they would hardly conform to the standard measure for a man's hand, which is one face length.

The Maidens in the Upper Row (from west to east, or left to right)

Maiden 1 has a tunic with a yellow ground applied over a light vermilion base, thin black lines, white wash, and thick, white, linear highlights. Her stole has a light blue ground, blue shadows, and black lines (Fig. 124). Maiden 2, at the center of the back row, has a tunic with a light green ground, black fold lines, thin blue wash highlights, and thick, white highlights. Her stole has a yellow ground, black lines, and white wash and thick, white highlights. Maiden 3, at the eastern end, has a blue stole similar to that of Maiden 1, and a tunic with a yellow-green ground, dark yellow green fold lines, thin blue wash highlights, and thick, white highlights.

The Maidens in the Front Row (from west to east)

Maiden 4, at the western end, has a stole with a light green ground, dark yellow-green shadows, black lines, blue wash highlights, and thick, white highlights. Her upper tunic has a green ground, grey shadows, black lines, blue wash highlights, and thick, white highlights. Her skirt has a light blue ground, blue shadows, black lines, and thick white linear highlights. This maiden has her head turned in the three-quarter-profile aspect toward the center of the scene. But in completing the facial features, the painter made a mistake which is unique in the 1192 paintings. He drew the nose with two nostrils showing, as would be appropriate for the frontal position, and he made

the shadow for the nose on the wider side of the face instead of on the narrower side. The rather Picasso-like caricature that results from these departures from the rules only serves to emphasize the importance of the standard system of painting (Fig. 125).

Maiden 5, west of center, has a stole with a light vermilion ground, red shadows, black lines, blue wash highlights, and thick, white highlights. Her tunic has a light green ground, yellow-green shadows, black lines, blue wash highlights, and thick, white, linear highlights. Her skirt has a grey ground, red fold lines that are particularly striking, black lines, blue wash highlights, and thick, white, linear highlights.

Maiden 6, east of center, has a stole with a light blue ground, blue shadows, and black lines. Her tunic has a discolored light vermilion ground, red shadows, black lines, blue wash highlights, and thick, white, linear highlights. Her skirt has a light blue ground, blue shadows, black lines, and thick, white highlights. Maiden 7, at the eastern end, has a stole with a discolored light vermilion ground, red shadows, black lines, blue wash highlights, and thick, white, linear highlights. Her tunic has a blue ground, grey shadows, black lines, blue wash highlights, and thick, white, linear highlights. Her skirt had a light blue ground, blue shadows, black lines, and thick, white highlights. Her right foot is not visible because it is hidden behind that of Joachim.

The Virgin in the Temple Is Fed by an Angel

The painter has illustrated this event in the upper arc of his panel. The rather squat, little figure of the Virgin is in three-quarter profile, and she sits on the edge of a cornice, high up above the altar ciborium. She has one hand on her knee, while the other arm is raised as she turns toward the angel swooping toward her.

Mary's halo intrudes into the upper red border of the scene, and it has a single white outline. Over her wimple she wears a maphorion that ripples generously over her upper body, and her long-sleeved undergarment falls into folds over her slippered feet. Her wimple and her undergarment are blue with black lines and outlines. Her maphorion has a red ground, black lines, and blue highlights, and the hem is decorated with a single white line. The segmenta on her forehead and shoulders are yellow, and her slippers are vermilion. The plaster for the area of the face was reworked. The figure is in very good condition.

At the top center of the panel, the half-length figure of the ministering angel floats forward with wings outstretched to either side of his haloed head. There is an impress mark delineating the top of his shoulder. The head is in three-quarter profile, and his right arm extends forward toward the Virgin as he proffers a rounded loaf of bread in his hand. His foreshortened left arm is held close to his body, and in his left hand he clutches a narrow yellow stave, traces of which can be seen extending upward from behind his halo. He wears a chiton with clavus under a himation.

The angel's halo has a single, plain, black outline. His hair is a smaller version of that of the angels in the dome, and he wears a blue ribbon within it. His face, which is that of a young man, is now much damaged. His chiton has a green ground and black lines, with white wash highlights overlaid with a further wash of blue highlights and thick, white, linear highlights. His himation has

a yellow ground, red fold lines, black lines and outlines, white wash highlights tinted with blue, and thick, white, linear highlights. The wings have a yellow ground with broad, black, outlines, long black pinion feathers, and covert feathers in red, tipped with pink, vermilion, and stubby black.

The angel's body appears to be sliced off diagonally across the middle, as if he were caught swerving around at right angles, or as if, like the Cheshire cat, he could only manifest his appearance slowly, in sections. The shortened body is less obtrusive in the overall composition than a full-length figure would be, and confines his importance to his minor role within the incident of the feeding of the Virgin.

Perhaps this peculiar truncated body, which appears elsewhere in Byzantine painting, derives from some early Christian representation of angels appearing out of the clouds. When plain backgrounds became the rule in the post-Iconoclast period, the angels in the sky still continued to be represented as if they were coming out of a cloud.

The painting of the Presentation illustrates very clearly that the 1192 master took particular pride in achieving equilibrium and harmony both in the composition as a whole and in the internal drawing of each of the figures. There is a strong movement from left to right in the west half of the panel as the maidens and Joachim advance in harmony with their right arms bent forward. The long diagonals of their right legs also form an insistent pointer toward the center. This strong movement is arrested by the verticals of Anna and Mary and the backward turning heads of some of the figures. The maidens form a compact independent group of figures within the neat green foreground, but their movement forms a link to the central figures of Joachim and Anna, who stand facing each other. Mary and Zacharias form another group, with their arms stretched out to each other, while the reaching hands of Joachim and Anna form a secondary movement linking Mary back to her parents.

Within the iconographic conventions for this scene, the painter has managed to express a great and tender understanding of the human drama unfolding. Anna looks back for reassurance to Joachim, and her hand reaches toward Mary as though she is acquiescent in the giving of her child, and yet, reluctant to part with her. The firmer figure of Joachim appears as protective, while at the same time his fingers express an admonition to his wife to be firm in their purpose. The child Mary and Zacharias reach forward to each other as if both have been waiting for this moment and know for certain that it is right. The chattering maidens in their beautiful, courtly dresses serve as a frivolity that enhances the central drama.

The persistent redesigning and modification of the central figures is a remarkable instance of the care in both design and execution that might be taken by a Byzantine wall painter, and while the damage can only be regretted, it does provide a revelation of the techniques of the painter and an insight into his thoughts about design and construction. His difficulty, in this case, was that he found that he, or a pupil, had taken up too much space with the background architecture, and left

himself too narrow a space for the principal figures. His final execution of the figures is elegant, in artistic terms, and sensitive in conveying the pathos of the event.

St. Nicholas [71]

(Figs. 111, 113; Text Figs. 35, 36)

This panel to the left of the north door measures 2.12 m in height and 82 cm in width, exclusive of the red borders, which average between 5 and 10 cm in width. The panel was plastered in a single section, and the area containing the saint's left hand was reworked. The painting sustained much damage over the years because of the lintel of the north door, which is set into the masonry in the area where the shoulders of the saint were painted. The movement of the wood has cracked the plaster repeatedly, right across the painting, and a number of repairs and repaints badly disfigured it. In the head of the figure, the paint layers have flaked back to the preliminary colors, and the lower background was much damaged. At some date, the original green upper background was overpainted with a copper blue. At the time of the fourteenth-century repairs, the damaged face was painted over with an orange-yellow, and the cracked area was roughly repaired and painted brown. In the course of conservation, it was necessary to repair the crack once again, and the areas of loss around it were toned down; the repaint on the head was cleaned away and the original lettering has been cleaned of the blue overpaint.

The titular inscription is neatly aligned on either side of the saint's halo; it is complete and unabbreviated. The saint is portrayed as an old man, and he stands stiffly upright with both body and head in the frontal aspect. His smooth, white hair recedes to the back of his head revealing the ears, and his short beard is neatly rounded under his chin. He raises his right arm in front of him, and the hand is in profile. In his left hand he steadies a closed book, with a richly decorated cover studded with jewels (Text Fig. 36.1a).

St. Nicholas wears the full episcopal regalia. His omophorion has a light grey ground with broad, white edges, and it is decorated with large, black crosses and small, black circles in the intervals between the crosses. It is looped over his left arm to fall in a vertical panel. The phelonion has a light red ground, red shadows, dark red and black fold lines, and thick, white highlights. This loose-flowing garment is caught up over both of his raised forearms, and it thus reveals the epigonation and the epimanikion. Both of these have yellow grounds with washes of white to simulate the sheen of gold, and they are decorated with linear patterns in dark red, and white pearls (Text Fig. 35a).

The vertical panel of the epitrachelion is revealed below the central folds of the phelonion, and it falls to ankle level. It has a yellow ground with a variety of patterns drawn on it in umber lines, and white pearls (Text Fig. 35a). His sticharion is much damaged and discolored. It was painted with a light umber ground color, and the folds and shadows appear to have been made with umber, dark grey, and black, with the highlighted areas in thick white. The hem of the sticharion folds back to reveal black slippers.

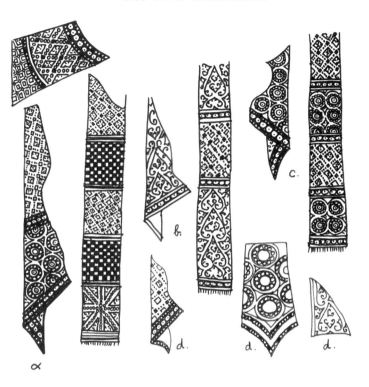

Text Fig. 35 The episcopal regalia worn by: a. St. Nicholas [71]; b. St. Lazaros [124]; c. St. Kyprianos [125]; and d. The bishops in the Koimesis [138]

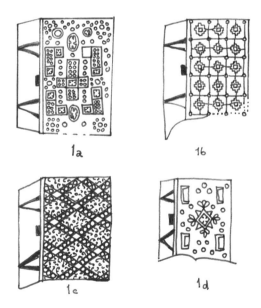

Text Fig. 36 Designs for the covers of books held by saints and bishops: 1a. St. Nicholas [71], a variation of the design for the book held by Christ in the dome [1]; 1b. St. Akepsimas [128]; St. Aithalas [134]; St. Hermolaos [146]; and on the throne in the Etoimasia [3]; 1c. The two bishops in the Koimesis [138]; 1d. St. Symeon Thaumaturgos [79]; and St. Lazaros [124]

Paintings of St. Nicholas are to be found in every Cypriot church. His face is always that of an old man, and his hair and beard style are similar to that of his earlier image in the apse (Fig. 23). In this particular painting, the slender figure carries a certain authority that is substantiated by the voluminous articulation of the phelonion.

The Holy Tile and the 1192 Donor Inscription [72] [73]

(Figs. 7 and 188)

The panel measures 117 cm in width and 58 cm in height, exclusive of the red borders. The painting represents an oblong ridged tile that is "imprinted" with the head of Christ, inscribed within a halo. Beneath the tile is the donor inscription for the 1192 series of paintings. (The donor inscription is discussed above, pp. 65–66.) There is some damage in this panel caused by the warping and moving of the wooden lintel of the door. The lower edge has flaked, and there is a diagonal crack down the center of Christ's head.

The lettering of the titular inscription is aligned vertically on either side of the tile (see Chapter Three). Within the tile the letters of the sigla IC XC are aligned horizontally on either side of the head of Christ. The lettering of the 1192 dedication was overpainted in the fourteenth century with broad brush line in thin, grey-white paint. In the course of conservation, this overpaint was removed to reveal the exact forms of the original inscription beneath.

Christ is represented as a young man, with smooth, flowing hair that is gathered over to the right of his head. The head is in the asymmetrical frontal aspect, with the wider side of the face and the widest width of the hair to the right side. His beard narrows downward to the base of his neck and divides into two loose curls under the chin. The edges of a brown robe can be seen on the side of his neck. Despite the youthfulness of Christ's face, his forehead is seared with the winged lines of age or, in this case, suffering. The ringlets of his beard compare ill with the "well-groomed" appearance of the beard of the majestic Christ [1] in the dome [Pl. 9, Fig. 42]. A similar contrast can be made between the dome Christ [1] and the Christ in the Mandylion [92] (Fig. 187).

The background of the tile has a blue ground, and all the inscriptions are in white lettering. The tile, which is ridged on its longer horizontal sides, has a yellow ground; thin, dark yellow shadow and thick, dark yellow outlines; but no black outlines. To each side of the halo the tile ends are decorated with two crossed diagonal lines in the form of dark yellow chevrons. Christ's halo has narrow black and white outlines and it extends over the upper ridge of the tile. The halo and neck of Christ do not overlap the lower ridge of the tile. The cross bars within the halo are white with a dark blue and grey shadow and a black outline to one side. Each bar has five round vermilion jewels, each outlined with a black line.

Despite the damage, this large disembodied head of Christ remains very impressive, and the stern impassive glance pursues the beholder wherever he stands. In most faces that are painted in

the asymmetrical frontal aspect, both the pupils are placed off-center so that the gaze is directed sideways across the wider plane of the face. In the head of Christ on this tile, the pupil in the smaller, rounded eye is off-center, and the pupil in the elongated eye in the wide side of the face is centered. It is this positioning of the pupils that creates the pursuing gaze.

The representation of the Holy Tile is complementary to the Mandylion, or holy handkerchief [92], in the center of the west face of the bema arch (Fig. 187).

St. Symeon and St. John the Forerunner [74, 75]

(Pl. 28; Figs. 133–136, 282)

Exclusive of the red borders, the panel measures 2.12 m in height. Across the top it measures 1.36 m in width, but narrows to a width of 1.23 m at the base. It contains the two standing figures of St. Symeon, holding the Christ child in his arms, and St. John the Forerunner.

The panel is traversed by a bad horizontal crack caused by the movement of the wooden lintel over the north door. This has created an area of damage across both the figures at waist level. The crack was repaired and toned in during the course of conservation. There is also the normal damage to be found in paintings on the ground register, resulting from the constant pressure of the congregation. Supplicants stuck lighted candles onto the images of their patrons, and the heat of the flame has turned yellow ochre into burnt-red ochre.

The figures stand on a green foreground that rises to one-third of the height of the panel. Unlike many of the other paintings in the ground register of the naos, the blue of the upper background to these figures is the original twelfth-century pigment, and not a later overpaint of copper blue. This upper background has a horizontal "interruption" line at a level some 39 cm above the line marking the meeting of the two background colors. The blue is darker and more intense above this "interruption" line than beneath it. It is possible that this change of color marks a staging level, as it lies some 170 cm above floor level and 1 m from the top of the panel. In the area between the figures, the green foreground was badly burned to an extent that suggests that at some time fires were lit in the naos. The plaster in the northeast corner of the naos contains an abnormally large quantity of straw, and the flames burned the surfaced particles, leaving quantities of holes. In the fourteenth century, the area was repaired with an indiscriminate overlay of a thin layer of lime plaster. This plaster layer was then colored in with green and with patches of yellow.

The titular inscription to St. Symeon is aligned horizontally above his halo, and the epithet is aligned vertically above his left shoulder. The sigla titling the Christ child are placed close together, to the left of his head, and are written in smaller characters than those for Symeon's title; the lettering is original (Pl. 28; Figs. 133, 134).

The image forms an abbreviated version of the Presentation of the Christ child to the Temple, with the tall figure of the holy Symeon standing alone, clutching to his bosom the sprawling figure of the Christ child. Symeon is represented as an old man with long, curling, white locks and a short

beard rippling to a point. His three-quarter-profile head is inclined steeply to the left as he enfolds the infant within his arms. His right forearm secures the child under his right arm, and his left hand catches the weight of the child under his right thigh. Symeon wears a chiton with black clavus under an ample himation.

The child sprawls across Symeon's chest, secure within the old man's uplifted arms. His head is in three-quarter profile, turning away to the left, and his face is characterized by a large, domed forehead and high, receding hair. The hair is smooth and curves around neatly to beneath his ear. His right arm dangles loosely downward while his left arm reaches forward as he clutches at the shoulder folds of Symeon's himation. Both his legs are bent at the knee; his right leg is hooked over Symeon's wrist while the other is kicking up and away. His right hand and his left foot were missing. They were shadowed in with a watery medium in the course of conservation and repair to the damaged panel.

Both figures have yellow haloes with black and white outlines, and both haloes were gilded at one time, although only a few traces of gold leaf now remain. The bars within the child's halo are white, shadowed with blue. Symeon's chiton has a light yellow ground, yellow and grey-green shadows, black lines and outlines, and fine, linear highlights painted in thick white. His himation has a yellow ground, grey shadows, and black lines and outlines. The child's tunic has a yellow ground with black lines. It was originally covered in chrysographia made with gold leaf, but this has almost entirely disappeared. The neckline is decorated with a thick, black line set between two narrow ones.

The child has the loose-limbed appearance of an Afghan puppy, and it is difficult to assess his proportions, in view of the informal pose. His halo has a diameter half the size of Symeon's halo. The measurements of parts of his figure are half those of the adult Symeon. The upper part of his head (top of head to level of upper rims of eyes) is larger than the lower part of his head (the level of the upper rims of his eyes to the base of his chin), in keeping with the natural proportions of the infant.

These two figures form a delightful composition that challenges the enigmatic nature of Byzantine images. St. Symeon envelops his precious burden with such protective tenderness, and the sprawling child within his arms, though large for his years, lacks the formal stiffness inherent in most Byzantine representations of the infant Christ. Only his head, with its solemn face, wide eyes, and sagacious, high forehead draws attention to the divine nature of the infant. The emotional content of these figures is thus implied in the Byzantine manner by the dramatic articulation of the figures. It is not suggested by the blank faces that remain totally enigmatic, with their features expressionless in repose.

Although the figure of St. John the Forerunner is contained within the same panel as that of St. Symeon, he belongs in the narrative sense to the Solicitation or Deesis composition placed at the entrance to the sanctuary, (see pp. 174, 221, 311–16; Figs. 135, 136) but the inscription upon his scroll also links him with Symeon and the Christ child.

The 1192 Decoration

The lettering of the abbreviated title of St. John is original, and it is aligned vertically on either side of his halo. His name is abbreviated to an iota and an omega and the letters of his title are also abbreviated. His scroll has seven lines of script, which are taken from the Gospel according to St. John 1:29 (Fig. 282).

In contrast to the bowing figures on either side of him, the tall, skinny figure of St. John stands very upright. He is seen in the frontal aspect, with his right arm flexed alongside his body with the hand raised vertically, palm forward (Text Fig. 14.1a). The two central fingers are bent toward the thumb, and both forefinger and little finger are upright. His left arm is foreshortened as he grips his unfurling scroll. In the crook of his left arm he steadies a tall stave with a short and a long horizontal bar at the top. His right leg is in the anterior aspect, and his left leg is turned outward. A loose cloth enfolds his skinny body, folding back to reveal his naked torso, right arm, and long, emaciated left leg. He goes barefoot, with no trace of sandals.

St. John is portrayed as a middle-aged man, with brown hair and beard styled in loose, curling locks. His head is similar to his image in the Anastasis [50]. His face is heavily lined, and it differs from that of the other mature saints in this series of paintings in that the cheeks have repetitive lines marking the contour of the cheekbones and the hollows beneath them. These lines emphasize the loosening skin and gauntness that come of prolonged fasting. His eyes gaze across the wider side of his face toward the east. St. John's thin body is further distinguished by the ruddy color of the skin, which is covered with neat, horizontal rows of linear tufts of hair. These attributes serve to emphasize the harshness of life in the wilderness. The two other ascetic saints in the paintings of 1192, St. Onuphrios [81] and St. Mary of Egypt [150], are both given similar characteristics. St. John's cross is yellow with no outlines, and his body cloth has a yellow ground, grey-green shadows, and black lines and outlines.

St. John's very slender body contrasts strongly with his large, tousled head. The bared chest reveals some interesting anatomical feature lines. Two curved lines mark the base of the breast. The center of these lines, which indicates the pit of the stomach, is very high; in nature, the pit of the stomach or top of the sternum lies one head length from the base of the chin. In this figure the breast measurement is equal to only three quarters of the head length, or one face measurement. This very high breast line is characteristic of the proportional ratios used by the 1192 painter (see below, pp. 284–86). As a consequence, figures with waist sashes, such as the prophet Daniel [23] or Zacharias in the Presentation to the Temple [70], appear to have very high waists.

The Reveals of the North Door [76, 77]
The Reveals of the South Door [152, 153]

(Figs. 141–144, 262, 263; Text Figs. 3, 4, 8)

Each reveal is decorated with a panel containing a cross, with inscriptions above a smaller square panel with a marble dado pattern [53]. The upper panels measure an average 124 cm in height by 67 cm in width, inclusive of the red border. They are divided into a white, upper background and a green, lower foreground. The green foreground occupies a little less than one-third of the total height of the panel. Each panel contains a large, two-armed cross with a foot bar, and a small, green wreath encircles the crossing of the upper bars.

The upper background has a number of abbreviated inscriptions above the central horizontal bar, and below it, each panel has a long horizontal inscription set between double lines. All the inscriptions are in black lettering, and the double lines above and below the long inscription are in yellow. In addition, the west jamb of the north door contains a number of incised graffiti of medieval date within the white background.[103] The green foreground is furnished with wavy clumps of black-bladed grass. The four panels are much damaged due to the movement of the wooden lintel above, the constant friction of people coming and going, and the swinging of the doors back and forth.

Each cross appears as a vertical pole averaging 100 cm in height, with three shorter poles laid across it horizontally. The upper bar is about 20 cm in width, and in each case it lies some 12 cm from the top of the cross. The central bar is about 50 cm in width and lies an average of 50 cm from the lowest bar; the lower bar, which is diagonal, measures some 14 cm in width and lies about 10 cm from the base of the cross. The bars themselves are 3 to 5 cm thick. They all have rounded ends, except for the lowest bars, which have squared ends. The wood of the crosses has a light umber ground, red down the center, and black shadow to one side and beneath.

---

[103] A particular graffito is discussed on p. 51 above and is illustrated on p. 50 (Text Fig. 8).

12

THE BEMA

The Sanctuary Vault

(Pls. 26, 27, 29; Figs. 145–162)

The Ascension of Christ [78]

From north to south, the panel measures 5.86 m in length; from east to west, the width of the vault averages 1.74 m. The central section, north to south, from plaster join to plaster join, measures 1.96 m; and the north and south sections, exclusive of the red border, measure 1.87 and 1.84 m, respectively.

The scene occupies the whole of the sanctuary vault. The composition is divided into three parts. The figure of Christ sits at the center of the vault with his head to the west, within a mandorla of concentric circles supported by four angels; on the north side of the vault, a central archangel stands quietly amid six apostles straining and peering upward; on the south side of the vault, six further apostles surround the central figure of the Mother of God, who is standing upon a footstool.

The vault was plastered in three separate sections, each of which corresponds to one part of the composition. The two transverse plaster joins separating the three sections run from east to west on either side of the central composition. The joins are well worked over, and they are partly concealed by the textual inscriptions that are written over them. The framing plaster joins for the whole panel are at the outer edge of the red borders running around the edges of the vault. Within some haloes, thin plaster patches were inserted prior to the completion of the heads. However, in most cases the flesh areas of the face and neck, like those of the hands, the bare arms, and the feet, were simply reworked prior to the laying-in of the final flesh colors. The only incised guidelines are in the north section, and they were used to mark the separation and overlap of figures. Apart from general surface damage, two cracks run through the vault, one to the right of Christ and one to the right of the figure of the Mother of God. On the south side, some heads have flaked badly,

and there are many discolored patches. The only overpaint was found on the south side, where the fourteenth-century repainter daubed blue on one figure.

The background within this scene is very simple. In the central section, it is divided equally into a blue upper ground and a lower green (eastern) foreground. The background of the north and south sections of the panel is divided vertically into a green eastern side and a blue western side. In both these sections, the green foreground received a second coat of green to darken and distinguish it from the green of the upper background. The vertical divisions of the upper background into blue and green, which continue the green and blue divisions of the central section, are unusual for an Ascension scene in a vault. It is more common to find an overall blue background to the central panels that would be extended to form the upper background for the apostles on either side. It is likely that the painter, already short on his supply of blue, was seeking to economize in the extensive use of it, rather than wishing to break with traditional background color schemes.

The Inscriptions

All the lettering used in this scene is white and belongs to the 1192 period of painting. The titular inscription is placed at the central western edge of the panel, and it is separated into two parts by the meeting of the wing tips of the angels above Christ's halo (Pl. 26; Fig. 145). The letters for this inscription are smaller than those of the other inscriptions within the panel, because of the small amount of background space within the triangle formed by the angels' haloes and wings and the upper red border.

Two long, textual inscriptions run transversely, from west to east and from east to west, respectively, above the north and south sections of the panel. These single line inscriptions are written along the plaster joins separating these sections from the central composition, and the joins clearly served as a guideline for setting out the letters. The inscriptions are the traditional ones for this scene and are taken from the Acts of the Apostles 1:11. Both lines are preceded by a cross. The first part of the quotation runs above the northern section: "Ye men of Galilee, why stand ye looking up into Heaven?" The painter ran into trouble with his spelling and had to insert two missing taus above the written line to remedy his mistakes, one to replace a tau missing in βλέποντες and the other to stand as an abbreviation for the missing τὸν. There remains sufficient space to the right of the inscription to render deliberate abbreviation unnecessary (Pls. 26, 27; Figs. 145, 146).

The second part of the quotation runs above the southern section of the panel but is crammed into the western side of it to avoid overlapping the wing of the southwest supporting angel: "This same Jesus who is taken up from you into Heaven." The end words of this line run downhill, and the last two words are abbreviated, but the lettering remains both elegant and legible (Pls. 26, 27).

The remaining three inscriptions are titular abbreviations. The sigla $\overline{\text{IC}}$ $\overline{\text{XC}}$ are placed on either side of Christ's halo on the light blue band within the mandorla, and they appear rather

askew in relation to the horizontal bars of his halo. On the north side of the panel, above the angel's halo, are written the abbreviated words: "The angel of the Lord." On the south side of the panel, the title "Mother of God" appears in abbreviated form above Mary's halo.

The Central Section (Pl. 26; Figs. 145, 147–150)

The mandorla, with its five concentric circles, is placed at the center of the vault, with the seated figure of Christ at the center of the main circle. Four angels swing out from behind the mandorla, each with one arm outstretched to grip its edge.

Christ appears to sit upon two linear arcs that run from north to south within the mandorla; the upper arc is tangent to the centerpoint of the mandorla circles. His feet rest upon two smaller linear arcs at the eastern edge of the mandorla. Christ's slender figure is shown in the frontal aspect and in a seated stance with the left leg correctly foreshortened and with the right leg and foot extending downward in profile. His two arms form an S-curve as his right arm is extended upward and outward, with the hand poised in the gesture of blessing, while his left arm is extended downward and outward. His left forearm is foreshortened and the hand steadies the top of his tightly furled scroll, the base of which rests upon his left knee.

Christ is portrayed as a young man, with smooth, flowing, long hair gathered to the right of his face, which is frontal and asymmetrical. His short beard divides into two curls below the chin. He wears a chiton with a black clavus over an undergarment of which only one narrow sleeve with decorated cuff is visible. His ample himation entwines him in swirling folds, and one hem flies off his arm in windswept folds. His feet are shod in delicately corded sandals.

The center of the mandorla has a blue ground, and the surrounding concentric bands are painted with increasingly lighter tones of blue ending in white. The linear arcs suggesting Christ's "throne" and "footstool" are in vermilion. Christ's yellow halo has white bars shadowed with blue and decorated with five vermilion gems. His chiton and undertunic have a red ground, black lines and outlines, and broad blue wash highlights. The cuff is decorated with pattern 1a (Text Fig. 24). His himation has a yellow ground, red and umber fold lines, white wash highlights over which is applied a further wash in blue, and thick, white highlights. The scroll has a red ground, dark red shadow, and white highlights; the binding cords are vermilion with black outlines.

At an intermediate stage, the painter decided that Christ's halo was extended too far over to the right and he corrected this before he completed the final halo outlines. At a final stage in his work, he created an "aperture" to the right of Christ's groin, by painting in a blue area to separate the scroll from the himation folds across the lower abdomen and arm.

The two western angels curve inward toward Christ. Their outer arms are extended downward with the hands as if resting on the outer rim of the mandorla that conceals their lower limbs and their inner arms. The two eastern angels arch their bodies upward and outward. Their outer arms are flung backward over their heads, with the hands in a position to grip the edge of the mandorla rim below the level of Christ's feet. Their heads and torsos are turned outward in three-quarter profile, but their legs are joined together in profile. They bend backward at the knee so

that the feet, like the inner arms of the figures, are concealed behind the mandorla. All four angels have haloes, and all the heads are seen in three-quarter profile. The bulky, wiglike hairstyles are relieved by a wispy, white fillet with a central jewel. Their faces are unlined, like those of young men. Their wings are all poised in a similar manner. The outer wings swoop down behind their backs, and the long, feathered wing tips of the inner wings can be seen at the eastern and western edges of the mandorla. Each angel wears a himation over a chiton with a black clavus, but the western angels also reveal the narrow sleeve and decorated cuff of an undergarment.

The northwest and southwest angels have garments painted in similar colors. Their chitons and undertunics have a red ground, black lines and outlines, and light blue wash highlights. The cuff of the undergarments is yellow, and it is decorated with pattern 1a (Text Fig. 24). Their himations have a yellow ground, red shadows, black lines and outlines, white wash highlights washed over with blue, and thick, white, linear highlights.

The northeast angel wears a chiton with a grey ground that was applied over a yellow base, dark grey shadows, and black lines and outlines. His himation has a yellow ground, red shadows, black lines and outlines, blue wash highlights, and thick, white, linear highlights.

The southeast angel wears a chiton with a light red ground, red shadows, black lines and outlines, blue wash highlights, and thick, white highlights. His himation has a light green ground that was applied over a yellow base, umber shadows, black lines and outlines, blue wash highlights, and thick, white highlights.

The angels' wings are built up in a manner similar to that used for the wings of the angels elsewhere in the 1192 decoration (see p. 125). The covert feathers of the downward sweeping wings of the western angels are graded in tones of yellow, and those of the eastern angels in tones of vermilion.

The Northern Section (Pls. 29; Figs. 146, 151–154, 162)

The central archangel stands upright in the frontal aspect, while to either side of him are two full-length figures of apostles leaning backwards. The head of a third figure may be seen beyond them on each side. All six apostles tilt their heads backward as they gaze upward. The foremost apostles raise one arm over their heads to shield their eyes from the brilliance of the vision.

The archangel dominates this northern section of the Ascension, and his figure is constructed to a larger scale than that of the apostles surrounding him. He stands raising his right arm upward, with his hand pointing to the inscription and to the ascending Christ above. His left arm curves downward, steadying his narrow stave of office. His right leg appears to be jutting forward to emphasize the forward gesture of his right arm, but his booted feet point downward on a level with each other.

The angel's head is painted in the asymmetrical frontal aspect. The pupil of the larger eye is centered so that the angel has a compelling gaze that pursues the viewer from every angle. The clustered curls of his hair form a rounded mass around his head, wider to the wide side of his face, and narrowing to a small cluster of curls above chin level. A single earlobe is visible on the wider

side of the head. A narrow, white fillet is threaded through his hair with the knotted, wispy ends floating to either side of the head. The band has a central jewel picked out with pearls. This archangel and the archangel Michael [140] are the only two angels to show their heads in the frontal asymmetrical aspect in the whole 1192 decoration. All the other angels are seen in three-quarter profile.

The archangel wears a tunic with a bejeweled hem and a black clavus over an undergarment with fitted sleeves and plain cuffs. Over these he wears a himation with rippling folds, and his feet are clad in boots similar to those in Pl. 10. His tunic and undergarment have a red ground, umber shadows, black lines and outlines, and broad, light blue wash highlights. The cuffs are plain yellow with black lines, and the decorated hem pattern of the tunic is similar to that of the prophets David [35] and Solomon [17] in the drum of the cupola (Pl. 10e; Figs. 61, 69). The archangel's himation has a light yellow-green ground, dark yellow-green shadows, umber fold lines, black lines and outlines, blue wash highlights, and thick, white, linear highlights. His boots are red with black lines and white pearls, and his stave is red with a white finial topped with white drop pearls.

One of the archangel's wings is painted against the blue background and the other against the green upper background. The color buildup for the body of his wings differs from that used for the other angels in this decoration, presumably because of the parti-colored background. The scapular or body of his wings has a yellow ground with blue inner outlines and black outer outlines. The wings' feathers are built up, one over the other, in decreasing lengths of feather and with graded colors. The longest outer feathers are black, then come red ones, then, in shortening lengths, the feathers succeed each other in vermilion, vermilion plus white, pink, light pink, thin white, thick white, and finally a row of short, stubby, black feathers at the base of the scapular. From the vermilion feathers downward, each feather has a blob of lighter color on each tip. Most angels' wings in this series of paintings have long, inner feathers in black, but in the case of this archangel, they were blocked out of the design at an early stage in the painting of the figure, probably to enlarge the distance between the figure and the wing.

A vertical incision line marks the left edge of the angel's raised forearm where it overlaps Peter's elbow, and where both limbs overlap the top of the angel's wing. The incision was necessary as a guide at this point, where there was a tricky series of overlaps that might well have been misinterpreted in the course of painting.

St. Peter, to the west of the archangel, has the head of an old man seen in the three-quarter-profile aspect. He has short hair clustered into tight, white curls, and a short, neatly rounded beard in the manner traditionally used to depict St. Peter, as can be seen in the painting of him on the south wall of the naos [143]. The apostle in the Ascension stands upright with his body arching backward and his head almost horizontal to his neck. His left arm curves upward and forward, with the forearm arching back toward his head. He shields his eyes from the light of the mandorla with outspread hand. His right arm curves downward to grip the loose folds of his himation. His robust right leg curves backward with the foot extended downward in the frontal position. The receded

left leg is in quiet profile, arresting the forward movement of the figure and carrying the onlooker's eye vertically upward.

His chiton has a light blue ground, blue shadows, and black lines and outlines. The clavus is black. His himation has a yellow ground, grey shadows, dark grey fold lines, black lines and outlines, and white, linear highlights washed over with blue.

The apostle behind Peter has a damaged head and is partly concealed behind the bulky mass of Peter. His three-quarter-profile figure is squeezed between Peter and the western red border. His right arm is raised up, but the forearm and hand are concealed behind Peter's halo. He appears as if advancing toward the center with his right leg forward, and the ankle and heel are awkwardly concealed behind Peter's substantial right foot.

The apostle's head was completed on a thin plaster patch. The paint layers have largely flaked off, but the head appears to represent a young man with short, curly hair and the beginnings of a curly beard. His chiton has a light red ground, red shadows, black lines and outlines, and light blue highlights. His himation has a light green ground, dark green shadows, black lines and fold lines, and light blue highlights.

The apostle to the rear on the west side can be glimpsed between the two apostles in front of him. Only the head, neck, and part of the halo of this beardless, young apostle can be seen. His face is in three-quarter profile, and his smooth, light brown hair sweeps down behind his ear. The upper layers of paint in his hair and across his lower brow are badly flaked. His chiton is visible at the neckline, and it has a red ground, black lines and outlines, and broad blue highlights. His himation, a short section of which can be seen between the two overlapping figures in front of him, has a yellow ground, red shadows, blue lines, and white highlights.

The apostle to the east of the archangel has the head of an old man with receding, white hair and a pointed beard neatly contouring the chin. The stance of his three-quarter profile figure echoes that of St. Peter as both bodies arch backward, and their movement is reinforced by giving prominence to the diagonal of the outer leg. His chiton has a light red ground, dark red shadows, black lines and outlines, white wash, and thick, white highlights. His himation has a light grey ground, dark grey shadows, black lines and outlines, white wash, and thick, white highlights. The top of his left shoulder and the outlines of the left arm are incised in order to mark him out clearly from the figures behind him.

St. Andrew, the easternmost apostle, has the three-quarter-profile head of an old man, with the long, white, tousled locks of hair and the white, straggly, pointed beard associated with portraits of this saint. His body is squeezed in behind the previous apostle and partly concealed by him and by the eastern red border. To counteract this awkward effect, the body is given added breadth and substance by the bulky articulation of his himation. His chiton has a light green ground, green shadows, black lines and outlines, white wash, and thick, white highlights. His himation has a yellow-brown ground, light red shadows, black lines and outlines, white wash, and thick, white highlights.

The 1192 Decoration

The eastern apostle, to the rear, is mainly concealed by the two figures in front of him. He has the three-quarter-profile face of a young man, with smooth, light brown hair and an incipient mustache and beard. His chiton has a red ground, umber shadows, black lines and outlines, and broad blue wash highlights. His himation has a light red ground, red shadows, black lines, white wash, and thick, white, linear highlights.

The Southern Section (Pl. 27; Figs. 155–161)

The still figure of the Mother of God stands upon a footstool at the center. To either side of her, three apostles cavort in upward, surging movement. The stance of these six apostles is very similar to that of their six colleagues on the north side.

The Mother of God is seen in the frontal aspect. Her figure is constructed on a larger scale than that used for the apostles, and she dominates them by her height and by her quiet, contained stance and flat garment folds. Her arms are held close to her body, the forearms slanting upward and inward, the hands palm-outward over her chest. Her stiff vertical stance is broken by the slight forward flexing of her left leg. She wears a close-fitting wimple under a maphorion with segmenta that encircles her head. It falls from her shoulders in ample folds, and its hem is decorated with double yellow lines. Her tunic has narrow, fitted sleeves with decorative bands near the wrists. The tips of her slippers appear below the hem of her tunic.

Her wimple is light blue, and her maphorion has a red ground, dark red shadows, black lines and outlines, and broad, thick washes of blue. The segmenta, the decorative bands on the hem and the cuffs, are yellow, and they are picked out with blobs of light yellow. Her tunic is blue with grey shadows, dark grey fold lines, and black lines and outlines. Her slippers are vermilion. Her footstool has narrow jeweled edges that are visible on three sides. It has a yellow top with a single decorative black line. The jeweled borders are black with a yellow lattice pattern filled with double rows of pearls alternating with a green or red jewel. The pattern is similar to the one used for decorating the edges of loroi (Pl. 11).

The foremost eastern apostle has a bald head that is in three-quarter profile, and his face is that of an old man. A soft tuft of white hair crowns his bald pate, and three tight curls pile up above his ear. His long, white beard comes to a point beneath the neatly outlined chin. The head is tilted backward and joined unnaturally to the upright neck. He raises his left arm over his head, with his hand to his forehead, the fingers curling inward. His right arm curves downward, with the hand gripping the loose folds of his himation. His right leg and foot extend backward and as if outward into the real space of the church. His left leg is vertical and in profile, and the toes of the foot overlap the corner of Mary's footstool, extending the illusion that this apostle exists in front of the picture space. There is a strong impression of forward and upward movement generated by the position of his right leg, and this is echoed in the swirling bell folds of the hem of his tunic and the whorling folds over his abdomen.

His chiton has a light red ground, red shadows, umber and black lines, black outlines, and white highlights. His himation has a light umber ground, umber shadows, and dark umber fold

lines; black lines and outlines; and white, linear highlights washed with green.

The easternmost apostle is squeezed in behind his neighbor, who partially conceals his upper right arm and the inner side of his torso. He has smooth, brown hair drawn to the back of his head and a short, rounded, brown beard. Both are striated with blue linear highlights to suggest middle age. His right leg extends backward, echoing the stance of the figure in front of him, but most of this leg is curtailed by the red border behind him.

His chiton has a light red ground, red shadows, dark red fold lines, black lines and outlines, white wash, and thick, white highlights. His himation has a light green ground, green shadows, black lines and outlines, white wash, and thick, white, linear highlights.

The eastern apostle to the rear is only partially visible. Only his halo and his head and neck can be seen above the haloes of the two figures in front of him. A small portion of one of his garments is also visible, between the two lower figures. His head is tilted backward, and it is that of a middle-aged man. His smooth hair and short beard are brown, but his forehead is heavily lined. The visible portion of his garment has a yellow ground, light red shadows, and umber and black lines.

The foremost apostle on the west side, a middle-aged apostle, has a long, pointed, brown beard and a bald pate with a single wisp of hair upon it and a few strands over his ear. He stands upright in three-quarter profile. His left leg appears to stride firmly forward and outward, with the toes of his foot overlapping the corner of Mary's footstool. His inner right leg reaches backward on tiptoe. His head is tilted backward, almost to the horizontal, as he gazes up at the ascending Christ. His right arm is raised upward and bends backward as he shields his eyes with outstretched hand. His left arm descends in a reverse curve, the forearm foreshortened, as he grips the loose folds of his himation. Although his torso is vertical, it appears to lean backward due to the diagonal slant of the ovoid folds of his himation across his abdomen. This effect is reinforced by the diagonal of the shoulders and the almost horizontal tilt of the head.

His chiton has a light red ground, red shadows, black lines and outlines, and light grey highlights. His himation has a grey ground, dark grey shadows, very dark grey fold lines, black lines and outlines, and light grey highlights. Parts of the surface of this figure have suffered from flaking, and the abdominal region was touched up with blue paint in the fourteenth century to conceal this damage. This overpaint was removed in the course of conservation.

The westernmost apostle has the heavily lined face of an old man, with a wisp of hair on the top of his bald pate and a vestige of hair over his ear. His short beard is rounded, and it neatly contours the chin. Both hair and beard are brown and heavily highlighted with blue striations. His stance is similar to that of the easternmost apostle, but the articulation of his garments and their color are different.

His chiton has a light green ground, dark green shadows, black lines and outlines, and white highlights. His himation has a bright yellow ground, light red shadows, black lines and outlines, white wash, and thick, white highlights.

The western apostle to the rear has the face of a young man. Only the head and neck can be seen; he is beardless and his smooth hair falls off his high forehead to bunch behind his ear. Part of what is probably his himation appears between the two apostles in front of him, and this has a yellow-green ground, green shadows, black lines and outlines, white wash, and thick, white highlights.

The Ascension keeps to well-established iconographic tradition. The omission of rocks and trees is probably due to the architectural limitation of the bema vault which, at Lagoudhera, is very narrow in relation to its length. In omitting the backdrop of traditional scenery, the painter was freer to negotiate both the size and the placing of his figures.

Each of the three sections of the composition approximates to a square, which is not the easiest space in which to organize a narrative figural composition. The great circle of the mandorla fits well into the central square, leaving four corners in which to fit the supporting angels. Christ's figure is bisected by the east-west diameter of the circle, and the upper arc marking his seat is tangent to the centerpoint of the circle. The slender, but imposing, figure of Christ, with its luminous pink and yellow garment hues, asserts a quiet authority as he looms forward out of the receding blues of the mandorla circles. The angels surge dynamically from behind the mandorla, and the arched and contorted bodies and the furling wings impart a sense of contained power and gyrating movement. The painter has partly concealed the angels' bodies, and the effect of this is to strengthen the emphasis on the figure of Christ as he appears to project forward into the church itself. The general effect of composition and color imparts an impression of whirling and receding movement that is dominated by the serene and masterful figure of Christ, whose himation hem alone is stirred by the heavenly wind.

The north and south sections of the panel are far too narrow to permit the frontal alignment of three apostles on either side of the Mother of God and the archangel. The painter overcame this difficulty by grouping the apostles closely together in order to leave a suitably large space for the dignity of the central characters. A generous margin is left above and below the figures, but the red borders to the sides crowd in on the figures nearest to them. The central figures, Mary and the archangel, are both bisected by a notional line bisecting the vault, but in the case of Mary, this bisecting line does not correspond to the dividing line between the green and the blue of the upper background.

The figures of Christ, Mary, and the archangel are constructed to the same proportional constants as those of the apostles and the angels, but they are larger in scale, in a ratio of 6:5. This increase in their size and the generous width of space left on either side of them isolate Mary and the archangel from the jostling apostles. In each of the four groups of apostles, the bodies of the three figures overlap each other, providing an illusion of recession and depth. The foremost, thrusting apostle of each group either overlaps or underlaps some part of the central figure, with shoulder over wing, with arm under arm, or with foot over footstool. This skillful interweaving of the spatial relationships between the elements of the composition reinforces the illusion that the apostles

are bunching together beneath the vault and exist within the real space of the church. With the absence of confining background detail, the carefully thought-out overlaps give to each group an encircling depth, so that they appear to enfold the central figure within the group. This is perhaps an echo of the compositional scheme for the Ascension when it was painted in a dome. It may be for this same reason that the central mandorla is round, and not in the form of an ellipse.

The archangel's static frontal stance, his downward sweeping wings, and firmly planted feet give him a dignified predominance over the arching and writhing apostles with their agitated robes. In the same manner, Mary's composed and contained figure contrasts with the surging apostles to either side of her.

All the stylistic characteristics of the 1192 master painter are present in this painting of the Ascension. Although often delicate in color and line, it attains great forcefulness through the use of striking contrast between swirling and straight lines, dynamic movement and static serenity, agitated and flat garment folds, and the use of cold and warm hues.

There are further hints in this painting of the hand of a second painter of ability working alongside the master painter. It is the presence of an apprentice, himself nearing the status of an independent master painter, that is so tantalizing (see above, p. 128; below, pp. 317–18). One peculiarity that suggests a different hand is the shaping of the eyes, which are in some cases more oval than elongated, and have heavier outlines. This was a peculiarity noted in some of the angels in the dome (for example, angel [11] (Fig. 54) as opposed to the other angels). The difference between the heads of the eastern angels (Figs. 149, 150) supporting the mandorla and most of the apostles versus the heads of Christ and of the western angels (Figs. 147, 148) in the Ascension forms a similar contrast. In the case of the Ascension, this characteristic could, of course, be explained not as the work of a different painter, but simply as the master painter's method of portraying wide-open eyes expressing amazement and wonder at the sight of Christ.

Another indication of a difference lies in the taste and emphasis in the overall color schemes. Grey is more frequently used as a color for garments in the Ascension than elsewhere in the church. In two of the figures in particular, the foremost apostle on the northeast side and the foremost apostle on the southwest side, the use of strong recessing darks to the rear of the figure are more pronounced than in other scenes. The color differences could be attributed to the fact that this was among the last paintings to be made in the 1192 series of paintings, and that the painter was running short of some pigments. But even if this is taken into account, there is still a difference in the feel of the color scheme. There are enough of these divergences to suggest that there was a second painter at work alongside the master on this scene.

The Walls of the Bema

The north and south sides of the sanctuary are similar, except that the north wall has a niche and the south wall does not. The layout and iconography of the painted panels are similarly bal-

anced, and the choice of saints is echoed between them. There are poets and hymnwriters in roundels, medallions with crosses, Passion crosses in niches, stylite saints on tall columns on the piers, bishops in opposing blind arches, and deacons on the east reveals with their swinging censers. Only the anchorite on the north-west reveal is discordant with St. Lazaros on the south-west reveal. This harmonious exchange is linked by the bema arch with the mandylion at its center.

The dadoes and niches were all plastered separately. The rest of the north and south bays were each plastered in three sections, with the plaster joins running along the edges of the red borders. The faces of the pier and the spandrels beyond it were each plastered in one section, the reveals and soffits of the blind arches are each one section, and the north and south walls of the bays are each one section. The edges of the plaster of the north and south pier fall deliberately short of the western edge. A narrow area was here left free of plaster to allow for the original Communion rail or templon. The present iconostasis dates from the seventeenth century.

There are no traces of incised or impressed lines in the plaster, and no fresh plaster patches were made for the heads of figures. There is general evidence that the flesh areas of head, neck, and hands were reworked before the final layers of paint were applied.

At the top of both the north and south walls, a long, wooden beam runs from west to east at the base of the vault. Movement in the wood has caused the plaster to fall away along the level of the red border marking the divide between the Ascension and the painting beneath it. At some period, a brick stove was built against the wall below the niche of the prothesis. In the course of conservation, this was removed to reveal the 1192 dadoes behind it.

The lettering of all the inscriptions is in the original 1192 script. The background of the roundels and figures is green; the foreground of the standing figures was given a second layer of green paint to differentiate it from the upper ground.

The North Wall [79–80]

The pier face and the spandrel above the north bay were plastered in one section with the exception of the dado. To the west appears St. Symeon Thaumaturgos on his column [79], and a roundel with St. Joseph the Poet occupies the spandrel to the east.

St. Symeon Thaumaturgos [79] (Fig. 165)

Symeon Stylites the Younger is placed appropriately on the south face of the northeast pier. The panel occupies approximately 192 cm in height, and at its narrowest, it measures 24 cm, exclusive of all red borders.

The waist-length figure is encaged behind a grille and placed on a broad capital over a long, slender column. The figure and inscription take up the broad area of the west spandrel, while both capital and column occupy the narrow length of the pier.

The Bema

The saint's inscription is placed on either side of his halo. Only a part of his name survives on the left, as the panel was damaged when the support beam of the seventeenth-century iconostasis was inserted into the wall at this point. The ἅγιος is abbreviated. The epithet remains undamaged in four lines to the right of the halo.

The saint is portrayed as an old man with a neatly rounded beard. His white hair is mostly concealed beneath his pointed black cowl, which adds both height and emphasis to his head. Both his head and torso are seen in the frontal aspect, and the face is asymmetrical in relation to the nose. His figure is tightly enfolded within his somber overrobe. His damaged right hand is raised against his chest, and he carries a closed book with a jeweled cover in the crook of his left arm. The lattice of white "ironwork," which encloses the figure to shoulder level, is picked out with decorative spikes. The upper bar to this railing is continued at a sharp diagonal on either side of the waist-length figure, thus enclosing it. The capital itself has a stylized leafy center that is sandwiched between two horizontal blocks representing cushion and abacus. The shaft of the column and the cushion and abacus are painted to look like marble.

The saint's cowl has a black ground. It is decorated with a broad linear pattern in white, the design of which is shown schematically without regard to the folds and convolutions of the cowl that it decorates. Three bands of pattern are placed to the top and sides of his face, as if forming the three arms of a cross, and a further band decorates the loose edge of the cloth. Each band consists of three rows of alternating crosses between two sets of parallel lines. The cowl also features single crosses in the space between the bands.

Symeon's somber overgarment has a yellow ground applied over a grey base, blue shadows, black lines, and yellow highlights. His book has vermilion page ends and a black lock, and the page ends are bound with black ties. The cover has a yellow ground, and it is decorated with a complicated linear pattern in umber that is picked out with green and vermilion gems and white pearls (Text Fig. 36.1d).

The column and the abacus and cushion of the capital have a light red ground, red shadows, dark red "veining," and black lines and "ties," the latter suggesting the joining of marble slabs. The dentils on the cornice of the capital are picked out with white to suggest relief. The central part of the capital has a yellow ground with the foliage drawn in red lines and picked out with pearls along the edges. The interstices are dark brown.

The painter clearly made deliberate use of an actual pier to give added emphasis to Symeon's column. It is long and thin and fits well on the pier. The wider area of the spandrel gives enough space for the figure with its halo and inscription. In a late adjustment, the painter enlarged the diameter of the halo to measure seven nose lengths rather than the standard six nose lengths, presumably because of the increased size of the head with its high pointed cowl. The center of the halo lies half a nose length above the inner corner of the right eye and not, as is customary, on the eyeline. The improbable relationship between the size of the figure and the column that he occupies was an established convention of Byzantine painting. It successfully conveys the importance of

the image without resorting to a realistic approach, which would have demanded a massive column and a minuscule figure.

St. Joseph the Poet or Hymnwriter [80] (Fig. 163)

The waist-length figure of the monk is in a roundel in the east spandrel. The roundel itself overlaps the red borders around it, and it is cut away by the arch of the bay below it. The roundel has a diameter of 44 cm. It appears very cramped in this small space, and there was no room for a wide yellow border similar to that of other roundels, but it is the roundel that suffers and not the image of the saint. His halo outlines surmount the roundel outlines, and this gives the illusion of projecting him forward into the real space of the church.

The titular inscription is placed outside the roundel, to the left above the arch. The epithet is abbreviated, and the saint's name and profession are written on two lines in well-spaced white letters. The saint's scroll is curtailed by the arc of the roundel, and it contains six lines of black lettering.[104]

The saint is portrayed as a middle-aged man with a lined face and a bushy, neatly rounded, brown beard highlighted with fine, white lines. His head is bound with a turban of black cloth, with a design in white line of crosses between parallel lines, similar to the pattern on the cowl worn by his neighbor, St. Symeon [79]. St. Joseph turns his head and body eastward in three-quarter profile, and the fingertips of his left hand overlap the top of his unfurling scroll.

The double outlines of both roundel and halo are black and white, and the interior of the roundel has a vermilion ground that enhances the black lines of the somber figure within. His enveloping outer garment has a dark grey ground, black lines and outlines, and yellow highlights. His scroll is white, with pale green shadows and script bands.

The North Arch [81–83]

The reveals contain the standing figures of St. Onuphrios [81], to the west and St. Stephen the Protomartyr [83], to the east. A roundel with a cross [82] occupies the soffit. There are no horizontal red borders separating the elements in this panel, which was plastered as a single section. The dadoes and the prothesis niche were plastered separately. The figures and the roundel were painted against a green background that was reinforced with further green at the lower end of the figures.

St. Onuphrios [81] (Figs. 167, 184)

The width of the reveal averages 63 cm, and from the eastern border to the apex of the arch is 79 cm, excluding the red borders. The gaunt, nude figure of the ascetic occupies the west reveal

---

[104] See Nicolaïdes, "Panagia Arakiotissa," scroll of St. Joseph the Hymnwriter [80], pp. 33–34.

and a part of the soffit. His inscription is placed in vertical alignment on either side of his halo.

The saint is portrayed as an old man with smooth, flowing, white hair and beard; two long locks of hair fall down over his back, and his long mustache and beard neatly outline the chin before falling to a tapering point above his middle. The saint stands upright in the three-quarter-profile aspect as he turns toward the center of the bema. He stands with his legs together and with his feet spread apart, one above the other. His arms are flexed at the elbow, and with both hands he reaches forward to receive a small flat bread that is proffered to him by a hand extending out from Heaven. Heaven is indicated by a vertical arc aligned against the red border above him. His high-breasted, thin figure is covered in regular horizontal rows of black linear Y-shapes indicating the hairiness of the anchorite. The "powder puff" foliage of a tree conveniently conceals his middle.

The arc of Heaven and the bread have a light umber ground, white wash, and thick, white highlights. The cuff of the hand is decorated with cuff pattern 1a (Text Fig. 24). The tree trunk has a light umber ground, deep umber shadow, and a thick black outline to the right. The "puff" of foliage is made up of needlelike strokes of paint overlapping each other, with tones of light red overlapped by strokes in thin and thick white at the center and black strokes at the outer edge. The saint's bare skin is painted with a ruddy yellow ground, green contour shadows, and dark umber lines and outlines. The tufts or twists of hair are painted in dark umber line.

The long, slender figure of this saint, with its soft curves, has a certain dignity. The nude body is particularly interesting, as it confirms the Lagoudhera master's short measurement for the chest; this is the distance lying between the base of the chin and the top of the sternum or the base of the breast muscles.[105]

The Roundel with an Inscribed Cross [82] (Fig. 175)

The roundel is set at the top of the soffit of the arch against the overall green background. It has a yellow border outlined with black lines, and the background within it is vermilion. The cross in the center has two horizontal arms and a diagonal foot bar, and there are inscriptions on either side of it. The roundel has a diameter of 50 cm and the border has a width of 4 cm. The bars of the cross average 2.5 cm in width. The upper horizontal bar measures 11 cm in length, the middle bar 26 cm, and the lowest bar 8.5 cm.

To either side of the upper bar are the sigla abbreviations $\overline{IC}$ $\overline{XC}$, and below the middle bar $\overline{NI}$ $\overline{KA}$ in white lettering. The cross is painted to simulate rounded poles with the horizontal bars overlapping the vertical bar. The poles have a yellow ground and are shadowed in umber, with black to the left of the stem and at the under edge of the horizontal bars.

St. Stephen, the Protomartyr [83] (Figs. 168, 176, 181)

The full-length figure of this young deacon saint is painted above the prothesis niche. The inscription is abbreviated, and it is placed in horizontal lines behind his back, except for the word

[105] See below, Proportion, pp. 283–85. Text Fig. 44.

"μαρτυς," which is in front of him. The words "ὁ πρωτώ/μαρτῦς" are written in smaller script than the name.

The saint stands upright in the three-quarter-profile stance as he turns toward the altar. His head inclines forward. With his right hand he swings a flaming censer, while in his left hand he holds a jeweled incense box. The saint is portrayed as a beardless young man with short, smooth hair reaching to just below his ear, and with a slight tonsure at the top. Under his billowing sticharion, he wears a dark tunic with a jeweled cuff, and his narrow orarion falls in a stiff vertical from his left shoulder. Over his left arm he carries a dark napkin. His feet are spread well apart and are clad in pointed boots or slippers.

Stephen's tunic has an umber ground, dark umber shadows, and black lines and outlines; the napkin over his arm is built up in colors similar to those of his tunic. His sticharion has a light grey ground, light green shadows, fine black lines and outlines, and thick, white, linear highlights. His orarion has a thick yellow ground, and it is picked out with small, black crosses spaced between black horizontal bars. His slippers are black. His cuff is decorated with pattern 1a (Text Fig. 24). The patterns for the incense box and the censer are illustrated (Text Fig. 31.1b, 2a). The interior of the censer is painted red to suggest hot charcoal.

This slightly hunched figure of the deacon Stephen, with his inclined head, has a demure but purposeful look. He steps forward over the niche with his censer swinging forward over the red border line, in a manner that projects him forward into the real space of the church. Within the lower folds of Stephen's sticharion is the inscription in black script made by the visiting Russian monk Barsky, when he was traveling in Cyprus in 1735 (Fig. 176).[106]

Vermiculated Square Pattern [84]

To the right of Stephen is a narrow, patterned panel at the base of the springing of the apse arch. Between the red and white borders, there is a green and white parti-colored ground over which is laid a black linear pattern of squares bisected by diagonals and filled with vermiculation. This vertical row of single squares piled one upon the other is repeated on the other side of the bema, on the abutment to the east reveal of the south arch [120]. The pattern of squares is also similar to window pattern d (Pl. 11). It is clearly a painted simulation of glazed wall tiles. This and the actual fragments of ceramic wall decoration at Patleina in Bulgaria suggest that ceramic wall decoration, which is common in the Islamic world, may once have been a regular feature of Byzantine buildings.

The Prothesis Niche [85] (Fig. 174)

The conch of this semicircular niche is decorated with a two-barred cross with a foot bar set amid instruments of the Passion of Christ and flanked by abbreviated incantations. The niche is 47 cm wide at the front, 47 cm deep, and 80 cm high at the center front.

---

[106] See above, Situation and History, pp. 53–54.

The panel is contained between red, white, and black borders and has an upper ground of white and a low foreground of green; the latter is picked out with short, vertical, sinuous lines of black to imitate grass. On the white background on either side of the cross are written the letters of the abbreviated laudatory titles.[107]

The cross is painted in a similar manner to that in the roundel above [82], but at the crossing of the center bars it is contoured with a small green wreath, evocative of the crown of thorns. Four large black nails are stuck into the foot bar. Standing on the base of the niche, on either side of the cross, are two spears, of which the one to the left bears a sponge at the top.

The North Bay [86–89]

The lunette is occupied by St. Hypatios [86]. Below him, a square niche bears an inscribed cross [89]. The reveals and walls to either side of the niche are decorated with patterns [87, 88]. The wall was plastered in a single section with the exception of the niche and the dado beneath.

St. Hypatios [86] (Figs. 171, 172)

The half-length figure occupies the lunette on the north wall of the blind arch, above the square niche. The panel measures 108 cm at its base and 90 cm at its greatest height, exclusive of the red borders. The entire background of the figure has a green ground that at some period was overpainted with another green that obscured the inscription; the overpaint was removed.

The titular inscription to the half-length figure of this prelate is placed on either side of his head and shoulders on the plain green background. The scroll that the saint unfurls between his hands bears an inscription.[108]

The saint is portrayed as an old man with white, receding hair and a long, pointed beard. His head is in three-quarter profile and inclines slightly forward, but his torso is frontal. His left arm is bent forward as he appears to tender the scroll forward and outward. Over an undergarment of which only the jeweled cuff can be seen, he wears a voluminous phelonion. His epitrachelion falls vertically to his waist, where it loops upward and over his right arm. This stole is decorated with a broad black cross on each shoulder and on the fold over the arm. The cuff is decorated with pattern 1a (Text Fig. 24). His phelonion has a light umber ground, dark yellow and umber shadows, black lines and outlines, and thick, white highlights. His epitrachelion is thick white.

This is a cool, luminous panel, and the color effects are unusual because of the overall light green background that sets off the large amount of white.

The Patterns to the West and East of the Square Niche [87] (Fig. 171)

The western panel measures an average 30 cm in width by 68 cm in height, exclusive of the red borders. The pattern in black line is closely similar to that of [84]. The difference is that there

---

[107] Abbreviations in Prothesis niche [85], Fig. 174.
[108] See Nicolaïdes, "Panagia Arakiotissa," scroll for St. Hypatios [86], pp. 17, 18.

are two vertical rows of squares joined to each other and painted onto a parti-colored ground divided into vertical green and yellow bands. The general effect is that of the simulation of eight glazed tiles. The eastern panel measures 13 cm in width by 68 cm, exclusive of the red borders. The ground is divided vertically into narrow green and yellow stripes, which are overlaid with a vermiculated scroll pattern executed in black line (Fig. 171).

The Square Niche [88, 89] (Figs. 171, 173)

The interior faces of the niche are rectangular in form but irregular in surface. The niche is approximately 42 cm deep, 68 cm high, and 60 cm wide. The east and west facets are painted with panels containing a slightly simpler version of the vermiculated square pattern described in [84] and [87] (Figs. 171, 174). The rear face contains a damaged painted panel with the remains of a two-armed cross with foot bar and with black letters flanking it on the white background.[109]

Only the two upper horizontal bars remain across the truncated stem of the cross, which is made of "wooden" poles painted with a dark ochre ground, red shadows, and black lines and outlines.

The South Wall [117, 118]

With the exception of the dado, the panel was plastered as a single section. To the west appears St. Symeon the Archimandrite on his column [118], and a roundel in the eastern spandrel contains St. Theophanes the Poet [117]. There is no red border separating the figure and roundel, which were painted against an overall green background.

At the western edge of the pier is a fragment of pattern [119] of a later date (see below p. 332). This fragment, like the figures of the two stylite saints, suffered much damage when the seventeenth-century iconostasis was inserted.

St. Theophanes, the Poet [117] (Fig. 164)

This roundel in the east spandrel overlaps the upper red border of the panel as well as the red border beneath it outlining the arch. The horizontal diameter of the roundel measures 51 cm, but the vertical diameter is rather shorter, despite the overlapping of the borders to the panel. The halo diameter measures half the horizontal diameter of the roundel. The titular inscription is placed on the green background of the panel to either side of the roundel. The saint clutches the top of an unfurling scroll with an inscription.[110]

The saint is portrayed as an old man with his white hair receding back from his forehead and a beard that neatly outlines the chin and falls to a rippling point. His head is in three-quarter profile as he turns toward the east. Only the tips of the fingers of his right hand can be seen. The rest of the

---

[109] Lettering around cross in niche of north wall [88], Figs. 171, 173.
[110] See Nicolaïdes, "Panagia Arakiotissa," scroll for St. Theophanes the Poet [117], pp. 34–35.

waist-length figure is concealed beneath a voluminous and somber overgarment. The background is vermilion and the saint's robe has a dark red ground, umber and black lines, and no highlights.

St. Symeon, the Elder [118] (Fig. 166)

This stylite saint occupies the face of the west pier. His titular inscription is written in white letters to the left of his halo. The total height of the panel between the upper and lower red borders is 127 cm, and its width below the figure averages 40 cm. Above the column, the spandrel widens considerably, giving ample space for the haloed figure.

The saint is represented as an old man with a short fringe of white hair just visible below the close-fitting, pointed hood that frames his face and neck. His beard neatly outlines his chin, and its fine, white tresses gather to a point beneath it. His head is in the asymmetrical frontal stance with the eyes gazing eastward across the wider side of the face. Just below waist level, the saint's figure is cut off by the capital that tops the marble column. Iron railings painted in white lines enclose his body from waist to shoulder level, with the sides of the railings angled backward behind his body. In his right hand he carries a fine, white cross. He wears a close-fitting, black, pointed hood decorated with a linear design in white of small crosses contained within double parallel lines. The pattern is arbitrarily geometric and set out in the form of a cross. It makes no attempt to contour the folds of the material or the shape of the head. A voluminous, light overgarment envelops his body, concealing all but his right hand.

His overgarment and the sleeve of his undergarment both have a yellow ground, dark grey shadows, black lines and outlines, and grey wash highlights. The column and capital and the white linear grille are built up in a similar manner to those belonging to St. Symeon the Wonderworker [79] on the facing wall. In general, the two stylite saints in the bema are much alike and complement each other well as they face each other across the sanctuary. They each dominate the narrowing space allotted to them, and both direct their gazes eastward.

The South Arch [120–124]

St. Romanos the Melode [122] stands in the east reveal above the diakonikon niche with its inscribed cross [121]; to the left is a long vertical strip of pattern [120]. A medallion with a cross [123] decorates the soffit, and St. Lazaros [124] stands in the west reveal.

With the exception of the dadoes and the niche, the arch was plastered as a single section, with no plaster join at the center. Like the north arch opposite, the figures and roundel were painted against an overall green background, with a further coat of green applied over the foreground. The lack of a blue background further confirms that the blue pigment was becoming scarce.

Pattern to East of St. Romanos [120] (Fig. 169)

This narrow section is 165 cm high and it varies from 10 to 20 cm in width. It was plastered

as a single separate section and contains a linear vermiculated design that is similar to and complements the pattern on the abutment on the opposite side of the apse [84]. Both patterns simulate square, glazed tiles.

The Cross in the diakonikon [121] (Fig. 178)

The niche that served as the diakonikon is placed some 18 cm above the present floor level. It is round-arched and shaped as a semicircle carved into the wall. At the center front, it measures 38 cm in width and 84 cm in height, and it has a maximum depth of 51 cm. The interior was plastered and decorated with a painting of a two-armed cross with a footrest standing amid the instruments of the Passion. It is now much damaged. Four black letters, $\overline{\Phi}\,\overline{X}\,\overline{\Phi}\,\overline{\Pi}$, placed to either side of the cross, are abbreviations for the incantation "The Light of Christ is the Light of the Ruler of All." A long sentence, now illegible, was written around the niche just above the foreground.

The niche is contoured with a red border. The upper background is of unpainted white plaster, and the lower foreground is green. The foreground occupies about a quarter of the whole height of the niche, and it was originally painted with sinuous, black blades of grass, of which only traces now remain. The two-barred cross has a small, green wreath signifying the Crown of Thorns looped about the center bar. To the left of the cross stands a spear and to the right a spear with a sponge transfixed upon it. There are no nails in the foot bar, as in the cross in the prothesis niche [85]. The rounded bars of the cross are painted with a light umber ground, dark umber shadows, and black lines beneath and to the right side of the bars.

St. Romanos, the Melode [122] (Figs. 169, 182)

The young saint is in the north bay of the sanctuary, and he occupies a position complementary to that of St. Stephen [83]. His long inscription is aligned vertically on either side of his halo. He is portrayed as a young man with short hair layered over his forehead and gathered into curls behind his left ear. He wears a slight mustache, and a short beard darkens the edge of his chin. He stands upright in a three-quarter-frontal stance, and his slightly bowed head is turned in three-quarter profile toward the apse. His right arm is bent upward at the elbow and is slightly foreshortened as he grips the chain of a swinging censer in his right hand. In the crook of his left arm, he carries a jeweled incense box that rests on a dark napkin thrown over the foreshortened forearm. His censer is similar to that carried by St. Stephen [83] and his incense box is like that carried by St. Abibos [67] and St. Joseph [135]. He is clad in a dark undertunic with close-fitting sleeves and jeweled cuffs under a figure-hugging sticharion. A long, thin orarion falls stiffly down from over his left shoulder. His feet are shod with plain, black boots.

The tunic and the napkin both have a red ground, dark umber shadows, and black lines and outlines. His sticharion has a light grey ground, yellow-green and then dark green shadows and lines, and thick, white highlights. The cuff, the orarion, the censer, and the box all have a yellow ground with linear patterns in dark umber, and they are decorated with pearls.

This slender young man with his slight mustache and beard derives much grace from the

close-fitting folds of his sticharion. The garment molds his abdomen with a great oval sweep and then falls in rippling outlines to shape his left leg, which juts forward.

The Roundel with a Cross, Soffit of South Arch [123] (Fig. 177)

Placed within the roundel circle is a two-armed cross with a foot bar. On either side of the cross are white letters on the vermilion background, with the abbreviations for "Jesus Christ, the Son of God": $\overline{\text{IC}}$ / $\overline{\text{XC}}$ // $\overline{\text{VC}}$ / $\overline{\theta\text{V}}$.

The outer band of the roundel has a yellow ground, and it is outlined with a black inner and outer outline. The cross has a yellow ground, umber shadows, and black lines beneath the bars and to the right of the vertical.

This roundel is similar to that in the soffit of the north blind arch of the bema [82], although the inscriptions are different. However, the southern cross is shadowed to the left, and the northern cross is shadowed to the west, as if in both cases the light source could be considered as coming from the center of the bema.

St. Lazaros [124] (Figs. 170, 183; Text Fig. 36.1d)

The titular inscription lies on either side of his halo. He is represented as an old man with a bald head, save for two white curls above his ear. With the exception of his tufty, tilted eyebrows, his face is hairless, with deep hollows beneath the heavily underlined cheekbones. His head is in the three-quarter-profile stance as he gazes into the center of the bema. His body is represented in the frontal aspect. He holds a jeweled book in the crook of his left arm, which is enveloped in garment folds. His right arm is bent at the elbow as his hand gestures across his chest. The saint wears an omophorion with black crosses over a voluminous phelonion, and both these garments are caught up over his left arm under the book. His epigonation is partly revealed, and he has an epimaniphion around his right wrist. The lower end of his long epitrachelion flows from beneath his phelonion and over the gathering pleats of his sticharion, which fold back over his black slippers.

His sticharion has a light yellow ground, light green and dark green shadows, and black lines and outlines. His phelonion has a light yellow ground, yellow shadows, black lines and outlines, and thick, white highlights. His omophorion has a thick, white ground; broad, black crosses; and white bobbles at the hem. His collar, cuff, epitrachelion, and epigonation all have a yellow ground with white wash highlights upon which various decorative designs are picked out in dark umber or black line. His collar has a vermiculated design; his epimanikion has the standard washer design at the cuff, with a vermiculated square design beneath; his epigonation has a washer design at the edge, and a vermiculated palmette design within; and his epitrachelion has rectangles filled with alternating designs of vermiculated squares and vermiculated palmettes separated by horizontal corridors with the washer design (Text Fig. 35b). The saint's book has a vermilion side with black ties and outlines, and the front has a yellow ground with a foliated gem at the center, oblong jewels at each corner, and large, white pearls between. The design on the book cover is

similar to that on the cover of the book held by St. Symeon the Wonderworker [79] (Fig. 165; Text Fig. 36. 1d).

This is the only saint of venerable age to be depicted without a beard or mustache, and his lower face is very similar to that of the elderly Eve in the Anastasis [50] and to that of the unbearded Moses [33] in the dome. Perhaps St. Lazaros's lack of facial hair can be linked with his return from the dead, since the lack of beard in a revered divine is unusual.

The South Bay [125]

Apart from the dado, the lunette was plastered as a single section and it contains the figure of St. Kyprianos [125]. The damage to the head reveals much evidence as to the 1192 painter's technique in building up layers of colors for the head (see below, pp. 309–11). The standard diameter for the halo, which measures six nose lengths, was increased to seven nose lengths, in the case of this figure, in order to accomodate the extra breadth of the heightened shoulders (see below, p. 287).

St. Kyprianos [125] (Figs. 185, 186)

The full-length figure of this bishop and martyr occupies the whole of the south wall above the dado. Below the curve of the arch, the width of the panel averages 125 cm, and from the base line to the apex of the arch the height is 186 cm. The background of the figure is green, and a further coat of green was applied to the foreground area reaching up to about knee level. Particular damage occurred to the face of the figure where the left eye socket area has flaked back to the preliminary yellow of the halo.

The saint's inscription is placed on either side of his halo, and he carries a scroll with an inscription in black letters.[111]

The saint is portrayed as an old man with receding hair and a long, white beard, which comes to a point beneath the neatly outlined chin. He inclines his head forward in a three-quarter-profile stance turning eastwards. His torso is frontal, but his legs and feet are in three-quarter profile. His left arm is bent at the waist, and the hand unfurls the lower end of a scroll, which is held up by his right hand. He is dressed as a bishop, and his feet are clad in black slippers.

The saint's sticharion has a light yellow ground, yellow shadows, and umber and black lines. His phelonion has a light umber ground, light red shadows, umber and black lines, and white highlights. His omophorion has a yellow base upon which was laid a thick, white ground, leaving the yellow as an outline. The large crosses are solid black, and there are white bobbles at the bottom edge. His epigonation, epimanikion, and epitrachelion all have a yellow ground with white wash highlights, and designs in umber or black line. His epigonation has a washer design at

---

[111] See Nicolaïdes, "Panagia Arakiotissa," scroll for St. Kyprianos [125], p. 15.

the edge and a pattern of concentric circles decorated with pearls and a central cross, and the interstices are decorated with vermiculation. His epitrachelion has panels of vermiculated diaper design alternating with a panel of concentric circles and divided by bands of washer pattern (Text Fig. 35c).

The West Face of the Bema Arch [90–94]

(Pls. 30, 31; Figs. 10, 179, 180, 187, 189, 190; Text Fig. 37)

The face of the arch is very narrow at the base, and it widens to reach 72 cm in vertical width at its apex. It was plastered in three sections: the upper central section contains all the decorative, painted elements, and the two lower sections are confined to the base of the arch at either side. The two plaster joins probably represent staging levels, as the bema arch is too high and wide to be accessible from ground level.

The background of the various elements within the panel is divided between an upper blue ground and a lower green ground; the latter reaches up the sides of the panel as far as the first figural roundel. All the figural roundels are outlined in fine black and white lines, similar to those for the standard halo.

The Decorative Roundels [90a] (Fig. 10; Text Fig. 37)

Above the springing of the arch, to each side of the panel, are pairs of decorative circles imitating a marble revetment. Each is painted with two central circles of marble contoured by a band of black and white opus sectile. The outline band of the upper circle entwines with that of the lower circle to form a figure eight. The diameter of the circles is 17.5 cm, and the width of the outline band is 2.5 cm. Measured down the arch, the total length of each entwined pattern is 34 cm. The upper central circles have a dark umber ground flecked with light umber, and the black triangles in the outlining band turn their apex outward. The lower central circles have a dark grey ground flecked with light grey, and the apex of the border triangles are turned inward. These decorative roundels are similar to the 1192 dado pattern [53].

The Roundel of St. Stachios [90] (Fig. 179)

The roundel has a diameter of 39 cm and the halo a diameter of 22 cm, inclusive of the outlines. The background within the roundel has a grey ground applied over a red base, and this provides a somber foil to the light colors of the waist-length figure within it. The inscription for this young deacon saint is in white letters placed within the roundel on either side of his halo, and the second word is abbreviated.

The saint's head is in three-quarter profile, and he turns toward the apse. His beardless, unlined face is contoured by smooth, flowing hair that falls to the level of his chin. In his right

Text. Fig. 37 The decorative roundels on the west face of the bema arch that simulate opus sectile [90a]

hand, he grips the ring and chains of a censer, while an incense box is propped against his left arm (Text Fig. 31.2b). Beneath his sticharion, the saint wears a dark tunic, and his orarion trails over his left shoulder .

The censer chains and the incense box have a yellow ground and are patterned with black lines, like those carried by St. Stephen [83]. His orarion has a yellow ground with decorative bars in black. This young St. Stachios looks like the twin to St. Nicanor [94], the young deacon on the opposite side of the arch, and their heads and the colors used to paint them are almost identical.

St. John of Damascus [91] (Pl. 31; Fig. 189)

The somber, waist-length figure of St. John is contained within a bright vermilion roundel above that of St. Stachios. The diameter of the roundel measures 51 cm, inclusive of the black and white outlines. The white letters of his inscription are distributed on either side of his halo, and the first two words are abbreviated. He carries an unfurled green and white scroll with a long inscription in black letters.[112]

He is portrayed as an old man, and his head is in the three-quarter-profile stance as he turns toward the apse. He wears a turban of decorated cloth around his head that conceals all his hair except for a small fringe in the middle of his forehead. His long, white beard neatly contours his chin and falls into tapering locks beneath it. Only a few fingers of his hands are visible as they steady the unfurled scroll. The halo has a diameter of seven nose lengths, which is one nose length longer than the standard measurement. The extra measure was made necessary by the voluminous turban.

The turban has a dark red ground, black lines and outlines, and a pattern of fine, white lines in the form of small crosses between parallel double lines. His overgarment has a dark green

---

[112] See Nicolaïdes, "Panagia Arakiotissa," scroll for St. John of Damascus [91], p. 32.

ground, black lines and outlines, and yellow-green washes. In color and design this saint much resembles St. Kosmas [93] in the roundel on the opposite side of the arch, except that St. John's overgarment has broad areas of shadow color, while St. Kosmas's garment has prominent linear folds.

The Mandylion [92] (Pl. 30; Fig. 187)

The Mandylion is placed at the apex of the apse arch. A fringed, oblong, white towel with decorative bands at either end displays at its center the haloed head of Christ. Inclusive of the fringe, the towel has a length of 80 cm, the fringe measures 1.75 cm, and the width of the towel is 37 cm. Inclusive of its single outline, Christ's halo has a diameter of 36 cm. The inscription is written vertically in large vermilion letters on the white background of the towel. The sigla $\overline{\text{IC}}$ $\overline{\text{XC}}$ are also written on either side of the halo.

Christ's face is that of a young man with a furrowed forehead, and his smooth, flowing hair is drawn to the right. He wears a short mustache, and his fine, thin beard is divided beneath the chin in two pointed ringlets. His head is in the asymmetrical frontal stance, with the wider side of the face to the right and the gaze focused across it toward the right. The base of his neck coincides with the base of the halo. Part of a garment can be seen on either side of it. Christ's halo extends above the towel to overlap the blue upper background of the arch panel. This is another example of the painter's habit of projecting his image forward into the real space of the church.

The towel is painted in thick lime white with the fringes laid out in fine horizontal lines. The vertical bands in vermilion at either end of the towel are made up of a broad, central band lying between two thin lines. Christ's halo has a single black outline decorated with lines of four single pearls alternating with a bright red or green jewel. The bars within the halo are painted in thick white with a green shadow, over which are painted five central vermilion jewels outlined in black lines. Christ's hair and beard are colored like those of a young man. The visible parts of his robe are colored in dark red and have some black lines.

There is a contemporary alteration to the bars within the halo that was made after the application of the white ground. The horizontal bars were enlarged downward, the upper bar was extended to the right with a further application of white, and the opposite edges were painted out with broad lines of yellow ochre to a depth of 1 cm. Below Christ's halo is a nail that was inserted into the wall at some period to support a hanging lamp.

The Mandylion forms a striking focus of attention at the center of the bema arch where it can easily be seen from the naos, looming above the iconostasis. The head of Christ is a particularly good example of the asymmetrical frontal face. It illustrates the uneven relationships of the head measurements across the eyeline, which were later to be tabulated by Panselinos (see below, pp. 287–90). The single, jeweled, black outline of Christ's halo is particular to a very few figures in this decoration. It can only be found in the Presentation of the Mother of God [70], where it is used for the haloes of Joachim, Anna, Zacharias, and Mary, and in the Nativity [142],

where it is used for the halo of the Mother of God.

Christ's forehead is seamed with a winged U-line in green, which is characteristic of the faces of old men in the 1192 paintings. The same winged U-line appears in the face of Christ on the Holy Tile [72]. Another characteristic of these two heads of Christ lies in the shaping of the beard, which is divided into wavy ringlets. In the other portraits of Christ, like that in the dome, the beard divides into rounded curls, which are neatly combed and striated.

St. Kosmas, the Hymnwriter [93] (Fig. 190)

Below the Mandylion to the south is a roundel containing the waist-length figure of another elderly saint in a turban, bearing an unfurled scroll. His name is written on either side of his halo on the vermilion background, and the epithet is abbreviated. The inscription on his scroll is in black letters.[113]

Apart from the inscriptions, St. Kosmas and St. John of Damascus [91], who is opposite to him on the north side of the arch, could be regarded as mirror images of one another. St. Kosmas has a distinctive incision line marking the outline of his left shoulder.

The Roundel of St. Nikanor, the Deacon [94] (Fig. 180)

This lies below St. Kosmas on the south side of the bema arch. The diameter of the roundel is 39 cm. The inscription in large letters is spread on either side of the halo, on the dark red of the background within the roundel, and the epithet is abbreviated.

The young saint with his smooth hair rippling to chin length closely resembles St. Stachios [90] opposite him on the north side of the arch. Like him, he carries the ring and chain of a censer in one hand and an incense box in the crook of his arm. His face is in three-quarter profile as he turns to gaze northward into the apse. He wears a sticharion with an undergarment that is visible at the neck, and his orarion hangs over his left shoulder.

The saint's sticharion has a thick, white ground, blue shadows and lines, and light blue washes. There are no black lines. His undergarment has a blue-green ground that is painted over the white ground of his sticharion. The latter is picked out with grey and black lines. His orarion and his censer chains have a yellow ground and are picked out with red and black lines. His incense box is similar to that of St. Stachios (Text Fig. 31.2b).

[113] See Nicolaïdes, "Panagia Arakiotissa," scroll for St. Kosmas the Hymnwriter [93], p. 33.

13
THE SOUTH BAY UNDER THE DOME

The South Wall [127–141] (Pl. 4)

The lunette is occupied by the Koimesis [138] and the ground register beneath by two large panels, the Mother of God Arakiotissa [139] to the east, and the archangel Michael [140] to the west. Within the arch, Christ Antiphonetes [127] stands in the east reveal and St. Anthony [137] in the west reveal. The soffit is adorned with eight roundels with Saints [128–136]. The dadoes, with their "marble" roundels, were plastered separately.

Christ Antiphonetes [127]

(Figs. 138, 140, 284)

This imposing figure forms part of the Deesis composition, which is divided by the archway of the bema (Pl. 2; Figs. 136–138; pp. 174, 194). It is to him that the Mother of God Eleousa [69] appeals as she stands on the east reveal of the opposing arch, clutching her scroll with its written dialogue of intercession. Her escort, St. John the Baptist [75], stands behind her on the neighboring but separate panel on the north wall under the dome.

The width of the reveal at the base of the south arch averages 72 cm, and the height of the panel is 176 cm, inclusive of the red borders. The upper and lower red borders measure 8 cm in width, but the vertical border on the north side is only 1 to 2 cm in width because of the narrowness of the reveal. At an early stage in painting, the vertical red border to the right of Christ ran up the corner, as it should do, marking the junction of the arch and the south wall. This initial version of the border was painted out with green, and the painter transferred the southern red border to the south wall when he came to paint the adjacent panel of the Arakiotissa [139] next to Christ. He left space on the eastern side of the figure to allow for some background and a broad red border, thus completing the enclosure of the Antiphonetes panel. The intrusion into the space of the south wall is some 15 cm wide, and it runs up to the full height of the Redeemer panel. By so treating the sides of the panel, the painter achieved a maximum space on the east reveal for the figure of Christ, and he was able to maintain the canonical ratios of width to height for the figure seen in a frontal stance. The complementary figure of the Eleousa on the opposing arch stands in the narrower, three-quarter-frontal stance. The painting is in good condition apart from some general flaking,

stains from an oil lamp, and a hole in the plaster of the knee area. There are no overpaints, and the lettering is original.

Christ is painted against a green background, the lower part of which received a further coat of green to darken and differentiate it from the upper ground. The sigla $\overline{\text{IC}}$ $\overline{\text{XC}}$ are placed high up on either side of Christ's halo, and the epithet Antiphonetes is aligned vertically on either side of the lower part of the halo. The sigla are in bold lettering, but, because of the restricted space, the letters for the epithet are too small to balance well with the substantial figure.

The open book, which Christ holds up in his left hand, has an inscription written on it in neat horizontal lines down one page, then down the other. The lettering is in fine, black lines on the white pages of the book (Fig. 284). The text is taken from the Gospel according to St. John, 8:12–13: "I am the Light of the World: he that followeth Me shall never walk in the darkness, but shall have the Light of Life."

Christ stands in the frontal stance with his feet apart, on a footstool with jeweled edges. His right arm is bent upward at the elbow as the hand gestures, palm forward, in the act of blessing. His foreshortened left arm and hand support the base of the open book. His right foot is in profile and his left foot is extended forward and downward so that he appears to float above the cushion of his footstool, which is not indented by his weight.

His halo contains three white bars with five jewels at the center of each bar, and his head is in the asymmetrical frontal aspect; the wide side of the young face lies to the right, and although the pupils of the eyes are not centered, his gaze is almost direct and follows the onlooker. The long, wavy hair is pulled over to the right side, and his beard separates into two short, rounded locks beneath the chin. The smooth contour lines of the eyebrows, suitable for a young man, were picked out with a feathering of black lines in a naturalistic manner unusual for the faces of young men in this decoration. Only the Christ in the dome has such eyebrows [1].

Christ's halo is yellow with plain black and white outlines. Its crossbars of thick white are shadowed with blue and decorated with five central vermilion jewels outlined in black. He wears a chiton with black clavus over an undertunic of which only the jeweled cuff is visible and a bulky himation. His feet are shod in sandals. The footstool has a jeweled front border and is topped by a plump cushion.

His ornate cuff has a double row of pearls around the washer pattern at the wrist; a diaper pattern of pearl-lined corridors with vermiculation in black is painted over the yellow ground, which has white sheen highlights, cuff pattern 1b (Text Fig. 24). His chiton is vermilion with umber shadows and black lines and outlines. His himation has a yellow ground, yellow-brown and dark brown shadows, red fold lines, black lines and outlines, blue-tinted wash highlights, and thick, white highlights. His book has white pages with thick, white frames for the inscription lines. The lettering is in black except for the initial E and the accents, which are in red. The sides of the book are vermilion with red shadow lines. The plump cushion on his footstool is vermilion with red fold and crease lines, but the vermilion is much blackened. The border has a black ground with yellow frame lines for the jewelled sections, where three rows of nine pearls alternate with a square vermilion jewel set in yellow lines.

The hands are beautifully built up with three flesh colors over the green ground, vermilion highlights, and outlines in black. The creamy yellow highlight carefully picks out the fingers, which are shown in profile, shaping the half-moons of the nails and outlining them, then marking out a short underline, followed by a long vertical line to mark the first joint of the finger (Text Fig. 38).

Text Fig. 38 The right hand of Christ Antiphonetes [127], illustrating his delicate gesture and the pattern of white highlights (marked in black).

This is an impressive figure; the length ratios of the proportional system are nicely counterbalanced by the large size of the hand, which is given a full face length, and by the substantial feet. Christ's himation was not painted blue. This may again be the result of the painter's need to economize on this precious pigment, but it may also be that the combination of yellow hues was more suitable to a Christ asserting himself as the "Light of the World."

The painter or painters of the 1192 decoration did not make any general use of the artificially linear striations known as chrysographia. Such a technique would have been appropriate for the figure of Christ, and the painter's rejection of such a technique in this case may provide further evidence of his giving to figures the illusion of their real presence in the church. The only exceptions are the chrysographia in gold leaf for the neighboring images of the Mother of God Arakiotissa and the Christ child [139], where they were used extensively, probably at the direct instigation of the donor who is commemorated in the inscription, and for the figures of Symeon and the Christ child on the south wall [74].

Roundels in the Soffit of the South Arch [128–136]

(Figs. 191–198, Text Fig. 25)
The panel within the south arch is outlined with red borders, and its width is irregular. It

measures 5.87 m from east to west and has an average width of 65 cm, inclusive of the red borders. The eight roundels within the panel have an average diameter of 64 cm, and the distance separating them averages 4 cm. The distance between the roundels at their widest point from the enclosing red borders averages 7.5 cm.

The soffit of this arch was plastered in a single section. Observation of the edges of the south arch suggests that the pendentives above were plastered before the soffit of the arch and that the "Koimesis" panel [138] in the bay below was plastered afterwards. The eastern and western ends of the soffit panel extended over the wooden cornice, which marks the springing of the arch to either side of the bay, but because of the movement in the wood, most of the plaster has now fractured off.

In the course of painting, the 1192 master laid in fresh plaster patches for the heads of the saints. Each patch was fitted neatly into the halo space, with the edges neatly smoothed and thinned with a spatula. Fractures in the plaster patches reveal that they were applied over the yellow base color of the halo. The heads that were built up on the patches were made over a green base. The plaster areas for the hands were not reworked, and the paint has flaked quite badly.

There are no incision lines, but impressed guidelines were made at the top of some shoulders and down the exterior lines of the arms. The impress lines were made at a preliminary stage in the painting, and this is confirmed by the fact that the final adjustments to the figures, such as the tidying up of the neckline, the enlarging of some shoulders, and the final black outlines, extend beyond these preliminary guidelines. Similar practices were observed in the making of the angel roundels in the dome above (see p. 122).

In the course of time, the panel sustained considerable damage, particularly at the outer edge, where much flaking occurred. Also, the vermilion has faded to grey or black. In the fourteenth century, the damaged areas were crudely overpainted with little regard to the original work, and the repaint often concealed surviving layers of original paint beneath it. In the course of conservation, the overpaint was removed where it clearly overlapped the original twelfth-century painting.

The eight medallions have yellow frames outlined in black line, and the backgrounds of the figures within alternates between green and red, starting with green at the eastern end of the panel. The background of the roundels has a yellow ground upon which was built up the floral pattern [136] (Text Fig. 26b).

The titular inscriptions are much damaged, but most of the saints have clear traces of their names. The letters of the inscriptions are elegant in shape and size; they are written on either side of the head and fitted vertically between the levels of the top of the forehead and the breast line.

The heads of all the saints are in the asymmetrical frontal stance, with the wide side of the face nearer to the outer edge of the arch, and they all direct their gazes across it into the naos. Their bodies are aligned in the frontal aspect, and with the exception of St. Eustratios [131], their left hands are concealed within the folds of their costumes. The number and dimensions of the roundels are well balanced in relation to the arch that they occupy. The layout of the roundels follows the underlying

construction described for the roundels in the opposing arch (pp. 171–74, and Text Fig. 25).

St. Akepsimas [128] (Fig. 191)

The original letters forming the title to the saint's inscription are lost, and only the letters ΓΙΟC can now be seen in the fourteenth-century grey-white repair. Of the name only the A and the final MAC can be clearly discerned and the traces of a K and C between them, to the right of the figure, on the green ground.

This roundel has a similar diameter to those above it, despite the fact that the panel narrows abruptly at this end of the soffit. The painter achieved this by making the roundel frame intrude over the red border. There are impress lines in the plaster to mark the outlines of the saint's shoulders.

The saint is portrayed as an old man with receding white hair and a long, straggly beard that comes to a point beneath the neatly outlined chin. In the crook of his left arm he carries a closed book, and his right hand is raised across his chest, revealing his jeweled cuff. He is dressed as a bishop and wears an omophorion with broad, black crosses over a voluminous phelonion. Both garments enfold and conceal his left hand. The paint layers within his face and right hand have greatly flaked away.

His phelonion has a light yellow ground, red shadows, black lines and outlines, white wash, and thick, white highlights. The omophorion has a light yellow ground with broad, thick white lines at the edges; the broad, black crosses have a fine, black line bisecting the angles at the crossing. The cuff has a yellow ground with patterns in umber lines, a washer pattern at the edge, and a vermiculated diaper pattern between pearl-lined corridors beneath it, cuff pattern 1a (Text Fig. 24). The side of the book is painted vermilion and the clasps are black; the cover is decorated with a diaper pattern with stepped crosses, as in loros pattern II (Pl. 11.1b; Text Fig. 36.1b). The paint layers within his face and hand have much flaked away.

St. Mardarios [129] (Fig. 192)

Apart from the blurred OC of his title, this saint's inscription is complete. It is written with elegant white letters neatly arrayed on the vermilion ground.

The saint is portrayed as a middle-aged man, with flowing locks to below the ear and a neat, rounded beard. In his right hand he carries a thin, two-barred white cross with fine serifs at the edges and a pearl on the top. He is attired in rich robes and wears a hat shaped like a "beanbag." His tunic has a heavy, decorated collar with indented edges and a jeweled cuff. The cloak that swathes his lower figure is lined with fur, the curls of which show at its edges.

The hat is vermilion and outlined in black line. His tunic has a blue ground, black lines, and thick white highlights. The ornate collar and cuffs have a yellow ground with white sheen highlights over which are painted designs in red line (Text Fig. 24.1a, 2a). The cloak has a yellow

ground with black lines and outlines; the fur tufts have an ochre ground but are picked out with light green and white lines.

This courtly martyr in his lavish dress well illustrates the middle-aged style of face affected by the painter. The hair is brown with a few grey lines; the eyebrows remain smooth and untilted; however, there is a winged U-line above his eyebrows and a deep cleaving line to either side of the nose, and the cheeks are deeply hollowed.

St. Eugenios (?) [130] (Fig. 193)

The only traces of lettering for his name are E–Γ–––O– to the right of his head, but these would fit well with Eugenios, a martyr associated with the four other martyrs from Cappadocia— Eustratios, Auxentios, Mardarios, and Orestes—all of whom are present in this panel.[114]

The saint is portrayed as a middle-aged man with smooth hair gathering into locks below his ear. His beard neatly outlines his chin and then falls into two short points. In his right hand he carries a white cross like that of St. Mardarios [129]. He is richly attired in a tunic with a heavy, ornate collar. Of the undergarment only the decorated cuff is visible. His cloak is swept back over his shoulders and reappears around his waist, and it is pinned at his breast with a single pearl.

His tunic has a blue ground with black lines and thick, white, linear highlights, and his collar and cuff are similar to those of St. Mardarios [129]. His cloak is vermilion with red and black lines.

Within the medallion, two impressed lines in the plaster delineate the upper curves of the shoulders, but these lines lie well below the finished shoulder line, which was extended upward at a late stage in painting. Also at a later stage of painting, the cuff was narrowed and probably the hand as well, but it has flaked badly and the evidence is not entirely clear.

Eugenios and Mardarios bear a close resemblance to other middle-aged martyrs portrayed in roundels within the church. Some examples are Sts. Akindinos [64], Viktor [47], Samonas [66], and Apthonios [62]. Their garment style is also very similar.

St. Eustratios [131] (Fig. 194)

Despite bad flaking within the vermilion background of the figure, the saint's inscription has survived intact. He is portrayed as a middle-aged man with smooth hair to below his ears. The paint layers within the head are badly flaked, and his appearance is blurred, but he appears to have had a long, pointed beard. In his right hand he holds the martyr's cross, and he raises his left hand palm outward across his chest; both hands are much flaked, as the plaster was not reworked before completion. He wears a tunic with ornate cuffs under a rich cloak with jeweled borders and appliqué roundels on the shoulders. The cloak is fastened with a large rectangular brooch lined with pearls.

His tunic is blue, and his cloak has a vermilion ground with broad washes of blue that give it an impression of shot taffeta. The circular shoulder badges, the brooch, the cuffs, and the borders

---

[114] For an account of the Five Martyrs of Sebasteia, see *ODB* 2: 789.

to the cloak all have a yellow ground with white wash highlights to simulate sheen. Over this ground the badges are painted with a design of vermiculated palmettes in umber line, and they are outlined with a black band lined with single pearls. The brooch is made up of three oblong jewels in red and green outlined with pearls, and the border trim to the cloak is filled with alternating bands of double pearls and single vermilion or green jewels. The cuffs have a washer pattern at the wrist edge and a vermiculated palmette pattern executed in umber line, cuff pattern 1b (Text Fig. 24). His cross has a short top bar, a longer middle bar, a stubby lower foot bar, and a dot over its summit; it is painted in thick white over a yellow base.

Impress lines in the plaster delineate the curving of the saint's shoulder and mark out the exterior outline to his right arm. At a later stage in painting, after the cloak was completed, the shoulders were extended upward, and the color layers forming this adjustment have flaked quite badly.

St. Auxentios [132] (Fig. 195)

On the green background of the figure, the saint's title is complete in the original 1192 lettering aligned to the left. Of his name only three letters survive to the right of his halo. These three letters, Αυξ, suggest that he is St. Auxentios, one of the five martyrs from Cappadocia.

The saint is represented as an old man with soft, wavy, white locks flowing to below his ears, and with a long, white beard whose tresses gather to a point beneath the neatly outlined chin. He carries a cross in his right hand, and his bent left arm is concealed under his heavy cloak. He wears a bulky tunic with a heavy embroidered collar and a decorated cuff.

His tunic is light green with dark green lines, white wash, and thick, white highlights. The collar and cuffs are yellow and are decorated with linear designs in umber and black line; both have a washer pattern at the edge of the wrist and neck, and a vermiculated palmette design beyond, cuff pattern 1b (Text Fig. 24). His cloak has a vermilion ground with black lines, and it is joined at his breast by a single white pearl. This saint much resembles St. Pigasios [63] and St. Akindinos [64], both in the stylization of the head and in the garments.

St. Orestes [133] (Fig. 196)

The inscription is complete, and it is written on the vermilion background of the figure. He is represented as a soldier, and he is the only military saint to survive in the 1192 decoration. He is shown as a beardless young man with soft hair flowing to below his ears. He carries a spear in his right hand, and he has a shield slung behind him by a strap crossing his breast. The shield is circular, and only half of it is visible. He wears a tunic of chain mail with a decorated cuff and an embroidered collar. Over it he wears a cloak, the loose folds of which envelop his waist, and a rounded fall of it droops over his shoulder. A decorative chain with a pendant cross hangs around his neck.

His tunic and collar have a yellow ground with white sheen highlights emphasizing his breast and the side of his arms. Green shadows underline the breast, and black lines define the chain mail and the linear palmette pattern on the collar. Both the hem of the collar and the edge of the arm of

the tunic are outlined with black linear corridors containing rows of single pearls alternating with a green or red jewel. His cuff has a yellow ground and a vermiculated diaper pattern with pearls and a washer pattern at the wrist, cuff pattern 1a (Text Fig. 24). The chain and cross are drawn in thick, white paint. The chain is in the form of S-links, and the single barred cross has pointed ends. His cloak has a light blue ground painted over a green base; it is rather untidily painted. His spear has a vermilion shaft with black outlines, and its blade is thick white. The shield has a green ground with some curious scriptlike markings in grey across the center. These consist of a reverse S and some curve-ended verticals. The border contains bands of double pearls alternating with red or green jewels on a yellow ground, and the strap is black.

At a late stage in the painting, the shoulders of this figure were widened and the arms extended outward. In the latter case, the pattern of the collar and chain mail was extended over the enlargement, and the pigments have flaked badly. The upper layers of paint that were used for building up the flesh colors for the face and hands have also suffered from flaking.

St. Aithalas [134] (Fig. 197)

The inscription is badly damaged and the gamma from the epithet is missing, as well as the foremost letters of the saint's name. Only the last three letters, ΛΑΣ, remain on the green background to the figure.

St. Aithalas is portrayed as a middle-aged man with receding brown hair and a long, pointed beard. His right hand is palm down across his chest, and the two forefingers and the little finger are extended. In the crook of his left arm he holds a closed book with a jeweled cover. He wears an undergarment with a narrow, decorated collar and decorated cuff. An overgarment is draped over his tunic and around his shoulders, and it conceals his left arm and hand.

The collar and cuff of his undergarment have a yellow ground with a white sheen highlight. The collar is decorated with a black vermiculated scroll design, and the cuff has a washer pattern at the wrist and a vermiculated diaper design beneath, cuff pattern 1a (Text Fig. 24). His tunic has a yellow-brown ground, red shadows, black lines and outlines, yellow-tinted white wash highlights, and thick, white highlights. His upper garment has a red ground, black lines, and blue wash highlights. The book has vermilion page ends and black clasps. The cover is decorated with a jeweled diaper pattern with linked, stepped crosses as in loros pattern II (Pl. 11b; Text Fig. 36.1b). Both the outlines of his shoulders and the outline of his left arm have guidelines deeply impressed into the plaster.

St. Joseph [135] (Fig. 198)

The inscription is now quite clear, with the fine twelfth-century lettering standing out on the vermilion background of the figure. Prior to conservation, the original lettering was obscured by the repaint of the background with red paint and a new inscription in stubby grey-white letters. The repaint was recorded and removed.

The saint is portrayed as a young man in a deacon's robes. He has a curly fringe across his

forehead and smooth hair that gathers into curls behind his prominent ears. The face is much damaged, but it appears to have been beardless, although it is possible that he had a slight mustache. In his right hand he grips the top of the chains for a censer, and in the fold of his left arm he cradles a jeweled incense box. He wears a tunic with a decorated cuff beneath a phelonion, and an orarion falls vertically from his left shoulder.

His tunic is red with black lines and outlines and blue wash highlights. His phelonion has a thick, white ground with blue shadow lines. Both the orarion and the cuff have a yellow ground, and the cuff has a vermiculated decoration that is mostly gone. The censer chains are yellow with black lines; the incense box has a yellow ground and is decorated with a vermiculated diaper pattern in umber and black lines (Text Fig. 31.2a).

Heavy impress lines were made in the plaster at a preliminary stage of painting to mark the contour of the shoulders and the outline of the figure's left arm. The head was painted on a fresh plaster patch, like all the other saints in this arch, but despite this measure the upper layers of paint on his face have flaked badly. The plaster for his hand was not reworked before the flesh colors were applied, and they also have flaked badly. The fourteenth-century overpaint was applied over these badly flaked areas, and it has penetrated into the plaster itself, giving this figure a fuzzy appearance.

The floral background [136] (Fig. 192; Text Fig. 26b)

Within the panel the background to the roundels was filled with a delicately painted, lacy floral pattern that has now much flaked and faded away. Enough of it is left to appreciate its colorful intricacy and to suggest that this is a similar pattern to that which decorated the background to the roundels in the soffit of the north arch [68] and the roundels in the west vault [49].

The pattern was painted on a yellow ground, which contrasts well with the alternating green or red backgrounds to the figures within the roundels. At the base of each spandrel, and to either side and between the roundels, the painter made a trefoil arrangement of three, broad leaf shapes, with their bases resting upon the panel outlines. From between the leaves spring stems whose meanders fill the angles of the spandrels with coiling tendrils topped with flower buds.

The leaves of the trefoil bases were given a light yellow ground, and then half of each leaf was painted bright blue with a deeply scalloped edge toward the center of the leaf. The outline of each leaf was then drawn in fine white line, and the concave areas of blue within were picked out with furling dot-and-tails in white. The stems were first drawn in red with a broad brush on the yellow ground of the panel; a narrower brush then was used to overpaint the red meanders in light yellow, leaving the red exposed at some edges to provide a shadow outline or relief. Finally, a thin, white line was drawn along the center of the yellow stems and tendrils. The flower buds were painted blue and picked out with dot-and-tails in white. The fussy floral pattern with its cursive irregularity and lacy, linear highlights contrasts with the stately regularity of the roundels and the solemn figures within them.

The 1192 Decoration

We have seen that in the painting of this particular sequence of roundels, the painter ran into serious trouble with the plaster. This southern arch was plastered in a single long section, unlike the soffit of the opposite arch under the dome. By the time the painter started on the flesh areas of the hands and head, the plaster ground was drying quickly. This accounts for the use of plaster patches inserted within the halo. The plaster patches were added in a thin lime slurry that did not prove to be particularly satisfactory, and some of the heads are badly flaked because the plaster slurry was too thin. The hands that were not reworked before the laying on of the flesh colors have also flaked back to the ground and base colors. And in the case of the floral background pattern, only part of the upper layers of colors defining the intricate pattern to the roundels has survived. This again indicates that the plaster had become too dry and unreceptive to the final layers of paint. Perhaps a day or two of particularly warm, dry weather occurred at this time, which made the plaster set too quickly. The different plaster patterns for the north and south arches could provide circumstantial evidence for the work of two different painters.

St. Anthony, west reveal [137] (Figs. 199, 200)

The panel measures 2 m in height by 57 cm in width, exclusive of the red borders. Within it the full-length figure of St. Anthony, the founder of monasticism, stands with unfurled scroll in hand, his head turning toward the naos.

The titular inscription is original. In the course of conservation, it was rescued from beneath a fourteenth-century overpaint of copper blue and fuzzy grey lettering. The saint's scroll was much damaged at an early period and has been completely overpainted. Only a small fragment of the original may be observed on the right-hand side. The present scroll is grey-green with yellow lines demarcating the areas for writing. The lettering is black and quite different from that of the twelfth-century inscriptions within the church. This late lettering is characterized by the central swelling in the vertical of the epsilons and sigmas (Fig. 199).[115]

Originally, the background to the figure was green, with two coats of green applied over the grey base of the foreground. In the fourteenth-century repair, the upper background to the figure was repainted with a copper blue. The base of the painting and a large area of the central part of the panel were much damaged, and these areas were overpainted by the repair painter. In the course of conservation, overpaints were removed as far as possible, but the scroll with the fourteenth-century lettering was retained, as so little of the original remained.

The saint is represented as an old man standing in three-quarter profile as he turns slightly toward the naos. His balding head, which is also in three-quarter profile, recedes realistically within the hollow of his monastic head cloth. Beneath the rounded chin, his long, white beard divides into two coiling tresses. His right arm is bent, and his much-damaged hand was probably laid in a gesture across his chest. His left arm is foreshortened, and he grips the top of an unfurling scroll in his right hand, which is also much damaged. His cloak closely enfolds his shoulders but falls open

---

115 Nicolaïdes, "Panagia Arakiotissa," scroll of St. Anthony, p. 118.

at the waist to reveal a voluminous habit with black stripes, which falls in loose folds over his black slippers. One end of his head cloth loosely enfolds his head, while the other is wound firmly around his neck. St. Anthony's costume is different from some of the other monkish saints in this decoration. St. Andronikos, for example, is bare-headed and wears knotted ropes over his dun-colored robes.

St. Anthony's cloak has a yellow ground, grey wash shadows, and black lines and outlines. His robe has a light red ground, umber shadows, and black lines and outlines. A fine white line outlines it at the front edge. His head cloth has a light red ground, umber shadows, and black lines and outlines. A pattern in fine, white lines decorates the ends and the center of the cloth, and it runs from the back to the front of the head. It consists of two pairs of parallel white lines with a row of simple crosses running down the central corridor and the odd single cross between these patterns.

The head of St. Anthony is a particularly fine example of the Lagoudhera master's method of painting the face of an old man. In this case, the head is given high relief within the depth of the head cloth, and the folds of it loosely frame the head. This impressive and realistic effect is in curious contrast to the placing of the simple white ornamental pattern on the head cloth. The design of parallel lines runs straight across the cloth in an arbitrary manner, regardless of the articulation of the folds of the head cloth or the form of the head beneath it.

The Koimesis, or Dormition of the Virgin [138]

(Pl. 23; Figs. 201–223, 289; Text Figs. 39, 40)

The height of the composition at its center, from the bottom border to the apex of the lunette, is 2.28 m, inclusive of the red borders. Its width along the base border is 3.4 m. The height of the foreground is 28 cm, the height from the bottom line to the top of the bier is 56.5 cm, and the width of the top of the bier is 29.5 cm. The bier itself is placed in the forefront and at the center of the composition. A notional vertical line bisecting the panel would run from the apex through the neck of the angel, passing tangent to the right edge of Christ's mandorla and to the raised arm of the bishop with the censer, before descending to bisect the bier.

Compositionally, the painting can be divided into six parts. A central section has the Mother of God on her bier. The two upper sections above her contain Christ in his mandorla with St. John the Divine below him and the three bishops. Two lateral sections contain the group of mourning apostles on the left, including St. Peter, and the group of apostles on the right. The angel straddles the notional central vertical line high above all the figures.

Originally the lunette was plastered in a single section with the plaster joins running around the red borders of the scene. However, in the course of painting, a complete new section of plaster was inserted into the center of the composition. Pictorially, this includes Mary and her bier and the hands of St. Paul, who bows over her feet. The plaster join can be traced all around this inserted section, which is extremely smooth in contrast to the uneven texture and relief of the plaster for the rest of the scene (Text Fig. 39). The painter once again used the device of concealing a plaster

join by placing an inscription over it. The **MP ΘV** is written across the upper line of the plaster join, thus hiding the hard horizontal of the plaster join, which might have disturbed the composition (Fig. 202).[116]

Each of the heads of the figures on the surrounding section of plaster was painted on a neat plaster patch inserted into the confines of the halo. The plaster area of Mary's hands was reworked to give a fresh surface before the flesh colors were built up. The hands of the other figures did not receive this treatment, and as a consequence, they have all flaked to a varying extent. The feet of five of the foremost apostles are visible, and the plaster for these was reworked before the completion of the flesh colors; as a result they are in good condition.

There are no sharp incision lines, but the painter frequently made impress marks in the plaster. The most important one is to the west side of Christ's mandorla, where there is a vertical sweep line some 4 to 5 cm wide, marking the center of the composition. Other impress marks were used to mark out the contour of the shoulders. An impressed line also marks the position of the tilted shaft of St. Peter's cross.

The general appearance of the painting is affected by a fine haze, as if some overall glaze has deteriorated, and this detracts from the original brilliance of the colors. This could have resulted from a misguided attempt to clean the painting (see above, p. 55). The haloes are badly discolored because of the thin plaster patching system used for the heads. The thin, attenuated edges of these patches have often flaked, and the yellow color appears uneven as a result. Fourteenth-century overpaints in this scene are limited to the application of an orange-yellow over the flaked flesh areas of some of the hands. The same orange-yellow was painted over the flaking areas within the haloes.

The titular inscription to the scene is distributed horizontally to either side of the central hovering angel. The lettering was executed freehand without any apparent guidelines, and the letters vary little in length, though the alignment undulates. The spacing was fairly well calculated, except that the final letters of the abbreviated "Θεοτόκου" are squashed up against the right-hand border. The letters average 4.5 cm in height; the first part of the inscription, exclusive of the star cross, measures 34 cm, and the second part 44 cm.

The sigla $\overline{\text{IC}}$ $\overline{\text{XC}}$ are placed to the upper left of Christ's mandorla and, exclusive of the decorative abbreviation lines above them, they measure 4 cm in height. Above the $\overline{\text{IC}}$ are traces of lettering that suggest the placement of the titular inscription originally had been planned at a lower level. This idea was no doubt rejected, because it would have brought the lettering into collision with the top of the mandorla, and the sigla would have been squashed below it. The only other inscription is the shortened title of the Mother of God, which is placed just above her halo. The

---

[116] Other examples of this device occur in the Ascension [78], where the long quotations of the inscriptions are written along the two plaster joins linking the central plaster patch to the two side patches making up the composition in the vault (see above, p. 197, Fig. 145). In the Presentation of the Virgin [70], the painter painted in a window along the vertical plaster join for the inset patch for the standing figure of the Virgin (see above, p. 183; Text Fig. 32; Figs. 123, 130).

Text Fig. 39 The Koimesis [138], indicating work on the plaster surface. ·–·– indicate impressed guidelines made in the plaster after the preliminary drawing and painting; ····· outline those areas that received fresh plaster patches before the painting was completed

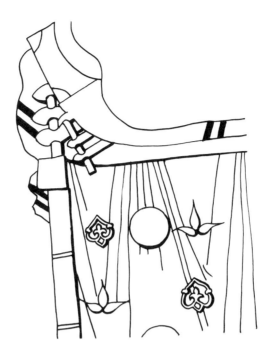

Text Fig. 40 Detail showing the carpentry of the trestle and the pillow and cloth supporting the head of
the Mother of God in the Koimesis

letters are 3 to 3.5 cm tall. All the inscriptions have letters whose neat serifs and fine lines have the
distinctive elegance of the 1192 script.

The backgrounds (Pl. 23; Fig. 201)

The foreground of the scene is made up of a narrow green strip to either side of the bier. This
green foreground is interrupted along the bottom of the picture by a band of darker green with an
undulating upper edge about 8 cm high. This is not unsimilar to the thin, white band at the
bottom of the green foreground to the roundels of the angels in the dome (see above, p. 122). In
the case of the angels, the undulated white band was later painted out with green. An upper
background of blue appears at the center of the scene above Christ and the bishops, and between
the architectures placed to either side of the scene. Behind the apostles rise architectures that are
cut off at the base by the arbitrary horizontal line marking the top of the green foreground. Both
blocks of architecture have a small barrel-vaulted building at the apex. These buildings are roofed
with rounded tiles above a patterned cornice. The sides of the buildings are shown as facing toward
the center, and they have round, arched gables over open doors. Below the buildings are walls that
can be seen to either side of the panel as the lunette widens toward its base. The walls have
horizontal cornices and arched or flat-topped windows. At a late stage in painting, the inner side of

the left, or eastern, building was sliced off, and one side of the door and gable was painted out with blue. Presumably, this adjustment was made in order to bring the building into alignment with the wall beneath, since it would otherwise appear to be leaning perilously forward.

All the architectures have a yellow ground upon which the architectural detail was built up. The walls are shadowed in tones of red and highlighted with washes and thick lines of lime white. The highlighted areas of the walls are placed toward the center of the composition so that the buildings help to throw emphasis on it. The interior of doors, windows, and gables is black, and the surrounds are in dark yellow. Each is picked out with a fine, linear, white outline on the side nearest to the center of the scene. The yellow tiles are outlined in umber and black line, and are highlighted with blue wash. There are three cornice patterns: a chevron pattern of alternating red and blue rectangles with vermiculation at the interstices; a dentil pattern, which was made with a dark yellow ground, a white square on top, and a black one to one side; and an acanthus pattern, which was made with a dark yellow ground, umber outlines, and scalloped edges heavily outlined in white. No draperies enfold these architectures, which suggests that the mourning took place outside Mary's house in Ephesus.

The Mother of God (Figs. 201, 208, 222; Text Figs. 39, 40)

Mary lies flat upon the top of the bier, but her head and neck are raised up and rest against a flat pillow. Her head is seen in three-quarter profile; her eyes are closed, and her hands are crossed palm downward over her chest. She wears a maphorion over a long tunic, and her feet are concealed by the figure leaning at the base of the bier. The bier is supported by two wooden posts at either end, and an elaborate trestle arrangement of poles provides adjustable head support (Text Fig. 40). Mary lies on a white cloth decorated at intervals with double vermilion lines. The cloth passes under the pillow to feed through the trestle and fall downward beyond it. The bier itself is draped with a rich coverlet that billows into five triangular folds at the front. These ample folds of material are decorated with a design of trefoils, palmettes, and solid circles. The design is superimposed on the undulating pleats of the cover, with no regard to its articulation (Text Fig. 40). The plain, low footstool at the center front of the bier shows three of its sides.

Mary's long, thin body is constructed to a larger scale than that of the other figures in this scene. The 1192 painter normally gave his figures a shoulder width equal to the diameter of the halo, but in the case of Mary, her shoulder width is one-sixth less than the width of her halo. This difference may be due to an awareness of perspective and the need to foreshorten a figure that is horizontally flattened. For this same reason, her figure appears very thin in comparison to its length. Mary's hands are small; from the wrist to the top of the medius they measure less than the full face length.

Mary's tunic has a blue ground, dark grey fold lines, and black lines and outlines. The cuff has double bands of yellow on it. Her maphorion has a red ground, broad washes of blue, and black lines and outlines. Around her head, the hem of her maphorion has a broad yellow outline, but the

lower hem is decorated with double yellow lines. The yellow segmenta on her head and shoulders are picked out with cream highlights.

The woodwork of the pillow rest and the bier posts have a yellow ground, red shadows, black lines and outlines, and creamy white highlights. The flat pillow has a vermilion ground with a yellow scallop at each corner. The bed cloth has a thick, white ground and vermilion stripes. The bier cloth has a red ground, and the triangular folds are painted with broad washes of blue to contrast them with the recessing areas. The superimposed design consists of a quincunx of solid yellow discs outlined in black line. The central disc is larger than the others; the trefoils and palmettes that appear between the discs are yellow with black outlines and creamy yellow highlights. The base of the bier cloth has a broad hem of yellow. The footstool has a yellow top and plain black sides. At first sight it looks as if the footstool was either an afterthought or an overpaint. It was in fact part of the original design, as can be seen from the lines defining the pleats of the bier coverlet, which were painted so as to take into account the presence of the footstool.

The eastern group of apostles (Figs. 201, 204–207, 210)

Five apostles are grouped at the head of the bier. St. Peter and another, younger apostle stand at the forefront, partially concealing another full-length figure immediately behind them. The head and shoulders of two more apostles appear above and behind them. St. Peter stands immediately behind the bier. He has the style of hair and beard associated with St. Peter, and he carries a two-barred cross (Figs. 210, 253). He stands in three-quarter-profile stance, bowing forward stiffly from the waist. He is portrayed as an old man, with his hair gathered into a band of two tightly clustered rows of white curls. His rounded beard is short and neatly outlines the chin. Intense grief is expressed by the elongated eyes, the contorted lines of the eyebrows, and the deeply furrowed forehead. The sorrow of his countenance is strengthened by the addition of "tear lines." These single, dark lines run down the cheeks from the inner corners of the eyes.

The saint's right arm is extended downward, as with thumb and forefinger he steadies the stem of his elongated, narrow cross. His left forearm appears from behind Mary's pillow, and the hand extends palm downward across his throat.

His chiton has a blue ground with black lines and outlines, and his himation has a yellow ground, brown and black fold lines and outlines, and grey wash highlights. His cross has a yellow ground and brown and black outlines. The top of the cross, including the short upper bar, overlaps the halo of the apostle behind him. This apostle's head was painted on a fresh patch of plaster that covers the area of the halo, and with it the top of Peter's cross, which therefore had to be repainted over the edge of the patch. This part of the cross has flaked quite badly.

The eastern apostle is a middle-aged man (Fig. 204). He is shown in full length, three-quarter profile, leaning forward from the waist. His shoulder overlaps the red border along the eastern curve of the arch, creating the effect of bringing him forward in front of the picture space. His brown hair has flaked badly. His neat beard ripples across the chin into a curly point. His eyes are elongated, his forehead creased in grief, and his cheeks bear tear lines.

His right arm is bent upward with his hand lying palm downward across his chest. His left arm is foreshortened, and he grips a rolled-up scroll in his left hand. He wears a chiton with a black clavus under a voluminous himation, of which one end loops up in a quiet bell fold behind his leg. His left foot is to the rear, and it advances in profile, while his right leg twists forward to present the foot in the frontal view.

His chiton has a vermilion ground, red fold lines, and white wash and thick white highlights; the vermilion has discolored to grey-black in some areas, particularly on the shoulder. His himation has a light green ground, green shadows, black lines and fold lines, and white wash and thick white highlights. His scroll is white with a blue shadow and vermilion outlines.

The apostle behind Peter is only partly visible (Figs. 204, 207). The figures of the eastern apostle and Peter appear to stand forward of him, and their haloes and the top of Peter's cross overlap his halo. He has the three-quarter profile head of an elderly man, with smooth white hair to below his ear and a long beard that ripples to a point beneath his chin. Grief is apparent in his face, where his forehead is creased, his eyes are elongated, and "tear lines" sear his cheeks.

Part of the apostle's right forearm is visible, and his hand is raised palm downward across his chest. He wears a chiton with a black clavus and a himation. The thigh fold of this robe is cut off abruptly by a black line in direct horizontal alignment with the base of the decorative cornice to the background wall. It would appear that either two painters were at work or one painter was of two minds as to whether the lower aperture between the two apostles in front should reveal the figure or the wall behind them. Within this area both the chiton and the himation appear to be contemporary overpaints executed at a late stage in the painting of this scene. Possibly, at an even later stage of tidying up the whole scene, the master painter mistakenly continued the black cornice across the white highlighted knee, without realizing that the area related to the figure of the apostle.

The chiton has a light green ground, yellow-green shadows, black lines and outlines, and white highlights. Where it is visible, the himation has a vermilion ground, black lines and outlines, and white highlights.

The rear apostle to the east reveals only his head and shoulders (Figs. 204, 205). His bowed head and figure are in three-quarter profile. His smooth brown hair falls down to the middle of his neck, and his young face is beardless. Such a young man would normally have an unlined face, but lines of grief pucker his brow, his eyes are elongated, and two tear lines furrow his cheeks. His right hand lies palm downward across his chest, and he supports his inclined head within the palm of his raised left hand. The little finger and the fourth finger come forward to support the cheekbone in a very realistic manner. He wears a black clavus painted over a chiton, which has a vermilion ground, red fold lines, black outlines, and thick, white highlights. His himation has a green ground, black outlines, and thick, white highlights.

The rear apostle nearest to Christ is in three-quarter profile, and only his head and shoulders are visible as he bows sharply forward (Figs. 204, 206). He has brown hair set in tight curls in a similar manner to the white curls of St. Peter, but scant hair is on his crown. This suggests that he

237

may be St. Luke, who is often portrayed as a middle-aged man with a tonsure. His mustache is short, and his beard is a sparse growth of black hairs edging his chin and exposing the deep furrows of his cheeks. His forehead is crisped in pain, his eyes are elongated, and two tear lines sear his cheeks with no regard to the salients of the face beneath. Part of his right hand is just visible above Peter's halo. It has suffered much damage from the flaking away of paint layers. His chiton has a blue ground with black lines, and his himation has a yellow-brown ground, umber lines, and black outlines.

The small central figure of an angel swoops down from the apex of the scene, and it fits neatly between the two sections of the titular inscription (Figs. 201, 208). His head is almost horizontal, while his body descends at a sharp diagonal. The acute angle of the body is counterbalanced by his wings, which sweep upward and backward, and by the curve of his outstretched arms as they reach downward to receive the soul from Christ. Both the angel's head and body are in three-quarter profile. His head is exactly half the size of those of the apostles. The figure is heavily foreshortened, which imparts a sense of movement through space. His halo has a single white outline. It is very large for the size of the figure, and it is not an accurate circle since it was widened on the upper side after the head was completed. The angel has a similar three-quarter-profile head to the angels in the dome, with a similar hairstyle of abundant tight curls ending in a ripple of locks at the neck, but the whole buildup is simplified. His hair ribbon is plain white with knots in the free-floating end. His large eyes have solid black pupils and no irises. His face is very small and measures some 7 cm from crown to chin. The painter employed a simpler and more emphatic technique to build up the colors. The angel wears a chiton with a black clavus under a himation of which one end flows over his extended arms in folds that conceal the hands. This provides a suitable cradle in which to enfold the soul of the Virgin. His chiton ends abruptly with an arbitrary diagonal about mid-thigh, which suggests that his body is swinging around sharply. Whether or not this is a deliberate contrivance must remain uncertain, but the figure of the angel does fit remarkably well into the space assigned to it.

His chiton has a vermilion ground (now discolored), red shadows, black lines and outlines, and white highlights with a blue wash over them. His himation has a light yellow-green ground, dark yellow-green shadows, black lines and outlines, white wash highlights, and thick white highlights washed over with blue.

Christ in his Mandorla (Figs. 202, 208, 209, 223)

The three-quarter-length figure of Christ stands upright with his halo fitting within the apex of the mandorla. The elliptical mandorla has an inner background of blue and a broad outer band of light blue. Its fine, scalloped outline in thick white has now mostly flaked away. His head is in three-quarter profile and inclines slightly to the left; his torso is in the frontal stance, and his lower body turns toward the right, counterbalancing the head. His right arm is bent upward as his hand steadies the lower end of the swaddled infant. His left arm is foreshortened as his hand comes up to

grip its shoulder. Christ wears a chiton with a black clavus over an undertunic of which only one sleeve and cuff are visible. Over the chiton he wears a himation, one end of which is pulled back over his left arm with one corner flying free in an arching bell fold.

The whole of Christ's figure is outlined with a thick white line. He has a yellow halo with black and white outlines and cross bars of thick white shadowed with blue but with no jewels. His chiton has a dark yellow-brown ground, fine black fold lines, and chrysographia in bright yellow. The sleeve and cuff of the undertunic are built up in a similar manner to the chiton, but two broad black lines mark the edges of the cuff. His himation has a red ground with broad blue washes and fine black fold lines and outlines.

The swaddled infant, or soul of Mary (Figs. 202, 208, 213)

The infant has a yellow halo with a single outline in white. The diameter is half the size of that of Christ. Only the face of the babe is visible beneath the hood of the enfolding cloths that closely envelop it. The rough lines of the swaddling bands indicate that the arms of the babe are bent up to the middle of the chest and mark the separation of the lower limbs. This is no plump infant but a waif with narrow shoulders and a narrowing body. The linen cloths swaddling the infant are made up of a ground of very thick lime white, which stands out in strong relief from the wall. Upon this ground, the outlines of the limbs, the shadows, and the fold lines are shown in blue with some black lines. The child has a very small head, like that of the angel above it. It measures 7 cm from crown to chin, and the eyes have large black pupils but no irises.

The apostle below Christ (Fig. 217)

St. John is hunched forward with his upright head turned in three-quarter profile as he appears to gaze into Mary's face. A few white curls adorn the top of his bald pate and the side of his head above the ear. His long, white beard neatly outlines his chin before it falls in tresses to the level of the bier. He wears a himation that has a yellow ground, dark grey folds, and black lines and outlines. His shoulder and back are further outlined with a fine, white outline, presumably reflecting or limiting the light of the mandorla behind him.

The three bishops (Figs. 201, 211, 214, 215)

They stand together behind the western end of the bier. They bear no inscriptions and could be any three of the four bishops who were said to be present at this event. They are represented as old men and have similar hair and beard styles. Their faces bear none of the signs of grief that visit the faces of the twelve apostles.

The censing bishop leans forward and is presented in three-quarter profile. With his right hand he raises the censer high in front of him, while with the forefinger of his left hand he steadies the swinging bowl. His receding, smooth white hair curves in to the back of his ear, and his beard closely outlines the chin and then falls into loose tresses. He is clad in full episcopal regalia, with an

omophorion with crosses looped up over his bent left arm. From under his polystavrion appears a jeweled epigonation, and an ornate epitrachelion hangs over his sticharion, which has jeweled epimanikia (Text Fig. 35d).

His omophorion has a thick, white ground, green shadows, light blue outlines, and round white tassels; the broad, single-armed black crosses are bisected at the center with short, fine, black lines. His polystavrion has a thick, white ground, dark yellow fold lines, and bracketed, broad black crosses. The epigonation, epitrachelion, and epimanikia have a yellow ground and white sheen highlights. The epigonation has a design of circles in red line containing jewels and pearls with an edging of pearl bands and a washer pattern (Text Fig. 35); the epitrachelion has a palmette design in red line; and the epimanikia are overlaid with a pearly diaper design with a washer pattern at the wrist (Fig. 24.1a). His sticharion has a red ground with broad washes of blue, and black lines and outlines. The censer has a yellow ground and white "sheen" highlights, and it is decorated with a palmette design in red line with a washer design on the rim. The interior of the bowl is vermilion, and the chain consists of a black line overlaid with yellow S-shapes to indicate the links (Text Fig. 31.1a).

The bishop to the west stands upright in the frontal stance, but his head turns in three-quarter profile as he gazes toward the center of the panel. The style of his hair and beard are similar to those of his neighbor. He bends his right arm upward, and the palm of his hand gestures forward to the figure on the bier. In the crook of his left arm, he carries a closed book with a jeweled cover. He wears episcopal regalia, but his phelonion is plain.

His omophorion has a thick, white ground, blue shadows, and crosses like those of his neighbor. His phelonion has a yellow ground, vermilion shadows, red fold lines, black lines and outlines, blue wash highlights, and thick white highlights. His epimanikia, epigonation, and the cover of his book all have a yellow ground with white sheen highlights. This ground is overlaid with a jeweled diaper pattern filled with vermiculation or palmettes in red line. The cuffs and knee cloth have a border with a washer pattern (Text Figs. 24.1a, 35d). The book has vermilion page ends and black clasps (Text Fig. 36.1c).

The bishop to the rear stands upright in the frontal stance, but he is partially obscured by the censing bishop in front of him. His head is in the frontal aspect, and his receding white hair curves round his head to reveal both ears. His beard falls in tresses down across his chin. His right hand can be seen overlying the jeweled book in the crook of his left arm. His omophorion is looped over his left arm, and the phelonion is pulled back to reveal a jeweled epimanikion on his right arm.

His omophorion has a thick, white ground, green shadows, and crosses like those of the other bishops. His phelonion has a blue ground, red and umber shadows, and black lines and outlines. The epimanikion and the book are similar to those of the bishop to his right.

The apostles to the right of the bier (Figs. 216, 218–221)

In this group of six apostles, the foremost, St. Paul, stands hunched over the end of the bier with three apostles standing in a line behind him. The figure immediately above and behind Paul

has the hair and beard style associated with St. Andrew. The apostle behind him conceals his stricken face in the palm of his supporting right hand. The westernmost apostle stands upright in a three-quarter-profile stance. He supports his sorrowing head on the fingers of his cupped right hand, while he grips the loose folds of his himation with his other hand; this figure is similar to portraits of St. John in many scenes of the Crucifixion. Above these four apostles are the head and shoulders of two additional apostles. The apostles stand in three tiers, but despite the narrowing curve of the arch there is no effect of overcrowding. The technique used for depicting grief in the faces of these remaining six apostles is similar to that described above, and except where an individual adaptation occurs, the descriptions are not repeated.

St. Paul is shown in three-quarter profile, and his upper body is hunched heavily forward to the front of the bier, concealing the upright post. His right hand is raised as he clutches a bunched fold of his himation under his cheek. His left arm is bent forward and the hand gestures toward the Mother of God. Both his legs are in profile, and his feet seem to hover in front of the bier, so that his figure appears to be out in the actual space of the church itself.

His head is in three-quarter profile as he raises it to peer at the Virgin's head beyond him. He has the bald head with a single curl on top and the bushy beard associated with representations of St. Paul. He wears a chiton with a black clavus under a himation of which a tail end loops over his left forearm to hang down in front of the corner post of the bier. His chiton has a light red ground, broad blue washes, red fold lines, black lines and outlines, and thick white highlights; the broad blue washes give the effect of a lavender color. His himation has a light red ground, red lines and fold lines, blue wash highlights, and thick, white, linear highlights.

Near the right side of his head, where the shoulder meets the plaster patch made for the head, the blue wash of the himation was replaced by a green intermediate highlight. This is a particularly clear example of the kind of final touching up that was needed when a head was painted on a patch. It demonstrates without doubt that the whole of the color buildup for the garment was completed before the new patch of plaster for the head was inserted. The new patch inevitably disturbed some of the completed work, and it needed tidying up. When he came to do this, the painter had no blue wash at hand, since blue is not one of the pigments used for building up flesh colors, and so he used what was at hand and made do with a green that he was using for coloring the flesh. The difference cannot be noticed except under close examination with a powerful light.

St. Andrew, the apostle behind St. Paul, is a three-quarter-profile figure that is mostly concealed by the overlapping bodies of the previous two apostles. The tousled white hair and beard are characteristic of Byzantine portraits of St. Andrew, but at Lagoudhera this type of head also serves for prophets and saints, and for Adam in the Anastasis [50]. St. Andrew hunches his shoulders, but his head is erect. His right forearm is raised up, and the hand is concealed in the voluminous folds of his himation, which is wrapped round his shoulders. His left hand gestures forward. The himation has a yellow ground, yellow-brown shadows, dark red and umber fold lines, black outlines, blue wash highlights, and thick, white, linear highlights.

The young apostle to the right is in the frontal stance except for his three-quarter-profile

head, which inclines toward the left, and his right foot, which is painted in profile. He supports his face in his cupped right hand, while his left arm extends languidly downward as he grips the bunched folds of the end of his himation as if to imprison it from the levity of flying free. He has a beardless face, and his layered hair ripples down to the base of his neck. He wears a chiton with a black clavus under a himation. His chiton has a light red ground, red fold lines, black lines and outlines, and thick, white, linear highlights; all the white highlights are washed over with light blue. His himation has a yellow ground, light red fold lines, black lines and outlines, blue wash highlights, and white, linear highlights.

A middle-aged apostle in full length can be glimpsed between St. Andrew and the young apostle. He wears a himation that has a light yellow-green ground, dark yellow-green shadows, black lines and outlines, and thick, white, linear highlights. His chiton has a yellow ground, a black clavus, vermilion shadows, red fold lines, black lines and outlines, blue wash highlights, and thick, white, linear highlights.

His bowed head is supported by his right hand, which lies palm downward across his face. His tilted eyebrows and closed eyes mime a paroxysm of grief that is strengthened by the bowed stance of his body and by his left hand, which clutches and draws up the folds of his himation.

The closed eyes for a living person and the covering of half the face with the hand are both features that run contrary to the conventions for the real presence of an image in a Byzantine church. The face is unusual in Byzantine art of its date, and although we cannot be certain that the type was the invention of the Lagoudhera master, since we have no Constantinopolitan painting of this date, the credit is certainly his for this particular and masterly expression of grief.

The middle-aged apostle above St. Andrew has only his head and shoulders visible. His shoulders are in the frontal stance, but his three-quarter-profile head turns away from the center toward the apostle next to him. His upright head is bald, save for a wisp of hair across the cranium and a lingering of hair above his ear. His round and scalloped beard is brown with white highlights, and it neatly outlines his cleft chin. The upright stance of this apostle is exceptional, and it is clear that the painter adopted it in order to use him as a compositional link between the bishops and his fellow apostles. He wears a blue chiton with a black clavus. His himation has a yellow ground, yellow-brown shadows, black lines and outlines, and thick, white, linear highlights.

The young apostle at the top west turns his bowed head and shoulders toward the center of the scene and holds up to his cheek a bundle of himation folds, as if wiping away his tears. The mouth line curves downward at each end, and his chin is cleft with a line that, although it is unnatural, adds to the expression of grief. He has the head of a young man with a thin mustache and slight beard, and his smooth brown hair curves round to below his ears. He wears a blue chiton with a black clavus. His himation has a yellow ground, vermilion shadows, red fold lines and outlines, some reinforcing black lines, blue wash highlights, and thick, white, linear highlights.

The iconography of the Koimesis requires the presence of a considerable number of figures gathered round a prominent bier. To achieve such an assembly in the architectural space provided by

a lunette, with its inward sloping sides, is a challenge that the 1192 master met with considerable skill.

The Virgin on her bier looms at the center and forefront of the composition, and her figure is constructed to a larger scale than that of the other figures. Her horizontal body is seen in aerial perspective, and because of the peculiar angle of her head, her halo is larger than standard. These compositional measures give a three-dimensional substance to her figure and her bier. The bier is thrust to the fore of the picture plane, and the presence of the footstool in front of it and the overlapping feet of St. Paul strongly suggest that the pictorial space is not limited behind the red borders of the picture frame. It extends outward into the space of the church itself and thereby increases the impact of the real presence of the scene for the worshipper.

The architectures have a minimum impact in this scene. They serve simply to limit the picture space and to form a backdrop to the figures of the apostles. Their strong verticals function well in holding up the line of the lunette so that the leaning figures in the corners do not appear too weighed down by it. The scale of the architecture is miniature in relation to the figures, as in other scenes in this decoration.

The grouping of the apostles is given depth by the use of overlap and by the elevation of the rear figures. With the exception of the rear right apostle, all the heads and upper torsos are inclined toward the center of the panel, and their three-quarter-profile stance draws the eye inward in depth. The figures of the apostles and that of Christ are drawn to a similar scale. They are smaller than the figure of the Virgin but larger than those of the bishops and the angel. Christ's figure very properly appears to be larger in scale than those of the apostles, and the painter has achieved this by painting him in the frontal stance. The swooping angel has a smaller head and body, and his head and shoulders are constructed to half the scale allowed for the apostles.

Two linked but separate dramas are represented in this tableau: the apotheosis of the Virgin, which is enacted by the central figures with their stolid bodies and enigmatic faces, and the death or falling asleep of the Virgin accompanied by the mourning apostles, with their dramatic stances and grief-stricken faces. The horizontal Virgin on her bier links both dramas, since her body is the focus of the bowed apostles and her soul is the subject of the apotheosis. The Falling Asleep of the Virgin is reflected in the circular composition in which all the figures, except the angel, are in-cluded. The apotheosis breaks the circular movement at the center of the composition by adding a sense of movement upward from the horizontal figure, achieved in a steep arching movement that echoes the actual arch of the lunette. In order to combine these two separate events and compositional themes, the scene was composed like a triptych, with the Virgin on the center panel and the apostles on the side panels. The bishops appear as solid witnesses, and while one holds high a censer in homage, the others stand stiffly upright with totally bland faces. Although Christ in-clines his head, he, too, stands stiffly upright in a frontal stance, and the breadth of his figure is emphasized by the soul he carries, the windswept tail of his himation, and the broad enclosing ellipse of the mandorla. In contrast, the apostles are seen in three-quarter profile, hunched forward in grief. The majority gesture in pain, with one hand palm down across the chest, and all their faces

are contorted in sorrow in a more emotionally intense manner than in any other surviving representation of the Koimesis. The faces of the young apostles have a forehead creased with winged U lines, and all of the apostles' faces have tilted eyebrows and tear lines. This is one of the few scenes in Byzantine painting in which the bodies of the figures and the heads are in complete emotional harmony and in which both are used to create in graphic mime the emotion of grief.

The painter shows a particular awareness of light in this painting, just as in the Presentation of the Mother of God [70]. The architectures are built up on both sides of the painting, with an emphasis on placing the highlights to the side nearest the center of the scene. There is also a particular manifestation of light in the form of the mandorla enclosing the figure of Christ. Where the light from the mandorla hits a figure within it, such as that of Christ or the shoulders of the apostle beneath Him, it rebounds, and each figure is outlined with a white line. Christ is further illuminated by the use of chrysographia upon his chiton. The normal Byzantine conventions governing the use of light are applied to the rest of the figures in the scene, which are encased within their black outlines. They are highlighted and shadowed to bring out the volume of each figure, independent of any general light effects in the background. It is a great pity that the overall haze on this painting detracts from the original brilliance of its coloring (see above, p. 232).

The strong vertical and curving movement provided by the ogival pyramid of the central composition and the curving masses of the groups of apostles under the arching sides of the lunette is counteracted by the solid ellipse lined with the heads of the remaining figures. The Lagoudhera Koimesis is remarkable for its economy in the use of space, for the harmony of the elements within it, and for the intense and single-minded expression of grief.[117]

The Arakiotissa [139]

(Pl. 32; Figs. 224–227; Text Fig. 41)

This tall panel, on the east side of the center bay's south wall, enshrines the slim figure of the Mother of God enfolding the Christ child in her arms. She stands upright against a backdrop of a throne and a long prayer in the form of a poem to Our Lady of the Vetches. The image is of the Virgin of Sorrows, Our Lady of the Passion, and to either side of the Virgin's shoulders an angel bows, holding forward instruments of the Passion of Christ: one holds the spear and the sponge, and the other a long, narrow cross. It is clear that the donor, Lord Leon, regarded the icon as the focal point of his church, and he gave most lavishly toward the completion of the painting. It was rich in blue and vermilion pigments and embellished with the sumptuous use of gold and silver leaf. This magnificent panel must have shimmered gaudily in the candlelight.

The appellation of the Mother of God is written to either side of her, as is the first line of the long prayer of supplication, which fills the background of her figure and throne from her waist level downward.

---

[117] For a different assessment of the Lagoudhera Koimesis, see R. Cormack, *Writing in Gold* (London, 1985), 174, 175. See also H. Maguire, *The Icons of Their Bodies* (Princeton, 1996), 64–65.

"The Arakiotissa, Most Full of Grace"

This part of the invocation is written in larger letters than those for the long prayer written beneath it. The title $\overline{\text{MHP}}$/ $\overline{\theta V}$ appears at the top of the panel to either side of her halo, in letters of a similar size to her title below. The sigla $\overline{\text{IC}}$ $\overline{\text{XC}}$ also appear to the left of the Child's halo, but these are inscribed in smaller lettering. (The inscribed prayer is recorded and discussed in Chapter Three, see above, pp. 66–68.) The panel measures 152 cm in width by 224 cm in height. It was plastered as a single section with plaster joins within the red borders framing the icon, except at the eastern end, where the plaster join is in the background of the figure of the Christ Antiphonetes [127], whose panel overlaps the south wall (see above, p. 222). The plaster for all the flesh areas of the figures was reworked before the final colors were laid in. Within the figure of the Mother of God are traces of flattened curves in the plaster surface, where it has been reworked in the manner noted on the face of the Christ in the dome [1] (see above, pp. 111–12). This reworking runs down her figure from the level of her hands, and it shows as horizontal depression lines that occur at 3 mm to 1 cm intervals, leaving impress lines about 2 mm wide. The reworking does not continue up the torso or within the area for the Christ child.

The eastern angel has two incised lines marking the diagonals of the shafts for the spears. The cross held by the western angel does not appear to have an incised diagonal, but it may be concealed by the thick paint on the central shaft. The figure of the Mother of God has numerous incised and impressed guidelines. The left outline to her maphorion, from beneath Christ's halo to its hem, has a deeply impressed line and a ridged disturbance in the plaster. Two fine incision lines mark the golden hem of her maphorion where it crosses at the base of her neck. The outline to Mary's left shoulder and upper arm is impressed, but the line does not continue down the outline to the maphorion. There is a heavy ridging of the plaster where the hem of her chiton hitches up over her feet and footstool. This ridging may be due to the accumulated plaster from the reworking of the plaster for the robe above. Impressed and incised lines mark the upper and lower outlines to the bolster and the outer vertical outlines to the throne. The plaster surface in general is very irregular, with shallow hollows and bumps.

The upper background to the figures was originally painted with a blue ground over a grey base. At some later date it was given an overpaint of copper blue, and this has now darkened significantly. The blue overpaint was applied in a manner so as not to intrude over the lettering of the poem, and the overpaint thus forms a frame round it. The lower background is green. The fourteenth-century painter also painted out and remade quite a lot of the jeweled decoration around the arms of the throne. Some pearls were covered over with black, like those of the jeweled edging to Mary's footstool in the pendentive [40] (see above, p. 146), and where he thought of it, he put in his own greyish pearls. The bolster's decorated tapered ends were also overpainted.

The very thick dirt over the lower part of the painting is evidence of centuries of veneration to the patroness. Other figures in the lower register were far less encrusted and greasy. The upper

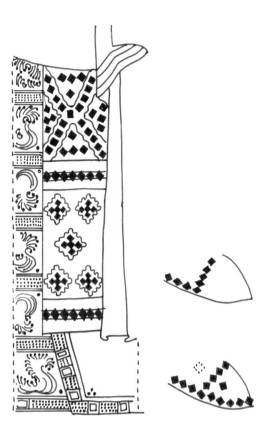

Text Fig. 41 Decoration of the throne and slippers of the Mother of God
Arakiotissa [139], showing the stamped pattern of gold- and silver-leaf squares

part of the panel was cleaned, and the faces especially were scrubbed in this century by a schoolmaster restorer who was also responsible for the coat of varnish applied over it, and perhaps also for the fuzzy coating over the painting of the Koimesis above. This unfortunate cleaning has removed the upper layers of flesh color from the faces and limbs of the two main figures, and also much of the upper layers of paint and such of the gilding as was left on the robes.

The figures of the angels and the Mother of God are different in size but are constructed on the same modular system. The femininity of the Virgin is emphasized by shortening her hands by one-eighth of a face length. The measures for the child's head, hands, and feet, like those of the other infants portrayed in this decoration [39, 74, 142], follow proportional ratios in keeping with nature (see below, pp. 293-96).

The importance of this dedicatory icon was emphasized with gold and silver leaf. The haloes of the figures were gilded, and gold leaf was applied in the form of chrysographia to the tunics of both the child and the Mother of God. The hems of her maphorion were decorated with single or double yellow bands formed of gold leaf, over which were applied highlights in creamy yellow.

The toes of her slippers were also impressed with squares of leaf. Silver leaf was applied in the form of impressed squares to form diamond and cross shapes amid the decoration within the cloth covering of the seat of the throne (see description below and Text Fig. 41). The impressed squares where traces of leaf were found have a geometric accuracy that suggests they were cut to a standard template, and the average measure of each side is 1.5 cm.

The Mother of God and Christ child

The Virgin stands upright in the frontal aspect, but her head is slightly inclined in the three-quarter-profile stance as she gazes down at the Christ child. Both her arms are bent as she brings her hands forward to meet loosely at waist level. Her right shoulder turns inward so that her upper left arm is in profile. She wears a maphorion with segmenta and decorated hem over a tunic with traces of chrysographia. Her pointed slippers are picked out with gold leaf. The child lies across her arms, his head and halo against her right shoulder, while Mary's hands form a cradle for him against her body. His right leg is bent upward and outward across her forearm, while the other is tucked underneath so that only the sole of his left foot is visible. He raises his right arm in blessing, while with his left fist he grips a rolled scroll. His head is in three-quarter profile, and a delicate pearly earring dangles from his right ear. He gazes upward, apparently toward the western angel of the Passion rather than to the inclined face of his mother above him. The child has the Byzantine characteristics of infancy, which are the high forehead, a snub nose, and broad cheeks. His head and halo are half the length and width of those of his mother. He is a substantial infant, although he appears to weigh little in Mary's arms. The painter has created an impression of great tenderness between the two figures, so that the mother seems to seek to enfold and protect the child's curving body.

The whole of Mary's upper figure, from one side of the bolster to the other, is outlined with a fine, white outline that stands outside the black outline to her maphorion. This ample upper garment enfolds her head and shoulders and falls down her back, while the front ends are looped over her forearms and gathered into folds beneath the child. The maphorion has a vermilion ground, umber shadows, and black lines and outlines. Where the maphorion frames the head, the hem has a single broad yellow band, but the lower hem folds have double yellow bands. All these bands were gilded and then highlighted with blobs of creamy yellow. The segmenta on her shoulders and the tassels falling from the folds on her shoulders are in fine, white lines. The wimple fits closely round her face, and it is blue with fine, black gather lines. The sleeves of her undergarment are also blue with fine fold lines in black, and they have double yellow bands at the wrist, similar to those edging the maphorion. Mary's tunic has a yellow ground, light red shadows, and red and black lines and outlines. There are definite traces of gilding in the tapering and sharply defined grey-brown diagonal and vertical striations that appear all over this garment, like the shadows of chrysographia. Her slippers are vermilion with an umber shadow and a heavy black underline. They were picked out with rows of diamond shapes in gold leaf (Text Fig. 41).

The yellow halo of the Christ child has white bars shadowed with blue and pinpointed by

five vermilion jewels. He has light brown hair that recedes from the top of his forehead to fall in loose curves to below his ear with its earring of pendant pearls. His tunic is yellow with vermilion lines and black lines and fold lines, and it still bears the tapered, angular traces of chrysographia in gold leaf. His stole has a ground of thick lime white, blue lines and fold lines, and a decorative pattern of double bands of vermilion enclosing a simple cross. His scroll is vermilion with gilt edges.

The throne with bolster, cloth, and footstool

The throne and its accouterments are partially concealed by the central figure of Mary. The two sides of the throne are decorated with an acanthus pattern bedecked with pearls. The top is crowned by a plump bolster, which is creased and indented to either side of Mary so that she appears to be resting her weight upon it. From beneath the center of the bolster a richly decorated white cloth falls to the level of her footstool. From the top of the bolster to the base of the panel measures 95 cm, and the bolster averages 33 cm in height.

The bolster has a vermilion ground with umber shaping lines. At each end it is drawn to a point by a white looped tassel with three pearls at the base. The gathered ends originally had two bands of white outlining their curve, but these were overpainted, possibly in the fourteenth century, by a design of black lines over yellow ochre.

The cloth has a thick white ground, and it is decorated with twin horizontal vermilion bands that divide the cloth into two sections of white. Each double band and the narrow gap of white between them were overlaid with a row of "diamond" shapes in the form of squares of gold leaf. The upper white section of the cloth has a diagonal cross formed by a double outline of chevron lines in black. Within the corridors of the chevron and at the interstices are traces of silver-leaf squares. The lower section has a pattern of irregularly stepped crosses with traces of five silver-leaf, diamond shapes within them (Text Fig. 41).

The sides of the throne have a single, tall panel divided into six rectangles. These are separated by horizontal bands of yellow outlined in black. Within the yellow bands are triple rows of pearls alternating with a vermilion jewel. The outer outline to the throne consists of a black band that is 1.5 cm wide and is filled with a continuous line of single pearls. The inner rectangles are each filled with an acanthus shape that has a light umber ground, dark red shadows, and umber and black lines. The inner outline is picked out with dot-and-tail pearls in creamy yellow (Text Fig. 41).[118] The dais or footstool upon which Mary stands is rectangular with a rich, jeweled border. The sides are set to a slight diagonal. The top of the dais has a yellow ground with a black inner and a light yellow outer outline. The surface is marked out with tapered vertical lines that are now a red color but were probably gilded. Three pearls in a triangle mark the center and corners of the

---

[118] This ornate acanthus pattern can be found on the throne of Christ in the Deesis panel on the north wall of the cell in the cave church of St. Neophytos, Paphos. C. Mango and E. J. W. Hawkins, "The Hermitage of St. Neophytos and Its Wall Paintings," *DOP* 20 (1966), 119–206; Stylianou, *Painted Churches*, fig. 206.

base area. The broad black borders are marked out with a linear yellow corridor with alternating rectangles and squares. The former contain triple lines of pearls and the latter a vermilion or green jewel.

The angels of the Passion (Figs. 226, 227)

An elegant angel hovers in each upper corner of the painting, above the inscription to either side of the Mother of God. Although perfectly proportioned, they are constructed to a scale less than half that of the Mother of God. Each full-length figure bows forward in the three-quarter-profile stance with arms bent forward and the front leg advancing forward across the other leg. Both of their wings are furled downward behind them. The three-quarter-profile heads with their heavy mass of curls, white jeweled fillets, and young faces are similar to those of the angel roundels in the dome [4–13] (Figs. 48–59). Both angels have haloes, which were previously lined with gold leaf. They are dressed in a chiton with a clavus under a himation with an eddying fold to the fore. Both wear boots decorated with pearls.

The figures are outlined, from their halo to their boots, with a white line painted outside the usual black outline to the robes. The scapular of their wings has a yellow ground, green edge shadows, black lines and outlines, and off-white highlights. The feathers run from long black feathers through dark red, vermilion, pink, and white ones, each with a daub of the lighter shade at the tip. The angels' boots are vermilion with umber underlines, and they are decorated with a double row of white pearls at the ankles and across the toes. A triangle of three pearls is placed on the toes, and a circlet of pearls on the dorsum of the foot. The western angel wears a chiton of light red, with umber lines and shadows, black lines and outlines, white wash highlights washed over in blue, and thick, white highlights. His himation has a yellow ground, dark red lines and shadows, black lines and outlines, white wash highlights tinted with a blue wash, and thick, white highlights. The chiton and himation of the eastern angel are colored in reverse to those of the western figure. Both angels exhibit the sleeves of an undergarment that is colored like their chitons. The cuffs of these undergarments are gilded and picked out with black bands lined with pearls. The spears have yellow shafts with fine black outlines, the bare spearhead is white, and the sponge is ochre with red speckles. The cross has a yellow ground, fine black outlines, and thick shadow underlines.

This richly decorated icon was made with costly materials. It has now lost much of its magnificence with the rubbing away of the gold and silver leaf and the scrubbing of the subtle coloring of the flesh areas. These losses cannot spoil the graceful composition, with the delicate, slender figures of the angels counterbalancing the heavy furnishing of the lower part of the painting. Their arching bodies act as ushers to the central figures beneath them. Despite their enigmatic features, the mother and child, with their interfolding stances, impart a sense of formal tenderness at the center of the composition that outweighs the dread significance of the ministering angels.

In the general iconographic layout of the church, the Mother of God is neatly counterpoised by the figure of the devout Symeon on the north wall opposite, holding a more lively Christ child in his arms, but with the same enveloping tenderness.

The Archangel Michael [140]

(Figs. 228–230, Text Fig. 42)

The archangel is placed to the west side of the Arakiotissa [139] in the ground register of the bay. The height and width of the panel are 2.20 cm by 1.54 cm, respectively, exclusive of the red borders. The panel is dominated by the majestic life-size figure of the archangel Michael, who stands upright upon a richly decorated footstool. His right arm curves upward as he grips his tall stave of office, and his left arm curves downward as he balances a large globe in the palm of his hand. The great wings are spread outward and downward to either side of the figure. He is richly clad in a loros with faceted jewels worn over an ample dalmatic with a stiff jeweled hem, and his feet are shod in boots decorated with pearls.

The titular inscription is abbreviated, and the shortenings are placed to either side of the halo. Despite the high relief of the thick, white lime pigment, the letters are elegant and finely executed. The inscription was painted on the original upper background of green. Three words are written on the yellow ground within the rectangular standard of the archangel's stave in white letters (Text Fig. 42): ΑΓΙΟС ΑΓΙΟС ΑΓΙΟС (holy, holy, holy). The final word climbs up around the side of the rectangle. The globe in the angel's left hand bears the sigla $\overline{\text{IC}}$ $\overline{\text{XC}}$ in vermilion letters on the white ground.

The panel was plastered in a single section, and there are no plaster patches. At some early period a bad hole appeared to the right of the archangel's neck above the scapula of the wing, and it was repaired and colored in at various times. The plaster for the hands was reworked before they were completed. There are traces of several incision lines: one marks the base of the footstool and one is above Michael's right shoulder, marking the outer curve of the wing between the neck and the hand. A long impress line in his left wing runs through the covert feathers and marks the base of the main body of the wing and its inner downward curve.

At a final stage of painting, the angel's tunic was narrowed in the area of the left underarm, and the wings were extended upward and outward by a thick, black line. The long diagonal shaft of the angel's stave is not very straight. This may well be due to an adjustment of the stave when painting from a stage of scaffolding. It has a distinct kink at the top where it runs through the angel's fingers under the knob.

The original background of the figure was painted green, and the foreground received a further coat of green to differentiate it. The upper background was overpainted, probably in the fourteenth century, with a copper blue, and many other areas were crudely overpainted with black and red. Much of the damage to the original painting was superficial. It can now be seen that the plaster contained an over-generous quantity of chopped straw, which was too near the surface, and the thin coating of lime has flaked off, taking with it quantities of paint. With the exception of the blue over the upper background, the overpaints were removed in the course of conservation. The pasty, flat yellow appearance of Michael's face is largely due to the scrubbing it received at the same time that attempts were made to clean the Arakiotissa [139] in the adjacent panel. Because of this,

Text Fig. 42 The archangel Michael's [140] stave and boot, footstool, and reverse pattern to his loros

the careful buildup of flesh colors in the face and neck has been reduced to a flat yellow with smears of vermilion that now contrast starkly with the dark green and umber contouring of the face.

The archangel stands firmly with his feet apart and with his body in the frontal aspect. His head is also in the frontal stance, and the face is asymmetrical in relation to the nose. His face is wider to the right side of the nose, and his gaze is directed across it to the west. His face is that of a clean-shaven young man, and his abundant hair is clustered in tight curls that taper to the back of his neck. The jeweled fillet with flying ends is woven through his hair. The hair style is similar to those of other angels in this decoration, but only Michael and the angel of the Ascension [78] are shown with their heads in the frontal aspect.

Michael wears a long-sleeved undergarment with jeweled cuffs under a dalmatic with an embroidered neckline and jewel-encrusted hemline. The long, narrow, richly jeweled imperial loros entwines his figure, and one long end is caught up over his left forearm, revealing its patterned lining, before falling down again in a chevron pattern of folds (Text Fig. 42).

The archangel's undertunic has a red ground and black lines and outlines, and his jeweled cuffs are similar to pattern 1a (Text Fig. 24). The hem of this garment was overpainted with

251

vermilion and given additional black lines; this was a contemporary alteration and may reflect some attempt to unite this garment with the dalmatic above it. His dalmatic has a vermilion ground with black lines, and the collar is decorated with a meander pattern in umber line on a yellow ground. The decorative hem band is outlined with narrow black bands, where lines of six pearls alternate with a green or red jewel. The yellow ground of the band is filled with a diamond net pattern in dark red line. The corridors within the pattern are lined with single pearls, with jewels at the intersections. The squares within the pattern are filled with vermiculation. The cuffs are decorated in a similar manner with a washer pattern and additional pearl bands at the wrist. The neckline or collar has a narrow black border with groups of single pearls, and the yellow corridor is filled with a vermiculation in dark red (Text Fig. 24.4b).

The archangel's loros entwines his figure, and the sections are uneven in width as they appear to the front of the figure. It has broad black borders marked out with a linear corridor of yellow squares and rectangles. The squares are filled with a red or green jewel set in yellow lines, and the rectangles are lined with a double row of pearls. The area between the black borders is filled with a net pattern of squares and rectangles marked out in black line on a yellow ground. Both the large and the small squares contain green or red jewels in white, linear settings. All the jewels are faceted, each seemingly bisected diagonally, as one half is painted in a darker tone than the other; the diagonals follow the same direction in each panel (Pl. 11c, loros pattern III). This suggestion of faceting effectively gives the impression of a rich relief within the garment, and it helps to break up the mass of this otherwise rather stolid figure. The tail end of the loros, which is caught up over Michael's arm, shows the reverse lining to it. The reverse panel ascending up to the arm has a dark red ground and umber shadows on which is applied a delicate chain-and-pearl pattern in lime white. The loose loros folds falling from the archangel's arms have their reverse painted in vermilion, and blue and white tassels hang from the edges. In these folds the border pattern to the jeweled panels has two additional corridor patterns, one with washer circles in umber line on a yellow ground, and the other with a single black band lined with pearls (Text Fig. 42).

The archangel's boots are vermilion with red and umber shadows to the inner outline. Double black bands lined with single pearls run across the top of the foot and across the ankle. A circlet of pearls marks the center of the dorsum, and a triangle of three pearls marks the toe of the boot.

The great wings are built up in a similar manner to that of the other angels, and the covert feathers are graded from dark red to very light pink. The archangel's stave is taller than he is, and the shaft is very thin. It has a yellow ground with a heavy black outline on the right side. The rectangular standard has a yellow ground with white outlines, and the contour is picked out with ten stiff finials of double white pearls. The orb is spherical and painted in thick lime white with a crescent of grey shadow at its base. A three-armed cross decorates the middle of the orb, and both the cross and the sigla IC XC to either side of it are painted in vermilion.

Only the front side of the footstool is shown in the form of a horizontal band of yellow, where double rows of nine pearls alternate with a red or green jewel. The feet of the archangel do

not rest on the footstool, and this traditional device pushes the figure forward and makes him appear to hover in the space of the church itself. The richly decorated, plumped-up cushion has a ground of red, and it is outlined in umber line. The surface has a diamond-net pattern of single white pearls set in corridors of yellow lines. Enclosed within the irregularly shaped interstices is a single green or red fleur de lys, each with an upper outline in white (Text Fig. 42).

The archangel Michael is a very impressive figure, with his authoritative stance and rich imperial garments, and with his orb and stave of office. The strong verticals of the body and the wings are relieved by the horizontal S-curve of the arms and the upper outline of the wings. The faceting of the great green and red jewels of the loros breaks up the mass of the flat, static body and almost sets one blinking. This would have been a dazzling image when it was first painted.

14

The South Side of the West Vault and the Southwest Bay

The Birth of Christ [142]

(Pls. 22, 33–35; Figs. 231–249, 295)

The birth of Christ is set in the curve of the southwest vault, which forms an irregular rectangle. The panel measures an average 2.93 m in width at the top and 2.84 m in width at the base, and the height of the scene is 2.44 m at the west side.

The scene follows a standard iconography that portrays in one painting all those events associated with the birth of Christ. The Mother of God is in the cave with the Christ child wrapped in swaddling bands and laid in a manger, where he is warmed by the breath of the ox and the ass; Joseph sits in isolation to one side with his donkey. Around the painting are the annunciation to the shepherds, the washing of the child by midwives, and the visitation of the Magi led by the star. All of these characters and events are brought together in the one painting with no regard for unity of time and action, and in this composition they all revolve around the central reclining figure of the Mother of God.

The background picture space is composed in eight sections, of which six are mountains and two are sky. The central and largest mountain contains the black, jagged-edged cave with the recumbent Mary on her white mattress. The manger appears to float forward into the space in front of her. High in the sky above looms an eight-pointed star, whose slanting linear rays descend toward the Christ child. Beneath the star, in a section of sky to the left, stand three angels with wings streaming behind them, their bodies partially concealed by Mary's mountain. One angel turns his head back to look at the approaching Magi while he gestures upward to the star; the other two angels bow forward, with their hands reaching across to Mary. To the right of Mary's mountain another angel exhorts the shepherds; one young shepherd playing the flute sits high on one mountain, while below him two more shepherds on another mountain gaze up at the angel. In keeping with tradition, one of the latter is the bucolic, bent, old man with a large red nose and trusty stick. His

youthful companion, crook and pelaska lying unheeded across the landscape, gestures upward to the angel, while he steps forward onto the mountain below him, where sheep graze among the bushes. This mountain also forms the background to the two midwives who are busy washing the Christ child at the bottom of the painting. One turbanned midwife is seated on the ground as she holds onto the child in the basin, while the other midwife stands, pouring water from a ewer. In the bottom left corner of the painting, Joseph, who is seated on his wooden donkey saddle, leans forward with his head in his hand, facing his small donkey, who is tied to a bush on the hill. Above Joseph, against another hill, the three Magi approach, one behind the other.

The title to the scene is written in fine, white letters in the sky at the center of the top of the scene. It occupies one horizontal line, and the name of Christ is abbreviated. To the upper right of the scene in the sky above the announcing angel and the flute player is a four-line inscription:

Fear not: for behold I bring you good tidings of great joy, which shall be to all people.

The quotation is traditional for the birth and is taken from the Gospel according to St. Luke, 2:10. Several titles in white letters also are scattered through the scene. The abbreviation $\overline{\text{MHP}}$ $\overline{\theta V}$ is neatly aligned to either side of Mary's shoulders on the black background of the cave. The letters stand 5 cm high and are finished with neat serifs. The sigla $\overline{\text{IC}}$ $\overline{\text{XC}}$ for the Christ child are placed just above his halo. The $\overline{\text{IC}}$ was repainted on the particularly damaged background, but the smaller $\overline{\text{XC}}$ is original. The child in the bath also has the sigla $\overline{\text{IC}}$ $\overline{\text{XC}}$ written close together in small letters above his halo on the mountain background. St. Joseph's inscription, written in small letters, is placed behind his halo. The epithet is laid out horizontally, and the name is aligned vertically beneath it. The elegant lettering forms a T-shape against the background of the two eastern mountains just behind Joseph's head.

The panel was plastered in a single section with the plaster joins lying in the red borders. A number of the heads of figures were painted on fresh plaster patches. The plaster for other heads, hands, and feet was reworked as was the plaster for the body of the nude Christ child. Incision lines were used to mark particular features. Among these are the upper outlines to the mountain behind the midwives, the shaft of the young shepherd's crook, the outlines to his bag and the straps hanging from it, the long stick held by the old shepherd, and the outlines of the arms of the midwife with the ewer. Impress lines were also used to mark some contours, such as the curving shoulder of St. Joseph and the right edge of his mountain.

Some bad damage occurred in the area of the two lower Magi and the crib, and in the mountain area behind Joseph. In the fourteenth century these damaged areas were overpainted with little regard to the surviving original. Where repair painting overlapped the original, it was removed in the course of conservation.

The upper background against which are seen the titular inscription, the star, and the four angels is colored with the clear twelfth-century blue. The lower background is divided into six distinct, overlapping mountain shapes. Mary's mountain dominates the center of the scene as it rises to a snow-capped, rounded summit that is placed slightly to one side of the notional center

vertical of the scene. Three tall mountains are to either side of hers: that of the three Magi at the east, and that of the flute player to the west, and below his, that of the two other shepherds. Joseph and his donkey are backed by their own low mount in the lower east corner. A slightly higher mount serves as background to the busy midwives, who share it with the sheep and their manger, in the western corner. The mountains are, sadly, damaged by patches of discoloration, and bad flaking has occurred in the hillsides behind Joseph and the Magi, and at the eastern edge of Mary's mountain. It looks as if the damage was the result of water leaking through the west vault at an early period before the secondary roof was added to the church.

Mary's mountain has a dark yellow ground, thin umber shadows, black lines to the west side, and thick, white highlights on the east side. The snowy crags on the crest have a white wash and thick, white caps underlined with black. From the top of the mountain to the bottom border of the picture measures 194 cm.

The flute player's mountain has a very pale red ground and thin reddish umber shadows with umber shadows over them. From the top of his mountain to the bottom border measures 221 cm.

The shepherds' mountain is very discolored. It has a light umber ground with red and umber shadows and white wash highlights at the eastern edge. The trees have a light umber ground, umber side shadow, green highlight to one side, and stubby, black definition lines. From the top to the bottom border measures 150 cm.

The midwives' mountain has a pale reddish brown ground with two darker tones of shadow, black lines delineating the ridges to the west, and white wash highlights marking the eastern edges. The trees have a yellow ground with black definition lines. The ground beneath the seated mid-wife and to the side of the basin is painted as a dark umber shadow. Beneath the feet of the standing midwife, the ground is painted in a contrasting light yellow. From the top of the mountain to the bottom red border measures 110 cm.

Joseph's mountain has a yellow ground, red shadows, some umber shadows, black lines on the west side, and a grey white crag. The trees have an umber ground, a light umber ground on the shadowed area of the mountain, black definition lines, and green highlights. From the crest to the bottom border the height is 81 cm.

The mountain of the Magi has a light red ground, thin and then thick red shadows, some umber shadows, and a black crest line. From the apex to the bottom of the picture measures 200 cm.

The Mother of God and the Child in the manger (Pl. 33; Figs. 232, 233)

Mary's upper body is frontal, but her legs are drawn up in a lateral stance, and she places her hands upon her knees so that her figure forms a soft, restful curve. She is painted to a larger scale than the other figures in the scene, and the center of her body marks the centerpoint of the whole painting. Her yellow halo has a single black outline beaded with rows of four pearls that alternate

with a single green or red jewel.[119] Her head was painted upon a fresh plaster patch applied within the halo, and it is in fine condition. She has a young face with smooth brows beneath her close-fitting blue wimple. She wears a long tunic under her enfolding maphorion, and her feet are clad in jeweled slippers.

Mary's tunic has a blue ground with black shadow lines. Her maphorion has a vermilion ground with dark red shadows, black lines, and a yellow hem picked out with lighter yellow highlights. The hem carries no tassels. A single segmentum decorates her forehead, but none is on her shoulders. Her maphorion has some badly bleached patches on it. Her slippers are vermilion with red shadows and traces of pearl decorations on the toes. The plaster for both her hands was reworked before completion, and their length was shortened in keeping with the painter's convention for women's hands.

The cavern in the mountain is painted solid black, and it has jagged edges with a thick white outline. Mary's mattress is curved like a bean, and it fits snuggly within the black cave surrounding it. It has a thick, lime white ground and is decorated with two sets of broad double lines in vermilion.

The Christ child raises his head, but his body is tightly bound up to his neck with swaddling bands and is laid in a stiff, horizontal position within the rectangular manger. The horned head of the ox and the long-eared head of the ass can just be seen above his halo.

The child's halo is yellow with a single thick, white outline and cross bars that are also white but may have been shaded with blue. His swaddling bands are white with alternate bands tinted with pink, and they are picked out with red lines. The manger has a white ground with a brown tint, light grey wash, and thick, white highlights, and the interior is black. The ox has a light red ground with umber lines; the ass is grey. These two animals were entirely painted out by the fourteenth-century repairer. The overpaint was removed in the course of conservation to reveal what is left of them.

Joseph and his donkey (Figs. 249, 295)

The plaster of Joseph's face and arms was reworked, and there are deep impress marks for the contour of his shoulders. He is portrayed in three-quarter profile and sits on his wooden saddle in silent communion with his tethered donkey. Together they form an intimate if isolated group relegated to the bottom east corner of the painting. Joseph's reflective pose is reminiscent of *The Thinker* by Auguste Rodin. Resting his elbow on his left knee, he supports his bowed head within the open palm of his left hand; his right arm lies passively along his profile right leg. Joseph was an old man, and his tight white curls and neatly rounded, short beard are of the type for St. Peter. Joseph's chiton has a light blue ground, blue shadows, black lines, and fine white highlights. His

---

[119] This single, jeweled halo appears in only five other haloes in this decoration: those of Joachim, Anna, Zacharias, the standing Virgin in the Presentation of the Virgin [70], and that of the head of Christ in the Mandylion [92]. The head of Christ is the only one of the six heads that was not built up on a fresh plaster patch.

himation has a pale red ground, thin brown shadow washes, red lines, black lines and outlines, and thick, white, linear highlights.

Joseph's saddle is similar to the standard wooden saddle still used on donkeys in the Middle East. It has a slightly concave, oblong wooden base and upright, horn-shaped, wooden lashing posts at the corners. It had a yellow ground with black lines and outlines and white, linear highlights. The saddle is now only partly visible because many of the paint layers have flaked away.

Joseph's donkey is loosely tethered to a miniature tree on the side of the mountain. He is a handsome, well-shaped animal seen in profile, with well-articulated, slender limbs, but his size is diminutive in relation to that of Joseph. He wears a bridle on his head that is connected by a chain to the rein. He is painted with a grey ground, blue shadows, black lines, and white highlights. His bridle and rein are black, and the chain is made of S shapes in white.

The two midwives and the Christ child (Pl. 35; Figs. 241, 244–248).

The three figures form another small group absorbed in each other. The seated woman supports the figure of the Christ child with one hand flat under his chest, while with the other hand she gestures upward to her standing colleague. The standing midwife, in the costume of a maiden at court, bows her head as she pours water from the slanting ewer. Her right hand is curled around the curving handle, and her left hand is beneath the pot, supporting its weight. This little vignette is separated from that of Joseph and his beast by a tree.

The seated midwife has one leg tucked under the other in a manner similar to that of the Christ child in the arms of the Arakiotissa [139]. Her head is in three-quarter profile, and she has a young face. Her brown hair shows beneath her turban, which fits closely over her ears. The turban is enriched with a decorated band, and its long train winds round her neck to fall all the way down her back. She wears a long tunic girdled at the waist, with the sleeves rolled back to leave her arms bare. Her feet are clad in black slippers like those of the Hebrew virgins in the Presentation of the Mother of God [70].

Her turban has a thick, white ground and yellow-green shadows. The decorative bandeau has a yellow ground and black outlines; it is overlaid with a vermiculated scroll pattern in red between the black outlines. Beneath the turban are traces of a vermilion wimple. Her tunic has a light grey ground, green shadows, black lines and outlines, and white wash and thick, white highlights.

In the golden basin full of water, the Christ child is shown as a nude figure in three-quarter profile. His head is craned back while his body leans forward with his legs drawn up beneath him. Both arms reach forward, and one hand rests on the midwife's knee and the other hand on her arm. The child is bald except for a little hair at the back of his head. His halo has a single white outline, and the bars are white with blue and black outlines. The flesh colors of his figure were carefully built up, and most of his body was overlaid with fine, undulating, horizontal lines in thin white to simulate the transparency of water.

The circular basin on its pedestal is seen both from above and from the front. The water within the wide circle of the bowl is painted with a thick lime white except where it covers the

child. Two narrow, pearl-lined black bands mark the rim of the basin, and the rest of the bowl and its pedestal are painted with a yellow ground and white wash sheen highlights. A vermiculated scroll and palmette pattern in dark red overlies the yellow of the bowl, while the pedestal is encrusted with a vermiculated diaper pattern with pearls (Fig. 244).

The standing midwife is turned in three-quarter profile, and she wears her hair loose down her back. Her head was painted on a fresh plaster patch, and since she has no halo, the disturbance in the plaster in the mountain area behind is very obvious and gives a pale aura to her head. She has a young face and wears a pearl-studded earring in her ear and two clasps on each bare arm. She is dressed in a long undertunic that billows into ample folds around her lower legs. Her thigh-length overtunic has a rich collar and hem, and the sleeves are folded back almost to the shoulder. The bare and shapely arms were each marked out with an upper incised line, and the armlets are black.

Her overgarment has a vermilion ground, dark red shadows, and black lines. The round collar and heavy border at the hem both have a yellow ground with sheen highlights in white, and they are edged with narrow, black bands beaded with single pearls. A vermiculated scroll and palmette design in dark red line was applied over the yellow. Her undertunic has a grey ground, green shadows, black lines, and white wash and thick, white highlights. In the lower section of this tunic, a wash of yellow was applied over the finished garment, and shafts of thick, yellow highlight were painted over it in the manner of chrysographia. The painting of this hem is similar to that of the undertunics of the Hebrew maidens in the Presentation [70]. The standing midwife's narrow, short feet are clad in black pointed slippers. The ewer has a solid white ground, light blue shadows, and black lines and outlines.

The four angels and the star (Figs. 231, 238)

A white star with eight points rides high in the sky to the left of the panel. From one side of it two white shafts of light tinted with vermilion descend to just above the animals at the manger. From behind the mountains arise the three-quarter-profile figures of four angels with their wings streaming upward behind them as they turn to the west. They all have a yellow halo outlined in black and white. Their voluminous curls are threaded with white jeweled fillets. Their heads closely resemble those of the dome angels [4–13]. They all wear a himation over a chiton with a black clavus. All the wings of the angels stream upward behind them as if they had just alighted. The color buildup for the body of the wings and the tail and covert feathers is similar to that of the wings of the dome angels. The heads were all painted on plaster patches inserted within the halo area. The patch for the angel nearest to Mary has suffered from much flaking.

The three-quarter-length figure of the easternmost angel arises directly out of the cleft between the two mountains. He turns his head backward over his shoulders to gaze at the Magi, while he raises his right arm upward to point at the star. With his left hand he gestures downward to the manger beneath him. This left hand overlaps both of the star's rays, while the twisting end of his himation weaves through them overlapping Mary's moutain.

His chiton has a light red ground, red shadows, black lines and outlines, blue wash highlights,

and thick, white, linear highlights. His himation has a light green ground, green shadows, black lines and outlines, blue wash highlights, and thick, white, linear highlights. The cuff of an undergarment has a yellow ground, with a linear palmette design in brown and a washer design in black at the wrist (Text Fig. 24.1b). His wing feathers range from long, black pinions through shorter feathers in shades of blue to stubby, white feathers.

The half-length figure of the middle angel arches stiffly forward with both hands held out in open gesture toward Mary. Both his right hand and the tail end of his himation overlap onto Mary's mountain. He in turn is overlapped by the eastern angel and the descending rays of light. His all-enveloping himation has a light umber ground, umber shadows, black lines and outlines, blue wash highlights, and thick, white, linear highlights. His middle wing feathers are built up in shades of red.

The half-length figure of the upper angel bows stiffly forward, with both hands overlapping the mountain. The left hand has the open palm upward, and with his right hand he uses two fingers to point directly at Mary, whose halo lies in front of him. His himation has a light red ground, red shadows, black lines and outlines, blue wash highlights, and thick, white, linear highlights. The middle feathers of his wings are built up in shades of blue.

The fourth angel and the shepherds (Pl. 34; Figs. 238–240, 242–243).

The three-quarter-length figure of the angel appears from behind the western side of Mary's mountain, and his body turns toward the shepherds. His inclined head is in three-quarter profile, his shoulders and torso in a twisted, rear aspect, his abdomen in three-quarter profile, and the upper thigh in profile. The distortion in this figure is a very good illustration of the disadvantages of the sectional modular system of proportion, where the arbitrary planar divisions of the human figure and the limited choice of aspect for the head cannot take into account the flowing articulation of the human body in movement.

The angel's right arm is extended forward, and only the elbow of his left arm is visible, but both arms relate more or less correctly to the back view of the shoulder. His stave is carried by his hidden left hand and appears between wing and halo. Each of the sections of the figure is rational, but they do not interrelate.

His chiton has a light green ground, dark green shadows, black lines and outlines, white wash, and thick, white highlights; both highlights were washed over with blue. His himation has a light red ground painted over a yellow base that gives it an apricot hue, red shadows, dark red and black lines, white wash, and thick, white highlights; the latter were also washed over with blue. His yellow cuff has a design of vermiculated palmettes and a washer design at the wrist (Text Fig. 24.1b). The stave has a light brown ground, with dark brown lines and black outlines. The knob has a light brown ground with a linear, white design. The covert feathers of his wings are built up in graded tones of red.

It seems clear that while the painter was seeking to continue the direction of movement of

the other angels, he also sought to divorce this angel from the other three, as he belongs in the vignette of the shepherds. In this case the angel ought logically to be seen from a three-quarter rear view. The formulae that the painter knew did not permit him to represent a holy figure in the rear aspect, so he achieved his aim with this hybrid stance. From the point of view of the composition of the scene as a whole, the angel is entirely satisfactory, and it is only when it is dissected in isolation that the onlooker notices the anomalies.

The seated shepherd holds his flute up sideways to his mouth while he turns his head, as if interrupted, to gaze at the angel. He has a young face with rounded eyes and soft brown hair sweeping down to his shoulder. Both his head and his hands were painted on fresh plaster patches, and the irregularities in the plaster around his head can be clearly seen (Fig. 240). He wears a long-sleeved tunic with a decorative arm band and cuff. The skirt of his tunic is rolled back over his thighs to reveal legs clad in hose and calf-length boots. A loose cloak is swept back over his shoulders to bell out into loose folds at his right side.

His tunic has a light green ground, green shadows, black lines, white wash highlights overlaid with blue, and thick, white highlights. Both the cuffs and the arm band have a yellow ground and a vermiculated pattern in dark brown (as in Text Fig. 24.1b) but without jewels. His cloak has a discolored vermilion ground, light brown shadows, thick, dark brown and black lines. His hose have a light red ground, dark red shadows and lines, and black outlines. The boots have a yellow ground, grey shadows, brown outlines, and white highlight lines over the front of the foot and ankle. His flute is yellow with dark brown lines, dark brown for the stops, and some shadowing in grey.

The young shepherd's head was painted on a fresh plaster patch, but the hair has nevertheless flaked badly. He wears a short, long-sleeved tunic hitched up over his hips to reveal long legs clad in hose and boots. A long, thin cloak pinned at the shoulder is swept back to entwine itself around his raised arm, from which it falls in a wedge of folds. His tunic has a very light yellow ground, thin red shadows, thick red lines and fold lines, black outlines, and thick, white highlights tinted with blue. His cloak has a light red ground, red fold lines, and black lines and outlines. His hose are light red with red shadows and black outlines. His boots have a thick, white ground washed over with brown, red fold lines, and black lines and outlines. The shaft of his crook is yellow with a black underline and a white upper line, while the crook itself is white with black lines. The pelaska (shepherd's bag) is yellow with white decorations and straps, and black outlines.

The old man's head was not painted on a fresh plaster patch. The plaster for his hands was reworked. He wears a vermilion cap held on by red strings. He has bushy white hair and a pointed beard, and his wrinkled face sports a bulbous nose. He wears a V-necked tunic with three-quarter-length sleeves over a knee-length undergarment. The tunic is belted with a double cord at the waist. His thick legs are bare, and he has black ankle boots. His undergarment has an unlined ground in thick lime white, and the tunic has a blue ground with black lines and outlines. The cord belt is white with red lines, and the stave is umber with a black outline to one side.

The 1192 Decoration

The sheep have a yellow ground over which their bodies are blocked in in white, leaving yellow borders. Additional yellow lines indicate their woolly fleece. Their horns are umber with black underlines.

The Three Magi (Figs. 234, 236, 237).

The three full-length, slightly hunched figures of the Magi stand one behind the other on the eastern side of the panel. None of the heads was painted on a fresh plaster patch. The foremost figure rests his booted feet on Joseph's mountain, and he has his knees slightly bent. He reaches forward with his arms outstretched, as he proffers a gift. The box and incense spoon that are now in his hands are crude fourteenth-century repaints, and the originals have entirely disappeared. The two other Magi also lean forward, but their arms and gifts are concealed behind the figure in front. They are all in the three-quarter-profile stance, and each wears a small, three-section hat tipped with three pearls. Each also wears a pearl earring dangling from his ear. All three Magi wear long-sleeved tunics with a decorative collar and arm band enriched by a dark hem with chrysographia. Over the tunics they wear cloaks pinned at their right shoulder and flowing down their backs; the edges of the cloaks are trimmed with single pearls, and on the inside, the hem is trimmed with a decorative band. Only the feet of the first Magus are visible, and they are clad in boots decorated with pearls.

The fourteenth-century overpaint was poorly executed in muddy colors. The face of the foremost figure was repainted, but the repaint has now gone, leaving a grey shadow on the face. The repainted hands and gift remain in good condition. The head of the second figure is almost a complete repaint, and only the lips and some fragments of flesh color remain from the original. The fourteenth-century repainter also spread paint untidily over much of the bodies of the three figures. Where it covered original coloring, this blurred repaint was removed in the course of conservation.

The shape of the face of the foremost Magus and the remnants of his rippling white hair and beard suggest that he was an old man. His hat was vermilion with white pearls, as were his boots, which are similar to those of the archangels and kings elsewhere in the 1192 decoration. His tunic has a green ground, dark green shadows, black lines and outlines, blue wash highlights, and thick, white highlights. The lower hem has an umber band with dark umber and black lines and sunray chrysographia in creamy yellow. His arm band and collar have a yellow ground, with a diaper pattern of pearl and jeweled corridors filled with vermiculation and outlined with a fine, black border lined with pearls (Text Fig. 24.2a); the collar has a washer pattern at the edge of the neck. His cloak is vermilion with red shadows and black lines and outlines. The border is black with white pearls, and the hem band has a yellow ground painted over the vermilion, white highlight "sheen" areas, and a vermiculated palmette pattern in dark red line.

The central Magus has little of the original head left, but it seems that the repair followed the original. The characteristics are those of a middle-aged man with smooth hair to chin level and a short, rounded beard. His tunic has a yellow ground, thin umber shadows, red lines and black

outlines, white wash, and thick, white highlights; it has an umber hem with sunray highlights similar to those of the figure in front. The arm band and collar are much flaked, but like his cloak they are all similar to that of the foremost figure.

Most of the head of the young magus at the back is undamaged, and his brown hair flows smoothly to chin level. He has neither beard nor mustache. His cloak has a blue ground with black lines, and it is edged with a black band lined with single pearls. His tunic has a green ground, dark green shadows, black lines, and white highlights. Both the collar and the arm band are badly flaked, but they were probably similar to those of the other two figures. His hat has a vermilion ground, black outlines, and single pearls at the corners.

The iconographic pattern of the Nativity of Christ was well established, but each church painter faced the challenge of fitting the elements of the composition into the architectural space available. He could also interpret the rules and stamp the traditional picture with his own individual style.

The six vignettes that make up this complicated composition could each stand as an independent picture. All together there are sixteen figures, numerous animals, and various other features essential to the narrative. These elements are combined into a homogenous composition while they maintain a proper hieratic distinction among the various dramas. This was achieved in a variety of ways. In particular, the landscape features within the background were used to divide and link the various groups. A distinction between the figures was achieved by scaling their size upward or downward according to their relative importance.

The painting focuses on the Virgin and child in the manger against their snowcapped mountain, and this is central to the measure relationships within the panel. Notional vertical and horizontal lines bisect the scene at the center of Mary's figure. The lesser events associated with the drama are distributed concentrically around this nucleus.

The landscaped background has a narrative function in placing the action of the drama in a rural setting, and it serves as a structural backdrop for the composition. The pyramidal mountain shapes provide a geometry that gives stability, while at the same time they encourage the onlooker to read the story by directing his eye around it.

The painter made use of the backdrop for two paradoxical purposes. First, the mountainous divisions were used to isolate and give individual prominence to the subsidiary characters and their dramatic contribution to the scene. This can be clearly seen in the vignette of the midwives. Second, the painter allowed various figures or their attributes to overlap from one mountain backdrop to the other, thus relinking the parts to form an integral whole.

The lines of movement take the eye in spiral fashion from the central figure of the Mother of God outward through the infant Christ to the Magi. From the Magi the movement is upward to the angels and across the top of the picture to come down through the shepherds and sheep to the midwives with the Christ child. The donkey leads on to Joseph, whose bent pose directs the eyes back to the central figures of the Mother of God and Christ child in the manger. At each stage there are alternative and subsidiary lines of view. They run from the Magi and the angels inward to

the central figures, and from the shepherds inward by gesture and by the crook laid on the ground to point at the Mother of God. The various overlaps of foliage, feet, and hands are all calculated to link the otherwise disconnected pyramids of the mountain background.

There is no definable horizontal foreground along the base of the picture to anchor the two lower vignettes of Joseph and the midwives, and the line of the mountainside continues down to the red border. The painter gave stability to the midwives and the bath with the illusionist device of painting a hard-edged dark shadow below the seated woman and to the side of the pedestal of the bath, and he also marked out a hard-edged light area on the mountain beneath the feet of the standing midwife. It is possible that he treated Joseph in a similar manner, but the area around his figure and saddle is too damaged to be certain. Originally, both the midwife's foot and the base of the bath overlapped the bottom red border of the scene. The lack of a formal horizontal foreground contributes to the circular motion of the minor elements of the scene.

The overlapping details of the figures and their possessions and the lack of formal foreground add a three-dimensional quality to the painting. The mountain overlaps suggest a recession backward into the picture frame, while the overlapping features bring the figures forward into the church. The red border framing the picture defines its limitation within the architecture of the church, but it does not confine the action of the scene to the picture space within it. The drama thus seems to unfold both forward and backward of the frame.

The painter used one proportional convention for the figures and their relation to each other, and another for the proportional relationship between the background and the figures and other furnishings. The figure of the Mother of God is larger than the other figures, and the angels, the Magi, Joseph, and the midwives are in a ratio of 2:3 to her. The shepherds, including the flute player, are all drawn to a smaller scale still. The same diminishing treatment is given to the animals within the scene. The sheep are small in relation to the shepherds and would reach to their knee height. The donkey would reach to mid-thigh level on the Magi. Thus the size of the actors in the drama is in proportion to their hierarchical importance, as was the rule in Byzantine painting.

A similar adjustment of proportional scale was applied to the landscape backdrop of the scene. The largest mountain is that at the center of the painting, and it contains Mary's cave. To either side, the mountains of the Magi and that of the flute-playing shepherd rise higher within the painting, but it is Mary's mountain that is capped with snow. The mountains and the trees that grow upon them are miniature in scale in relation to the figures for whom they form a background. This adds to their decorative value but also serves to emphasize the figures and to thrust them forward in the picture plane. The painter thus provided a landscape in miniature in which the mountainous backdrop sets the scene unobtrusively, while at the same time it acts as a foil and a link for the figures and is an essential and positive element in the construction of the scene.

The proportional ratios may be disturbing to the eye trained to conventional illusionist perspective. In this painting, however, the deliberate elasticity in the ratios between the various elements leads to a highly decorative and well-balanced composition. The function of the dwarfed landscape and its features is like the miniature architectures in the pendentives, in that both of these

backgrounds ensure the unimpeded domination of the figures in the scene.

The hands of Mary and the midwives are shorter than the face length and conform with the 1192 master's practice of giving shorter hands and feet to the women. In the seated position Mary's figure is foreshortened, and her thighs and lower abdomen are folded upon one another. The visual problems are neatly concealed by the massed folds of her maphorion.

The two figures of the Christ child have measures that are half those of his mother. Both of his heads and haloes measure half the size of hers. The measures within his head follow the rules for the heads of infants as practiced by the 1192 painter (see below, pp. 296–98).

The articulation of the figures is for the most part felicitous. The supple stance of the elegant, little figure of the young shepherd who leans back to secure the attention of the old man contrasts well with the stiffly bent posture of the old peasant. The angel above them illustrates the problem of structural drawing based on arbitrary sectional measures versus studying from life, but his movements illustrate his purpose as a message bearer. The figure of the old shepherd was by tradition an exception, and he alone, of all the figures in this decoration, fails to run to type. His face and beard are conventional for an old man, but his nose is bulbous and lacks the straight aquiline quality of the standard 1192 nose. His figure is very stocky, and it lacks the elegant slimness of the other figures. His legs, knees, and arms are all thickly thewed, and his back is bent forward, seeking the support of his stave. The old man is an exciting exception, where we can see the Lagoudhera master free to paint an individual. The sheep, while pleasingly accurate in individual form, are grouped in tight, overlapping blocks of three. This antiquated convention for illustrating numbers of animals dates back at least as far as the practice of ancient Egyptian wall painters. The grouping of the three Magi shows the greater freedom of the Byzantine approach when dealing with groups of figures.

The condition of the painting with its large, damaged areas on the eastern side and the mottling of discolored patches does not convey accurately the fresh, clear-cut coloring that it had when painted. However, it does still retain something of its luminous quality. The light browns, light umbers, and light reds and yellows that wash the mountains with color form a pleasing foil to the figures, with their vermilions, blues, greens, and strong yellows picked out with black lines and outlines and strong, linear, white highlights. The variety and articulation of bright color in the less-important figures might well distract visually from the central figures of the Mother of God and child. The painter ensured their prominence by surrounding them with the shocking contrast of black and white. The white mattress in the womblike black cave with its white outlines makes Mary's figure stand out like a bright nut in its shell.

The painter made an unselfconscious use of details from the contemporary world, such as the donkey's saddle, the fat-tail sheep, and the shepherd's bag. The young shepherd playing his pipes could no doubt have been seen on the hillsides around the church, and he provides an idyllic note with his elegant figure, which is saved from instability by the crossed leg, giving him a firm, triangular structure. None of the elements in the scene is original, but the painter has given to it a dramatic, lyrical quality that makes it a masterwork among portrayals of the Nativity.

The Southwest Bay [143–153]

The bay is interrupted by the south doorway, whose reveals are decorated with inscribed crosses [152–153]. Above the doorway, in the narrow lunette, St. Christopher [149] presides in his roundel. To the east of the doorway, St. Mary of Egypt [150] bows forward to receive Holy Communion from St. Zosimos [151] on the west side.

The arch reveals support the standing figures of St. Chariton [145], to the east and St. Hilarion [148], to the west; the single panel in the arch soffit contains the half-length figures of the doctors, St. Hermolaos [146], to the east and St. Panteleimon [147], to the west.

St. Peter [143] stands on the north face of the pier, and the western spandrel contains a vermiculated pattern [144].

None of the heads in this bay was painted on fresh plaster patches, but the plaster for some of the hands was reworked. There are no traces of incision lines or impressed guidelines. General flaking of the upper layers of pigment was caused by dampness, which is also responsible for some staining and discoloration. The lower registers have suffered much from friction caused by the press of the congregation, and little now remains of the dadoes. The robes of Sts. Zosimos and Mary are greatly damaged at the hem, and St. Mary is the most heavily damaged figure in the 1192 decoration. The contractions of the wooden lintel of the south door caused fracturing within the paintings. The original upper backgrounds to the figures in the panels of the southwest bay were painted green. With the exception of the background to the roundel of St. Christopher in the tympanum, the upper backgrounds were overlaid with a copper blue at some later date, thus obscuring the original lettering. In the fourteenth century various damaged areas were restored with muddy colors, and a number of outlines were thickly reinforced with black. The panel in the soffit of the arch originally had an ochre background, and this was overpainted with yellow.

St. Peter [143] (Figs. 250, 253, 286)

The top of the panel is stepped, and it is higher on the west side, where it includes the spandrel of the arch of the west bay. The panel measures 2.22 m at the eastern edge and 63 cm across the center of the panel, inclusive of the red borders.

The life-size figure of Peter stands upright with his head turned eastward toward the apse. His right hand is caught up in the folds of his himation, and in his left hand he grips the top of an unfurled scroll, below which two keys hang from a rope wound around his wrist. In the crook of his arm he bears a long, thin, two-armed cross.

The background to St. Peter was originally green, with a second coat of green paint applied to the foreground to darken and distinguish it from the upper ground. At some later period, the upper ground was overpainted with a copper blue. The original titular inscription, which is written to either side of the halo, was overpainted in white. These letters seem to follow the original to

some extent, but the Π and the E are shorter than the original, traces of which can be seen beneath the overpaint. The inscription on his scroll is from the first epistle of St. Peter, 2:11 (Fig. 286). The scribe forgot to place a bar in the first alpha of the third row, so it appears as a lambda.

The panel was plastered in a single section and there are no plaster patches, but the plaster in the areas of the face, the feet, and the hands was reworked. The feet are substantial, and their size is in keeping with the large figure. There are no apparent incision or impress lines. The panel is relatively undamaged for a painting in the ground register, but there is some general flaking, and candle burns have turned the yellow ochres to red in a number of places.

The saint's figure is seen in the frontal aspect, but one leg is turned in profile, and his head is turned in the three-quarter-profile stance. His halo is larger than standard, with a diameter of seven nose lengths instead of six.[120] It is wider to the right, or west, side of Peter's head. Normally the painter centered heads within the halo, whatever their stance, but in this case the panel would have been too narrow at the left side to admit the Ὁ ἅγιος of the titular inscription. The position of the figure itself could not be adjusted in view of the narrowing panel beneath. In moving the halo over, the painter enlarged its size by one nose length. The enlargement created a better balance for Peter's rounded hair style and is in keeping with his solid figure. A halo with the usual diameter of only six nose lengths placed in an asymmetrical relationship would have been too close to the left side of Peter's head.

He is represented in the traditional type for St. Peter, as an old man with white hair dressed in tight white curls running low across his forehead and a neat, short, rounded beard outlining the chin. He wears a chiton with black clavus under a voluminous himation.

His chiton has a light vermilion ground, umber shadows, black lines and fold lines, white wash, and thick, white, linear highlights. His himation has a grey ground painted over a yellow base, light green shadows, black lines and outlines, and thick, white, linear highlights. His long stave and cross have a yellow ground with black underlining and side shadows. The keys are white, and the rope from which they hang is yellow with no outlines.

The pattern in the spandrel of the west end of the south wall [144] is almost the same as that in the spandrel opposite. See the description for the latter under [51], p. 159; Text Fig. 28.

St. Chariton [145] (Figs. 251, 254, 280)

The panel on the east face of the arch measures 2 m in height by 57 cm in width, exclusive of the red borders. St. Chariton wears the subfusc habit of a monk, and he stands upright in the frontal aspect with his head turning in three-quarter profile toward the naos. In his right hand he carries a white martyr's cross, and with his left hand he grips the top of an unfurling scroll.

His title is aligned vertically to either side of his halo, and the lettering is an overpaint, the original of which was obscured by the blue overpainting of the original green background

---

[120] See below, Proportion, p. 286.

The 1192 Decoration

(Text Fig. 30.1c). The inscription upon St. Chariton's scroll is in the original script (Fig. 280).[121]

He is portrayed as an old man with receding, smooth white hair and a long, pointed beard. He wears similar monastic garments to those of St. Andronikos [55], but the colors vary. The tunic has a light red ground, umber shadows, and dark grey and black lines and outlines; the cuff is marked with two black lines with a dot at the center. His overgarment has a yellow ground, grey-green shadows, and black lines and outlines. A wash of coarse umber was applied over it by the painter of the repair work.

Sts. Hermolaos and Panteleimon [146–147] (Figs. 256–258)

The panel within the soffit of the arch measures 188 cm and has an average width of 66 cm exclusive of the red borders, but the arch is very irregular and widens toward its apex. St. Hermolaos's [146] titular inscription is placed vertically to either side of his halo. Only the epithet is in the original 1192 lettering. His name was later rewritten in watery grey-white, and the alpha is different from those used in the 1192 inscriptions.

The waist-length figure is seen in the frontal aspect, and he has the standard asymmetrical frontal face, but the eyes gaze sideways and out into the naos. He is portrayed as an old man with receding, smooth white hair and a pointed beard. His right hand is raised palm inward, and in the crook of his enfolded left arm he carries a closed book with a jeweled cover. He wears an undertunic with narrow collar and jeweled cuff under a loose tunic that is overlapped by a generous mantle.

The collar and cuff are yellow with white sheen highlights, over which the collar has a vermiculated pattern in umber lines, and the cuff has a diaper pattern lined with jewels (as in Text Fig. 24b). His chiton has a grey ground, light umber shadows, black lines and outlines, and thick, white, linear highlights. His mantle is red with umber shadows and black lines and outlines. The book has vermilion pages, black clasps, and a bejeweled square-net pattern, as in loros pattern II (Pl. 11b; Text Fig. 36.1b).

The titular inscription of St. Panteleimon [147], which appears vertically to either side of his halo, is in the original script, but it lacks some accents and breathings as well as the crispness of the original because of the condition of the background paint layers.

The saint is portrayed as a young man, beardless with a mass of tight curls around his head, some of which have been crudely outlined by the repair painter. The head has flaked badly, and it has lost much of its original crisp quality. His waist-length figure is in the frontal aspect, but his gaze is directed sideways into the naos of the church. In the crook of his folded left arm he holds an open physician's box, and with his right hand he holds a long, white spatula or spoon. He wears an undergarment of which only part of the neckline and a jeweled cuff are visible under a loose-sleeved overtunic with a vertical collar. His himation, or upper garment, has a broad decorative hem (Text Fig. 24.4b).

---

[121] Nicolaïdes, "Panagia Arakiotissa," scroll of St. Chariton [145], pp. 119–20.

268

His undertunic has a dark red ground with black lines and outlines. His overtunic has a light yellow ground, dark yellow lines and shadows, black lines and outlines, and white wash and thick, white highlights. His himation has a red ground, black lines and outlines, and vermilion highlights. His cuff, his collar, the hem of his himation, and the box all have a yellow ground with white sheen highlights. The collar and hem have a vermicular decoration in umber lines, and the cuff and the box both have a diaper pattern of pearl corridors and vermiculated lozenges, with a line of washer pattern at the upper edges. Inside the box are round, white pills with black centers. The triangular shape of the box's lid is clearly meant to indicate a circular lid. It has a pearl at the apex and a "fluted" design in umber line. The spoon has a light yellow handle and a white bowl (Text Fig. 31.3b).

St. Hilarion [148] (Figs. 252, 255, 281)

The panel on the west face of the arch measures 148 cm in height and averages 65 cm in width, exclusive of the red borders. The figure stands upright in the frontal aspect with his head in the asymmetrical frontal stance. His gaze, however, is directed sideways across the wider side of his face and out into the naos. He carries a white, two-barred cross in his right hand, and with his left hand he grips the top of an unfurling scroll.

The titular inscription is aligned vertically to either side of his halo. In the course of conservation the copper blue overpaint was removed where it concealed the twelfth-century inscription. The inscription upon his scroll is original (Fig. 281).[122]

St. Hilarion wears similar monastic robes to those of St. Andronikos [55], but some of the colors vary. His tunic has a light red ground, dark red and umber shadows, grey highlights, and black lines and outlines. The overgarment has a yellow ground, grey-green shadows, and black lines and outlines.

St. Christopher [149] (Fig. 259; Text Fig. 30e)

The tympanum is wide and shallow, and it measures 183 cm in width exclusive of the red borders and 70 cm in height. Within it is a roundel with the waist-length frontal figure of St. Christopher holding up a two-barred cross in his right hand. There are two titular inscriptions. The original inscription lies on the green ground of the background to the medallion and is aligned to either side of it. The other inscription is aligned to either side of the figure within the medallion upon the vermilion background. It is probably from the fourteenth century, and it was painted in grey-white and has faded badly. There are differences in the spelling, and the letter shapes vary considerably between the two inscriptions (Text Fig. 30e).

St. Christopher is represented as a beardless young man with smooth hair that falls into a long lock on each shoulder. His face is in the asymmetrical frontal aspect, and his gaze is directed toward

---

[122] Nicolaïdes, "Panagia Arakiotissa," scroll of St. Hilarion [148], p. 120.

the east across the wider left side of his face. He is dressed in an undertunic with an ornate cuff and a heavy, ornate scalloped collar (Text Fig. 24.2a). Over these he wears a tunic that is pinned on his chest by a clasp dotted with pearls.

His tunic has a light yellow-green ground, green shadow and fold lines, grey shadows, black lines and outlines, and thick, white, linear highlights. His collar and cuff have a yellow ground and white sheen highlights, and both are overlaid with a vermiculated palmette pattern in dark red. There is a border pattern of washer design at the wrist, and the neckline and the lower edges of the collar are outlined with a broad black band lined with single pearls. His mantle has a dark red ground, umber shadows, and black lines and outlines.

St. Mary of Egypt [150] (Fig. 260; Text Fig. 30c)

The panel measures 162 cm in height and 60 cm in width, exclusive of the red borders. The full-length, emaciated figure of St. Mary is turned in three-quarter profile as her hands reach upward and forward to St. Zosimos in the panel of the other side of the doorway. Her titular inscription is placed behind her, between her halo and the corner of the wall. There are two inscriptions. The original one appears on the green ground. It was concealed when copper blue paint was applied over the upper background at some later date. The present inscription partly overlaps the original, where the blue overpaint has flaked away to reveal some of the original inscription, in particular the ἡ ἐγιπτία that was painted lower down than the overpainted title. Although the words are spelled the same in both inscriptions, the forms of the letters are different (Text Fig. 30c).

Mary's skinny figure has lost most of its head, but her white hair is gathered in short locks at the back of her neck. Her seminude figure is wrapped in a cloth that encircles her left arm to fall diagonally from her left shoulder to her upper right thigh. This diagonal is echoed in the loosely articulated hemline that runs up across her legs at knee level, revealing her thin, naked limbs below. Her nude upper body and arm are covered in short Y-shaped hairs, and the contours of her bare anatomy are marked out with lines. Two curving underlines mark the base of the breast, giving no indication of femininity. Curved lines mark the chest cavity and the inner line of the flank, and a long vertical marks her side. Her back is ridged, with small white "knobs" marking her backbone. The arms are very long, quite exceeding the measures allowed for an arm in the other figures in this decoration, and the elbow reaches down to well below waist level. The hands are small and probably follow the master's preference for giving women shorter hands.

The cloth that winds round her has a red ground, umber shadows, green shadows and lines, and light red highlights. The flesh of this saint, like that of the other ascetic figures, St. John the Baptist [75] and St. Onuphrios [81], is built up to a ruddy weather-beaten hue that is quite distinct from the flesh of other saints. The hairs are drawn in fine, umber line.

St. Zosimos [151] (Fig. 261)

The panel measures 166 cm in height by 53 cm in width, exclusive of the red borders. St. Zosimos stands upright, and his figure is turned in three-quarter profile toward the figure of St. Mary on the opposite side of the door. With his right hand he holds up a long spoon whose bowl overlaps the red border. With his left hand, which is enfolded in a napkin, he holds a chalice (Text Fig. 31.3a). His inscription lies to the side of his halo above the spoon, but the upper half of it is lost. The last five letters that remain belong to the late overpaint.

The saint is portrayed as an old man with smooth, white hair and a long, pointed beard. He is attired in a monk's habit similar to that of Sts. Chariton and Hilarion on the arch reveals next to him, and it is painted in similar colors. The figure is much damaged, and the upper layers of pigment have mostly flaked away from his lower robes.

To understand St. Zosimos' actions in administering the last rites to St. Maria of Egypt, it is once again necessary for the onlooker to assume that the saintly figures are with him in the real architectural space of the church, and that he is present at the occasion. Neither figure makes sense without the inclusion of the space of the doorway between them.

Part Four: Technique

15

The Layout of the Decoration, the Plaster, and the Preliminary Drawing

The Layout of the Decoration

The disposal of the subject matter over the wall, vaults, and dome of the building was the painter's first task, and in many ways it is one of the most interesting problems in Byzantine church decoration. The presence of the earlier paintings in the apse shows a pious desire to preserve that work, and the 1192 master fitted his own program to dovetail neatly with it in terms of scale. The small number of scenes painted to a large scale and the relatively large size of individual figures show that both painter and patron wanted to create a majestic and impressive decoration for this small church. Clarity of message counted rather than the creation of a confusion of small scenes with petty details.

Within the canon of rules laid down for the general iconography of church decoration was a considerable latitude of choice for discussion between patron and painter. The number of scenes and images of saints could be varied by adjusting their size, so that both large and small churches might have a few scenes and images on a grand scale, or many scenes and images on a smaller scale. When the decision had been made as to the list of subject matter and its location, the painter could proceed, working from the vault or the cupola downward. The preliminary approach consisted of determining the registers of paintings and their subdivisions so that the final trellis of red borders echoed harmoniously around the building. At the second stage and before plastering, some reckoning of the space to be occupied by the elements of the scene, or the module to be used for a single figure, took place. Such reckonings probably took the form of schemas on the masonry itself or on the roughcast plaster laid down for a panel.

The evidence for these vital stages of planning is therefore only available where the plaster and paintings have fallen off the walls to reveal the lines that marked the divisions and the rough work schemas. In repairing the damaged red border marking the base of the Nativity [142], a red snap line was observed on the masonry beneath. This would have marked the lower limit of the

275

plastered area for the scene. The final border is actually irregular, as it is divided by the apex of the arch of the west bay. Other such lines can be seen on the wall of the Hagia Sophia at Trebizond and at St. John Chrysostomos at Koutsovendis in Cyprus,[123] and there are no doubt many more examples awaiting record in ruined churches.[124]

At Lagoudhera the decoration is complete, and no physical evidence can be seen for the division of the wall space other than that mentioned above. The painter's method of carrying out his task, however, can be deduced from the finished paintings and from the modular proportional system that he used.

In the nature of his work the painter worked downward, and before erecting and mounting his scaffolds he would have already measured out, if only in his mind, the balancing of the size of the panels and the continuity of register levels where possible.

In the ground register of the 1192 paintings, the height of the register is defined by the height from the cornices of the piers to the ground; this allowed for life-size figures and a dado beneath. The red border marking the height of the register is continued right around the naos and the sanctuary. This fixed level was maintained even in the reveals of the bays, so that the heads of the standing figures are perforce on the surface of the springing of the arch; two examples are St. Andronikos [55] and St. Kyriakos [58]. The great scenes in the lunettes and vaults all have base lines along the upper borders of the ground register. In a similar manner, the upper and lower red borders outlining the dado also form continuous contour lines around the base of the naos, except on the reveals of the north and south doors, which contain no figural decoration.

The height of the ground register in the apse is lower than that of the 1192 painting. The base line and dado on the fragment of the earlier decoration found in the naos also had a base line and dado lower than the 1192 decoration superseding it (see pp. 59, 99).

The horizontal divisions are continuous and serve to unify the decoration. The vertical divisions mostly follow the verticals presented by the architecture. The dome presented a more difficult task of division in order to fit in the three registers that were not entirely dictated by architectural features (see above, pp. 58, 111). The general framework for the 1192 decoration is comparatively simple since the architecture and size of the church are modest.

For the construction of individual figures, a basic module would have been worked out and would remain standard for the single-figure panels throughout the ground register.[125] The proph-

---

[123] D. Winfield, "The Making of the Paintings," in *The Church of Haghia Sophia at Trebizond*, ed. D. Talbot Rice (Edinburgh, 1968), p. 188. C. Mango, E. Hawkins, "The Monastery of St. Chrysostomos at Koutsovendis (Cyprus) and Its Paintings," *DOP* 44 (1990), p. 93

[124] The authors noted a number of examples seen on their travels in the Balkans, Greece, Asia Minor, and the Levant, but unfortunately their notes were lost in a fire. Vladimir Mako, *Lik i broj* (Belgrade, 1998), has suggested that the dimension of the halo was fundamental in setting out the decoration of a church. We have never found evidence that the diameter of the halo was of prime importance. The Byzantine painter was primarily concerned with the human figure, and the halo was only a secondary attribute that required fitting to the figure (see below, p. 286).

[125] See pp. 283–86 , Text Fig. 43, pp. 276-78.

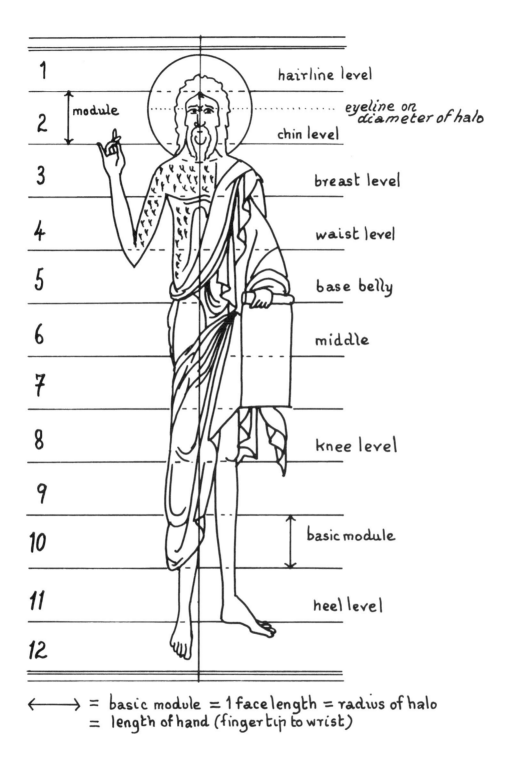

Text Fig. 43 Diagram of the modular method of laying out a panel with a single standing figure

ets in the drum also share a standard module. In the panels for single figures at Lagoudhera, the figure always occupies the maximum amount of vertical space, so that a minimum amount of space is left above or below the halo and the feet. In some cases, allowance was made for the presence of footstools, such as for the Christ Antiphonetes [127] or the archangel Michael [140].

When the painter came to work out his module for his single figure, he must have had some minimum references to guide him so as to maintain the balance between width and height. The minimum ratios given below suggest themselves for the standing figures at Lagoudhera, working backward from the finished figures.

Within a typical panel, twelve face-length modules account for a full-length figure with halo and at least one extended frontal foot within a panel with red borders. Text Figure 43 illustrates the practical use of the module and its application at the stage of preliminary drawing. When dealing with the upright figure divided into sections down a central vertical axis, the twelve equal measures are made up of one upper measure to account for the upper red border, including the upper halo and the hair; ten measures for the figure from the top of the forehead to base of heel; and one measure to account for the frontal extension of the foot and the red border below. These twelve measures or face-length modules are the minimum vertical requirements for a nimbed figure in a panel. Any surplus could be left to the upper background or the foreground.

The width of the figure in repose is two face-length modules or units, which corresponds to the width of the shoulders and the diameter of the halo. When the arms are flexed at the elbow in gesture or to hold forth a book or scroll, however, the width of the figure expands, so that a minimum of three modules would be required for the figure. Further account must also be taken of the space occupied by the red borders to either side of the panel and for a width of background to separate the figure from those borders. Thus, a width of four face-length modules would be desirable. An experienced painter would have little difficulty in the sizing of his module and figure on that basis. The actual module used on the wall could be established by finding the centerpoint of the panel and proceeding from there with dividers or compass to work out the sectional levels.

In the case of panels with a sequence of roundels, a median line was established upon which to base the centerpoint of the roundels so that a rough calculation of their diameter and positioning could be made (see above, pp. 88–90, 149; Text Figs. 18, 23, 25). Scenes were more complicated, and the painter's methods had to be very adaptable since lunettes and squares are difficult spaces in which to set out narrative scenes. The final paintings suggest a very simple allotment of spaces within a scene, so that the relevant subject matter could all be suitably fitted in. In some cases the notional divisions are reinforced by the presence of the painter's own impressed or incised guidelines, which can still be seen in the surface of the painting, for example, in the Presentation of the Virgin [70] (Pl. 24; Text Fig. 32).

Determining the centerpoint of the space available for each scene was essential to the painter's method, since in every case the principal figure or figures in the drama were placed in the center, and their size is always larger than the secondary participants in the action. It is possible to see how

the painter built up his composition around the central figures and linked the other elements to them in all the 1192 scenes.

Figures of different sizes are in most scenes for hieratic reasons or because of the diversity of subject matter. The proportional canon for the figures remains the same, and to maintain harmony it was only necessary to adjust the module controlling their construction. The proportional system that underlies the construction of figures is outlined below (see pp. 284–86).

When the painter was satisfied with the setting out of his scene and the measures controlling the layout within the panels, he could begin to plaster and paint.

The Plaster

The evidence for the painters having used only one layer of plaster for the decoration is incomplete, and it is therefore not certain. The paintings are for the most part in good condition, and it was only possible to verify the layering where the plaster had a hole. Near the center of the dome, where a hole was made in Christ's neck for the hook to carry the kandelion, the plaster was 10 cm thick and in one layer. In the drum and in the ground register of paintings, the plaster was also in one layer, but only 1 to 3 cm in thickness.

There are two possible reasons for abandoning the traditional two-layer system. Either the Lagoudhera master felt that the binder of chaff and straw stalks would retain enough water within the plaster to keep it fresh, or he felt that two layers were unnecessary since he would insert fresh patches of plaster whenever it dried out too rapidly. He may also have taken into account the important factor of climate and assumed that the cooler mountain air at 1,000 m would allow him a lot more time on fresh plaster than would the scaring heat and dry winds of the plains of Cyprus. It must be added that knowledge of the chemical process of carbonation in lime plaster, the speed at which it happened, and the effect of dry or humid weather on the speeds of the chemical change was all empirical and not scientific knowledge. The accumulated empirical knowledge of many generations of painters working over many centuries probably gave them a very accurate feel as to the behavior of the surface of their plaster and an understanding of when it was ceasing to be fresh and receptive to paint.

The Lagoudhera master certainly must have had this experience and accuracy of knowledge since without it he would never have dared to work his plaster surfaces so freely. The evidence is that he gave himself the receptive surface that he wished, and it would of course have been without the straw and chaff on the surface. It is likely that he overlaid his plaster with a thin covering of lime slurry to ensure a smooth, even surface.

Four methods of rendering the plaster ground were used by the Lagoudhera painters. First was the traditional rendering of a whole area for a scene, for one large figure, or for a group of smaller figures.

In the second method, for a large subject such as the Ascension in the sanctuary vault, the area was rendered in three sections. The sections were planned to take into account the subject matter, so that a join did not cut across a face or another vital detail. They also took into account the position of scaffolding for the convenience of painting. The Italian term for divisions of this type is *pontata*. The Ascension at Lagoudhera has a rendering at the center of the vault that was large enough for painting the mandorla with Christ and the four angels. The other two sections cover the sides of the vault, one with six apostles and the angel, and the other with six apostles and the Virgin. The same method was used to divide groups of figures in roundels and for the prophets in the dome, where the join between plaster sections was made as neatly as possible through the empty space of a background.

Using the third method, the painters rendered the plaster for a whole scene, as in the first method, but because of the amount of detailed work and adjustments in composition, they scraped down certain areas within the scene and re-rendered them with a fresh surface plaster, or *intonaco*. The Koimesis and the Presentation of the Virgin in the Temple illustrate this method at Lagoudhera (Text Figs. 32, 39). In the scene of the Koimesis, it is the quantity of detailed work that caused the adoption of this method, and in the Presentation it was changes and adaptation of the figures at the center of the composition. The Italian term for this and for the fourth method is *giornata*.

For the fourth method, the painter used the first three methods for rendering large areas of plaster, but then scraped out and re-rendered the areas for the heads of figures and sometimes even for a hand. The edges of these patches can sometimes be detected as a physical disturbance of the surface at the join, and sometimes by late retouching of the colors. It is confirmed by the fact that heads on new patches were started with a green base layer, whereas heads on the original rendering were started over the yellow base color that filled the whole of the halo area. It is unlikely that it took the Lagoudhera master a whole day to paint even the finest of his heads, and he might well have painted three or four new patches in the course of a day's work. These small patches were made for heads in particular because the heads were the last part of a figure to be completed, and the plaster was often drying out too fast to receive the pigments. It is doubtful that this was a much favored alternative since it required meticulous care to scrape out and put in a neat patch, but it was forced upon the Lagoudhera master because he demanded a fine finish for the paintings, and this required more time than was allowed by the drying out of the plaster. The Koimesis [138] has eighteen heads painted on fresh plaster patches. Only the head of the Virgin is not on a separate patch because the painter made a whole new section for her body and bier (as in method 3), and the plaster surface was still receptive when he painted the head.[126]

---

[126] See pp. 233, 235, Text Fig. 39.

Preliminary Drawing

The evidence of preliminary drawing is limited as it is restricted to areas of damage where the paint layers have flaked back to reveal the base colors. Where visible, it takes the form of light red lines in watercolor that still show through the thin base layer of paint.

For some figures with more complex garment lines, a second drawing in dark grey was made over the base color. This drawing marked out the design of the garment folds, and the dark lines showed up faintly through the ground color which, though opaque, was often pale in tone. These same grey lines were eventually lost under the build up of dark shadow colors within the garment (see above, the prophet Gideon [25], Fig. 64).

In the case of single panels, such as the standing figures in the ground register, a rapid relaying of the basic module with the aid of the compass established the ratios of the divisions of the body and a compass point for the halo. Then the painter made a preliminary drawing that marked out the rough shape of the head, the articulation of the figure, and its garments (Text Fig. 43).

In the case of scenes, he marked out the divisions of the composition and then sketched within each division the appropriate layout of the figures, the architectures, and other elements.

One important feature of the drawing is that the master used his plaster ground not only as a passive surface for receiving paint but also as a malleable surface aid on which he could mark out more permanent guidelines. This was an important procedure since the painted preliminary drawing was quickly obscured by the buildup of opaque layers of paint.

His methods were either to impress outlines with a spatula or to incise outlines, probably with the point or narrow edge of the same tool. In the case of the roughly marked, vertical center line of the Koimesis, he may have even run his thumb quickly down the surface. Such permanent marks enabled him to retain the essential guidelines of his composition. Common examples in these paintings are the definition of the limits to the architectures and background features, the definition of complicated overlaps in groups of figures, and the marking out of difficult convolutions in a particular garment. He also often marked out the shoulder lines of figures; this was a particularly useful reminder since the width of the body was determined by the shoulders.

The setting out and drawing of the subject matter formed the essential basis to the painting of a panel, since they established the painter's control of the underlying harmony and proportion. Once the plaster rendering for the panel was completed, speed was imperative, and the master's drawing was limited to practical essentials. He did not make an elaborately detailed and highly finished cartoon. His drawing simply formed a secure foundation upon which he built up and articulated in color and line the established iconographic forms of his subject matter.

The use of the plaster and such evidence as we have of the painted drawings on the surface all point to speed of execution at this preliminary stage. Speed was essential in order to accomplish as much of the painting as possible on the fresh plaster. It may seem paradoxical to make our master

painter work at high speed on his preliminary drawing and then attribute painstaking care by him at the finishing stages, but it is only an apparent paradox since it was, after all, the finished painting that mattered rather than the preliminary drawing. Strong circumstantial evidence for speed and perfunctory drawing at the early stages may be drawn from the amount of revision carried out toward the final stages of his painting. Almost every figure bears traces of later adjustments to arrive at a better balance in the relationship of clothing to body and limbs. Sometimes there were major readjustments, such as in the simple symbolic composition of the Etoimasia [3], or in the radical alterations of figures in the complex composition of the Presentation of the Virgin [70]. Some of these alterations might be attributable to the master coming round to give a better finish to weak work by an assistant, but it is more likely that the master himself impressed, incised, and sketched in the preliminary drawings and that he made the final adjustments to the painting. The process of composition and the need for harmony and proportion preoccupied him right up to the finish of the painting.[127]

[127] The evidence for this can be seen throughout the descriptions given above of paintings by the 1192 master. The wider significance of this late adjustment of paintings at the finishing stages is suggested below, pp. 322–24.

16

PROPORTION

The emphasis at Lagoudhera, as indeed in all Byzantine church decoration, is on the holy figures who dominate every scene. The architectures, trees, and mountains are merely stage props or backdrops to actions performed by the figures. Within a single decoration the size of the figure varies considerably from panel to panel, and even within the same scene. Within the scenes the figures differ in size for hierarchical reasons, not in order to comply with the convention of diminishing perspective. All the adult figures are built to the same proportions. The male figures conform closely to the concept of the phrase "clothed nude," with the tunic and himation closely molding the forms of the bodies they conceal.[128]

It follows that the painter had to have some method of measuring out figures rapidly at the preliminary stage of painting and had to be able to adjust the scale of a figure to suit hieratic or panel requirements. While doing this he had to maintain harmony among all the figures in the decoration. At Lagoudhera the pattern of proportional relationships in adult figures is constant whether the size of the figure varies or not, and this confirms that a modular system of regulating proportion was employed. The virtue of such a system lies in the fact that once the size of the basic module had been fixed, it was possible to relay it rapidly between measure points with the use of a measure stick or compass. By enlarging or reducing the measure of his basic module, the painter increased or decreased the size of his figures while the ratios of the measures within the figures remained constant.

The vertical height of the upright figure was measured from the forehead (root of the hair) to the heel along a notional vertical in terms of ten face lengths. Along such a notional vertical the distance between standard anatomical reference points was measured either in face lengths or by the smaller module, which is referred to as the nose length.[129]

The head was painted in only two aspects, the frontal and the three-quarter profile. The frontal heads are asymmetrical in that the faces are wider to one side of the median of the nose than the other. There are 43 heads in the asymmetrical frontal aspect and 121 heads in the three-quarter profile aspect, for a total of 164 heads.

---

[128] For a general discussion of Byzantine proportion, see Winfield and Winfield, *Proportion*. Also see Torp, *Integrating System of Proportion*.

[129] The nose length was used by Vitruvius; see Winfield and Winfield, *Proportion*, 28–34.

Some of the frontal faces have an indirect gaze that appears to follow and communicate with the onlooker. The most striking examples at Lagoudhera are the frontal faces of Christ. In most frontal heads, however, the gaze is deliberately directed across the wide side of the face to compel the onlooker to look toward the center of the church or toward the east.

The main function of the three-quarter-profile head is to indicate communication between figures within major scenes.[130] It is used occasionally for the heads of single figures, in which case the head is always orientated to look either toward the center of the church or toward the east. In both aspects the measures for the length of the face are similar, but the measures within the width of the face vary.

Construction of the Human Figure

(Figs. 101, 133, 167; Text Figs. 43, 44)

The Christ of the Baptism [54] is the only nude figure at Lagoudhera that is convenient for measuring purposes. He wears no loincloth and his head is inclined sideways. The other seminude figures are those of St. John the Baptist [75], whose middle anatomy is concealed by a loincloth, and St. Onuphrios [81], whose modesty is saved by a tree. Both the nude and the seminude figures conform to a total height of ten face lengths from the root of the hair to the base of the heel. Using the individual face length and standard measuring points on all three figures, the proportional ratios were found to be constant.

These same ratios also remain standard in the clothed figure, and the face length and the nose length of the individual figure were used as modules. In the painting of clothed figures, both at Lagoudhera and in other Byzantine paintings and mosaics, it is clear that the designer used the modular system as a guide to determine the level at which he should place a particular feature, such as the waist, the knee, the elbows, etc. Within these levels he could and did articulate the body as he chose. These correctly proportioned sectional divisions make no allowance for the plasticity of the human form, whether static or in movement, because the painter constructed his figures according to the proportional rules and not by the observation of nature. Many of the 1192 figures bear witness to this limitation in that their bodies are contorted and occasionally are totally misaligned. There are striking examples of this problem among the prophets in the dome, as well as in the archangel Gabriel of the Annunciation and the shepherd's angel in the Nativity. These all illustrate that in the painting of the clothed figure, the proportional reference points served three positive, painterly purposes. Their first purpose was to measure correctly the anatomical parts of the body, a usage that is echoed in the canons of proportions of antique and Renaissance painters. The second and third purposes served the Byzantine painter in helping him to achieve the more specific needs of his own style. They served as a guide for the layout of garments and the articula-

---

[130] Demus, *Byzantine Mosaic Decoration*, pp. 7–8.

tion of their folds, and for the placing of shadows and highlights that finally molded the figure. The proportions used are as follows:

Body measures

Root of hair to heel	10 faces	30 nose lengths	7½ heads
Root of hair to chin	1 face	3 nose lengths	¾ head
Chin to pit of stomach (breast line)	1 face	3 nose lengths	¾ head
Pit of stomach (breast line) to waist	1 face	3 nose lengths	¾ head
Waist to base of stomach (belly)	1 face	3 nose lengths	¾ head
Base of belly to centerpoint (middle)	1 face	3 nose lengths	¾ head
Centerpoint (middle) to base of knee	2 faces	6 nose lengths	1½ heads
Base of knee to base of heel	3 faces	9 nose lengths	2¼ heads

Subsidiary measures

Heel to toe, profile foot	1⅓ faces	4 nose lengths	1 head
Ankle to heel	⅓ face	1 nose length	¼ head
Height of neck	⅓ face	1 nose length	¼ head
Ankle to end of toes	1 face	3 nose lengths	¾ head
Halo diameter	2 faces	6 nose lengths	1½ heads

Measures for the upper limbs

Height of shoulders (pit of throat to armpit)	⅔ face	2 nose lengths	½ head
Armpit to elbow (humerus)	1 face	3 nose lengths	¾ head
Inner elbow to wrist	1 face	3 nose lengths	¾ head
Exterior elbow to wrist	1⅓ faces	4 nose lengths	1 head
Wrist to tip of medius	1 face	3 nose lengths	¾ head
Wrist to tip of medius (the female hand)	1 face	2½ nose lengths	⅝ head

Measures of width

Width of shoulders	2 faces	6 nose lengths	1½ heads

The majority of the figures are clothed in the chiton and himation. Some figures wear tunics and cloaks, some the monastic habit, and the archangels and kingly prophets are clothed in imperial costume. This regal apparel consists of a tunic with a richly embroidered hem that is loosely belted with a white band at waist level. The tunic is worn under the entwining folds of the heavily bejeweled loros. The upper interior edge of the loros (ignoring the jeweled black borders) marks the base of the belly. The underline of the knee appears three face lengths lower in the tunic folds, as for the prophet David [35]. In those figures who are attired in the chiton and himation, the folds of the latter are usually thrown back over one shoulder to reappear around the waist. These folds

Text Fig. 44 Diagram of the modular proportions of the human figure in the 1192 paintings

sometimes droop low enough to mark the base of the belly, and sometimes they are high enough to reveal the notched line λ, with which the painter marked the navel. At least one knee is underlined within the lower folds of the garments, and the ankle is clearly illustrated as it marks the high point of the dorsum of the foot and the base of the robes in most figures. In the case of the female figures and those of monks, both of whom wear long skirted robes, the base of the heel marks the level of the spilling hem of the robes as they overlap the top of the feet. When the upper arm is alongside the body and the forearm is extended, the point of reference for the inner elbow lies at waist level, two face lengths from the level of the chin.

The sectional division of the vertical space to be occupied by figures was clearly vital to the Lagoudhera master both at the compositional stage and for the build up of his figures. Byzantine painters did not spend long hours studying the human figure in the "life" class, and so they lacked the benefit of seeing an endless variety of stances and observing the fluent integration of the human form. However, the Lagoudhera master was well aware of the plastic form of the human figure, and he modeled his figures in light and dark hues and tones. Patterns and flowing folds of swirling robes do much to smooth out the incoherencies of the arbitrary sections of the figures that he mapped out.

Proportion

Measures for the Head

There are three types of head, regardless of aspect or stance. These are the heads of young men and women, those of old men, and those of extreme youth.[131] The head lengths for old men are occasionally longer than those for young men, and the head length for one old man will sometimes vary from one to another. The variation lies in the enlargement of the distance from the top of the forehead to the apex of the head.

The proportional relationships for the frontal face and the three-quarter-profile face remain standard whether the head be young or old, despite any variation in head length, in physical characteristics, or in stance or aspect.

Another constant characteristic of adult heads is the way that their measures are related to the haloes. Thus the module for the face length also acts as the measure for the radius of the halo. This relationship remains standard, with only six exceptions among 130 figures with haloes.[132] The halo was marked out at a preliminary stage of painting, and its circumference was designed to separate the grey base of the background colors from the yellow base color of the halo.[133] A compass, which was indispensable for marking out the halo, was also the easiest tool with which to relay the modular lengths of the parts of the figure along any notional axis. It must be emphasized, however, that although there is a definite relationship between the face measure and the halo diameter at Lagoudhera, this relationship is not based on a buildup of concentric circles.[134]

The Asymmetrical Frontal Face
Pls. 9, 13, 26, 27, 30; Figs. 42, 61, 74, 88–91, 104, 106, 108–109, 113–121, 135, 140, 152, 165–166, 187–188, 191–198, 211, 229, 255–259; Text Fig. 45)
The frontal faces at Lagoudhera, in common with the vast majority of good quality frontal heads in Byzantine mosaics and paintings of the post-Iconoclast period, are characterized by their lack of symmetry.[135] In these faces, the gaze is indirect and summons the worshipper to look beyond the icon and into the church or eastward. This indirect gaze is achieved by placing the

[131] The proportions and measures used for the Christ child are discussed below, pp. 292–95.

[132] The haloes were occasionally enlarged to encompass head gear or the piled-up neck folds of cowls.

[133] One of the basic purposes of preliminary drawings was to separate areas of the composition or figures that would have a grey rather than a yellow base color. Blue and green backgrounds were painted over a grey proplasmos, whereas haloes and heads were built up over a yellow proplasmos, with red over a yellow proplasmos.

[134] Panofsky, "Die Entwicklung der Proportionslehre als Abbild der Stilentwicklung," *Monatshefte für Kunstwissenschaft* 14 (1921), 188–219. For a further discussion of the Panofsky observation in relation to Byzantine heads, see Winfield and Winfield, *Proportion*, 180–85. The concentric system as suggested by Panofsky is based on a centerpoint along the center of the nose of a symmetrical face. It presupposes a symmetrical face.

[135] If the Iconoclast condemnation of images was due to the idolatrous focus of the worshipper, then this may have implemented the change from the symmetrical face with its intimate, frontal gaze to the asymmetrical face with its indirect gaze. The latter leads the worshipper on and beyond the icon itself and may thus indicate that a deliberate compromise was made when images were again accepted.

pupils off-center. By contrast, the direct gaze in the symmetrical frontal face is achieved by placing the pupil in the center of each eye.

Another characteristic of the asymmetrical face is the deliberate difference between the shape of the eyes, even though the upper rims may remain level. The eye in the wide side of the face is usually narrower and frequently longer than the more rounded eye of the narrow side of the face. At Lagoudhera this is more or less constant, and it is a further characteristic of single figures in the panels or roundels that the wide side of the face with the longer and narrower eye is usually on the side of the nose across which the gaze is directed. Thus if a figure is gazing to the left, then the wide side of the face will be on the left side of the nose.

The frontal asymmetrical faces cannot be described as turning since, if they were, their gaze would be directed across the narrow side of the face to follow through the movement of turning. The nose is always shown with both nostrils, although the nostril on the narrow side of the face is frequently smaller than the other nostril. In general, the darker shadow to the nose is placed to the right, regardless of the direction of the gaze. The mouth is symmetrical, and the ears are level and equal in size when both are painted.

In single figures the direction of the gaze is governed by the siting of the figure within the church. At Lagoudhera, such figures were all made either with eyes looking into the naos or bema, or with eyes gazing eastward.

The Christ in the dome at Lagoudhera is an exception in that the wide side of his face remains to the right of his nose, and his gaze tends to follow the onlooker wherever he moves. This is achieved by placing the pupil of the eye in the narrow side of the face close to the nose and by centering the pupil in the other eye. Other exceptions are the archangel Michael [140], St. John the Baptist [75], and the archangel and the figure of the Mother of God in the Ascension scene [78].

The frontal faces are bisected by a vertical line that passes through the root of the hair and through the inner corner of the larger eye; the line is tangent to the outer side of the nostril and then runs down to the chin. Along this vertical line, the distances from the root of the hair to the root of the nose, from thence to the base of the nose, and from thence to the base of the chin are all of equal length. Thus the face is divided into three equal parts: the forehead, the nose, and the chin. The upper area of the head, from the root of the hair to the vertex, is equal to one nose length, but some old men have additional hair above the vertex, and some young men have a smaller scalp area.

A notional horizontal drawn across the upper rims of the eyes and through the nose root will intersect with the bisecting vertical at a point to the side of the nose. This point is used as the centerpoint for the halo. The haloes measure six noses or two face lengths in diameter, with some specific exceptions. In some cases the halo is enlarged to accommodate a turban or a cowl as, for example, for the heads of St. Symeon the Archimandrite [118] or St. Joseph the Poet [80]. In these cases, the halo centerpoint is placed in the middle of the forehead. A similar adjustment was made

for the monks in the lower register because of the visual distortion that would be caused by their folded cowls, which ride high up on their necks.

The width of the head is usually less than three noses, but in the case of the angels it is wider because of their voluminous hair style. The normal Lagoudhera ratio of width to height is less than 3:4 for the head. The width of the large eye in the wider side of the face is never less than half a nose, and the distance between the eyes never exceeds half a nose. The width between the pupils is most frequently less than one nose. When fully shown, the ears have a length of one nose and a width of half a nose; they are sited on a level with the nose.

The 1192 master took particular care when painting the heads of figures, although he did not paint them with a mathematical precision as to measure. Nevertheless, the evidence is overwhelming as to the asymmetry of the face planes in relation to the median of the nose. The same consistency of measure can be found in the tripartite division of the face into three equal parts. Other constant features are the indirect gaze, the differing size of the eyes, and the clear constructional link between the halo and the face measures. With these rules governing his drawing as a result of training and habit, the painter could draw his heads freehand, apart from the halo, without worrying about small measures. The evidence from preliminary drawings at Lagoudhera and elsewhere suggests that a line to mark the eyeline and the nose length was all that the painter bothered to put in at a preliminary stage.[136] The essential mastery of these proportional rules is demonstrated in the creation of the painting of the half-length figure of Christ in the curving dome away from daylight. Here, the modular ratios for the head came into their own, and they were indispensable for setting out this great figure (see above, pp. 111–19; Text Fig. 21).

The reference points for the head were simply marked out along the continuation of the notional axis line of the body (Text Figs. 23, 25, 43, 44). A point one face length up from the base of the throat marks the level of the eyeline, whether the head is in the frontal or oblique aspect, or whether it is upright or inclined in stance. This point is also the centerpoint for the halo, and it follows that, in nimbed figures, the eyeline that guides the measures of width for the head will always lie along a diameter of the halo.[137]

---

[136] To note just a few instances, the 12th-century wall paintings in the church of the Holy Apostles at Perachorio in Cyprus reveal a variety of such examples in heads of the figures in scenes and in single figures. In the 12th-century church of St. John Chrysostomos, Koutsovendis, there is a drawing on the masonry of the dome and a preliminary drawing within the damaged face of St. Ephraim of Syria. In the church of Eski Gümüş in Turkey, traces of these guide lines are seen in the face of the 12th-century image of the archangel Gabriel. All the above are illustrated in Winfield and Winfield, *Proportion*, pls. 1–6, but there are many other examples to be observed.

[137] The 12th-century figural paintings in many other Byzantine churches seem to conform to a system of construction for the head that is similar to that at Lagoudhera. The preliminary drawing provides no evidence as to the use of concentric circles.

The Three-Quarter-Profile Head

(Pls. 12, 14–15, 19, 21–29, 31–35; Figs. 48–57, 59–60, 72, 73, 75, 82–87, 92–97, 99–103, 107, 112, 122–127, 129–134, 137, 139, 147–151, 155–161, 163, 164, 167–172,179–186, 189–190, 200–210, 212–227, 233–251, 253, 254, 261; Text Figs. 23, 46)

The three-quarter-profile head is characterized by a profile nose with only one defined nostril, while the receding area of the face beyond the nose contains a rounded eye, but no temple is visible beyond it (Text Fig. 46). The broad side of the face, which is to the side of the single nostril that is depicted, contains the larger eye. This is usually drawn-out and narrowed, with the pupil in the corner nearest the nose, so that the gaze is directed across the narrow side of the face. The highest point of the head lies above the outer corner of the large eye.

The vertical axis of the head is a continuation of the median of the figure beneath, and the eyeline lies one module or face measure above the pit of the throat, in the same way that it does for the frontal face. In the three-quarter-profile head, however, the vertical axis intersects the eyeline at a point that marks the outer corner of the longer eye in the wide side of the face. This point also serves as the centerpoint for the halo and lies two nose lengths from the top of the head and two nose lengths from the level of the chin in both inclined and upright heads. The alignment of the features is still made with reference to the horizontal eyeline, and the distance from the axial intersection to the nose bridge is one nose length. In the case of the inclined head, the horizontal eyeline is replaced by a diagonal one. In upright heads, the eyelines and the notional verticals correspond with diameters of the halo because, as in the asymmetrical heads, the main axis for the heads is the continuation of the axis of the body. This angular construction accounts for the stiffness of the inclining heads in the dome angels [4–13] (Text Figs. 23, 46b).

The descriptions and drawings given for the construction of the heads are precise and geometric, and they indicate the basic geometry and patterns of measure relationships underlying their construction. The detailed schemas make it clear how versatile and adaptable this system can be. An experienced painter such as the Lagoudhera master did not apply these rules rigidly and precisely in the case of small heads. He relied instead on his own experienced judgment and a simple rule of thumb for the smaller measures.

Proportion

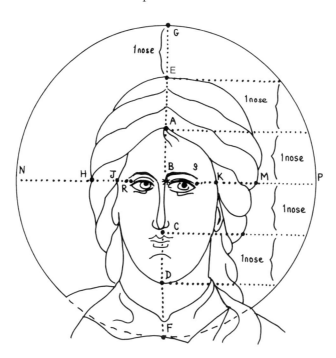

Text Fig. 45 Diagram of an asymmetrical frontal face

<u>The summary of the measures for the construction of the asymmetrical frontal head.</u>
(Text Fig. 45, see above p. 287).

Measures along the vertical axis

Vertex to chin: ED	4 nose lengths
Root of hair to chin, the face: AD	3 nose lengths
Vertex to root of hair: EA	1 nose length
Root of hair to root of nose: AB	1 nose length
Root of nose to base of nose: BC	1 nose length
Base of nose to base of chin: CD	1 nose length
Base of chin to pit of throat: DF	1 nose length
Base of nose to central lip line	¼ nose length
Base of nose to line of central chin cleft	½ nose length
Radius of halo: BF; BN; BG; BP;	3 nose lengths

Measures along the eyeline or horizontal axis

Root of nose to edge of the narrow side of the face: BJ	1 nose length
Root of nose to edge of the wide side of the face: BK	1 nose length min.
Root of nose to edge of hair on the narrow side of the head: BH	1½ nose lengths min.
Root of nose to edge of hair on the wide side of the head: BM	1½–2 nose lengths

Halo diameter along the eyeline: NBP	6 nose lengths or 2 face lengths

Other less-constant measures

From the outer corner of the large eye to edge of the face: SK	½ nose length min.
From the edge of wider side of the face to the edge of the hair: KM	⅞ nose length max.
Outer corner of the small eye to the edge of the face: RJ	¼ nose length max.
Edge of the narrow side of the face to the edge of the hair: JH	varies (JC = ½ nose length)
Width between the pupils	¾ nose length max.
Width of large eye,[138] corner to corner	½ nose length +
Width of small eye, corner to corner	under ½ nose length

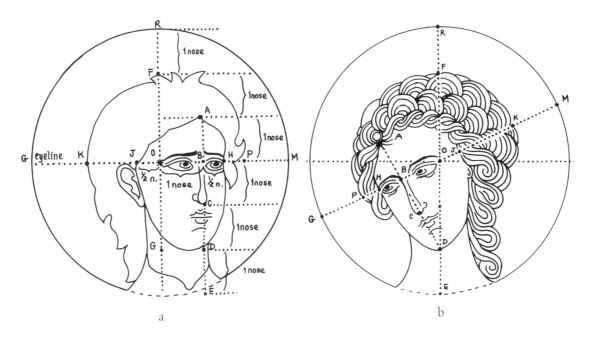

a   b

Text Fig. 46 Diagram of the three-quarter-profile head. (a) the upright head; (b) the inclined head

<u>Measures for the construction of the three-quarter-frontal, semiprofile, or oblique head</u>
Whether the head is upright or inclined, the measures are taken along an axis running from the vertex through the outer corner of the large eye to the chin, and the reference points are in parallel alignment with this notional line (Text Figs. 23, 46).

Vertex of head to chin: FG or FD	4 nose lengths

[138] Though differentiated in length and shape, the eyes are level.

Root of hair to chin: AD	3 nose lengths
Root of hair to root of nose: AB	1 nose length
Root of nose to base of nose: BC	1 nose length
Base of nose to base of chin: CD	1 nose length
Halo[139] centerpoint to vertex of head: OF	2 nose lengths
Halo centerpoint to base of chin: OG or OD (46b)	2 nose lengths

Measures along the horizontal or diagonal eyeline

Root of nose to centerpoint of halo: BO	1 nose length
Root of nose to edge of narrow side of face: BH	½ nose length
Root of nose to edge of broad side of face: BJ	1½ to 1¾ nose lengths
Root of nose to edge of hair on narrow side of the face: BP	½ to 1 nose length max.
Root of nose to edge of hair on broad side of the face: BK	2½ to 3 nose lengths
Width of face along eyeline: HJ	2 to 2¼ nose lengths max.
Width of head along the eyeline: PK	2¼ to 4 nose lengths max.
Radius of halo: OR	3 nose lengths or 1 face length
Width between pupils	1 nose length
Outer corner of large eye to edge of face	½ nose length
Pupil of large eye to edge of narrow side of face	¾ nose length max.
Edge of nostril to base of ear	1 nose length

The female head and figure are constructed according to the measures for the male. The females differ only in that they have shorter, narrower hands and feet, and most of them conceal their heads under wide hoods with wimples beneath. The characteristics of the female form remain concealed by loose robes, and they wear slippers on their feet. The scraggy figure of St. Mary of Egypt [150] is loosely enfolded by a cloth hanging off one shoulder. This reveals her upper body, which has a high breast line at the level of the armpit. Her torso is similar to that of St. John the Baptist and shows no concession to femininity.

The Christ Child

(Pl. 20; Figs. 134, 225, 232, 244, 247; Text Fig. 47)

The only frontal head of a child is the bust-length figure of the Christ Emmanuel [39]. There are three articulated figures of the child with the head in three-quarter profile: the child bathed by midwives in the Nativity [142], the child in the arms of St. Symeon [74], and the child held by the

[139] The halo centerpoint is on the eyeline at the outer corner of the large eye.

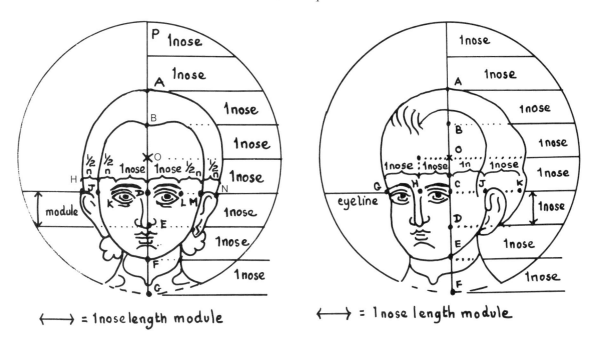

a. the frontal head   b. the three-quarter profile

Text Fig. 47 Diagrams of the head of the Christ child

Mother of God Arakiotissa [139]. From these figures it is possible to make certain observations regarding the proportions given to the child in contrast to those of the adult and to link the measures of the child with those of adult figures.

The heads and haloes of the child supported by adults have a vertical measure (apex to chin) and radius equal to half that of the accompanying adult; the body and limbs also seem to follow this ratio. The only exception is that of the midwives with the Christ child, where only the head measures can be related since the women have no haloes.

The Frontal Head of the Christ Emmanuel
(Pl. 20; Text Fig. 47a)

He has an asymmetrical face in relation to the median of the nose, and his gaze is directed to the right across the wider plane of the face. The nose is small with a broad tip, the cheeks are wide and rounded, and the forehead is tall and broad. The hair consists of a narrow band around the top of the head that gathers into a small, tight bunch of curls beneath the ears. The ears are large, prominent, and longer than the nose. The eyes are wide and rounded, but the eye in the wider side of the face is longer than the other eye.

The head retains the asymmetrical characteristics of the adult frontal face with its indirect gaze. However, as will be seen in the measures below, the subsidiary measures of the face and head

were altered in their ratio to the face length in order to establish the characteristic large brainbox and plump, rounded cheeks of infancy. Text Figure 47 illustrates the construction of the head of the Christ child seen in the frontal and the three-quarter aspect.

The face of the child is divided into four parts instead of three, and two parts are given to the forehead and one part each to the nose and chin. The face and halo relationship remains the same as for the adult, with two face lengths to the diameter of the halo. The reduced height of the lower face fattens the cheeks and shortens the nose. The height of the upper head (top of forehead to apex of head) measures less than one nose length. Having established his basic guide measures, the painter could paint the child's head without resorting to the careful measuring implied below; the balance and relationships of the form and size of the child would be second nature to him.

Measures for the asymmetrical frontal head of the child are as follows:

Vertical measures

Head: vertex to base of chin: AF	4+ nose lengths
Hair: vertex to root of hair: AB	1− nose length
Face: Root of hair to chin: BF	4 nose lengths
Forehead: root of hair to root of nose: BD	2 nose lengths
Nose: root of nose to base of nose: DE	1 nose length
Chin: base of nose to base of chin: EF	1 nose length
Base of nose to chin cleft	½ nose length
Base of nose to central line of lips	¼ nose length
Neck: base of chin to pit of throat: FG	1 nose length
Maximum height of ears	⅓ face length
	(−1 nose length)

Along a notional eyeline running through the top of the ears, through the upper rim of the eyes and through the root of the nose, the following measures can be observed:

Width of the head: HN	4− nose lengths
Width of the face: JM	3+ nose lengths
Width of the hair to either side of the face: HJ/MN: each	½ nose length
Root of nose to the edge of the narrow side of face: DJ	1½ nose lengths
Root of nose to edge of wide side of face: DM	1½ nose lengths
Width of temple on wide side of face: LM	½ nose length
Width of temple on narrow side of face: JK	½− nose length
Width between the inner corners of the eyes	½ nose length
Width between the pupils	1+ nose length
From pupil of large eye to edge of face	1 nose length

From inner corner of small eye to the   1 nose length
   edge of the narrow side of the face

The center of the halo, O, lies within the forehead in alignment with the root of the nose, D, and is equidistant from D and from the root of the hair, B. The measures indicate that the nose measure continues to be the module for the construction of the head, but the ratio of the nose measure to the face measure has altered from 1:3 (as in the adult face) to 1:4. The measures along the vertical and horizontal axes of the head therefore relate to a module that is one-quarter of a face length and not one-third of a face length.

By reducing the nose-length module and altering the ratios, the painter succeeded in distinguishing the infant from the adult. When comparing the child's head with infant heads in nature, it can be seen, however, that the child's ears are far too long and his upper head is exaggerated. The reduced size of the child's neck is in keeping with the characteristics of early childhood. His neck measures one-fourth of his face length, whereas in the adult figure, the neck measures one-third of the adult's face. As a result of all these adjustments to the subdivisions of the face, the center of his halo lies above his forehead and not on his eyeline.

The Oblique Head of the Christ child (Figs. 134, 225, 244, 247; Text Fig. 47b)

The three oblique heads of the Christ child present physical characteristics of an infant similar to those observed in the frontal head, namely, the broad, high forehead, the thickened nosetip, and the wide, lower face with rounded cheeks. The heads are turned sufficiently to conceal the further temple. The further nostril is either omitted or barely sketched. The hair is styled to recede high on one side so that it emphasizes the forehead, while on the other side it falls neatly in soft waves to the base of the ear.

The vertical axis of the head bisects the eyeline at a point just above the outer corner of the large eye. The eyeline, which runs across the upper rims of the eyes and through the root of the nose, bisects the distance between the vertex and the pit of the throat. The face is divided into four equal vertical sections of one nose length, and thus the nose (root of nose to base of nose) measures one-quarter of a face length. The vertical divisions of the head are similar to those of the frontal head except that the reference point for the root of the nose has been moved one nose length along the eyeline to lie just above the outer corner of the large eye.

The halo radius has a similar measure to that of the frontal head (four noses or one face), and its centerpoint also lies one nose length above the eyeline but in alignment with the outer corner of the large eye. The measures of width taken along the eyeline are as follows:

Width of the head: GK   4 nose lengths
Width of the face: GJ   3 nose lengths
Outer corner of large eye to edge of wide side of face: CJ   1 nose length

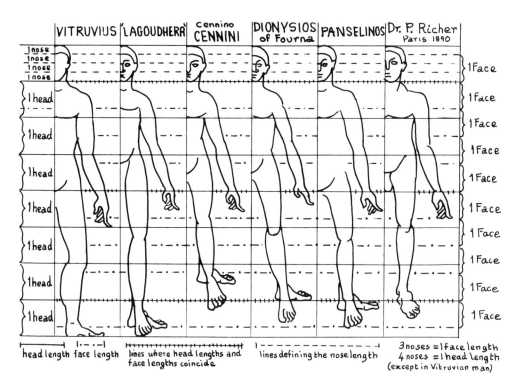

Text Fig. 48 The Lagoudhera system of figural proportion in relation to other known systems based on anatomical modules related to the head

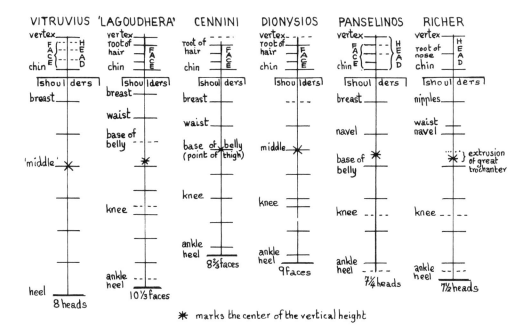

Text Fig. 49 An abstraction of the systems of proportion illustrated in Text Fig. 48, showing the differing aesthetic approaches to the human form

Outer corner of large eye to nose root on wide side of face: CH	1 nose length
Outer corner of large eye to edge of narrow side of face: CG	2 nose lengths
Outer corner of large eye to edge of hair: CK	2 nose lengths

In the 1192 paintings, the Christ child affects an air of ponderous sagacity largely because of the exaggerated size of his forehead, but this severe effect is softened by the plumpness of the cheeks. The three figures of the child are so varied in their articulation that it would be too speculative to suggest their bodily proportions and to relate them to those of the adult figures.

This system of proportion, when interpreted in the manner of the textbook formulae outlined above, may seem very complex for the average painter to master and to apply with comfortable speed. In practice, however, the system could be easily mastered and applied, and an apprentice working with his master on a church would find it an elementary and practical method to follow.

The modular system as used by the master set a standard from which he made little or no departure, for it was not used by him as a canon against which to measure the variations of the human figure in nature, but quite simply as a basis upon which to construct all figures. It was a system well adapted to the flat surface of a wall, but, because it was a simple sectional system, it had its limitations. It defined arbitrary distances within the human figure, and it did not and indeed could not take into account the fluent changes within the figure articulated in movement. It was left to the painter to coordinate his figures from joint to joint, and from limb to limb, and he sometimes encountered difficulties in connecting the parts of the body to build up a coherent, natural whole. However, he was adept as an artist at concealing his problems under the elegant articulations of garments. He used linear rhythms on the faces and in clothing to create a sense of drama far more powerful than any natural portrayal of movement and emotion.

The Lagoudhera system of modular proportion is one variant among modular systems that are to be observed in all good-quality Byzantine painting and in many western medieval church decorations (Text Figs. 48, 49).[140] The simplicity of such systems allowed Byzantine painters and mosaicists to cover large areas of church walls with speed and confidence.

---

[140] Segers-Glocke, *Forschungsprojekt Wandmalereischaden: Arbeitshefte zur Denkmalpflege in Niedersachsen*, vol. 2 (Hannover, 1994), 54–60.

17

COLOR, TEXTURE, MATERIALS, AND TOOLS

The pigments used at Lagoudhera are mainly earth colors, and many good-quality colors are still mined locally in Cyprus. The medium used for mixing the pigments was mainly lime water or lime white. The use of lime white gives the opaque pastel texture of so many of the colors. The darker colors, such as umber and dark red, were probably mixed with animal glues, casein, or egg. The colors have some interesting visual and textural characteristics.

The Colors

Black usually appears opaque and smooth. Where it is applied in broad bands, as in the ground for the borders of the imperial loros or the inner halo outline, it has a satinlike finish that reveals no trace of the brush. It is mainly used to outline and define figures and objects at a final stage of painting, but it is also used as a color in its own right for the loros bands, the crosses of liturgical robes, or for the slippers of monks and maidens, and to indicate interiors implied by open doors or windows.

Grey veers toward blue rather than brown. It is one of the colors used for drawing on fresh plaster and for laying-in as a proplasmos. In its latter form, it was probably black that was diluted with a heavily saturated lime water. As a proplasmos it was used under cooler colors, such as green and blue. In subfusc garments such as those of the monks, it was used occasionally over yellow. It appears rarely as a ground color or shadow color, but one apostle on the north side of the Ascension has a whole garment built up out of graded values of grey (p. 203). It would be possible to grade the grey by varying the admixture of white.

Blue is very grainy, and, without a proplasmos or another color beneath, it would have little opacity or body as it is very thin. Its main use was as a wash layer over grey for backgrounds. It was also traditionally used in this way for the garments of Christ and the Virgin. Where it is used as a ground for their tunics, it carries no highlights and is simply articulated with dark grey and black fold lines and outlines. A few other figures in this decoration have garments that have a light blue ground with blue shadows and thick, white highlights. The himation of St. Paul in the Koimesis

has a light blue ground, red and umber shadows, and the usual black definition lines and thick, white highlights.

Blue was used quite frequently as a wash highlight, and when thus applied over a garment with a green or a dark red ground, the color effects are filmy. Blue applied over dark red gives a somber purple effect, whereas when it was applied over a light red, the blue could assume a lavender hue. When blue wash was used as a wash highlight over yellow or green, the painter first put down a wash of white. The blue was applied over this and retained its blueness without turning muddy green. Thick, white highlights on yellow were also occasionally washed over with thin blue. Thick blue was also rarely used as a thick highlight, as on the final version of Anna's green tunic and on its yellow hem. Light blue was used as a highlight for architectural cornices and capitals of grey "stone." The range of tones in blue is well illustrated in the Ascension [78], in the deepening blues of the mandorla surrounding the central figure of Christ (Pl. 26).

Vermilion seems to vary from an orangy red to a bluer red. This variation is partly due to the quality of the pigment obtained and partly to how finely it was crushed. In the 1192 paintings at Lagoudhera, the red has the value and intensity of carmine to crimson. Where it is used as a background, as for the Christ in the dome [1] and the Etoimasia [3], the vermilion appears to be burnished, and it shines, unlike the other colors, which are matte (Pls. 1, 9).

The painter must have known that vermilion blackened in contact with lime, and it was never used directly on the wet plaster but always over a ground of yellow or as a highlight over a buildup of other colors. Vermilion also turns black with long exposure to light, and in this decoration a number of garments of "red" hue have blackened. A sad loss to the whole decoration is that many of the red borders were given a narrow central highlight line in vermilion, and this now appears as a greyish black line.

Some shades of pinkish red may be described as light vermilion and were used as grounds and shadows. Pure vermilion is also used as a highlight in dark red garments and in the buildup of flesh colors.

Umber is a ferric oxide compound with a large proportion of manganese. Cyprus has exported the pigment since the Roman period, and we found good-quality surface deposits of it in the valley below the church. It is a brown with the color tone of dark chocolate in its natural form, and it can be mixed with white to provide pastel shades. It is used extensively in both forms to build up garments, both as a light or medium value ground and as shadows on light umber or yellow garments. Dark umber is used as a subsidiary shadow to define garments, for the linear definition of faces, and as a ground for the buildup of colors for the hair.

Red ochre, which is an anhydrous ferric oxide, can be commonly found in Cyprus. Ample quantities of reds and yellows of various hues are on the tips of the iron ore mines near the foot of the Lagoudhera valley. The standard red ochre is of a reddish brown hue. It is used for the red borders, and it is commonly used throughout the paintings. Darker and lighter tones of red ochre were used, respectively, as grounds and shadows for lighter areas. On rare occasions, thin red was applied over a white wash highlight if the ground color was yellow.

Color, Texture, Materials, and Tools

Yellow in differing grades of ochres was widely used not only as a ground but also for the buildup of garments. The color tones were further varied by the amount of white mixed with them. The value of the yellows remains cool but never attains a citron or an orange tone. Angel [8] in the dome originally had an apricot-colored ground for his tunic, but this was overpainted with green. The original version would have clashed badly with the vermilion background of the figure. The apricot color, though intense in value, was not used elsewhere, and it must have been made by mixing yellow, red, and white in the pot.

A creamy yellow was used for chrysographia in the case of the garments of Christ Antiphonetes [127], Christ of the Ascension [78] (Pl. 26), and the Christ Emmanuel [39] (Pl. 20). The same yellow made the sunray chrysographia of the hems to the tunics of the three Magi in the Nativity [142] (Pl. 22). Yellow-brown is another variant to the yellow and red ochres. It was used mainly as a warm shadow on light yellows and as a ground for the tunics of some monks.

Green, in some instances, may come from a high grade of celadonite or terre verte that Cyprus produces. As a pigment, celadonite does not have much body, and it can vary from apple green to deep olive. Another possible local source of green was malachite, a green carbonate of copper. It was much used in the Middle Ages, and there are deposits of it on the island. The 1192 green is a cool rather than a grainy color, usually applied over a grey base; it is commonly used in this manner for foregrounds. In tone, green varies from light to medium and dark, and it was occasionally highlighted with thick, blue lines and blue wash. Green was nearly always used as a ground for the flesh colors and as a reinforcing shadow in the buildup of flesh colors.

Yellow-green is a second green similar to the above, but when it is applied over a yellow proplasmos instead of grey, the grainy pigment acquires a warmer tone.

White is thick and very white. The majority of the whites are undoubtedly lime white, and there may be a coarse and a fine grade of it since it varies in texture. It usually has a matte and rather grainy appearance, and it bears the imprint of brush marks very clearly. The white used for garment highlights and pearl decorations, however, often has a lucent pearly appearance and an unctuous texture. Pearls were made in high relief and are well rounded with a slight peak, as if dropped with an icing syringe. Such a tool could easily have been made with a bamboo tube and a plunger.

Lavender is blue applied over a light red ground, and it only appears for one small area of a tunic. There are a few other uncommon color mixtures where only small parts of garments are revealed. It looks as if the painter simply used up what was at hand for such small areas.

Despite the heavy use of lime white to mix colors, the color values remain intense and very clean. There is nothing watery or murky in their value. The whole decoration is dominated by light, bright colors, with the exception of necessarily subdued coloring for the monks. The medallion backgrounds alternate in bright vermilion and blue or vermilion and green, and the floral decorative patterns in the spandrels between the medallions were originally cheerful and decorative, although now sadly discolored. The architectures are similarly fretted with ornamental color, and

they contrast well with the strong, flowing effect of the figures where the color buildups are tonal. The overall effect of the decoration is of a cool crispness, despite the warmth of the vermilion, the yellows, and the reds. This complex and seemingly contradictory impression of color values is possibly due to the pastel quality of the lime white medium.

The Lagoudhera master shows a complete mastery of the three basic methods of using color: in solid blocks of color, in watercolor-like washes to soften or modify the solid color underneath, and in thick and fine continuous lines that show no hesitation in the wielding of the brush. It is the linear patterns that strike the onlooker, and it is obvious that the Lagoudhera master delighted in them, but the effect of these complex lines would be chaotic without the stabilizing force of the blocks of solid color underneath. The washes of color serve to add subtlety, grace, and texture where he wanted silken effects. And whenever there is a yellow to simulate the gold in panels and hems decorating garments, he always used a wash of white over small areas of yellow to simulate the glitter of gold.

His range of tones of color is greater than most Byzantine wall painters employed, and for the buildup of faces the Lagoudhera master used up to twelve tones or colors, whereas six or seven tones might be considered the average.[141] Apart from mixing different tones of colors in his paint pots, he increased this range of color effects by using the color of his proplasmos to intensify the surface colors and by using surface washes to modify ground colors.

Gilding and Silvering

This highly expensive treatment was reserved for the great icon of the Arakiotissa [139] (Pl. 32) and for the representation of Symeon holding the Christ child [74] (Pl. 28).

The haloes of Symeon and the Christ child were both gilded over yellow, which acted as the mordant. The whole area of the child's tunic was similarly gilded, forming a ground upon which the folds were delineated in fine, black line. The pattern at the neckline and the triple-line pattern of his clavus were all superimposed in black line over the gilding.

In the panel of the Arakiotissa [139], the haloes of the Mother of God and child and the angels were all gilded over the yellow. The child's robe has a yellow ground, vermilion lines, and black fold lines and outlines. Dark traces of chrysographia in the form of tapered, gilded lines can be seen on the yellow ground.

Both the single and the double decorative yellow bands on the edge of the Arakiotissa's maphorion were originally gilded, and blobs of white highlight were added over the gilding to pinpoint the center and corners of each fold. Her tunic is yellow, and it was shot with chrysographia, the traces of which can still be observed as long, diagonal, tapered grey marks. The cuffs of the sleeves of both angels were gilded, the fold lines were indicated in brown, and the decorative bands

141 See Winfield, "Methods," 137.

were black with pearls.

A second method of gilding appears to have been carried out with some sort of stamp. This delivered a square patch of gold or silver leaf, varying from about .5 cm to 1.5 cm square, usually set diagonally to form a diamond shape. It is possible that these patches were laid on and burnished in the normal way, but the regular square patches are more suggestive of a special tool for the job.

The vermilion slippers of the Arakiotissa were stamped with diamond-shaped squares of gold leaf (Text Fig. 41). The cloth that falls from beneath the bolster behind her has a ground of thick lime white. This is divided into two sections by twin, horizontal bands of vermilion, and similar double bands of vermilion decorate the hem edge. (The vermilion was not applied directly onto the white but over an undercoat of yellow.) The white line separating the twin bands between the double vermilion lines was stamped with a single row of diamond patches of gold leaf that overlap onto the vermilion (Text Fig. 41).

Two patterns are on the white ground of the bolster cloth as it appears to either side of the Virgin. There is an upper design of diagonal crosses with a stepped outline in black line. Stamped silver squares set in diamond shapes line both the corridors of the crosses and the white triangles formed by their arms. The lower pattern consists of large, scallop-edged, diamond shapes outlined in black that contain five stamped silver squares in the form of a cross (Text Fig. 41).

Materials and Tools

There is no local source of lime at Lagoudhera, and a caravan of camels or donkeys must have brought chalk or limestone along the mountain tracks throughout 1191 and 1192. Some small pockets of limestone are not far from Vyzakia, the village in the Mesaoria owned by the monastery. The best sources, however, were either on the southern slopes of Troodos or in the Kyrenia range of mountains. It would be interesting to know if the painter fired and slaked his own lime, since there is some advantage in the adhesive quality of freshly slaked lime. The straw and the chaff binder probably came from arable lands belonging to the donor family at the foot of the Lagoudhera valley.

As was mentioned above (p. 299), the yellow and red ochres that make up the bulk of the coloring might have been obtained from the iron mines in the foothills below Lagoudhera, and a good source of umber is very near the mine. The 1192 master was quite particular in his choice of high-quality colors, and it is likely that he brought the other colors with him, but some at least were probably produced in Cyprus.

The scaffolding timber could easily have been cut locally, since the area was almost certainly more heavily wooded than it is at present. The painter would have brought the tools of his trade with him, perhaps on his own donkeys or camels. He and his three assistants would each have had a donkey or a camel, and there must have been at least two baggage animals. These would have carried the pestles and mortars for grinding colors, pots for paint and vessels for water, plastering

tools, and string for setting out measures. The master would have brought with him his finer and favorite brushes, but other brushes would have been made up by an apprentice as and when the work required. Goat and camel hair and pigs' bristles would all have been obtainable locally and would certainly have been needed since wall painting work is quite hard on brushes, and the fine detail of the paintings must have been carried out with brushes in good condition.

The tools for gilding, silvering, and burnishing, together with supplies of gold and silver leaf, must also have formed a part of the master's equipment, although possibly the gold and silver leaf were provided by Lord Leon. His most prized tools must have been his compass and dividers.[142] These were his indispensable aids both in the general layout of the decoration and in the construction of each roundel, panel, and scene. Circumferences can be drawn or incised with the aid of a few nails, a stick of charcoal or a brush, and some string. To make the precise double outlines of his haloes, however, required great accuracy and dependability. We have noted above (pp. 278, 281, 283) that he must have had a special tool for this work, since the outlines have none of the small irregularities in the thickness of paint that would appear even with expert brushwork.

---

[142] Many Byzantine illustrations of the evangelists show these tools on their writing desks. Several 12th-century examples appear in the manuscripts of Mount Athos. See S. M. Pelikanides et al., *The Treasures of Mount Athos*, vol. 2 (Athens, 1975), 194, 195, pls. 323, 324, Monastery of St. Panteleimon, 12th-century codex 25, St. Matthew; St. Mark; ibid., 152, 153, pls. 274, 275, 276, Monastery of St. Panteleimon, 12th-century codex 2.

18

Painting Procedures, Light and Perspective, and Emotion

The Painting Sequence

The following description shows how the 1192 master went to work at painting a single figure in a panel. The procedure for scenes was not unsimilar, but it would have been more complicated.

Before plastering, the painter had to choose which figure to fit into the panel that he was decorating. He also had to assess in which aspect the figure was to be seen, the bodily stance and gesture of the image, together with its costume and any identifying paraphernalia, such as books or scrolls. With this information in mind, he then worked out the placing of his figure within the panel, and he worked out his basic module, which would control the proportion and structure of the final figure (see above, pp. 283–86; Text Fig. 43).

As soon as the panel was plastered, the master established a preliminary layout, marking out reference points for the various levels of his figure and the halo outlines. This required only a moment's work using a compass fixed at the radius of the basic module, the face length. He then made a brush sketch of his figure in thin, red paint. If a painting presented a particular problem or possibility of confusion at a later stage, he reinforced his drawing with incised or impressed lines, since such lines would not disappear in the course of painting. Once the figure was drawn out, the painter blocked in the first layer of color, or proplasmos. In general, the proplasmos was either grey or yellow, and was distinct from the light red drawing lines. The yellow proplasmos was painted over the whole halo, covering the head and neck included within it. The hands and feet and any other flesh areas were also painted with this preliminary coat of yellow. The same yellow proplasmos was applied in preparation for any ground colors from the warmer side of the spectrum: yellow, brown, umber, red, vermilion, and, more rarely, green for some garments. Dark grey was laid on as the proplasmos under the blue and green backgrounds, and dark grey was also used for any cool garment colors within the figure. Having blocked out his panel in this way, with no white plaster remaining, the painter sometimes resorted to marking complicated folds in dark grey. This was because most of the grounds were light in tone, with the exception of blue and dark red, and the dark grey would remain visible through them (see above, the prophet Gideon [25], pp. 136–37; Fig. 64).

There were several advantages to this preliminary application of color, or proplasmos. By rapidly blocking in preliminary washes of color, the painter delayed the congealing of the plaster's

surface. By blocking out all the glaring white of the plaster, he could then see the preliminary forms of his composition, and he was able to manage his color scheme more delicately. An additional gain was that the proplasmos served as a foundation for the second layer of color or ground, which would then appear more opaque as it gained more body. Without this proplasmos, grainy colors such as blue and green would allow the white of the plaster background to filter through and thereby weaken the impact and value of the ground colors.

After applying his proplasmos, the painter blocked in the ground colors upon which he would build up the colors that modeled the figure and other elements in the panel. Most of these ground colors were applied in a medium tone to act as a foil to the modeling in darker and lighter tones or hues. In simple panels, blue was applied over grey for the upper background, and green was applied over grey for the foreground. The hair was painted with a coat of umber. In the case of flesh areas, green was applied over the yellow base of proplasmos to serve as the ground for the buildup of flesh tones.[143] After completing the laying in of his ground colors, the painter proceeded to build up the garments of the figures and their impedimenta of books or scrolls. When painting large scenes, he completed not only the garments of the figures but also any background features, such as buildings or furniture, or landscape elements, such as mountains, trees, and sheep. He left the head and flesh areas of hands and feet to be painted last, whether he was painting a single panel or a scene.

Each feature or garment was built up with increasingly darker tones of color and then highlighted with transparent washes, followed by thick, white highlights applied in blocks or lines. None of these darks and lights was blended. The first dark tone would leave bare an area of ground; the second dark tone would be applied over the first, leaving it partially revealed; and the dark fold lines and outlines would also step back from the second dark tone like terracing. The highlights were also similarly layered and stepped over the remaining ground color; the wash highlight never totally covers the ground color itself. Sometimes the wash highlight was omitted altogether, and thick, white highlights alone pick out the remaining ground. Some garments have neither thin nor thick highlights.

The layering system is the basic technique of Byzantine painting, though some painters were more careful than others as to overlaps. There was no blending on the wall, just layering. Colors were darkened or lightened in the pot. This was in itself a skilled operation, as colors in the pot usually lighten when they dry out on the wall. An effect of blending was produced by the skillful use of the brush where particularly delicate effects were required. By deftly lifting the paint brush, the edges of a layer could be attenuated and appear to blend into the layer beneath. This is a technique used in faces, where one flesh color applied over another can appear to blend at the edges with the color beneath.

---

[143] The green base for flesh and faces may be a Byzantine innovation in painting technique. It has a long and distinguished usage. It can often be seen in portraits from the medieval period through the 19th century where a face has been overcleaned, to be left with "a morning after the night before" effect.

Painting Procedures, Light and Perspective, and Emotion

There were considerable variations as to the amount of layering. A very pale yellow ground might have four successive layers of shadow tones in graded darks and only one layer of thick, white highlights. The subfusc robes of monks sometimes have no highlights. Graded darks and lights could vary in number and hue, but the basic system of layering did not. Special textural effects were sometimes achieved. Dark red grounds were built up with broad blue washes to simulate purple. Blue wash highlights over a green ground give a diaphanous appearance, as in the robes of the maidens in the Presentation [70]. Occasionally thick white highlights were washed over with a thin color to soften the bright white and reduce it to a tinted highlight, presumably because a thin wash of tinted highlight would take on a muddy hue when painted directly on the ground color. Vermilion was used as a wash highlight or as a thick, linear highlight on dark red garments to achieve a rich textural effect.

At the end of this stage, the figure, its background, and impedimenta were all completed, leaving the face, the hair, the feet, the hands and arms, the halo outlines, and the inscriptions as yet uncompleted.

The Heads

Three types of adult head are found at Lagoudhera: the young, the middle-aged, and the old. The heads of young women are painted in the same manner as those of young men, and Eve, an older woman, has the face of a mature male, such as St. Lazaros, who is also beardless. The frontal heads are all held upright, but heads in three-quarter profile are often inclined forward, sideways, or even backward. The faces of the young people are smooth and unlined, whereas those of the middle-aged and elderly are seared with the lines of age. The difference between depictions of middle age and old age lies in the coloration of the hair and the degree of beard. There are no profile heads.

Throughout the decoration there is a considerable variety in the hair styles, which contributes to an impression of a diversity of heads. There is further differentiation and variation in the styles of beard and mustache. The young head is characterized by its hair style and color, the lack of full beard, and the smooth, unlined face.

Men of middle age have a grizzled, brown coloring to the beard and hair, whereas old men have white hair, mustaches, and beards. The heads of middle-aged and old men have the same characteristic features of the face, and the buildup of colors is similar. Both disport hair styles that either recede high on the forehead or reveal a bald cranium alleviated by a vestigial wisp or a few curls of hair.

In many figures of this decoration, the upper paint layers of flesh areas in the heads and hands have badly flaked, revealing the layering system beneath. For some heads the painter inserted patches. Sometimes he merely reworked the plaster area for heads, hands, or feet, because this troweling of the plaster brought moisture to the drying surface and made it more receptive once again to his paints (Figs. 45, 70, 98, 126, 132, 203, 245–246, 291, 296).

Both plastering and the sequence of paint layers confirm that areas of flesh were painted last. The neck was certainly painted after the robes beneath it, as were the arms and hands that lie across

the body of the figure. The reworking of the flesh areas often caused a disturbance in the plaster of a completed garment, and the necessary retouching of areas damaged in this way can be seen very clearly, particularly if the troweling interfered with the pattern of a loros. If the hair and beard styles of the young or old figure overlapped with the shoulders, the garment area was frequently reworked, and a suitable brown or green ground was then painted over the garment as a foundation for the darks and lights modeling the overlapping locks or curls (Pls. 14, 28; Fig. 97).

Having first completed the garments and other paraphernalia, the painter then redrew the features of the face, blocking in the socket of the eye and the design of the hair.

The Hair and Halo

If the figure in the panel was that of a young or middle-aged man, then the final colors of the hair were laid in over the umber ground. The hair and beard styles were modeled with the use of one dark brown and one yellow tone, and these were further picked out with black lines. The hair of a middle-aged man would be highlighted with blue streaks.

The final buildup for the hair of an old man would be made upon a thick, light green ground that was painted over the original ground of umber. The umber ground is occasionally apparent at the edge of the heads where the paint layers have flaked. Upon this second green ground two graded tones of dark green were used to model the hair and beard styles. The first shadow green was an olive green, and the second was a darker greenish brown.

At this stage the painter would put in the second coat or yellow ground to the halo. This permitted him to mask any modification of exterior outlines to the design of the hair and beard. This is well illustrated in the head of Joachim in the Presentation of the Virgin [70], where the final yellow of the halo has flaked away to reveal the original brown ground of the hair, which extends further than the final and present upper outline to the head (Fig. 129). At a final stage in painting, probably after the completion of the face, thick, black contour lines would further outline contours of the hairstyle, and the hair of an old man would receive the addition of fine, white, linear highlights. The darker the buildup of the hair, the more effective the highlight striations.

In all the heads, whether old, middle-aged, or young, the painter highlighted more heavily those areas of the head that are nearer to the edge of the face. In the case of a three-quarter-profile head, the hair at the back of the head was deliberately left without highlight striations. The sense of volume suggested by this deliberate shadowing of the recessing surfaces is always reduced, however, by the presence of hard, continuous outlines to the face and head. The finishing touches of shadow and highlight illustrate the skill of the 1192 master at creating a Hellenistic illusion of reality in his portraits, and the final stage of black outlines represents his rejection of reality in favor of assuring the spiritual presence of the image.

The painter would complete the halo outlines before finishing the face, since these are drawn with a compass, and the centerpoint of both circles lies within the face. It was not possible to interrelate accurately the sequence of laying in colors for the hair with the sequence used for the face because the sequence of all these procedures was only clear where damage revealed the over-

laps of built-up layers of color. The final white, linear highlighting for the heads of old men, however, was completed after the face was finished, and a general reinforcing in black line to neaten the edges of the hair and face was also done at a final stage, probably when completing the eyebrows in the case of older saints.

Naked Flesh

Bare flesh, such as forearms, feet, the occasional seminude figure, the ears, and the neck, is built up in a standard manner, and only the face varies in its greater technical complexity. For the flesh, the painter first put in a green ground layer, as described above. Upon this ground was laid a creamy flesh color, leaving areas of green to mark recessed areas and edges. Lines in dark green were used to define form, such as the curved lines marking the inner wrist, the bulge of the thumb, and the pit of the throat (Pl. 9). Highlight lines were used in a similar manner to pick out relief, as in the case of the hands, where yellow-tinted white highlights define nails and knuckles, and black outlines are often to only one side of the fingers, as in the hand of Christ Antiphonetes (Text Fig. 38). Some areas were also picked out with vermilion.

The Face

There are basically two kinds of face: the young and the old. Each can be further differentiated by the style and color of hair and beard that they were given. The young face is smooth and unlined with smooth, arching eyebrows that are unstressed by "hair" lines. However, Christ's smooth brows are sometimes picked out with black hair lines (Figs. 42–43, 140, 188). And we have seen that the head of Christ as shown in the Holy Tile [72] and the Mandylion [92] remains that of a young man, but his forehead is seared with lines, in particular the winged U over the eyebrows (see above, p. 220; Figs. 187, 188). In general, the face for old men is seamed and frequently boasts a ponderous forehead built up in high relief and riven with arched furrows (Pl. 15; Figs. 72, 73, 75, 112, 183, 200). The eyebrows of middle-aged men are more horizontal but tilt upward toward the nasal incision. The eyebrows of old men are tilted toward the nasal incision and are tufted at this point. All the eyes have an inner lid line and pupils set within an iris. In none of the faces are the eyes given eyelashes, but the final outline to the eyes is usually twice as thick for the upper rim as for the lower rim. This black outline to the eye is not joined where it meets the inner corner, and the resulting gap is sufficient to indicate the tear duct.

Apart from the heads of the apostles in the Koimesis [138], the facial features are cast in quiescent lines, and the gaze is, for the most part, directed away and beyond those who behold them.

The hairless areas of the head were built up in a very similar manner to the sequence of color applications for the flesh. The preliminary drawing for the head was overlaid with an initial wash or proplasmos of yellow, which was extended to fill the whole halo. It would still have been possible to see the preliminary drawing through this initial wash of yellow. When the painter returned to finish the head, he painted an umber ground for the hair and a green ground color for

the face, the neck, and the ears. Upon this green ground he redefined the features in brown line, filling up the eye sockets with solid brown color, as can be seen in the damaged faces of the prophets Moses [33] and David [35] (Figs. 75, 72).[144]

Having remapped the face, the painter then inserted the almond shapes of the eye within the brown sockets. These shapes are painted in a yellow green to a size larger than the final eye form. There is no evidence as to the timing of the placing of these green shapes within the sockets, except that it was the next move to follow the laying in of the flesh colors.

After the redrawing of the face came the blocking in of the areas of flesh color. The initial flesh color in yellow plus white was applied like a stencil or a cosmetic face mask, leaving the recessed areas in dark green. These are the edges of the face, the sides of the nose and the nose bridge, part of the under eye, part of the nostrils, the notch in the upper lip, the chin cleft, an area under the chin, and the pits of the throat and shoulders. Additional lighter coats of flesh color were then put on with sometimes as many as two or more in larger heads, with each layer receding further toward areas of high relief.

Vermilion was added in spare, attenuated strokes of the brush to prominent areas of the face, such as the higher points of relief in the forehead, the nose bridge and tip, the cheekbones, and the lips.

The second green used in the face is particularly prominent in the faces of old and middle-aged men. It is used mainly in linear form to reaccent the curves of the face, to reinforce the shadow to the side of the nose and the eyebrows, and to delineate the base of the eye socket and, in the faces of old men, the wrinkle furrows of the face.

The Lagoudhera master left his stylistic signature in the manner in which he used wing-shaped lines to mark the nasal incision and the lower brow, and a swirling curlicue where the line underlying the eye is continued across the cheekbone to denote its salient form (Pls. 15, 28, 29, 31; Figs. 72–73, 75, 96, 99, 106, 107, 112, 113, 135, 155, 160, 183, 184, 186, 189, 200, 253–256).

Having built up the complementary dark and light colors forming the relief within the face, the painter then proceeded to give it more definition. Feature lines, such as those of the ears, nose, mouth, and eyes, were reoutlined with dark brown. Particular care was taken within the eye, where the brown line marking out the upper rim of the eye was inserted below the upper edge of the green almond shape, leaving the light green above it to act as a highlight line. This is a subtle technique, and less meticulous Byzantine painters merely added a crescent of white line over the upper lid line at a final stage of painting.

Black line was used sparingly within the face. The eyebrows and the upper lid line are firmly and sleekly outlined, and so also are the iris and the pupil. The ear was defined and the nostrils underlined. Black was also used to clean up any untidiness in the interrelation of the hair and face,

---

[144] This technique of building up the eyes upon dark-colored eye sockets also appears in damaged faces in the 12th-century paintings at Antiphonetes, Cyprus. A similar method can be seen in the painting of the Winchester Bible miniatures, where unfinished painting shows blind faces with eyes awaiting further definition.

as well as the neck and garments. The cornea retains the yellow-green put in previously. The iris is ovoid and light brown in color, and its upper edge is delimited by the upper rim of the eye, but the curve of its black outline never quite touches the upper rim of the eye. Thus the iris appears to be partly concealed by the lid and well detached from the lower rim of the eye and well to one side of the eye. The pupil is a small, rounded dot that stands high at the center of the iris.

The final touch to the head was the use of thick lime white, mostly applied in fine lines. The cornea of the eye has two highlights, a thin wash highlight followed by a smaller, thick white highlight, and neither of them touches the rims of the eye. The integration of the face, hair, beard, neck, and neckline of garments was neatened by strong definition lines in black, which are only applied in "sketch" or "broken line" where they neaten the beard within the face. The white highlight lines within the beard and hair often overlap these and the flesh beyond them.

Where heads were painted on fresh plaster patches with or without a halo, the base color or proplasmos was green, not yellow, as was the case of the proplasmos for heads built up on the original rendering.

These very sophisticated and precise procedures employed by the Lagoudhera master do not necessarily make for more impressive wall paintings. Greater speed in execution can create an impression of spontaneity, even within a hierarchical system of decoration. By contrast, too much sophistication can lead to paintings that are too soft to have the necessary impact on high walls and vaults. The Lagoudhera master steered a middle line. While the closeup view of some of his heads reveals the delicacy of an icon painter with precise wrist control of the brush, the overall impression is of a vigorous painter capable of making strong, sweeping lines that hold the fine detail together. The paintings are the work of a mature master who shows no hesitation in his brushwork, and it is clear that by the time he came to Lagoudhera, he had gained that supreme freedom of using established methods not as something governing him but as a positive aid in the expression of his art. He used his proportional and coloring system to make up a complete church decoration that is integrated and harmonious, and his professional skill and judgment transmuted his painting system into the realms of fine art.

Light and Perspective

The two subjects can be treated separately in post-medieval art, but in Byzantine painting they are not easily separable, and both play their part in creating the Byzantine painter's conception of reality. The Lagoudhera master created volume and used the illusion of space in the Byzantine manner, which is very different from classical illusionism. The reality he aimed to create was the spiritual presence in the church of the guiding church fathers, and the sacred events in the ritual of the church of Christ. His principal means of achieving this lay not in creating the illusion of reality but in transcending reality by bringing all his people and events into the real space of the church. Both light and perspective play a vital role in creating this spiritual presence of the holy images,

which to us may be an illusion, but to the Byzantine was the reality of his spiritual home.[145]

While the 1192 painter added particular distinction to the Byzantine painting system by his subtle use of light and perspective, the technique is not in itself unique to this series of paintings. In the Lagoudhera paintings, illumination is not derived from a single light source that dictates the pattern of light and shadow. The painter used light to give substance and emphasis to his figures. Light does not fall upon the figures, but rather it belongs to them and steps out with them into the body of the church. A garment may be painted with both highlights and shadows, but these function to articulate the garment so that it molds the figure and gives it form and volume without the illusion of reality.

Perspective was used by the Lagoudhera painter to ensure the recognition of what was useful to his theme. The top and side of a building or a piece of furniture are enough for recognition and for giving it enough substance to project it forward into the church. Buildings function as a necessary backdrop that helps in the composition of a scene by concentrating the eye on the principal figures, but the perspective function of the backdrop is to close the picture and to propel the actors forward into the church. This is, of course, the opposite of classical illusionist architectures, which seek to deepen the picture space and distance the figures within it. The Byzantine interpretation of space was designed to project figures forward from the wall. For this reason there are no representations at Lagoudhera of the illusionist reality of an interior containing any of the principal figures within it. To contain the figures in this manner would not only diminish their impact, but would also defeat the Byzantine view of the real presence of the painted figures in company with the beholder in the church. Thus the context of an interior was better represented by the convention of a drapery around the exterior of a building.

The definition of "reverse perspective" that has been given to the Byzantine viewpoint is perhaps as good a definition as we can make, although the viewpoint is variously from above, below, and to the side, as well as from the reverse. The important point is to remember that a Byzantine church represents the reality of the spiritual world just as surely as *Alice in Wonderland* and *Through the Looking Glass* represent the reality of a fantasy world.

The perspective of buildings that close the picture space is paralleled by the mountain backgrounds, but with some modification. In the Nativity scene the painter used a version of the terraced landscape of antiquity, but the similarity is very limited. At Lagoudhera the painter needed his separate mountain pyramids as individual backdrops for the vignettes that accommodate the various events accompanying the Nativity. The mountains do not appear to take the onlooker back into the picture space but instead bring the events of the Nativity forward so that they become almost tangible, and we are there, present at this wondrous event.

[145] Forty years ago when I was making notes on the paintings of the Old Patriarchate at Peć, an old Serbian monk inquired about my interest. When I explained that it was the wall paintings, he kindly gave me an hour of his time to explain the real presence of the holy figures through their images and the eternal and actual continuum of the dramas depicted on the walls. But I was too young and the world was too much with me to comprehend what he was saying.

Painting Procedures, Light and Perspective, and Emotion

A number of aids were employed together with reverse perspective. There is often no foreground, so figures seem to float forward in a scene, and the feet never seem to touch the ground. Occasionally, they actually overlap a border in Baroque fashion. Angels overlap the red borders, as do the frames of the roundels, causing them to appear to float forward rather than remaining firmly pinned to the wall.

The limitation of language in describing this world makes it necessary to resort once again to paradox in pointing out that in coexistence with all the anti-illusionist devices, the painter was happy to approach the appearance of our realities quite closely. He used light and shadow in some of his architectures, such as the roof of the altar ciborium in the Presentation [70], to give a sense of roundness and recession (Fig. 123). In other buildings there is a light and a dark side to the same wall, but the light is not used to simulate recession or to mold form, but to direct the attention to the central figures for which they form the background. None of these background elements is brought into a realistic optical relation to one another with regard to size, and so they retain their unreality and can function as closure screens (Pls. 19, 23, 24; Figs. 76–83, 123, 201).

The same contradictions can be seen in individual figures where faces, such as that of St. Lazaros [124], have a powerful sense of individual character, and there is the illusion of volume and weight in the head, but all of this exemplar of painterly skill is prevented from becoming an imitation of a real person by the arbitrary thick black outline to the head (Pls. 12–15, 20, 29, 30; Figs. 73, 112, 113, 155–158, 183, 253–256). The figure of St. Anthony [137] is another example, with a powerful head set realistically within the depth of his cowl, but the painter used the same device of hard outlines and a quite arbitrary decoration over the cowl, which defeats the impression of realism (Fig. 200).

The limitation of allowing only two views of the human face, the asymmetrical frontal and the three-quarter profile, is in itself a rule that inhibits realistic or illusionistic perspective. Like other Byzantine painterly practices, however, the two views of the face are firmly based in reality, since the frontal measures of a human face are rarely quite symmetrical. The three-quarter-profile face and figure perform the necessary double role of allowing the image to be present in communion with the worshipper, while at the same time it can establish a communion with other images around it and can take a plausible part in a collective scene of action.

It would be wrong to deduce from these complex paintings that the Lagoudhera master did not know how to paint realistically. It is more plausible to suggest that our sort of illusion of reality was not appropriate for the decoration of a church.[146] The Lagoudhera painters did not invent this sacred world of church decoration nor the various painterly skills by which it is made to exist, but this little church does provide a supreme example of its success.

---

[146] A. P. Kazhdan and A. W. Epstein, *Change in Byzantine Culture in the Eleventh and Twelfth Centuries* (Berkeley, 1990), 142, make the point: "One might even suggest that the classicizing style, with its inherent concern with the manipulation of the eye of the beholder, is fundamentally anthropocentric, and thus potentially disruptive to a Christian, theocentric image, and less appropriate for monumental, communal, religious works." L. James, *Light and Colour in Byzantine Art* (Oxford, 1996), has a useful discussion of how the literate Byzantine looked at light and colors, pp. 125 ff.

Emotion

Byzantine church decoration has often been described as enigmatic, but contemporary writers described how the canonical scenes aroused powerful emotions and how the worshipper saw what he expected to see.[147] Most of what seems strange to the modern viewer is linked to the deep religious significance of scenes and figures and to an artistic language that follows conventions now alien to us.

The suggestion of emotion in the Lagoudhera paintings is induced directly by the subject matter, such as a death or a parting. It also can be conveyed by the articulation of facial features and by bodily posture, or it can arise from the cumulative effect of these devices. The use of static figures among agitated ones can stimulate the onlooker's sense of drama. The heavy, embroidered imperial garments or the quiet garment folds of a static figure anchor an image, whereas flying folds suggest imminent movement and drama. The juxtaposition of certain colors also adds to the beholder's impression of emotion and movement. Byzantine perspective propels the dramatic action of a scene forward out of the confining red borders into the body of the church itself. The spectator becomes directly involved in the sacred world that is given to him in images. He does not passively contemplate events that recede away from him in a distant image of reality.

The 1192 paintings are a fine example of this Byzantine method of communicating with the worshipper, and they illustrate several points of interpretative interest. Single, standing figures are often static, and their faces are shown in repose. As witnesses, they communicate either through gesture or by the message on their scrolls. The direction of their gaze consistently draws the worshipper on to the deeper spiritual significance of the church itself, to the celebration of the liturgy in the apse, to the Mother of God in the semidome, and to the Godhead in the dome. The standing figures in the ground register are static and solemn, and include the two "pillars of the church," Peter and Paul. By contrast, the prophets cavort in a lively fashion around the dome, and the angels bowl along in their roundels with their movement arrested and turned upward by the Etoimasia. They all unite to convert a flat decoration into a cohesive, animated whirl that culminates in the dominating Christ above them.

The gaze of the figures is among the crucial factors that give a unity of purpose to the whole church decoration. The frontal heads of Christ confront the worshipper, and Christ's eyes pursue him, even though his facial features remain at rest. The face of the great figure of Christ in the dome is impassive, with a smooth, unlined brow and features in repose, but it arouses strong subjective emotions in the onlooker. In contrast, the two frontal heads of Christ on the Mandylion [92] and the Keramidion [72] represent the suffering Christ on his way to Golgotha (Figs. 187–188). In these two images the faces suggest pain and distress. The eyebrows are tilted toward the nose bridge, and the forehead is furrowed by a winged U. The beard has a pointed, bedraggled

look. These two faces of Christ are in sharp contrast to all the other neutral heads of young men in this decoration and to the Christ in the dome, all of whom have smooth brows and unlined foreheads.

The Koimesis is a scene that by its context embodies drama and mourning, and it graphically illustrates emotion. The figures of the apostles and their faces are contorted in grief. The grouping of the bowed figures and the arching lunette both unite and enhance the dramatic portrayal of pain and loss.

The content of the narrative scenes was familiar and fundamental to the life of the Byzantine churchgoer in the form of feast days, and the context enabled him to form a correct interpretation of dramatic stances. The apostles in the Ascension [78] are tilted backward with their heads gazing upward to peer into the vault of heaven at the ascending Christ. The four foremost apostles raise their arms to shield their faces. All the movement suggests wonder, amazement, and possibly fear. All this emotional interpretation is suggested by the context, but it is not reinforced by any articulation of the faces. There are no gaping mouths nor frowns of anxiety, and no fear appears in the young faces. The central figures of Mary and the archangel, with their contrasting quiet stance, are thus posed to enhance the sense of emotive movement in their companions.

At the center of the Ascension [78], the luminous Majesty of Christ is thrust forward by the cool, receding blues of his mandorla. The placid geometry of the concentric circles of the mandorla is in turn given dramatic counterpoint by the gyrating forms of the supporting angels. An intimation of this human drama is conveyed to the tranquil Christ by the wild, flying fold of his himation, as if he might soon be gathered up in a whirlwind.

The Anastasis [50], with its figures of the dead, is a Stygian scene into which bursts the luminous, galvanic figure of Christ. He tramples down the doors of Hades and in a forceful, dynamic movement hauls the hunched Adam out of his yawning sarcophagus. The painter conveys not a passive symbol of redemption but a triumphant Christ bearing all before him.

The Nativity [142] is a spiral of gentle vignettes around the dominating central figure of Mary in her womblike cave. Each event is subtly interlinked so that the eye travels continuously around the scene, always returning to its center. The figures possess little of the extreme emotional movement of the other scenes, but the skillful interweaving of the vignettes illustrating the emotional events surrounding the birth expresses the joyful celebration of the New Dispensation that is open to mankind.

The emotions that are clearly recognizable through gestures are tenderness and love, as in the manner in which the old man Symeon holds the Christ child [74] (Pl. 28; Fig. 134). His face is impassive, but his whole upper figure enfolds the child, conveying the awe and tenderness of the old man actually holding the Promised One.[148] Tenderness and love are also superbly expressed in a collective way in the Presentation of the Virgin [70] (Pls. 24–25, Figs. 122–123). The importance

that the painter placed upon the impact of this drama is shown by his painstaking final alterations. Thus, in altering Anna to turn her head back toward Joachim, he heightened the tension between these two figures, while their gestures continue to link them to their child and the forward-reaching Zacharias. The emotion of the central group is further emphasized by antithesis. The pathos of a mother losing a child is vividly evoked in the figure of Anna, in contrast to the impersonal, chattering maidens. And in a similar way in the Koimesis [138], the impassive bishops emphasize the grief of the apostles (Pl. 23).

The language of emotion and drama is thus present throughout the decoration, but not by the imitation of reality as we understand it. It is worked by subtle suggestion in the composition of scenes, in gesture and the articulation of figures, in contrasts, and in the subtle use of color and lines. The worshipper and the figures in the paintings are all integrated into a powerful whole that swells out from the walls to pervade the church.

The Lagoudhera master might be likened to a conductor who has summoned his orchestra to a unified theme. The orchestra is the thronging crowd of images delivering different parts of the same message of salvation through Christ. The composer of the theme is Christ in the dome, and he gives the necessary equilibrium in the midst of all the movement. The church is the universe in which the action happens, and its rounded shapes harmonize with that cyclical notion of time that dominated perception before Newtonian physics made the change to a linear notion of progression. The medieval mind, whether western or Byzantine, conceived only of man's inward spiritual progression toward perfection, and the paintings at Lagoudhera assist him forward along that road. They do not purport to lead us either backward on a temporal journey to the antique world nor do they aspire forward to the Renaissance.

19

CONCLUSION

The Authorship of the 1192 Paintings

We have referred throughout the text to the Lagoudhera master, and we have raised the question occasionally of whether other painters were also at work. There is no doubt that one master painter planned and was responsible for the drawing, much of the execution, and certainly for the finished appearance of the paintings. Indeed, the unity of the 1192 decoration is such that it is exceedingly difficult to detect the work of assistants, but it is perhaps worthwhile to summarize the circumstantial evidence that has been noted.

There is a clear contrast, common in all good Byzantine painting, between the speed at which most of the work was carried out and the careful brushwork and buildup of color for the flesh of hands, feet, and faces. This may betoken the work of assistant and master, but the distinction is so regular as to suggest that it is an inherent part of the craft of Byzantine wall painting rather than a distinction between different hands.

At the fundamental stage of plastering in the dome, there is the difference of two plaster sections, each with three prophets, and one plaster section with six prophets. A similar division occurs in the angel medallions, with a division of three, three, and six. The soffit of the north blind arch under the dome, which has eight roundels, was plastered in two sections, whereas the eight similar roundels in the opposing arch were painted on a single section of plaster. Perhaps the master was confident enough to take on eight medallions or six figures at one sitting, while his more cautious assistant worked more slowly on fewer figures. Other irregularities occur in the band of angel roundels in the dome (see above, pp. 122, 129–30).

A few heads of young men have exceptionally large, rounded eyes, such as those of angels [7] and [8] in the dome and the young apostles in the back rows of the Ascension [78]. In the Ascension is an unusual amount of grey as a regular tone in the buildup of garment colors.

There is also some confusion in the patterns surrounding the naos medallions, where the absence of fine finish is not a result of surface damage. In particular, the half-finished state of the pattern around the west vault medallions is puzzling (Text Fig. 26a). Traces of a background pattern are around the figures in the soffit of the arch to the northwest bay; this pattern was never

completed because the space was needed for the titular inscriptions for the two figures occupying the panel [56, 57] (see above, p. 166). This confusion may indicate the work of another painter with a taste for filling empty spaces with colorful patterns.

The many pentimenti that occur throughout the decoration might indicate the master overriding or correcting the work of an assistant or apprentice, but they could equally well be alterations and additions of this fastidious master painter to his own work. It is more likely that the disparities noted above denote deviations that can occur in the best team work. All these divergencies may simply be ripples of individual craftsmanship in the otherwise calm sea of systematized uniformity that makes up Byzantine wall painting.

The master painter would have been supported by a team of assistants who mixed plaster, ground and mixed pigments, cleaned paint pots and brushes, and did the general fetching and carrying. At least one of these apprentices would be learning to plaster, and another would have been washing in background colors. Most Byzantine churches are small, and Lagoudhera is smaller than most. A team of four would fit such circumstantial evidence as we found, and it would have consisted of the master, a master-apprentice capable of independent work, and two or more apprentices together with a local assistant or two for cleaning, carrying, and fetching water and other materials, etc. The scaffolding at Lagoudhera would not have accommodated more than four people with any comfort.

There is no direct evidence as to how long Byzantine painters took for their work.[149] One piece of relevant but indirect evidence would be the number of separate renderings of plaster in a church, but conclusions to be drawn from this are tentative, since if one or more master painter was at work, two or three plaster patches might be worked on simultaneously. At Lagoudhera there are about fifty major plaster sections for the 1192 paintings, if we include a few hypothetical ones for the destroyed west wall of the church. In addition there are numerous smaller plaster inserts for heads or for sections of the larger scenes. The climate is such that there is no way in which the surface of the plaster could have remained fresh for more than a week, and in summer it would have become unreceptive to pigments within twenty-four hours. If we assume that the seven major scenes each took about a week to paint, and allow a week for Christ in the dome, this work would have taken the painter two months. The remaining forty-three sections might be allotted an average of three days each by allowing a generous time for some individual figures, and perhaps an underestimate for a section with six prophets; this would take another 130 days, or four to five months. If painting began in March or April, this total of eight or nine months might have allowed time for the painting of a small narthex as well, if there was one, and we have the inscription indicating that December was the month when the work was finished.

---

[149] Mango, *Art of the Byzantine Empire*, 255–56, quotes excerpts from the Novgorod and Troitskaia chronicles, stating that the painter Theophanes finished church decorations in one year.

The Place of Lagoudhera in Cypriot and Byzantine Art

One feature of the plastering methods at Lagoudhera is found a hundred years earlier at the monastery of St. John Chrysostomos near Koutsovendis in Cyprus.[150] This is the insertion of a fresh plaster patch in the middle of the scene of the betrayal on the north wall. It is important since it seems to be the only other early example of fresh sectional plaster patching within a scene that has been so far recorded. The painter of St. John Chrysostomos was a fine craftsman, and like the 1192 Lagoudhera master, he was constantly altering and correcting the balance of his figures right up to the finish of the painting. It can thus be seen that the interest in both design and execution was not just a peculiarity of the Lagoudhera master of 1192 but something that existed one hundred years earlier and is indeed common to all good Byzantine wall paintings.

There are only two contemporary examples of wall painting of the quality of Lagoudhera in Cyprus. One is among the paintings of the Encleistra of St. Neophytos at Paphos,[151] and the other is a single painting of St. George at Asinou.[152]

The St. George is on the wall of the south apse of the narthex at Asinou. It is a magnificent image that combines monumental size and splendor with a minute attention to detailed patterning in clothing, armor, and the trappings of the horse. The saint's tunic and the saddle cloth have a very similar pattern and coloring to the backcloth of the throne of the Mother of God in the apse at Lagoudhera. Both patterns have a black ground with patterning in vermilion, blue, and white line. Similarity with the painter of the Lagoudhera apse ends at this point. The painter at Lagoudhera worked quickly, and his faces are built up as fairly simple masks in the fashion of one of the early Monagri painters or the painter of the naos of the Encleistra at Paphos. The St. George is a superb piece of careful painting with quantities of minute detail, and the face is built up with colors so delicate in tone that they appear to be blended. The Asinou St. George, some of the paintings of the cell and bema of the Encleistra at Paphos, and the paintings of the 1192 Lagoudhera master show a lavish use of fine quality blue, vermilion, and the application of gold leaf. The chronology of the paintings of the Encleistra is not entirely clear,[153] but one of the painters, probably Theodore Apseudes, used two of the plastering techniques that have been described at Lagoudhera. He put in fresh plaster patches for some of his heads and reworked the plaster for other heads and hands.[154] He also used a similar method of burnishing the thick black paint of the decorative borders and simulated pearls with the same thick blobs of opalescent white in high relief.

---

[150] Mango, Hawkins, and Boyd, "Monastery of St. Chrysostomos," 82–83, 94, figs. 103–105.

[151] Mango and Hawkins, "Hermitage of St. Neophytos," 119–206.

[152] Wharton, *Art of Empire*, fig. 3.16, for an illustration of this painting.

[153] D. C. Winfield, "Dumbarton Oaks' (Harvard University) Work at Hagios Neophytos Monagri, Perachorio and Lagoudera, 1971, 1972, and 1973: A Final Report," *RDAC* (1978), 279–81.

[154] Ibid., pl. LXV. In a hypothetical reconstruction of the fragmentary inscription below the Baptism [54] at Lagoudhera, I put in the name of Theodore. See Winfield, *Panagia tou Arakos*, 16, 17. This has led to a firm statement

Technique

Some stylistic details are similar in both churches, notably the blob of white highlight in garments, with spidery lines coming out of the blob, one of them ending in a hook. There is also a general air of similarity that is hard to define. A detailed study of the bema in the Encleistra reveals a sketchy finish in the paintings of the Ascension of Christ and the Ascension of St. Neophytos. This is in striking contrast to the precise and almost academic finish of the Deesis and the exquisite fragment of the Crucifixion in the cell. At Lagoudhera there is occasionally a similar contrast in finish. In particular, some of the figures, for example in the Ascension [78], exhibit a certain perfunctoriness of line in their robes and are portrayed with faces that have a wide-eyed vapidity. This sketchiness of line and wide-eyed weakness contrast with the high-quality finish and meticulous attention to detail apparent elsewhere.

The paintings in the cell and in the bema of St. Neophytos need further study, and it is not clear which of them may be the work of Theodore Apseudes. There are enough similarities of color and technique, however, to warrant the view that the Encleistra and the church at Lagoudhera contain paintings by the same masters who were trained in the same workshop. It is also clear that the St. George at Asinou came out of the same workshop.

The agitated style of late twelfth-century Byzantine painting is well represented in the little church of Perachorio in Cyprus.[155] There is no suggestion of similarity in the style and manner of the painting with that of Lagoudhera, however. Several other Cypriot churches have paintings of the late twelfth-century style. The most important are the paintings of an eccentric but very competent master in the church of Christ Antiphonetes.[156] His portrayals of elderly saints are recognizably in the manner of the period, but they have a slightly fanciful air of caricature.

In the church of St. Michael the Archangel at Lefkara is a representation of the Mandylion that must be by a painter who had worked with the Lagoudhera/Neophytos workshop at some period. The clothing of the prophets in the dome at Lefkara is stirred by the same wind of agitation but show less resemblance to the Lagoudhera style than does the Mandylion. The Department of Antiquities of Cyprus has recently uncovered paintings at two more churches, St. Anthony at Kellia and St. Paraskevi at Yeroskipos. There are said to be paintings of the late twelfth century among them, but these have not been seen by the authors.[157]

Of direct relevance to the Lagoudhera master of 1192 are the two icons of Christ and the

---

that I believe the painter of the 1192 decoration at Lagoudhera and the painter of the Encleistra are the same Theodore Apseudes. *ODB* 1:169. This is not the case. For other interpretations of Lagoudhera and its place in Cypriot painting of the late 12th century, see Wharton, *Art of Empire*, 79–90. See Weyl Carr, *Byzantine Masterpiece Recovered*, and A. Wharton Epstein, "Phases of Construction and Decoration in the Enkleistra of St. Neophytos near Paphos on Cyprus," *Byzantine Studies/Etudes Byzantines* 10 (1983), 71–80.

[155] A. H. S. Megaw and E. J. W. Hawkins, "The Church of the Holy Apostles at Perachorio, Cyprus, and Its Frescoes," *DOP* 16 (1962), 279–348.

[156] Stylianou, *Painted Churches of Cyprus*, rev. ed., 469–85.

[157] Ibid., 447–50, for an illustration of the mandylion at Kato Lefkara. See Weyl Carr, *Byzantine Masterpiece Recovered*, text fig. 23, p. 69, for an illustration of the clothing of a prophet.

Conclusion

Virgin that were kept in the church until 1970, and they are certainly to be attributed to him. There are two other icons that are also clearly attributable to the workshop of the St. Neophytos and Lagoudhera group and a number of others that have a close similarity of workmanship.[158] The literary evidence that a painter might make icons as well as wall paintings seems to be limited to Theophanes the Greek and Epiphanios the Wise, working in Russia.[159] However, it does make general sense that an itinerant painter might work on a small-scale icon as well as on a large-scale commission for painting a church, and probably he was also competent at setting out mosaics, large and small. The painter monk established in a monastery might be more likely to specialize in icons and book illustrations. It is rare, if not unique, to have actual examples of icons and wall painting by the same hand preserved for us over a period of eight hundred years. The rightly conservative cleaning of the Lagoudhera icon of Christ has left a later green overpaint that obscures much of the clarity of the painting of the nostril and eye sockets, but even so it is instructive to look at how little a master painter needed to do to make his changes of scale. It was, of course, the modular system of proportion that allowed him to make the necessary adaptation to his measures without upsetting his style.

At the end of the twelfth century three, if not four, highly competent master painters were at work on the walls of Cypriot churches, together with three or four more painters who were competent and well trained. The inscription for the donor of the image of St. George at Asinou tells us that he was a trainer of horses, and this may be regarded as one piece of evidence for the economic prosperity that made possible the patronage of good painting. Cyprus was ideally placed as a peaceful emporium for supplying the Crusaders. Constant warfare in the Holy Land would not have been conducive to agriculture or to such activities as horse breeding and training. The number of monastic foundations and the quality of the wall paintings of the eleventh and twelfth centuries both reflect a thriving economy in Cyprus.

The number of Cypriot saints on the walls of Lagoudhera might prompt the question of whether anything specifically Cypriot is in the paintings that could point to a local style. In our opinion nothing at Lagoudhera suggests a local style. This is not to say that the master of the 1192 paintings might not have been a Cypriot trained in Constantinople. Byzantine church decoration is essentially an art with a recognizable program and a core of rules for painting. Perhaps only 1 percent or less of Byzantine church decoration survives and none at all of its secular painting. With this paucity of material evidence, the recognition of local styles becomes problematic, and we are indeed lucky if we can occasionally recognize a workshop style.

In the wider context of Byzantine art, Lagoudhera ranks with Nerezi in that these two churches present high quality but very different interpretations of the style of late twelfth-century painting. The work of the master painters of these two churches is separated by only twenty-eight

[158] A. Papageorghiou, "Δύο βυζαντινὲς εἰκόνες τοῦ 12ου αἰώνα," *RDAC* (1976), 267–74. Idem, "Εἰκὼν τοῦ Χριστοῦ ἐν τῷ ναῷ τῆς Παναγίας τοῦ Ἄρακος," in Κυπρ.Σπ. 32, 45–55. A. Papageorghiou, Ιερά Μητρόπολις Πάφου (Nicosia, 1996), pls. 94, 94a. A. Papageorghiou, *Icons of Cyprus* (Nicosia, 1994), fig. 24.

[159] Mango, *Art of the Byzantine Empire*, 256–58.

years, and their paintings were made at a time when the art of wall painting had reached a high stage of development. The Lagoudhera master adhered more closely to the rule book and made paintings of supreme elegance with a precision that in a lesser painter would have declined into academic emptiness. The Nerezi master made much freer use of the rule book, and he shows more interest in the narrative and human potentialities of his art than in the rarefied and hieratic themes of Lagoudhera. The manner in which the two masters handled such themes as the formal frontal portrait, the Presentation scenes, the heads of elderly, bearded figures, or the emotion of grief shows what diverse artistry and character might be achieved within the formal constraints of a single Byzantine style.

The diffusion of this style in the empire can be seen in a Sinai icon of the Annunciation, and in Greece at Kastoria and in the church of St. Hierotheos at Megara, attributed to the 1170s. In the Balkans are the high-quality paintings of 1164 at Nerezi and provincial paintings of some thirty years later at Kurbinovo. The style was exported successfully to Venice, whence it diffused into northern Italy and southern Germany and Austria, and from Byzantium it was exported to Russia and to Sicily.

It is clear that Byzantium preserved throughout its history both hieratic and narrative art forms, but it was the hieratic form that best suited the single-domed church with a semidome over the apse. This architectural form expresses an equilibrium that is not found in the basilican church, where the eye is necessarily directed eastward. We have seen that the Lagoudhera painter of 1192 invented little in the way of iconography, but he does stand out among Byzantine painters in his recognition of the correct size and proportion of his figures in relation to the architectural spaces. From the tranquility of Christ in the dome, the eye is set in motion and spirals through the angel medallions to the gesturing of the prophets and from thence downward and then eastward to the Mother of God in the apse. From there it moves freely over the vaults and wall surfaces to be drawn upward eventually and come to rest once again in Christ. In this way the painter achieved that ultimate art of emotion recollected in tranquility. There are numbers of other small, Byzantine domed churches, but none survives that achieves this perfect union of form and content.

Lagoudhera and the General Development of Wall Painting

A few particular aspects of the paintings can be usefully set in the wider context of medieval art and its transition toward the Renaissance.

At Lagoudhera we have shown how plasterer and painter worked together and that they were probably one and the same person. The painter used and valued the strength of fresco painting and enhanced its effects by using layers of opaque paint mixed with lime, and translucent layers of paint mixed with lime water or another medium.

The technical development of this art of Byzantine wall painting is as yet largely uncharted, but it must logically be linked with the art of mosaic since that also depended upon the use of fresh

Conclusion

lime plaster. Mosaic and wall painting both required a thorough comprehension of the behavior of lime plasters and the diverse methods of handling them. Both techniques involved sketching a preliminary guide drawing.

The plaster sections that make up the jigsaw of a mosaic picture were laid one after the other upon a base layer of plaster that was of the size of the panel to be completed. Upon this foundation the painter/mosaicist drew and painted a detailed version of his final composition. From this preliminary sketch he could estimate the size of a fresh patch of plaster for the day's work, and this would vary according to the complexity of the design. In the process of setting the cubes for each patch, which itself would have needed a preliminary drawing, he could remain aware of the final composition and maintain the coherence of his jigsaw of patches by relating each of these to the preliminary sketch on the plaster below.

The job of the mosaicist is petty, close work that requires firm finger and wrist control, and in the process of setting the cubes there is little opportunity for creative deviation. The setting of cubes is a painfully slow process, since only small areas of a composition could be completed at a time. It was necessary to adhere closely to the guide drawing, because if he strayed from the set design on a single patch of setting bed he could prejudice the success of the completed picture. Thus to the mosaicist, the importance of a detailed, measured, and accurate preliminary painted drawing was fundamental and indispensable.

Up until the twelfth century the wall painter, in contrast to the mosaicist, not only made a preliminary sketch on the plaster surface of his panel but also continued to build up his color layers on this same plaster. His preliminary drawing was minimal and essentially structural, as time was of the essence if he were to complete the composition before the plaster became unreceptive to pigments. At Lagoudhera little of this type of drawing can be seen because the paintings are in good condition, but some near contemporary and fine examples of rapid wall drawing can be seen at Perachorio.[160] Unlike the mosaicist, the painter did not employ a patchwork of fresh plaster sections, but if at a final stage of painting there were errors or changes to deal with, or if the surface of his plaster was drying too quickly, then he would scrape away the dried-out area and insert patches or even whole sections of fresh plaster.

Since the arts of mosaic and wall painting were continually practiced from the Roman period onward in both Italy and the Byzantine Empire, it is likely that sectional plaster joins were always made where large-scale compositions were painted, and that the various forms of fresco painting continued in use. The fact that few sectional plaster joins are recorded between the first and twelfth centuries does not reflect their absence but rather a lack of observation of them. We know that a sectional plaster join for the scene of the betrayal at St. Chrysostomos monastery in Cyprus dates to about A.D. 1100, and at the end of the twelfth century we have the paintings of the Encleistra, which also have sectional joins. The example of Lagoudhera in 1192 is more important since it represents an almost complete scheme of church decoration, with both sectional joins in the scenes

---

[160] Megaw and Hawkins, "Church of the Holy Apostles at Perachorio," 279–348.

and fresh plaster patches for heads, as well as abundant evidence of the reworking of plaster surfaces to ensure that they were fresh. From this evidence it is clearly misleading to claim that fresco painting on plaster patches is an innovation or an invention of Italian painters in the thirteenth century. The technical difference in fresco method that Italian painters evolved was that they began to paint a whole scene piece by piece on fresh plaster sections, whereas Byzantine painters began all except the largest scenes with a complete plaster patch and then modified it, if necessary, by scraping out and inserting fresh plaster wherever the surface had gone off.

The discoveries about techniques of painting that have been made as a result of conservation work in the past half century now make it possible to establish a more rational view of Romanesque and Byzantine wall-painting methods.[161] It is clear that painting on fresh plaster may be approached in two ways. Both methods belong technically under the description fresco, but each can produce a very different result in the finished product. At one end of the scale stands a watercolor technique using lime water as a medium, and at the other end is a heavily textured layering technique that uses a lime slurry as well as lime water for medium. Both were carried out on fresh plaster in order to bond together pigments and ground. The watercolor technique tends to produce soft and limpid paintings, whereas the textured layer technique tends to produce opaque and hard linear contrasts. Technical analyses have proved the truth of Cennini's dictum, "And know that everything that you begin in fresco you must bring to a finish in secco." This is true of Romanesque and Byzantine, as well as Renaissance, wall paintings.[162] The layered, linear effects are typical of Byzantine and western medieval wall-painting work, whereas a greater use of the softer watercolor technique typifies the work of Renaissance painters. The importance of the 1192 paintings at Lagoudhera is that they provide abundant factual evidence of the sophisticated use of fresco painting.

We have stressed the intimate connection between plaster and preliminary drawing at Lagoudhera, and this can be regarded as a characteristic of good Byzantine painting. From this premise it is possible to outline a new theoretical framework for the development of Byzantine and western medieval wall-painting methods that accords better with our present knowledge of them. Up to the end of the twelfth century, the Byzantine painter of churches had a familiar command of his subject matter that made model books largely unnecessary. In later centuries the complexity of individual scenes and the proliferation of the iconographic themes encouraged the use of model

[161] Segers-Glocke, *Forschungsprojekt Wandmalereischaden*, is a collection of conservation articles typical of many other conservation reports in recent years. It contains information about plastering, methods of painting, and proportion in various Romanesque churches.

[162] A. Oddy, ed., *The Art of the Conservator* (London, 1992), 89–107. The recent conservation of Michelangelo's frescoes in the Sistine Chapel by F. Mancinelli makes it clear that Michelangelo practiced each technique of fresco where he thought it appropriate, and what he thought appropriate for the wall was different from the technique for the ceiling. The one is a layered technique and the other is a watercolor technique, but both are finished off in tempera as necessary. D. Bomford et al., *Italian Painting before 1400*, National Gallery, exhibition catalogue (London, 1989), gives a series of technical studies of panel paintings that show the close similarities of Italian panel to Byzantine icon. Many of the technical observations apply to Byzantine wall paintings of an earlier date than the Italian panels.

Conclusion

books. Twelfth-century painters had at their command a modular system of proportion that enabled them to adapt their compositions with ease to any given architectural setting. Their method of laying out compositions and basic drawing was simple and reliable, and it required a minimum of application and delay. They were also adept at managing their plaster surface in the course of painting. The Lagoudhera master in particular appears totally uninhibited by the problems of his drying plaster surface. He was prepared to retrowel it, patch it, or even put in totally new sections.

Romanesque wall painters had much less of a settled repertoire of subject matter than their Byzantine counterparts. Neither do they seem to have possessed any generally accepted system of proportion for their figure painting or for the general division of wall spaces. It was because of this that the model book and preliminary drawing developed a more important and time-consuming role in western art than ever they did for the Byzantines. Western painters went to more trouble and took longer in sketching out their preliminary drawings and transferring them to the wall. Eventually this difference in the time taken at the beginning of a wall painting forced Italian painters to adopt the sectional plaster system for a whole scene as their regular method of work. By the late thirteenth century, Italian painters had, in effect, gone back to the plastering system for mosaic work. This system required a precise and detailed preliminary drawing. It was also better suited to the laborious transfer of a small-scale drawing into a large-scale drawing for wall painting on the base plaster, or *arriccio*, by using a cross reference of squared grids. Small areas of fresh plaster, or *intonaco*, enough for a day's work, were then laid over it. These *giornata* form a patchwork of plaster sections over the sketch on the *arriccio*. Like all sound and methodical craftsmen, the Italians were able to adapt their practices for new aims and ends. By the early fifteenth century, with the introduction of the manufacture of paper for which Ancona became famous, they evolved the *spolvero* system for transferring parts of a drawing from large sheets of paper to the wall on a full scale.

It is tempting to suggest that the fundamental element that Romanesque painters were trying to acquire was not a knowledge of the antique styles but the expertise in method that characterizes good Byzantine painting, such as that of the 1192 Lagoudhera master. He was in supreme control of the grammar of the Byzantine system of wall painting, and he used its inherent harmony and balance to produce a collective work of art that is a masterpiece of the language of Byzantine religious painting.

Part Five: Addendum, the Later Paintings

20

THE OLD NARTHEX

The Fourteenth-Century Paintings

(Figs. 300–302; Text Figs. 5, 50)

The new extension, or narthex, was probably constructed in the seventeenth century, and, to join it directly with the naos, a wide arch was cut out of the west wall. In the course of conservation work, the cement repair work to the soffit of the arch was removed. The masonry of the original wall was of uncoursed stone with a surface pointing of gypsum. At the western edge of the soffit, the arch had been trimmed with neat ashlar sandstone, along which ran an astragal molding terminating at the springing of the arch with a rounded molding. Both molding and astragal are similar to those on the exterior of the northwest door, which leads out of the new extension.

The enlargement of the building in the seventeenth century destroyed the twelfth-century decoration on the interior of the west wall of the naos. On the exterior of this wall, fragments of a later decoration, probably belonging to the fourteenth century, survive in the spandrels of the arch. Their presence confirms the existence of an earlier narthex at the west end of the church. In the course of conservation it was found that these fourteenth-century fragments of painting continued behind the present interior wall on the south side of the extension. The shape of the older narthex is uncertain, and there was no evidence as to its date. We do not know whether the original roof was barrel vaulted or not. Presumably a door was at the center, but whether this door had a tympanum in the manner of the north door to the naos is uncertain.

Three registers of painting were on this east wall of the older narthex: a central narrow lunette at the top, a middle register above a central door, and paintings on a ground register to either side of the door, and possibly a dado.

On the north side adjacent to the north wall is a fragment with a group of heads of apostles [154] that belongs to the middle register. On the south side is a large fragment with part of the decoration for the lunette. Only the red bottom border and the steeply inclined outer border survive, and a piece of green background within. Below this is part of a scene with the seated figure

329

of Christ on a mountain side [155]. In the lower register are the remains of two standing figures, St. John of Damascus [156] and St. Kosmas the Poet [157], and a fragment of a third monk on the north side of the arch.

There is no evidence as to what decoration occupied the upper register. The middle register is approximately 5 m wide and 1 m high, and it could have contained two or three scenes, depending on whether there was a tympanum to the door beneath. The ground register probably contained additional standing figures of monks, hymnographers, or ascetics. The dado fragment that survives beneath St. Kosmas has only unpainted plaster beneath the red border with no trace of pattern upon it. There are no traces of incised or impressed lines, or of the use of plaster patches in these fragments of painting. They were extremely dirty and much damaged.

The lettering and the painting technique link these surviving fragments with the repainting of the Panagia Achrantos (Fig. 8) in the tympanum of the exterior of the north door, as well as to the repainting of the scroll of St. Anthony [137] (Fig. 279) in the bema. The colors and the brushwork of the narthex link that painter with the repairer who carelessly repainted damaged areas of the 1192 paintings. The white lettering that survives on these fragments was executed in thick, white paint, and the letters are rather stubby. The black letters on the scroll are tall, and while they do not have the crisp elegance of the 1192 lettering, some care has been taken in their drawing.

After cleaning and conservation, the soffit of the extension arch and the sides were replastered with a lime plaster tinted yellow to distinguish it from the earlier 1192 plaster.

The Apostles [154] (Fig. 300)

The fragment shows a group of seven apostles on a mountainside. The base of the fragment cuts off the two lower apostles at bust level. Its northern side is marked by a red border running up the wall to the top of the fragment. The upper edge cuts off a background of sky and mountain, and the southern edge slices through the foremost apostle. The apostles overlap each other so that the only visible part of the three apostles to the rear is the top of their heads and haloes. Each apostle has an initial to indicate his name, except the apostle to the fore. The three apostles to the rear are, respectively, M—Mark or Matthew, Φ—Philip, and B—Bartholomew. At the lower front is the bust-length figure of St. Peter with Π in his halo, and behind him is the figure of St. James with an I in his halo. All the haloes are yellow and outlined in black and white. All the figures appear to turn toward the center of the arch. St. Peter has the white hair and rounded beard that is traditionally associated with his portrait, and St. James has brown wavy hair and a beard of curling locks.

Christ on the Mountain [155] (Fig. 301)

This fragment of a scene is approximately one meter high, exclusive of the red borders that outline it on three sides. The northern edge of the fragment borders the ashlar stones that were added to outline the new arch when the new extension was built.

Against a background of mountain and sky, Christ sits upon a hillock with grasses growing in

the crevices. Below him is part of a structure in masonry, with each yellow block carefully outlined in white. The very narrow green foreground undulates regularly in front of the masonry and the mountain, and in the right corner a miniature tree spreads out its branches. The mountains are built up in shades of brown or light umber and have some grey-white highlights. The grasses are drawn in black lines, and the tree has a light umber ground with some green in the clumps of foliage and grey-white highlight on the trunk and branches. Black outlines define it and shape and shadow the leafy branches. The portion of masonry at Christ's feet could be a stepped base, perhaps of a well. The scene takes place in the countryside, and it would appear that Christ is speaking, but it is uncertain which of the episodes of the Gospel is illustrated here.

The sigla $\overline{\text{IC}}$ $\overline{\text{XC}}$ are placed above and to either side of Christ's halo, which is a warm yellow with brown and white outlines. The cross bars are white, and they are decorated with dark brown lines and jeweled outlines. Christ is seated with his knees far apart and his feet coming together. In his left hand he holds a rolled scroll. He wears a light brown chiton decorated with creamy yellow chrysographia. His blue himation falls into loose folds within his lap, while a loose end streams out to one side.

St. John of Damascus [156] and St. Kosmas the Poet [157] (Fig. 302)

The background to the figures is blue and the foreground is green, and both these ground colors are applied over a black base or proplasmos. St. Kosmas [157] is the only complete figure. The head of St. John [156] is missing, and only half of his lower body remains. Of his titular inscription, only the letters κινος survive to the right of the figure. The titular inscription for St. Kosmas is aligned to either side of his halo: Ὁ Ἅγιος Κοσμᾶς ὁ ποιητής. Both inscriptions are in thick white letters. Each hymnwriter carries a scroll with a text in black lettering. Both scrolls have a thick white ground and grey separating lines (Text Fig. 50).

Both saints stand in the frontal position, and St. Kosmas turns his head in the three-quarter-frontal stance as he gazes into the church. He is portrayed as an old man with a neat, rounded beard and a fringe of curly white hair that has escaped from beneath his head-hugging turban. Both saints clutch the top of their unfurled scrolls in their left hands, and St. Kosmas raises his right hand, palm outward and fingers straight across his chest. Both saints wear a long-sleeved tunic under a cloak that is pinned together at the base of the neck to fall back over the arms into a ripple of folds to either side of their body. St. Kosmas's cloak has a fine white outline along its edge, and the hem is decorated with a pattern of double parallel lines separated by a row of diagonal crosses painted in white; a similar pattern decorates the hem of St. John's cloak. St. Kosmas also has a painted motif on either shoulder similar to that on the head of the Mother of God Achrantos in the tympanum of the north door. Both saints wear neck cloths whose end folds appear at the parting of the cloak. These are dark blue with black lines and fold lines, and they have a white, linear design along the hem. From beneath these gathered folds, a black, knotted cord belt descends to loop away to either side of the figure. Their tunics fall in heaped folds over their feet, and only the pointed toes of their black boots are visible.

Text Fig. 50 The text on the scrolls of St. John of Damascus [156] and St. Kosmas the Poet [157]

St. Kosmas's halo is a warm yellow and has black and white outlines. His turban is red with umber fold lines, and there is a decorative design of black across the folds in the form of a thick line between two fine ones. His cloak has an umber ground, dark umber shadows, and black lines and outlines. His narrow elliptical brooch is white and has four pearls. His tunic has a brown ground, with dark brown shadows and red lines and outlines.

St. John's cloak has a dark brown ground with black lines and fold lines. His tunic has a yellow ground, yellow shadows, black lines and outlines, and grey-white highlights.

Fragment of Pattern [119]

On the south wall of the bema, to the right of St. Symeon the Archimandrite [118], is a fragment of patterned plaster [119] at the western edge of the pier, which is partly concealed by the present iconostasis. The fragment consists of a vertical patterned band contained within yellow borders outlined in white, with a further wide, red border at the western edge. The pattern itself was painted on a deep red ground—like that of its border—and appears to consist of a small curling foliated pattern in dark green picked out in white. The yellow and red borders measured 10 cms and the remaining piece of pattern some 11 cms at its greatest surviving width. The western border of the fragment overlaps onto the red border of the Christ Antiphonetes [127] on the adjacent reveal.

The pattern, the colors, and textures of the pigments used, and the brushwork suggest that this pattern belongs with the painted repairs to the 1192 decoration, and to the fourteenth-century paintings in the narthex.

Technique

No trace of preliminary drawing was found in these fragments, because although there was much damage, the upper layers of paint have not flaked back sufficiently to reveal that stage of painting. The haloes were all drawn with a compass and follow the ratio of six nose lengths, that is, two face lengths to the diameter. The fourteenth-century painter was possibly using a similar module to that used by the 1192 master. The fragmentary nature of this fourteenth-century sequence of paintings makes it impossible to assess the proportional relationships of the module to the figure. The centerpoint to the haloes of Christ and Peter seems to fall in the corner of the large eye, but that of the turbaned head of St. Kosmas falls above it. In the latter case, instead of enlarging the halo to accommodate the turban in the manner of the 1192 master, the narthex painter simply placed the head lower in the halo.[163]

It was possible to observe something of the color technique used by the narthex painter. Both the heads of Christ and St. Kosmas indicate that the hair and the face colors were built up on a green ground applied over the base yellow of the halo. Christ's hair was given a light brown ground, and it was styled with brown lines and black lines and given yellow highlight lines. St. Kosmas' hair was given a further grey-white ground, and it was styled in thin, red lines and dark red lines, and then finally picked out with short, sketchy lines in white. The eyebrows of this figure were outlined at the drawing stage and received no further elaboration except for the addition of a tuft of white hairs at the nose bridge.

The features of the faces were first defined on the green ground with dark brown lines, and then the upper area of the eye socket, the narrow side of the face, and the upper lip were all filled in with brown. The first flesh color of warm orange-yellow was then applied stencil fashion across the forehead, the cheekbones, down the nose bridge, on the nostril, and to either side of the mustache. For the face of Christ, this orange-yellow was also applied in the chin cleft. In the case of Kosmas, who is an old man, the first highlight was not applied in solid blocks but split up, leaving channels of green to simulate the furrows of age and to give relief to salient cheekbones. The ears of St. Kosmas and those of St. James in the group of apostles well illustrate how to convey a rapid impression of an ear with broad brushstrokes and graphic simplicity. The ears are simply formed by a C-shape with a couple of blobs underneath applied on the green ground.

This fourteenth-century painter used a second flesh color of reddish brown, whereas in most Byzantine paintings this would be vermilion. Technically, this highlight would be applied sparingly in patch and line over the previous flesh color, but the painter was not a careful craftsman, and it overlaps onto the green beneath. This second flesh color also reddens the lower lip. Black lines were then used to provide further definition and to reinforce shadow areas, such as the

---

[163] The 1192 painter also adjusted his haloes to encompass figures whose voluminous headgear occupied too much space in the halo. See above, Part Four, Chapter Sixteen, p. 289.

outlines of the face, the solid pupil, and the eyebrow lines. Finally, a white highlight was applied over the eyebrow line, the forehead ridge, the inner corner under the eye, the inner eye, and other prominent points. The system of painting hair and face is not unlike that of the 1192 master, and both follow the same basic Byzantine system. However, the earlier master used at least one further flesh color and shadow color. Also, the buildup of the eye area was more complex than that found in St. Kosmas, whose head is a reasonable size for comparison. Much of the difference between the painters lies in the usage of the brush, its loading and lifting to attenuate edges, and most of all, the care and precision used. The narthex painter was a sketchy painter. He used fine line, particularly in the heads, in short brushstrokes tapered at each end and unjoined. The artistic difference is quite clear when the head of Peter in the apostle group or that of St. Kosmas is compared with the 1192 St. Peter [143] (Fig. 253) or indeed with the carefully built-up heads of other old men in the earlier decoration.

There is a contrast between the competent original work painted by this fourteenth-century artist and the apparent carelessness of his repairs to the 1192 paintings. The fact that he did repair the paintings rather than repaint them completely is also of interest.

Three factors may well account for the carelessness of the repaints. First, he used a rather unstable ladder instead of going to the time and expense of erecting scaffolding for the job. Second, it is inherently difficult to carry out neat work on an uneven and damaged plaster surface. And third, he was working by the dim light of a candle.

The Exterior of the North Wall

(Figs. 8, 303–308; Text Fig. 6)

The paintings appear to be from different periods, but the evidence is confusing, and so, apart from the tympanum of the north door, they are described from east to west rather than by period. A ground register apparently was made up of single, standing figures, but all that is left are the traces of the tops of haloes of four figures. Above this is a second register of painting beginning just above the level of the top of the door, and it is this register that is described first. The scant remains of the ground register are described at the end.

The Mother of God, the Immaculate, the Achrantos [158] (Figs. 8, 303)

The image is a waist-length figure of the Virgin orans in the recessed tympanum over the east door. Around the face of the tympanum arch is an inscription [159] (see above, pp. 68–69).

The internal dimensions of the tympanum niche are 1.12 m long by 77 cm at maximum height, and it is 10 cm deep. The inscription for the Mother of God is in the normal abbreviated form to each side of the halo in white letters 5 cm high. The epithet "Achrantos" is immediately below in white letters about 4 cm high. It seems likely that this title represents the original dedication of the church. The lettering is neat, with serifs and letter forms very similar to those of 1333 at Asinou. The decorative elaboration of the M is particular to both churches.

The plaster is a single layer of lime with a straw or chaff binding. Within the background of the painting are two or three areas where the general background color has gone, and there is a reddish yellow wash that belongs to a previous painting. At Asinou, the Mother of God Phorbiotissa in the lunette over the west door from the narthex into the church is certainly a repaint of 1333 over the original painting of 1106. It is quite possible that this Mother of God Achrantos is, in a similar way, a repaint of an original that was painted in 1192.

The general background has an overall black base with a blue wash over it. The Virgin's tunic is blue on a black ground and at the wrist are double lines of creamy ochre separated by yellow diagonal crosses. Her wimple is also blue, and it is decorated with creamy yellow lines, one thick line between two thin ones. Her maphorion has a dark red ground, black fold lines, and light red highlights. The edges are decorated with double yellow lines that join at the edges of the folds. On each shoulder and at the top of her head, the maphorion is decorated with motifs in yellow ochre.

Her halo is yellow with a red inner and a white outer outline. It was drawn with a compass, and the outlines are neat and regular. The horizontal diameter of the halo falls along the upper lid line and nose bridge, and the centerpoint of the circle lies on the inner corner of the right eye. The length of her hands, from wrist to the tip of the median finger, is less than one face length. The division of the head into four nose lengths, the placing of the head in the halo, and the shorter measure for the hand all agree with the proportional system of the 1192 master. The flesh coloring is built up like that of the figures on the east wall of the narthex (see pp. 333–34). The lettering of the inscription, the workmanship of the brushstrokes, and the coloring all combine to link this repainting of the Mother of God Achrantos to the paintings of the old narthex [154–157].

The Upper Register (from east to west) [160–169]

A Mounted Warrior Saint [160] (Fig. 304)

The rectangular panel measures approximately 75 cm in height by 103 cm in length. The inscription is now gone. The plastering is over a rendering of mud plaster with straw and chaff in it. The foreground is yellow, with black lines to give shape as if of a valley over which rider and horse are jumping. The upper background is black with a grey wash over it.

The horse is red, with darker red outlines and squiggles representing curly hair. The reins are black. The saint has a red tunic, red armor, and yellow leggings. His cloak is now black, but the billowing ends of it have traces of red color suggesting that it could originally have been vermilion now discolored to black. There are pearl-shaped decorations to the saddle cloth and to some of his clothing, which was possibly vermilion but is now black, and these also might originally have been vermilion. He holds the reins with his left hand, and a black sword is carried upright in his right hand. His face is beardless and in the frontal position. It was painted on a fresh plaster patch, but it is impossible to say whether this is original or a later repair patched into the painting because it was

damaged. In either case the patch was not successful, and the painter had great difficulty in making it adhere to the mud plaster beneath. The face is simply painted with red feature lines and outlines, and he has red hair. The hand was also painted on a plaster patch. The halo is yellow with thin red and black outlines. In the rocky foreground is an area of white plaster that the painter appears to have forgotten to fill in with color.

St. Theodore Stratilates [161] (Fig. 308)

The panel measures approximately 1 m square. The saint is identified by an inscription in white letters at the right-hand side of the top of his halo. Theodore is a lively figure with his horse rearing up as he plunges his lance through the head of the dragon. The dragon's two tails both end in heads that bite at the horse. Theodore's cloak billows out behind him in a similar way to that of the unknown warrior described above [160]. There is no foreground, and the whole background has a black base with a grey wash over it. The dragon has a black ground with a pattern of scales, some in grey dots and some made with white dots with black outlines. The creature has dark grey outlines that may originally have been black. The eyes are black and the teeth are white.

The horse is black with a solid grey wash over it and some circular patterning in a lighter grey to make it look piebald. The outlines are mostly black, but there are a few red outlines. The eyes are black. The trappings are red, and the saddle cloth is red with white decorations to it. The saddle is of the high-backed type, and it is yellow with an outline decoration of red with a few white pearls.

St. Theodore wears yellow boots and red stockings. He has a grey tunic with black fold lines and white highlights. His cloak has a red ground with large areas of grey wash highlight over it and a white pearl decoration. His armor had a red ground with yellow delineating lines for the shapes and white pearl decoration. His shield is of western shape, and it is made with white and red areas. The lance is yellow with red outlines. His face is yellow with red feature lines and red hair, mustache, and beard. His halo is yellow with a red inner and a white outer outline. The head is seen in three-quarter profile and turns west as he looks down toward the dragon.

St. Menas [162] (Fig. 305)

The panel measures 76 cm in width by 1 m in height. The inscription is conventionally placed with the Haghios to the left of the halo and the name to the right. The lettering is in bold, white letters about twice as large as those for Theodore. The alpha is in semicursive form whereas Theodore has capital alphas. The saint sits astride his galloping horse and faces frontally to the onlooker while the horse gallops westward. He is dressed as a civilian rather than as a soldier and holds a martyr's cross in his right hand and the reins in his left hand. The whole of the background and foreground are black, but the background is differentiated by having a white wash over it.

The horse appears to be made with a black ground and an overall grey wash. This is overpainted with circles in light grey to give a piebald effect. The forms are outlined in red and black. He has red trappings partly turned black, which may indicate the use of vermilion. The saddle cloth is

yellow with white pearls and red squiggly decoration, and the saddle is black with red outlines and white pearls. The horses' hooves overlap into the bottom border of the painting, and it has been left unpainted at this point.

The saint's tunic has a red ground with light red highlight lines. A grey undergarment shows only on the forearm, and it has yellow embroidered cuffs with red outlines and white pearls. The lining of his cloak is yellow, and the outside is red in places but has partly turned black, perhaps indicating vermilion.

The halo is yellow, and it has a white inner and a red outer outline. His face has a yellow ground with red feature lines and white highlights. The hair and beard have a grey ground with white highlights shaping the curls and lines.

The Ancient of Days [163] (Fig. 303)

The panel is approximately 2.5 m long by 1 m high and is placed above and around the tympanum to the north door. There is no inscription for the scene. It shows a central mandorla with a bust-length figure of an old man with long, white beard and hair, dressed in white with a halo with a cross in it. The image symbolizes Christ's oneness with the Father. Here the association of this image with the Holy Trinity is confirmed by the presence of a red triangle that lies behind the Ancient's head with its points in the cross bars. The arms of the Ancient are stretched wide apart so that the hands extend beyond the edge of the mandorla, and the fingers are bent in blessing. An archangel is placed to either side, each swinging a censer forward.

The composition appears to be lopsided because it was cut short on the right-hand side by one of the upright wooden posts that must have originally supported the roof of an older peridromos. The left-hand archangel floats freely forward with its wings arranged in elegant curves that lead the eye up to the Ancient. The right-hand archangel is cramped into a semiupright position. Both archangels gesture with their inner hand toward the Deity while the other hand swings a censer forward.

The base color for the foreground and background is black. The foreground, which occupies about two-thirds of the height of the scene, is made with a bright green painted over the black. The upper third of the background appears to have been given a light grey wash over the black ground, but most of this has gone.

The mandorla is circular with a broad, white band forming the outer circle. The central circle is made with grey. The Ancient has white robes with a white ground and grey fold lines. The clavus is made with light red and dark red lines. The flesh coloring has a yellow ground and red and black outlines. He has a yellow halo with a red inner and a white outer outline. The cross within it is made with red lines and the triangles are red. The face is frontal, and the halo was drawn with a compass.

The eastern archangel looks to the west with his face in the three-quarter-profile aspect. The wings curve gracefully, but the body is shortened into a broad, lumpy caricature that gives the impression that he is wearing a misshapen crinoline. Both archangels have haloes that were drawn

with a compass, and they have a yellow ground and a red inner and a white outer outline. The archangels have the traditional hair style of tight curls and tresses at the back of the neck held by a white ribbon. The hair has a red ground with yellow styling lines. The buildup of the flesh colors is difficult to assess, but there appears to be a yellow ground and some reddish yellow areas with white highlights. The feature lines are strongly drawn in red.

Their yellow boots are outlined in red. Their dalmatics have a red ground with extensive areas of white highlight and a decorative hem with red, linear scroll work. The body of the dalmatic of the eastern angel is overlaid with a linear floral pattern. Each has a narrow, jeweled loros that is wound around his body and loops over one arm. The loros is yellow, with borders outlined in red line and lined with pearls; the central panel is studded with large, diamond-shaped red jewels alternating with square green ones. The jewels are outlined in red and edged with pearls. The lining to the loros is white. The primary and secondary wing feathers have a yellow ground, strong red outlines and some green shading. The tertiary wing feathers have a grey ground with white highlights. The censers are white with red outlines, and the chains are black.

A Bishop and a Prophet [164 and 165] (Fig. 307)

The panel measures approximately 58 cm in width by 1 m in height. The two figures are united within the one panel. They are separated from the Ancient of Days by a gap in the plaster for an upright post supporting the older peridromos roof. No inscriptions survive.

The background has a black base over which the foreground is painted with a green ground up to five-eighths of the height, and the area above the background has a wash of grey. Both figures stand in the fully frontal aspect with their feet extended downward.

The bishop is the eastern figure, and he stands fully frontal with his left hand holding a closed book and his right hand raised across his body in blessing. His tunic is white with blue shadow lines, and two pairs of red lines presumably denote a vestigial clavus. At the neck is a collar that may be part of the tunic; it has a yellow ground with brown outlines and white pearls. The upper garment has a light and dark area; the dark areas are folds around his waist and folds at the hemline. The light area has a red ground, dark red fold lines, and light red highlights. The darker part has a dark red ground, darker red fold lines, and no highlights. The epitrachelion has a white ground, blue fold lines, and black crosses and a horizontal black stripe at the bottom. The bishop's feet are shod in sandals, and the flesh is yellow with black outlines and black straps indicating the sandals. His book has a yellow ground with black outlines and decorative lines for the cover, which has a round, red jewel in the center surrounded by white pearls. The page lines are indicated in red.

His face is yellow with umber wrinkle lines very prominent in the forehead and dark umber feature lines. There is green shading at the sides of the face, but it is impossible to see if the green was used as a base color. His hair and beard are grey, made with a black base, a grey wash covering nearly all the black, and white lines delineating the hair.

The prophet stands in the full frontal stance like the bishop. His right hand gestures toward the Transfiguration in the next panel, and his left hand holds an open scroll with five lines prepared

for lettering, but no lettering is on it. He wears a white tunic that has blue fold lines and a black stylized decoration across the hem, similar to the design on the dalmatic of the eastern archangel [163] (Fig. 303). The cuffs are yellow with black lines and outlines and large white pearls. His cloak appears to have a light red ground covered with white. The fold lines are red and the border has a similar pattern to the cuffs of his tunic. His boots are yellow with brown outlines, and his hat is blue. The scroll is white with green lines on it.

His face and hair are made in the same way as that of the bishop, and the haloes of both figures are yellow with dark red inner and white outer outlines. The robes of the bishop are traditional and have none of the floral elaboration or polystavroi that might be expected of a late Byzantine painting. However, they do lack the epimanikion and epigonation.

The Transfiguration [166] (Fig. 306)

This panel is 1 m wide by 1.28 m high. There is no red border. The background and fore-ground occupy roughly equal areas of the scene. Apart from the sigla for Christ, there is no inscription, and the canonical six figures are placed in two tiers, but they do not appear to have been labeled. The upper tier has the transfigured Christ at the center with the prophets Moses and Elijah to either side of him. The lower tier has the three apostles Peter, James, and John tumbling forward out of the picture, as in the words of St. Matthew 17:6, "They fell on their face and were sore afraid."

The background has a black base with a grey wash over it. The foreground is made up of a rocky landscape of ravines and crags conforming to the "high mountains" where the event took place. The mountains are divided from the sky rather unusually by an arbitrary horizontal line. The rocks are in three colors and are built up quite elaborately. Yellow rocks have a yellow ground, brown shadow lines, black shadow lines, and white highlights. The red rocks have a red ground, dark red and black shadow lines, light red highlights, and white highlights. In the center the rocks are purplish, and perhaps they were made with hematite. The ground is light reddish purple, with dark reddish purple and black shadow lines, and light purple and white highlights. The trees are made with a light red–purple ground, green foliage, and white delineating lines.

Christ is a frontal figure framed within a square and an elliptical mandorla. He stands in the fully frontal position with his feet extended downward. He holds his right arm bent across his chest with his hand up in blessing. In his left hand he holds a scroll. The sigla $\overline{\text{IC}}$ $\overline{\text{XC}}$ are scrawled untidily to either side of his halo.

The square mandorla has a central white square that is surrounded by a dark grey band and a grey outer band outlined in thick white. The elliptical mandorla that appears above and below the square has a grey center and a white outer band.

Christ's face has a yellow-green ground. The green could just be a shadow color. There is also at least one reddish yellow flesh color, and the feature lines are made in dark red and black. The hair has a yellow ground with light yellow and black defining lines. The cross bars of his halo are formed in the same way as for the Ancient of Days, with the corners of a red triangle appearing

339

from behind his head. Christ's chiton has a white ground and red fold lines. Thin, blue lines for the clavus show at the shoulder. His himation has a white ground, blue fold lines, and a few black fold lines. His scroll is white with grey and black lines on it. His feet are yellow with black lines marking the straps of his sandals.

The prophet to the east is shown in three-quarter profile as he turns toward Christ. His arms are folded across his body; his left hand clutches the hem of his cloak, and with the other he gestures toward Christ. His title of prophet is untidily written above the top right-hand corner of his halo. It would customarily be placed to the left to leave room for his name to the right of the halo. In this case there is no trace of any lettering for his name, but the figure should represent Elijah.

He wears a yellow tunic made with a yellow ground, brown fold lines, and white highlights. The tunic only appears below the cloak at his ankles. His cloak has a hematite purple ground, dark hematite purple fold lines, black fold lines, and light hematite purple highlight lines. It has a thick fur trimming made with a grey ground and white highlights. His feet and hands have a yellow ground with brown outlines. The sandals on his feet are indicated by black strap lines and outlines. His face has a yellow ground with red feature lines. His hair was made with a yellow ground, some grey areas over the yellow, black defining lines and outlines, and white lines delineating the hair.

The prophet to the west is also turned in three-quarter profile toward Christ. His arms are bent forward together, and the hands, which are concealed by his himation, support an inscribed tablet as if he were offering it to Christ. He has no name but must represent Moses holding the Tablets of the Law. The title prophet is untidily inscribed to the left of his halo. His chiton has a white ground, hematite shadows, and dark hematite lines and outlines. His himation has a hematite ground, dark hematite fold lines, and a few black lines for the buildup of dark areas. The light areas are built up with light hematite and white. The tablet has a white ground, green lines, and black lettering that appears to be purely decorative. The feet have a yellow ground with green shading and brown delineating lines. The sandals are indicated by black strap lines and outlines. He has short brown hair and a beard.

The eastern apostle has no name inscribed, and the face is destroyed, but the curly grey hair and bushy beard suggest that this is the figure of Peter. On his knees, Peter falls forward out of the picture space and overlaps the edge. His head is turned in three-quarter profile as he turns back to look up at the Christ above.

His hair has a yellow ground, black lines, and light yellow and white lines delineating the hair. His chiton has a white ground and light blue fold lines with a dark red clavus. His himation has a light hematite ground, dark hematite fold lines, lighter hematite highlights, and white high-lights. His feet are yellow with black sandal straps.

The center apostle has no name and the face is destroyed, but it appears as if he had no beard, so this figure must be the apostle John. He has fallen forward on his hands and knees and supports himself on his left hand, which he thrusts over the edge of the picture as if to stop himself from falling out of it. His head is turned downward and is seen in three-quarter profile, and his right

hand was placed over his face, presumably to hide his eyes from the vision. His hair has a dull yellow color, but it is too damaged to analyze. His chiton has a white ground with blue fold lines. His himation is made up of shades of hematite purple. It has a hematite purple ground, dark hematite fold lines, and light hematite and white highlights.

The western apostle, by elimination, must be James, who was the third apostle present at the Transfiguration. He too is down on his knees and huddles into the western corner. His head, which is much damaged, is in three-quarter profile. His body is in profile and curls up upon itself, and his arms bend upward to shield his head.

He wears a chiton with a red ground, light red areas, and white highlights. His himation is almost equally divided into dark and light areas built up in tones of hematite purple. The dark area has a hematite ground, broad, dark hematite shadows, and black lines and outlines. The light areas have a hematite ground, light hematite intermediate highlights, and white highlights.

The halo of each of the five figures in the scene is yellow, and has red inner and white outer outlines. The border to the scene is clearly marked, but it shows no sign that it was ever painted. The scene is recognizably the same as the Sinai mosaic of the Transfiguration of perhaps a thousand years earlier. There is a convincing impression of galvanic movement in the apostles, which is echoed in the lines of their garments. This is enhanced by the exaggerated linear forms of the rocky background, which looks like a petrified waterfall. The lack of a titular inscription is odd, as is the flat top of the mountains, but in its simple way this is still a remarkably alive and expressive painting.

Unknown bishop [167] and St. Herakleidios [168] (Fig. 309)

The panel measures 85 cm in width and is approximately 1.5 m in height. The plaster for this panel overlaps the plaster for the panel of the Transfiguration, and it was therefore painted after that scene. It has a painted red border with a white inner outline. The upper part of the plaster for the panel has fallen away, leaving the bishop to the east without shoulders or head, and St. Herakleidios to the west has lost most of his head.

The remaining inscription is written in clear white letters to the west of the figure, between the halo and shoulder. The horizontal bar of the delta is at the base of that letter and is easy to distinguish from the alpha with a diagonal bar.

Each bishop holds a book in his left hand, and St. Herakleidios blesses with his raised right hand. The flesh color is yellow with red defining lines. His halo is yellow, and it has thin, red inner and white outer outlines that are distinct from the thick halo outlines of the central panels on this wall. His beard has a yellow ground.

The foreground occupies rather less than half the height of the panel. It appears to have a yellow ground and a distinctive bright green covering the yellow. The upper background is black, and it may have had a grey wash over it.

The painting of what remains of these two bishops is identical, and they are described together. Their robes come down to the red border at the bottom, and no feet are shown. Both wear

a polystavrion, which has a grey ground, dark grey fold lines, black fold lines, black crosses, and light grey highlight areas. The epimanikion has a yellow ground, red defining lines, grey jewels, and white pearls. The epigonation is made in the same way. Their stoles have black crosses on a grey ground at the shoulders, but the section that drops down over the knees at the front center has a yellow ground with black linear patterns and white pearls. The books have a yellow ground with grey jewels and white pearls, and the page ends are red.

This panel shows some marked differences with the central panels on this wall. The vivid green of the foreground, which contrasts with that of the central panels, is probably due to the fact that it was painted over a yellow base, whereas the greens of the central panels were painted on black. The outlines to the halo of St. Herakleidios are very thin compared with the broad outlines of those to the haloes of the central figures. The episcopal robes of this pair of bishops are also distinct from those of the central panels, which lack the epimanikion and epigonation. The central pair of bishops have squat figures, whereas this pair are more elongated and better proportioned, and they wear a polystavrion.

Unknown bishop [169]

This is approximately 58 cm wide (to where it continues under the buttress) by 1.25 m in height. The plaster of this panel overlaps the neighboring panel to the east. On the west side it continues under the buttress. The painting is of a bishop with receding white hair and a long beard. His inscription does not survive. He stands in the fully frontal stance and holds a closed book in his left hand. His right hand lies across his breast, and his long, sinuous fingers extend in the gesture of blessing.

The background and foreground, if any, have a black base that serves as a ground. There is no trace of grey wash or green ground, but the paint surfaces are very damaged, so it is impossible to be certain.

The bishop's halo is yellow with a single white outline. His hair has a yellow ground, brown feature lines, and overall white shaping lines. The flesh colors are uncertain but appear to be built up over a yellow ground. There is some green, but it is indeterminate as to whether this is an overall ground color under the yellow or merely a shadow layer. The feature lines are drawn in red and brown, and there are strong, creamy yellow highlight lines.

The bishop wears a polystavrion that has a grey ground and black crosses, but it does not appear to have any fold lines. The epimanikion has a yellow ground with brown outlines and white pearls. The epigonation has a yellow ground with brown outlines, white pearls, and a red jewel in the center. The stole has a white ground with black crosses at the shoulders, and it ends in a panel with a yellow ground, black floral decoration, and white pearls. The book has a yellow ground, brown outlines, white pearls, and a red jewel in each of the four corners. The page ends are yellow, and the clasp is black. This panel is differentiated from its neighbor by the lack of green ground, a different halo outline, and the drawing of the hands and the books.

The Lower Register

Four Standing Figures? [170]

All that remains are the tops of two haloes to the west of the northeast door and two rather narrower panels with the tops of haloes to the west of the door. Both panels were outlined in yellow and have white borders. A part of a foot survives for one of the western figures, giving a height of 1.55 m, which is roughly in scale with the upper register.

It may be fortuitous, but the foot and the fragment of red border that are now at about 1 m above the present ground level were at about the height to which earth had accumulated against the north side of the church until it was cleared away in 1955. This would argue a later rather than an earlier date for the paintings.

The haloes have a yellow ground with a red inner and a white outer outline. The background color is red. The fragment of foot has a yellow ground with green over it.

Other Fragments [171]

To the east of the northeast door are remains of a red border that is similar to the dark red used by the fourteenth-century painter. The plaster is of varying thickness. There is a thin, rough-cast layer of a few millimeters in thickness, followed by the surface plaster of lime with a chaff binder, varying from 1 to 3 cm in thickness.

On the roughcast to the east of the door, a rectangle has been marked out in red with a few lines of preliminary drawing, but the subject matter is not clear. There are also traces of green wash on the white ground. On the surface plaster to the east of the rectangle is some additional red preliminary drawing, which may represent the upper half of a figure holding a lance or staff in a diagonal position. The three horizontal red lines, each equidistant at 3 cm crossing a vertical line, could represent the proportional schema for a face. The plaster of the ground register of painting at the west end continues under the buttress. There is a black background and a vertical red border line.

The paintings of the north wall can be differentiated in color, technique, and style, but it is not easy to assign dates except for period one.

Period One [158, 159] The tympanum painting and inscription are of the same style as the Lagoudhera narthex paintings and agree well with the style of the 1333 paintings at Asinou (see above, pp. 68–69).

Style A [161, 162, 163] The upper register to the east of the east door has three saints on horseback. There is no green or blue in these three figures, who seem to be entirely made up of white, red, yellow, and black. They have similar red borders for each panel with no white outlines. The halo outlines are slightly different in each case, and the eastern saint has plaster

patches for his face and a hand, so there could be a case for further subdivision by painter or by period.

Style B [163, 164, 165, 166] The Ancient of Days, the two bishops west of the door, and the Transfiguration share a similarity in the dumpy figures and in the coloring, notably the choice of hematite purple. The haloes are all similar, and so are the untidy borders that appear to have been only partially painted in red.

Style C [167, 168] The two bishops west of the Transfiguration.

Style D [169] This bishop is very close to Style C, but the outlines to the panel and the halo outlines are different.

Style E [170, 171] Not enough is left to qualify these small fragments.

Dating

None of the styles has any parallel in the neat paintings of the nearby church at Sarandi, which probably dates from the sixteenth or seventeenth century. Nor is there any parallel with the naive and fantastic paintings of the church at Vyzakia, which was a dependency of Lagoudhera.

The styles could represent different periods of painting, when a monk who had trained as a painter joined the brotherhood of the monastery; or they could be a collection, made over a few centuries, as itinerant painters passed by the monastery.

Exterior of the South Wall

On the south side of the apse are obscure traces of red drawing, including three crosses, each of which has two bars to it.

On the buttress to the east of the south door is a fragment of painted background consisting of a black ground with green over it. The border is red with white outlines.

Iconographic Index

Abibos 171, 172, 174, 214; Text Fig. 31; Fig. 121

Adam 153, 154, 155, 156, 158, 241, 315; Figs. 92, 97–99; Pl. 21

Aithalas 228; Text Fig. 36; Fig. 197

Ancient of Days 76, 337, 338, 339, 344; Fig. 303

angels 58, 66, 71, 79, 114, 116, 120–28, 129, 130, 141, 144, 149, 162, 164–65, 176, 180, 187, 188, 196–99, 200, 204, 205, 224, 231, 232, 234, 238, 239, 243, 244, 245, 246, 247, 249–53, 254, 255, 259–65, 280, 284, 289, 290, 301, 302, 313, 314, 315, 317, 322, 338; Text Fig. 23; Figs. 51, 53–56, 59, 102, 103, 145, 147–50, 226, 227, 235, 238, 239; Pls. 12, 25. *See also* archangels

archangels 71, 76, 77, 83, 84–88, 99, 103, 104, 106, 107, 108, 121, 122, 124–28, 146, 164n, 196, 199, 200, 201, 204, 205, 262, 285, 288, 315, 337–38, 339; Text Fig. 17; Figs. 48, 49, 50, 52, 57, 58, 146, 152, 153, 154, 162, 293, 296, 299, 303; Pl. 10c

   Gabriel 70, 83, 86, 88, 142, 144, 284, 290n; Figs. 10, 11, 81a; Pls. 6. 19

   Michael 70, 71, 83, 84, 87, 88, 132, 161, 164n, 200, 221, 250–53, 278, 288, 320; Text Fig. 42; Figs. 10, 12, 228, 229, 230

Akepsimas 225, Text Fig. 36.1b; Fig. 191

Akindinos (?) 171, 173, 226, 227; Fig. 118

Andrew 156, 201, 241, 242

Anna 176, 178, 179, 180–84, 188, 219, 257n, 300, 316; Text Fig. 34; Figs. 123, 126, 127, 128; Pl. 25

Anempodistos 173; Fig. 114

Andronikos 158, 165–66, 169, 170, 231, 268, 269, 276; Figs. 104, 106, 276

Anthony 221, 230–31, 313, 320, 330; Figs. 199, 200, 279

Aphthonios 173, 174; Fig. 116

apostles 72, 73, 196, 197, 199, 200–205, 231, 232, 234, 236–38, 239, 240–44, 280, 299, 309, 315, 316, 317, 329, 330, 333, 334, 339, 340, 341; Figs. 146, 155–62, 204, 205, 207, 216, 219, 220, 221, 300, Pl. 27, 29. *See also* individual apostles by name

Athanasios 92, 96; Figs. 26, 33

Auxentios 226, 227; Fig. 195

Auxibios 72, 89, 91; Fig. 17

Barnabas 72, 97; Fig. 39

Basil 92, 95, 96; Figs. 25, 31, 36

bishops 72, 73, 76, 92, 93–94, 97, 98, 102, 103, 206, 216, 225, 231, 234, 239–40, 242, 243, 316, 338–39, 341, 342, 343, 344; Text Figs. 19, 31, 35, 36; Figs. 211, 214, 215, 307

bishop, unknown 341, 342

Chariton 266, 267–68, 271; Text Fig. 30; Figs. 251, 254, 280

Christ 58, 70, 71, 73, 79, 80, 111–19, 120, 121, 124, 135, 140, 141, 142, 152, 153, 154, 155, 156, 157, 158, 161, 162, 163, 164, 165, 174, 175, 191, 192, 193, 196, 197, 198, 199, 203, 204, 205, 210, 214, 215, 219, 220, 239, 243, 244, 245, 254, 279, 284, 288, 289, 299, 300, 309, 314, 315, 316, 318, 320, 321, 322, 330, 331, 333, 337, 339, 340; Text Figs. 21, 22, 36; Figs. 42–45, 92, 93, 202, 209, 223, 301; Pls. 9, 21

Christ Antiphonetes 72, 83, 99, 175, 221–31, 234, 237, 238, 245, 278, 301, 309, 320, 332; Text Fig. 38; Figs. 138, 140

   book of Christ Antiphonetes Fig. 284

Christ child 66, 70, 71, 74, 84, 85, 103, 104, 106, 107, 108, 114, 131, 144, 145, 176, 192, 245, 247, 249, 254–58, 263, 265, 287n, 293–96, 302, 315; Text Fig. 47; Figs. 10, 13, 133, 134, 244, 247; Pls. 28, 35

Christ Emmanuel 71, 146, 301; Pl. 20

Christ in a mandorla 231, 232, 238–39, 280; Fig. 145; Pl. 26

Christ in the Mandylion 180, 191; Figs. 145, 187. *See also* Mandylion

Christopher 23, 266, 269; Text Fig. 30c; Fig. 259

crosses 53, 63, 64, 73, 87, 90, 93, 94, 95, 96, 97, 98, 99, 118n, 123, 124, 125, 150, 153, 155, 158,

Index

PLATES

Numbers in square brackets indicate the location of the image on the iconographic plans,
pp. 36–39; Text Figs. 1–6

Photographs by R. Anderson and D. Winfield

1 Dome and pendentives

2 Naos looking east

3 North wall under the dome

4 South wall under the dome

5 Apse conch

6 Apse conch, head of the
archangel Gabriel [95]

7 Apse, roundel with St.
Zenon [98]

8 Apse, St. Meletios of Antioch [107] and St. John Chrysostomos [108]

9 Dome, head of Christ [1]

10 Patterns from the 1192 decoration: (a) bolster from the Etoimasia [3]; (b) embroidered panel, Daniel [23];
(c) boot, as worn by archangels and kings; (d) crown, as worn by Solomon [17] and David [35]; (e) hem of
dalmatic, as worn by David [35] and Solomon [17]

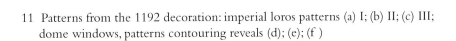

11 Patterns from the 1192 decoration: imperial loros patterns (a) I; (b) II; (c) III; dome windows, patterns contouring reveals (d); (e); (f)

12 Dome, south roundel with angel [6]

13 Dome, the prophet Daniel [23]

14 Dome, the prophet Isaiah [37]

15 Dome, head of the prophet Jeremiah [15]

16 Dome, beard of the prophet Ezechiel [29]

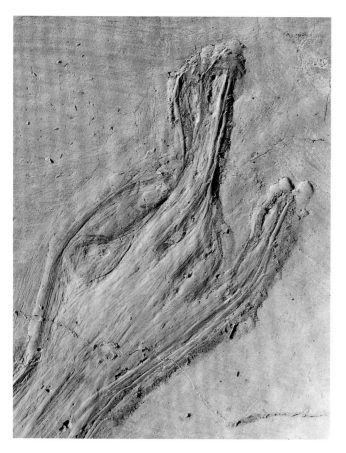

17 Dome, hand of the prophet Habakkuk [27], illustrating the reworking of the plaster and the texture of the paint

18 Dome, robes of the prophet Jeremiah [15], illustrating the buildup of color layers

19 Northeast pendentive, the archangel Gabriel [38] of the Annunciation

20 Between the northeast and southeast pendentives, Christ Emmanuel [39]

21 North half of the west vault, the Anastasis [50]

22 South half of the west vault, the Nativity [142]

23 South wall under the dome, the Koimesis [138]

24 North wall under the dome, the Presentation of the Virgin [70]

25 North wall under the dome, the Presentation of the Virgin [70], Joachim, Anna, and the child Mary, detail

26 Bema vault, the Ascension [78], Christ in the mandorla borne up by angels

27 Bema vault, the Ascension [78], south side, the Mother of God and six apostles

28 North wall under the dome, the Holy Symeon and the Christ child [74]

29 Bema vault, the Ascension [78], north side, three apostles to the east of the archangel

30 Apse arch, center, the Mandylion [92]

31 Apse arch, north side, St. John of
    Damascus [91]

32 South wall under the dome, the Mother of God Arakiotissa [139]

33 Southern half of the west vault, the
   Nativity [142], head of the Mother of
   God

34 Southern half of the west vault,
   the Nativity [142], heads of two
   shepherds

35 Southern half of the west vault, the Nativity [142], midwives bathing the Christ child

FIGURES

Numbers in square brackets indicate the location of the image on the iconographic plans, pp. 36–39; Text Figs. 1–6

Photographs by R. Anderson and D. Winfield

1 Church in its setting viewed from the northeast

2 Exterior of the church viewed from the southeast

3 North side of the church in
   1955 during the restoration
   of the secondary roof
   (courtesy of the Department
   of Antiquities, Cyprus)

4 General view of the cupola and the western extension during the 1955 restoration, showing the
construction and the secondary roof (courtesy of the Department of Antiquities, Cyprus)

5 Exterior view of the apse from beneath the
secondary roof

6 Exterior view of the western extension before the
1955 restoration (courtesy of the Department of
Antiquities, Cyprus)

7 Lintel, north door under the dome, the 1192 donor inscription [73] with the Holy Tile [72]

8 Tympanum, exterior north door, with votary inscription to the Mother of God Achrantos [158]

9 Naos, south wall, the Mother of God Arakiotissa [139] with votive inscription to either side of her figure

10 Apse conch, pre-1192, the enthroned Mother of God with Christ child attended by the archangels Gabriel and Michael, with the roundels of Cypriot church fathers beneath [95-104]

11 The archangel Gabriel [95]

12 The archangel Michael [97]

13 Apse conch, the enthroned Mother of God with Christ child [96]

14 Apse, middle register, St. Herakleidios [102]

15 Apse, middle register, St. Philagrios [100]

16 Apse, middle register, St. Tryphillios [104]

17 Apse, middle register, St. Auxibios [101]

18 Apse, middle register, St. Nikon [99]

19 Apse, middle register, St. Makedonios [103]

20 Apse, middle register, head of St. Philagrios [100] revealing the preliminary drawing

21 Apse, middle register, head St. Herakleidios [102] revealing the preliminary drawing

22 Apse, middle register, head of St. Zenon [98]

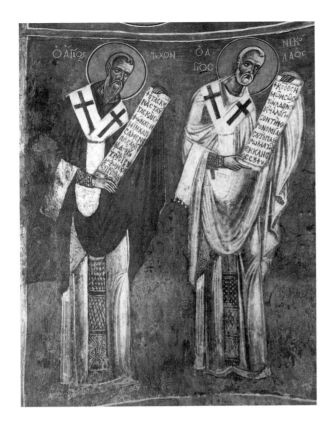

23 Apse, ground register, St. Tychon [105] and St. Nicholas [106]

24 Apse, ground register, St. Meletios of Antioch [107] and St. John Chrysostomos [108]

25 Apse, ground register, St. Basil [113] and St. Gregory the Theologian [114]

26 Apse, ground register, St. Athanasios [115] and St. John the Almoner [116]

27 St. Tychon [105]

28 St. Nicholas [106]

29 St. Meletios of
Antioch [107]

30 St. John
Chrysostomos [108]

31 St. Basil [113]

32 St. Gregory the
Theologian [114]

33 St. Athanasios [115]

34 St. John the
Almoner [116]

Apse, scrolls of the church fathers, ground register (pre–1192)

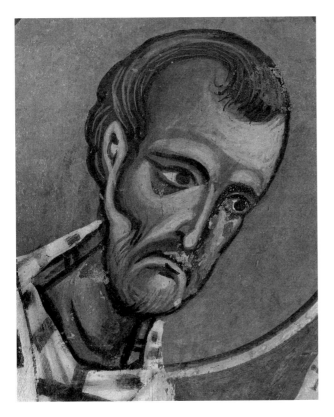

35 Apse, ground register, St. John Chrysostomos [108]

36 Apse, ground register, St. Basil [113]

37 Apse, ground register, St. Meletios of Antioch [107]

38 Apse, ground register, St. Gregory the Theologian [114]

Pre-1192 paintings

39 Apse, pre-1192, mullions between the windows, St. Epiphanios? [109] and St. Barnabas [110]

40 Apse, pre-1192, roundels in the panel beneath the windows, St. Spyridon [111] and an unidentified saint [112]

41 Fragment of pre-1192 painting [141] removed from below the Mother of God Arakiotissa [139] on the south wall below the dome

42 Dome, 1192, general view, image of Christ [1] and the chevron pattern [2]

Paintings of 1192

43 Christ's eyes

44 Christ's nostrils, mouth, and beard

45 Christ's right hand under raking light showing
incised guidelines and the reworking of the
plaster surface prior to completing the hand

46 Dome, east, the Etoimasia [3]

47 Dome, the Etoimasia [3] in raking light, showing alterations to the dove and the impressed guideline marking the outline of the cross

48 Dome, northeast archangel [13]

49 Dome, southeast archangel [4]

50 Dome, north–northeast
    archangel [12]

51 Dome, south angel [6]

52 Dome, north-northwest archangel [10]

53 Dome, south-southeast angel [5]

54 Dome, north angel [11]

55 Dome, southwest angel [8]

56 Dome, northwest angel [9]

57 Dome, south–southwest archangel [7]

58 Dome, south–southeast archangel [5], showing the adjustments to the loros pattern after the disturbance caused by
reworking the surface plaster prior to completing the hand

59 Dome, head of the southwest angel [8]

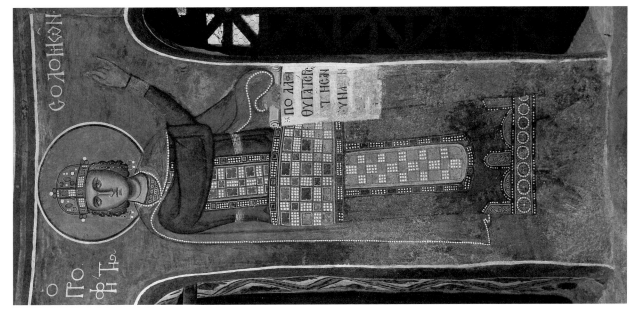

62 Dome, drum, the prophet Elijah [19]

61 Dome, drum, the prophet Solomon [17]

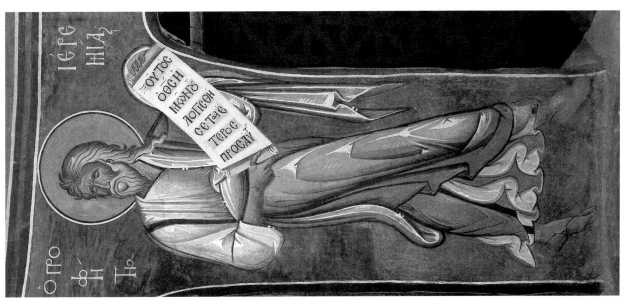

60 Dome, drum, the prophet Jeremiah [15]

65 Dome, drum, the prophet Habakkuk [27]

64 Dome, drum, the prophet Gideon [25]

63 Dome, drum, the prophet Elisha [21]

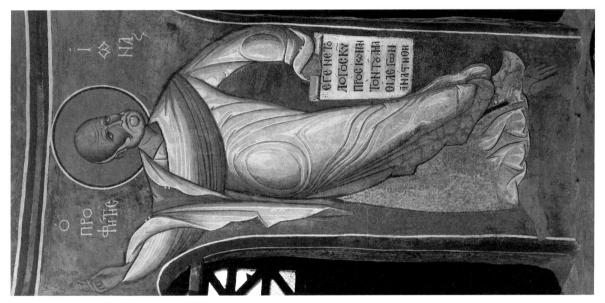

68 Dome, drum, the prophet Moses [33]

67 Dome, drum, the prophet Jonah [31]

66 Dome, drum, the prophet Ezechiel [29]

69 Dome, drum, the prophet
    David [35]

70 Dome, drum, right hand of the prophet Daniel
    [23] in raking light, showing the reworking of the
    plaster prior to the final painting of the hand

71 Dome, drum, loros of the prophet David [35]
    in raking light, with high-relief white pearls

72 Dome, drum, head of
   the prophet David [35]

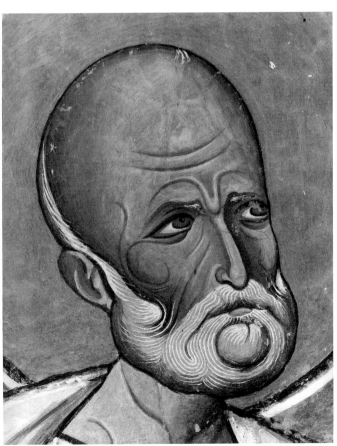

73 Dome, drum, head of
   the prophet Jonah [31]

74 Dome, drum, head of
the prophet Daniel [23]

75 Dome, drum, head of
the prophet Moses [33]

77 Pendentive, southeast, south side of the Mother of God [40]

76 Pendentive, southeast, east side of the Mother of God [40]

78 Pendentive, southwest, south side of St. John [41]

79 Pendentive, southwest, west side of St. Luke [42]

80 Pendentive, northwest, west
side of St. Matthew [43]

81 Pendentive, northwest,
north side of St. Mark [44],
rotunda with porch

81a Pendentive, northeast, the Annunciation, archangel Gabriel [38]

81b Pendentive, southeast, the Annunciation, the Mother of God [40]

82 Pendentive, northwest, St. Matthew [43] and St. Mark [44]

83 Pendentive, southwest, St. John [41] and St. Luke [42]

84 Pendentive, northwest, head of St. Matthew [43]

85 Pendentive, northwest, head of St. Mark [44]

86 Pendentive, southwest, head of St. John [41],
fourteenth-century repaint

87 Pendentive, southwest, head of St. Luke [42],
fourteenth-century repaint

88 Naos, center of west vault, roundel, St. Tryphon [45]

89 Naos, center of west vault, roundel, St. Vikentios? [46]

90 Naos, center of west vault, roundel, St. Viktor [47] against a faded floral background [49]

91 Naos, center of west vault, roundel, St. Menas [48] against a faded floral background [49]

92 Naos, west vault, north side, general view, the Anastasis [50]

93 Head of Christ

94 Solomon

95 Head of Eve

96 Head of St. John

97 Head of Adam in raking light, showing the fresh plaster patch inserted prior to the completion of his head

98 Adam's forearm in raking light, showing the incised
outlines and the reworking of the plaster for the
flesh areas

100 Naos, northwest bay, north wall, St. Paul [52]

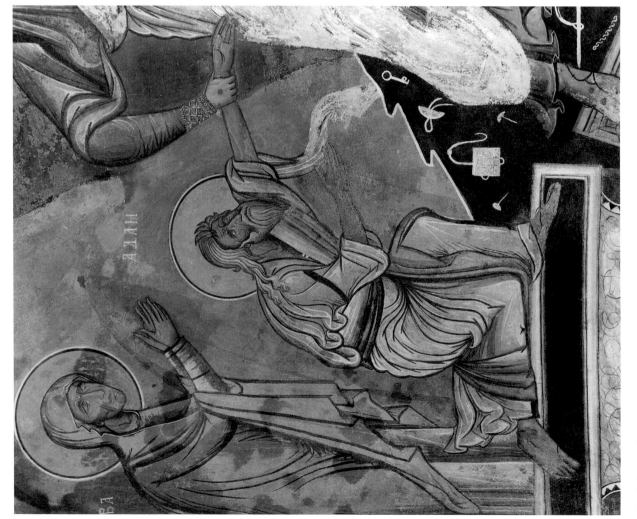

99 Adam and Eve

102 Head of the upper angel

103 Head of the lower angel, still retaining heavy

101 Naos, northwest bay, north wall, general view, the Baptism [54]

107 Head of St. Kyriakos [58]

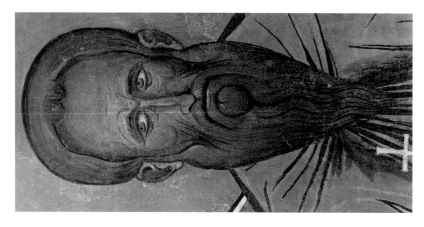

106 Head of St. Andronikos [55]

105 Naos, northwest bay, reveal of arch, east side, St. Kyriakos [58]

104 Naos, northwest bay, reveal of arch, west side, St. Andronikos [55]

108 Naos, northwest bay, soffit of
     arch, west side, St. Kosmas [56]

109 Naos, northwest bay, soffit of
     arch, east side, St. Damian [57]

113 Head of St. Nicholas [71]

112 Head of St. Sabas [59]

111 Naos, north bay under dome, west side of door, St. Nicholas [71]

110 Naos, north bay under dome, west reveal, St. Sabas [59]

114 Soffit, north arch under dome, St. Anempodistos [60]

115 Soffit, north arch under dome, St. Elpidiphoros [61]

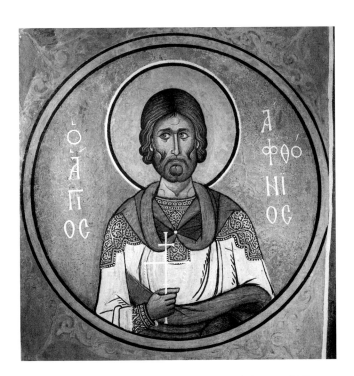

116 Soffit, north arch under dome, St. Aphthonios [62]

117 Soffit, north arch under dome, St. Pigasios [63]

118 Soffit, north arch under dome, St. Akindinos? [64]

119 Soffit, north arch under dome, St. Gourias [65]

120 Soffit, north arch under dome, St. Samonas [66]

121 Soffit, north arch under dome, St. Abibos [67]

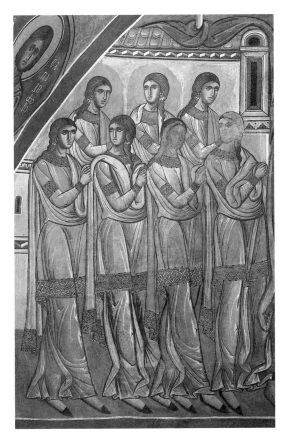

122 Naos, lunette, north bay under dome,
Presentation of the Virgin [70]: west side,
Hebrew maidens

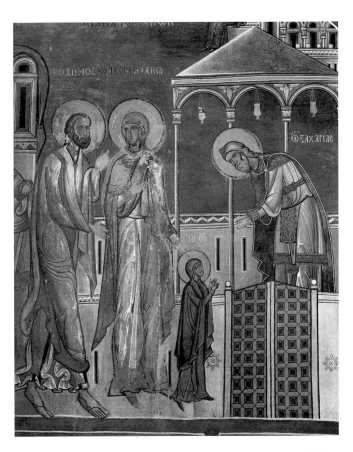

123 Naos, lunette, north bay under dome, Presentation of the
Virgin [70]: east side, St. Joachim and St. Anna, Mary and
St. Zacharias

124 Head of the western maiden whose nose is
incorrectly oriented, lower row

125 Head of a maiden, upper row

126 Head of St. Anna

127 Head of St. Anna in raking light, showing the plaster patch for the final version of her head, the slight rectification to that version, and the initial halo outline and the incised lines marking the shoulders of the initial figure

128 Hem of St. Anna's tunic, showing the outlines of her initial garment and the bell folds of the hem

129 Head of St. Joachim, showing the plaster patch for the final version of his head and the flaking of the jeweled black halo line revealing the initial halo that had black and white outlines

130a Child Mary outside the temple gate

130b Child Mary in raking light, showing the plaster patch inserted before painting the figure of the Virgin

131 Head of St. Zacharias, showing the original halo that was never given definitive outlines

132 Head of St. Zacharias in raking light, showing in high relief the plaster patch for the final version of his head and the incised line delimiting his right shoulder

134 Christ child in the arms of St. Symeon [74]

135 Head of St. John the Baptist [75]

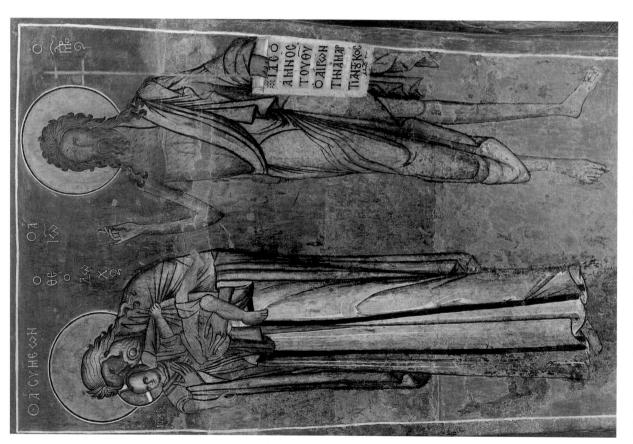

133 Naos, north wall under dome, east side of door, St. Symeon the God-bearer holding Christ child [74], and St. John the Baptist, or Forerunner [75]

138 Naos, east end, south arch under the dome, the Deesis: Christ Antiphonetes [127]

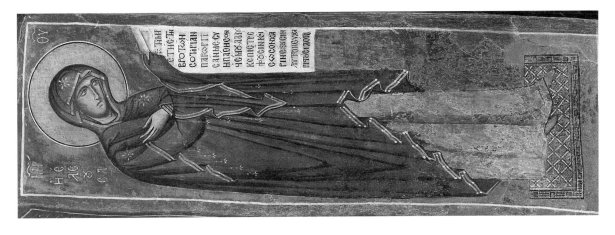

137 Naos, east end, north arch under the dome, the Deesis: the Mother of God Eleousa [69]

136 Naos, east end, north bay under the dome, the Deesis: St. John the Baptist [75]

139 Head of the Mother of God
     Eleousa [69]

140 Head of Christ Antiphonetes
     [127]

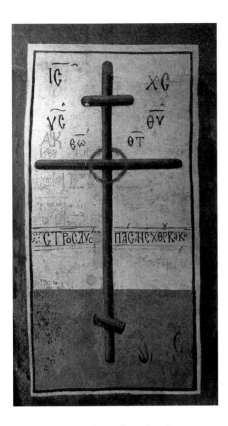

141 Naos, north wall under dome, west reveal of door, cross with inscriptions [76]

142 Naos, north wall under dome, east reveal of door, cross with inscriptions [77]

143 West reveal [76] in raking light, showing graffiti

144 East reveal [77] in raking light, showing graffiti

145 Sanctuary vault, center, the Ascension: Christ in a mandorla borne up by angels

146 Sanctuary vault, north side, the Ascension: the archangel standing amidst six apostles

147 Head of the northwest angel

148 Head of the southwest angel

149 Head of the southeast angel

150 Head of the northeast angel

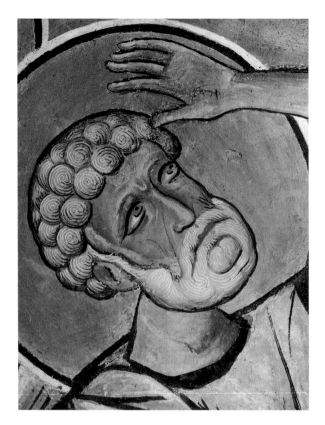

151 Head of St. Peter

152 Head of the archangel

153 The archangel, garment folds over the thigh

154 The archangel in raking light, with the left wing showing buildup of the feathers

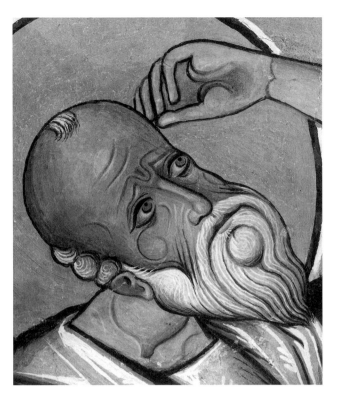

155 Head of the apostle, east side of the Mother of God

156 Head of the apostle, west side of the Mother of God

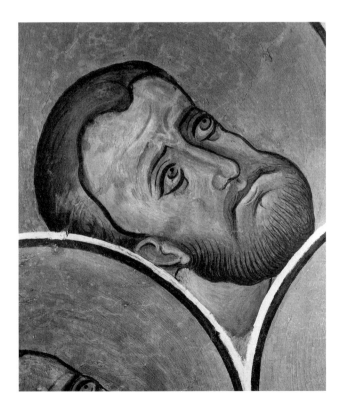

157 Head of the apostle, east side of the Mother of God

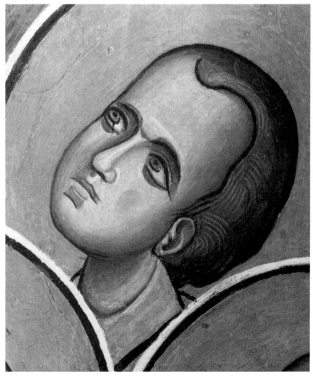

158 Head of the young apostle, west side of the Mother of God

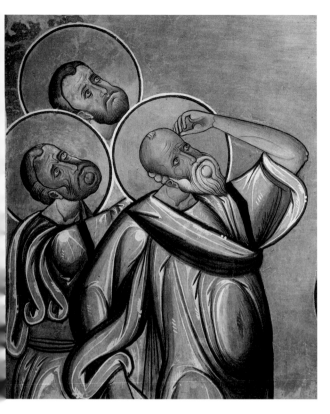

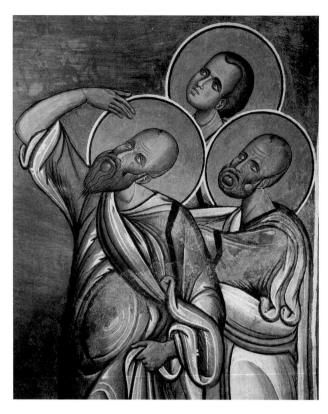

159 Group of apostles, east side of the Mother of God

160 Group of apostles, west side of the Mother of God

161 Head of the apostle, east side of the Mother of God

162 Apostle east of the archangel, bell folds of his chiton

163 Sanctuary, north wall, east side, roundel, St. Joseph the Poet [80]

164 Sanctuary, south wall, east side, roundel, St. Theophanes the Poet [117]

165 Sanctuary, north wall, west side, head of St. Symeon Thaumaturgos [79]

166 Sanctuary, south wall, west side, head of St. Symeon the Elder [118]

170 Sanctuary, south arch, west
reveal, St. Lazaros [124]

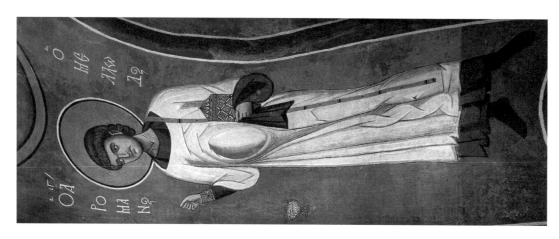

169 Sanctuary, south arch, east reveal,
St. Romanos the Melode [122]

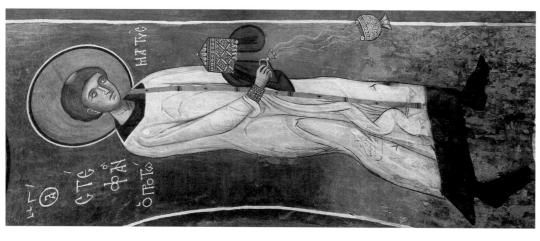

168 Sanctuary, north arch, east reveal,
St. Stephen the Protomartyr [83]

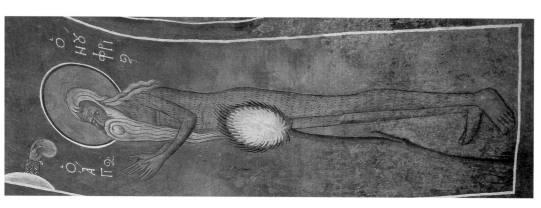

167 Sanctuary, north arch, west
reveal, St. Onuphrios [81]

171 Sanctuary, north bay, general view of the north wall [86-89]

172 Lunette of the north wall, head of St. Hypatios [86]

173 Niche, cross with inscriptions [89] and imitation tile patterns [88]

174 Sanctuary, north bay, prothesis niche, cross with instruments of the Crucifixion [85]

175 Sanctuary, soffit of north arch, roundel with cross [82]

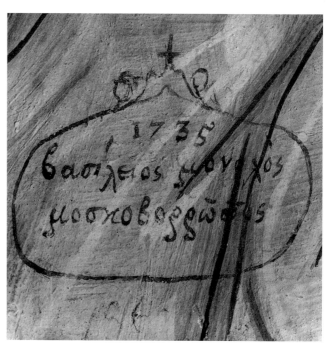

176 Sanctuary, north arch, east reveal, St. Stephen [83],
      with signature of the monk Barsky

177 Sanctuary, soffit of south arch, roundel with cross [123]

178 Sanctuary, south arch, east reveal, diakonikon niche,
      cross with instruments of the Passion [121]

179 Sanctuary, reveal of the apse arch, north side, roundel, St. Stachios [90]

180 Sanctuary, reveal of the apse arch, south side, roundel, St. Nikanor [94]

181 Sanctuary, east reveal, north arch, head of St. Stephen the Protomartyr [83]

182 Sanctuary, east reveal, south arch, head of St. Romanos the Melode [122]

183 Sanctuary, south arch, west reveal, head of
     St. Lazaros [124]

184 Sanctuary, north arch, west reveal, head of St.
     Onuphrios [81]

185 Sanctuary, south bay, lunette, St. Kyprianos
     [125]

186 Sanctuary, south bay, lunette, head of
     St. Kyprianos [125]

187 Sanctuary, center of the reveal of the apse arch, the Mandylion [92]

188 North bay, under dome, lintel over north door, the Holy Tile [72] and the 1192 inscription [73]

189 Sanctuary, reveal of the apse arch, north side, head of St. John of Damascus [91]

190 Sanctuary, reveal of the apse arch, south side, roundel with St. Kosmas the Poet [93]

191 Naos, soffit, south arch under dome, St. Akepsimas [128]

192 Naos, soffit, south arch under dome, St. Mardarios [129]

193 Naos, soffit, south arch under dome, St. Eugenios (?) [130]

194 Naos, soffit, south arch under dome, St. Eustratios [131]

195 Naos, soffit, south arch under dome, St. Auxentios
     [132] and floral pattern [136]

196 Naos, soffit, south arch under dome, St. Orestes [133]
     and floral pattern [136]

197 Naos, soffit, south arch under dome, St. Aithalas [134]

198 Naos, soffit, south arch under dome, St. Joseph [135]

200 Head of St. Anthony [137]

199 Naos, west reveal, south arch under
dome, St. Anthony [137]

201 Naos, lunette, south bay under dome, general view, the Koimesis [138]

202 Christ and the soul of the Virgin in raking light,
showing the textures of the plaster and paint, the
impressed vertical to the right of the mandorla,
and the painted-out edge of the architecture

203 Head of St. Paul in raking light, showing the
plaster patch inserted prior to the completion of
his head and the final adjustments to his garments
this entailed

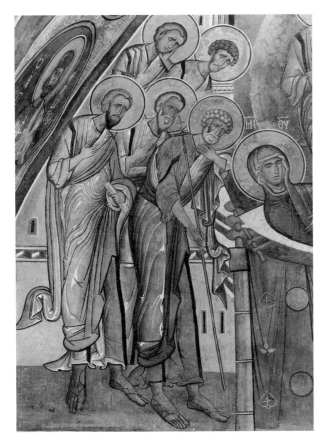

204 Mourning apostles to the east of the bier

205 Head of the young apostle behind St. Luke

206 Head of St. Luke

207 Head of the apostle behind St. Peter

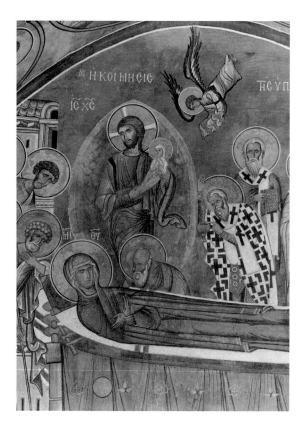

208 The Assumption of the soul of the Virgin

209 Head of Christ

210 Head of St. Peter

211 Head of the middle bishop

212 Head of the Mother of God

213 Soul of the Mother of God

214 Bishop to the west

215 Bishop holding a censer

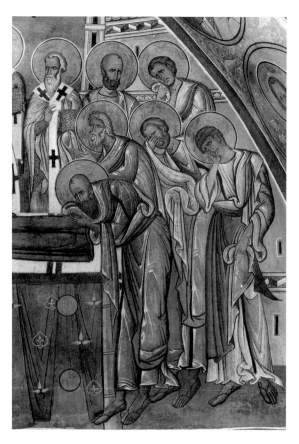

216 Apostles to the west of the bier

217 Head of St. John, at the head of the bier

218 Head of St. Paul, at the foot of the bier

219 Head of the young apostle behind St. Paul

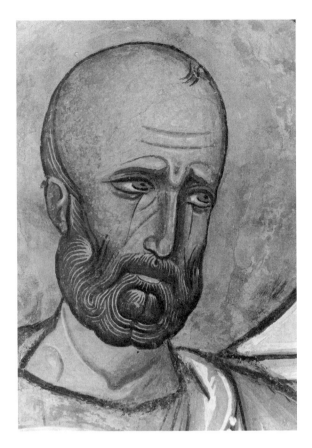

220 Head of the bald apostle next to a bishop

221 Head of the apostle with closed eyes behind St. Andrew

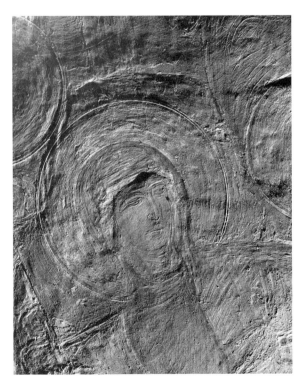

222 Head of the Mother of God in raking light, showing the upper joins of the fresh plaster inserted for her bier and figure and her inscription across the join

223 Christ and the soul in raking light, showing textures, in particular the high relief of the thick lime white used for the figure of the soul

224 Naos, south wall under dome, east side, the Mother of God Arakiotissa [139]

225 Christ child in the arms of the Mother of God

226 Angel to the east, holding the spears and sponge

227 Angel to the west, holding a cross

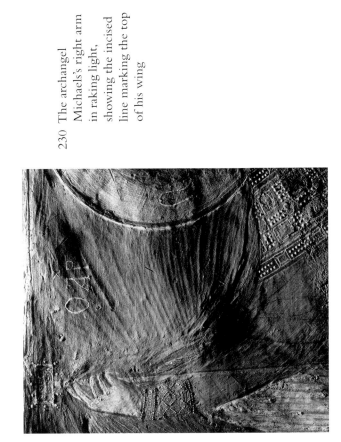

229 Head of the archangel Michael

230 The archangel Michael's right arm in raking light, showing the incised line marking the top of his wing

228 Naos, south wall under dome, west side, the archangel Michael [140]

231 Naos, south side of the west vault, general view, the Nativity [142]

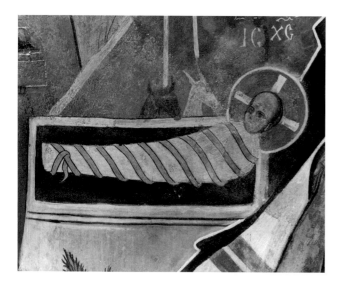

232 Christ child swaddled in the manger

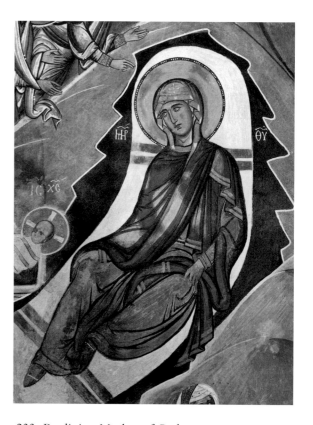

233 Reclining Mother of God

234 Three Magi

235 Head of the angel guiding the Magi

236 Head of the young Magus

237 Head of the middle-aged Magus

238 Shepherds' angel, his message, and the flautist shepherd

239 Head of the shepherds' angel

240 Head of the shepherd playing the flute

242 Heads of the two lower shepherds

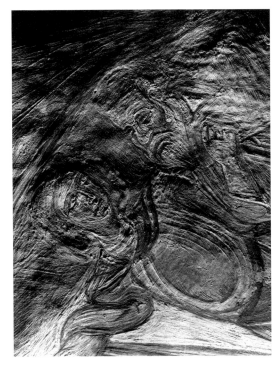

243 Heads of the two lower shepherds in raking light, showing plaster patches for heads and the texture of the paint and plaster

241 Standing midwife, shepherds, and their sheep

244 Midwives bathing
Christ child

245 Head of the standing midwife

246 Head of the standing midwife in raking light, showing
the reworking of the plaster before the completion of
the head and the overpainting of the disturbed
background

247 Seated midwife bathing Christ child

248 Seated midwife in raking light, showing plaster and paint textures, the rough thickness of the lime white paint for the water in the basin, and the glossy smoothness of the child's naked body

249 Joseph and his donkey

252 Naos, southwest arch, west reveal, St. Hilarion [148]

251 Naos, southwest arch, east reveal, St. Chariton [145]

250 Naos, southwest bay, east side, St. Peter [143]

253 Naos, southwest bay, east side, head of St. Peter [143]

254 Naos, southwest arch, east reveal, head of St. Chariton [145]

255 Naos, southwest arch, west reveal, head of St. Hilarion [148]

256 Naos, soffit of southwest arch, east side, head of St. Hermolaos [146]

257 Naos, soffit of southwest arch, east side, St.
     Hermolaos [146]

258 Naos, soffit of southwest arch, west side, St.
     Panteleimon [147]

259 Tympanon, south door, St. Christopher [149]

260 Naos, east side of south door, St. Mary of Egypt [150]

261 Naos, west side of south door, head of St. Zosimos [151]

262 South door, east reveal, cross with inscriptions [152]

263 South door, west reveal, cross with inscriptions [153]

264 Drum of the dome, the prophet Jeremiah [15]

265 Drum of the dome, the prophet Solomon [17]

266 Drum of the dome, the prophet Elijah [19]

267 Drum of the dome, the prophet Elisha [21]

268 Drum of the dome, the prophet Daniel [23]

269 Drum of the dome, the prophet Gideon [25]

270 Drum of the dome, the
     prophet Habakkuk [27]

271 Drum of the dome, the
     prophet Ezechiel [29]

272 Drum of the dome, the
     prophet Jonah [31]

273 Drum of the dome, the
     prophet Moses [33]

274 Drum of the dome, the
     prophet David [35]

275 Drum of the dome, the
     prophet Isaiah [37]

276 Naos, St. Andronikos [55]

277 Naos, St. Kyriakos [58]

278 Naos, St. Sabas [59]

279 Naos, St. Anthony [137]

280 Naos, St. Chariton [145]

281 Naos, St. Hilarion [148]

282 Naos, St. John the Baptist [75]

283 Naos, Mother of God Eleousa [69]

284 Naos, Book of Christ Anti-phonetes [127]

285 Naos, St. Paul [52]

286 Naos, St. Peter [143]

287 Sanctuary, St. Hypatios [86]

288 Sanctuary, St. Kyprianos [125]

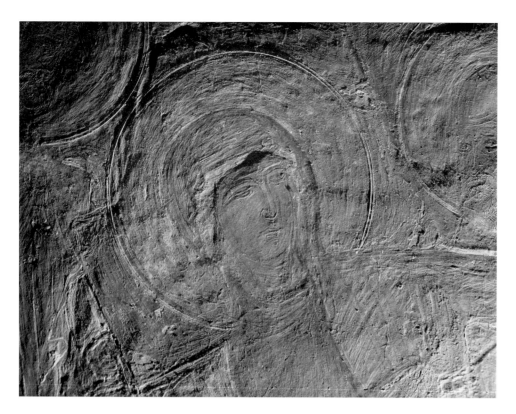

289 The Koimesis [138], head of the Mother of God in raking light, showing the upper
     edge of the plaster join for the large inserted plaster patch and the reworking of the
     plaster prior to the completion of her face

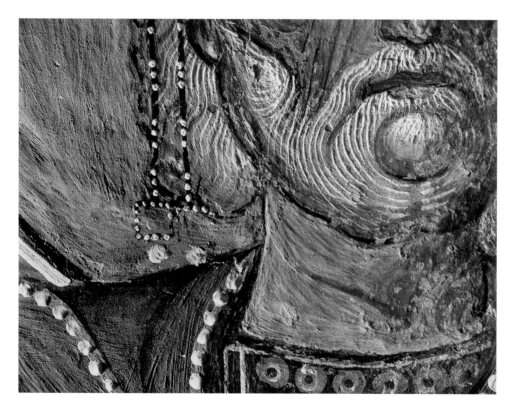

290 The prophet David [35] in raking light, showing the layering and texture of the paint
     on the side of his head

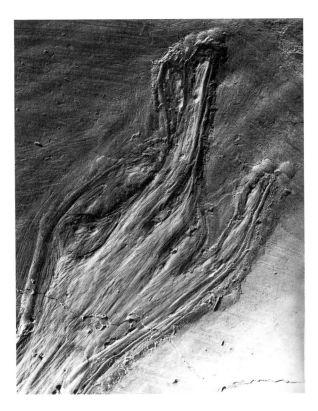

291   The prophet Habakkuk [27] in raking light,
      showing the reworking of the plaster on his hand
      prior to the application of the final flesh colors

292   The prophet Ezechiel [29] in raking light,
      showing the fine brushstrokes in lime white
      articulating his beard

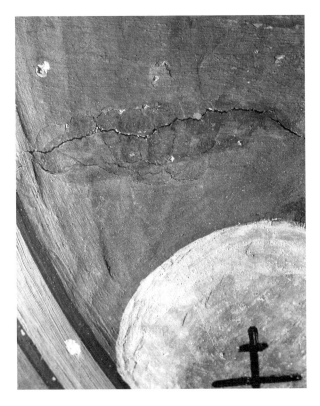

293   The archangel in the southeast roundel [4],
      showing the repair to the plaster made with
      impressed thumb

294   St. Paul [52] in raking light, showing the buildup
      of fold patterns in his himation

295 The Nativity [142] in raking light, showing the relief of the buildup of paint layers, the impress marks
     outlining Joseph's shoulders, and the reworking of the plaster prior to the completion of the arm,
     hands, and face

296 The archangel in the southeast
     roundel [4] in raking light,
     showing the final adjustments
     made to the loros pattern after
     the disturbance of the plaster
     due to the completion of the
     hand

298 The prophet Habakkuk [27] in raking light, showing impressed lines marking the adjustments to the arms and the overpainted error made at the preliminary stage of planning the figure

299 The archangel in the southwest roundel [4], showing the impressed black paint within the borders of the loros

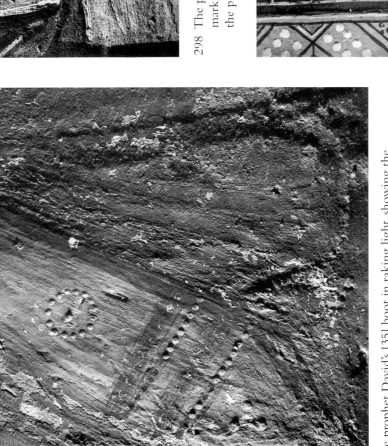

297 The prophet David's [35] boot in raking light, showing the fourteenth-century overpaint with a watery black paint

300 Narthex, east wall, north side, fragment of an unidentified scene, heads of a group of apostles [154]

301 Narthex, east wall, south side, fragment of an unidentified scene, seated figure of Christ [155]

302 Narthex, east wall, south side, head of St. Kosmas [157]

303 Exterior of north wall, tympanum of the door, the fourteenth-century Mother of God Achrantos and her votive inscription [158, 159], and above the tympanum, the Ancient of Days flanked by archangels with censers [163]

304 Exterior of north wall, east of the door, warrior saint [160]

305 Exterior of north wall, east of the door, St. Menas [162]

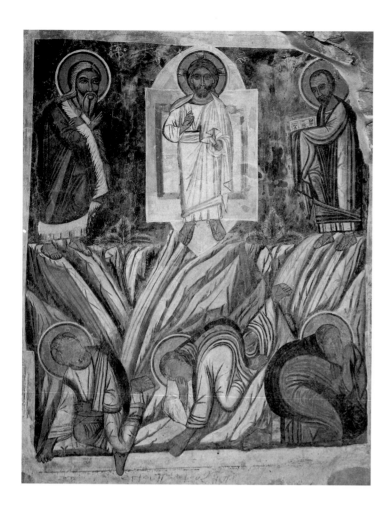

306 Exterior of north wall, west of the door,
the Transfiguration [166]

307 Exterior of north wall, bishop and
prophet [164, 165]

308 Exterior of north wall, east of the door,
St. Theodore Stratilates [161]

309 Exterior of north wall, west of the door, St. Herakleidios [168]

D1568206